DATE DUE

SEX AND GENDER

The Development of
Masculinity and Femininity

Robert J. Stoller, M.D.

Professor of Psychiatry,

Department of Psychiatry,
School of Medicine
University of California at Los Angeles

MARESFIELD LIBRARY

LONDON
KARNAC BOOKS

ISBN 0 946439 03 6
Reprinted 1984 by
H. Karnac (Books) Ltd.
56-58 Gloucester Road, London. SW7 4QY

Acknowledgements:

The author wishes to thank the following for granting permission to include materials published by them:

Chapter 4, "The Hermaphroditic Identity of Hermaphrodites," was first published in *The Journal of Nervous and Mental Disease,* 139:453-457, copyright 1964, The Williams and Wilkins Company, Baltimore, Maryland.

Chapter 5, "The Sense of Maleness," was first published in the *Psychoanalytic Quarterly,* XXXIV:207-218, copyright 1965.

Chapter 6, "The Sense of Femaleness," was first published, in somewhat different form, in the *Psychoanalytic Quarterly,* XXXVII: 42-55, copyright 1968.

Parts of Chapter 7, "A Biological Force in Gender Identity?" were first published as "A Contribution to the Study of Gender Identity," in *The International Journal of Psychoanalysis* 45:220-226, copyright 1964, and in the *Psychoanalytic Forum,* Vol. 2, copyright 1968.

Chapter 8, "Male Childhood Transsexualism," was first published in somewhat different form, in *The Journal of the American Academy of Child Psychiatry,* Vol. 7, No. 1, copyright 1968, International Universities Press, New York.

Chapter 9, "The Mother's Contribution to Boyhood Transsexualism," was first published in somewhat different form as "The Mother's Contribution to Infantile Transvestic Behavior" in *The International Journal of Psychoanalysis,* 47:384-395, copyright 1966.

Chapter 18, "Transvestites' Women," was first published in somewhat different form in *The American Journal of Psychiatry,* 124:333-339, copyright 1967, American Psychiatric Association.

Parts of Chapter 20, "Treatment of Patients with Biological Abnormalities of Sex," were first published in somewhat different form as "Psychiatric Management of Intersexed Patients," co-authors listed as Garfinkel, H., and Rosen, A. C., in *California Medicine* 96:30-34, copyright 1962.

Chapter 21, "The Treatment of Transvestism and Transsexualism," was first published in *Current Psychiatric Therapies,* Vol. VI, edited by Jules Masserman, now reprinted by permission of Grune & Stratton, Inc. New York, copyright 1966.

Printed in Great Britain by BPC Wheatons Ltd, Exeter

For Sybil

Personal Acknowledgments

This is no way to pay debts, and I set about it reluctantly, for I owe more (and should like to be more personal and private about it) than the listing below permits. However, the reader should at least know that these are my friends and colleagues, the research team which helped shape the form of this book:

Howard J. Baker, M.D.
Peter M. Bentler, PH.D.
Edward L. Burke, PH.D.
Hannah Fenichel, PH.D.
Harold Garfinkel, PH.D.
Richard Green, M.D.
Ralph R. Greenson, M.D.
Martha J. Kirkpatrick, M.D.
Nathan Leites, PH.D.
Leonard Loren, M.D.
G. Craig MacAndrew, PH.D.
Lawrence E. Newman, M.D.
Alexander C. Rosen, PH.D.
Alan S. Ruttenberg, M.D.
Richard W. Shearman, M.A.
Donald G. Siegel, M.D.
Richard E. Whalen, PH.D.
Robert Zaitlin, M.D.

I wish especially to thank Dr. Greenson and Dr. Leites; their thoughts and enthusiasm are present throughout, enriching areas that had been very underdeveloped.

My secretary, Thelma Guffan, did her usual superb job. Without her, the book would still be unfinished.

Finally, the generosity of Mrs. Lita Hazen and of the Foundation for Research in Psychoanalysis has given a continuing stability to all of us in the Gender Identity Research Clinic at UCLA.

Preface

In the last fifteen years or so, an increasing interest and an increasing body of information have been developing in the study of sexuality. During this time, advances have been made by geneticists, embryologists, biochemists, neurophysiologists, endocrinologists, and others studying the biological substrates to human sexual behavior, while the studies of zoologists and psychologists on lower animals and the collecting by clinicians of masses of data by interviews, questionnaires, and actual observations of the physiology of sexual excitement, have also contributed to the crescendo of interest and information. As in many other areas of the study of human behavior, this new information has outstripped a capacity to synthesize it, a wholesome change from the not too distant past when scholars felt freer to philosophize without the encumbrance of data.

It is not the task of this present work to attempt such a synthesis. However, within discrete areas there has been a congealing of concepts and theories around some of the new data, and it is in one of these circumscribed areas that I have been working and thinking for the past ten years. This book reports on those findings which permit some generalization, and so I wish now to present information regarding the development, maintenance, and manifestations of masculinity and femininity, and also to discuss certain syndromes, the findings of which seem to cluster around describable etiologies, and to express some preliminary thoughts regarding treatment.

While the work of our research team has been associated with the term *gender identity*, we are not militantly fixed either on copyrighting the term or on defending the concept as one of the ˙ splendors of the scientific world. It is a working term. We know that though it deals with another realm of feelings, thoughts, and behavior than that encompassed by, say, *sexual activity*, the two terms are contiguous and at times inextricably intermingled. With *gender* difficult to define and *identity* still a challenge to theoreticians, we need hardly insist on the holiness of the term "gender identity."

One need not—one cannot—summarize the literature in which *sex, sexuality*, and such terms are used; then, too, there is the problem that one is often confused when an author uses such a term before he has carefully described the data to which he is referring. For instance, the word *sexuality* usually does not communicate much, for it covers so much. Trying to be more precise, we have split off "gender" as a distinguishable part of "sexuality."*

Dictionaries stress that the major connotation of *sex* is a biological one, as, for example, in the phrases *sexual relations* or *the male sex*. In agreement with this, the word *sex* in this work will refer to the male or the female sex and the component biological parts that determine whether one is a male or a female; the

---

* As did Freud years ago (1920) in "The Psychogenesis of a Case of Homosexuality in a Woman,"[1]† in which he listed three characteristics of (homo)sexuality: (1) physical sexual characters; (2) mental sexual characters (what we are now calling *gender*); and (3) object choice. He said these "up to a certain point, vary independently of one another, and are met with in different individuals in manifold permutations."

† This and other superscript figures used throughout refer to the numbered references to publications consulted found under chapter headings at the end of the book. (Shortened titles are used, each work being cited in full in the Bibliography.) —ED.

word *sexual* will have connotations of anatomy and physiology. This obviously leaves tremendous areas of behavior, feelings, thoughts, and fantasies that are related to the sexes and yet do not have primarily biological connotations. It is for some of these psychological phenomena that the term *gender* will be used: one can speak of the male sex or the female sex, but one can also talk about masculinity and femininity and not necessarily be implying anything about anatomy or physiology. Thus, while *sex* and *gender* seem to common sense to be practically synonymous, and in everyday life to be inextricably bound together, one purpose of this study will be to confirm the fact that the two realms (sex and gender) are not at all inevitably bound in anything like a one-to-one relationship, but each may go in its quite independent way.

This first became clearly evident in those monumental works *The Interpretation of Dreams* and *Three Essays on Sexuality*, wherein Sigmund Freud forced the world to recognize that much of what was called sexuality was determined by one's life experiences from infancy on and was not simply a matter of inheritance, biochemistry, and other organic factors. While his work was amplified and refined by subsequent analysts, no such profound or simple statement has supplemented or supplanted Freud's original work.

In recent years, building directly upon this knowledge of postnatal learning experiences as essential to "sexuality," Money and the Hampsons have clearly drawn the thesis that sex and gender are not necessarily in a one-to-one relationship. To develop this thesis, they have turned especially to "natural experiments," in which the variables of sex and gender have been manipulated by fate. For example, they cite that classical "experiment" in which two children are born with adrenogenital syndrome; both are genetically, gonadally, and endocrinologically female and have the normal internal sex structures of females, though their external genitalia are masculinized. If at birth one of these children is correctly designated as a female and the other incorrectly labeled a male because of the apparently male genitalia, by the time these children are about five years old, the one who was unequivocally believed to be a girl has no question but that she *is* a girl and the

one believed to be a boy knows he is a boy. What determined the
gender behavior of these children, then, was not their sex (biological) but their postnatal life experiences, a very complicated
process that begins with the authoritative labeling of the infant
by society as being male or female.

So much for the moment for *sex* and *gender*. As regards the
word *identity*, my treatment of that word will not be more
adequate. The purpose of this work is not to arrive at a compre-
hensive or even useful definition of the term *identity*, or to enter
into the controversies now very much in the forefront of psychoanalytic theorizing as to the differences and similarities, usefulness
or distortions of such terms as *ego, self, self-representation, identity,
sense of identity* and the like.* At this point in my studies, I am
using the word *identity* to mean one's awareness (whether one
is conscious of it or not) of one's existence and purpose in the
world or, put a bit differently, the organization of those psychic
components that are to preserve one's awareness of existing. After
much struggle, I cannot see, when actually observing a person,
what is *identity* as different from *self, ego identity, self-representation*, and so forth. All the efforts at definition in the literature
blur terribly for me in facing real life.

Yet these terms represent our yearning for theory that will
help us to better understand data. Take this statement: "I am
going to the store." Where has this "I" gone when dissected into
ego, superego, and id? *Identity* or the other words (synonyms?)
represents our honest but at times pathetic attempts to get the
whole personality back into metapsychology.

*My colleague Nathan Leites, Ph.D., has concluded after a review of the
literature that the term *identity* has little use other than as fancy dress in which
to disguise vagueness, ambiguity, tautologies, lack of clinical data, and poverty
of explanation. In his words: "I would call the 'gross product' of 'identity's' rise
to prominence during the last ten years the totality of hypotheses formulated in
that period which (a) contain the word, (b) refer to clinically observable
events, (c) were novel in content, and not only in wording, (d) do not seem
clearly false. In my guess this gross product is exceedingly low. I would call the
corresponding 'net product' of 'identity' theory that fraction of its gross product which could not without notable loss of convenience be reformulated in
the language of psychoanalysis *minus* 'identity.' At this time I believe *that*
to be zero."[2]

Obviously, then, this book will not be a review of the literature or a study of theory; nor will it attempt the disciplined approach to the data that the proper application of metapsychological principles would demand. It can be looked on as a preliminary clinical report.

This research project has gone on now for ten years. During that time, I have studied 85 patients who especially illuminate the area of gender identity, and in addition have studied 63 members of their families. The word "studied" stands for a variety of clinical experiences, from a one-hour psychiatric evaluation to a classical psychoanalysis. Recently, several colleagues have joined me in seeing a few patients for treatment; nevertheless, except where specifically noted, the findings and interpretations of findings in this work remain my own responsibility.

It will be apparent to the reader that, in addition to side-stepping a serious attempt to define *gender* and *gender identity*, I have not discussed in depth here many types of people who might be considered under that rubric. Thus, for example, the great issue of homosexuality is looked at only peripherally and only as it has related to the specific patients with gender identity problems who are discussed in this work. In addition, that rather large and very important group, the fetishists, are ignored, except those whose fetishism is an essential part of their cross-dressing. People with other perversions, such as exhibitionism, voyeurism, and sado-masochism, also have not been a part of this research, since they were not felt necessarily to suffer primarily from gross distortions of their gender development.

The perspective used in my clinical work is psychoanalytic. This particular interest must therefore modify the data collected and certainly the way in which these data are conceptualized. However, psychoanalytic terminology has been purposefully minimized; as much as is possible within the limitations of language, I have tried to rely primarily on what one can observe in the patients and have made a conscious effort to note whenever I have filled gaps in the data with psychoanalytic terminology which has concretized itself from a concept to an apparent clinical fact. Unhappily, there is no way around the problem that one cannot know what an author really has observed unless one has been able to see the author's patients with him. That being impossible, the author is under a special obligation to try to choose words that will come as close as possible to approximating what he actually observed. Since that requires the skill of an artist (with all the dangers that are latent in poetic privileges with language), and since I am not an artist, I must make do with relatively simple, nonabstract, nonimaginative language. While not writing for a psychoanalytic audience only, I trust that this compromise in writing style will not also be found to be too meager for a non-analytic audience.

Having nothing to say that would add anything to the argument of whether it is better to present relatively superficial data that can be managed by statistical techniques versus the in-depth study of a few cases, I will not introduce that argument. I would simply note that I am aware of the power that seeing many cases can give one, but I am also especially impressed with the richness of data than can only be collected by the intensive study that psychoanalysis alone permits. I also feel that, along with the dangers inherent in it, there is an advantage in the fact that these patients have been seen by one person, whose technique of collecting and arranging the findings and of writing about them are contained within the limits of his own personality. This makes for a homogeneity which tends to keep out certain artifacts; at least all the biases are mine.

At this point, I should note the very important fact that this whole study is not concerned with much of the crucial part of gender identity development that has been studied by psycho-analysts since Freud's pioneering work—that aspect which has to do with the defensive maneuvers of an individual to protect himself from the felt traumas relating to his gender and sexual development. Thus, for example, I shall not discuss such crucial aspects as the development and resolution of the Oedipal situation in males and females, the defenses raised against castration anxiety, the vicissitudes of penis envy in females, the cultural manifestations of pressures against freer expression of sexual drives, and the like.

My conclusions to date are easily summarized. (And I might

add that my present opinions are often not those with which I started.) I now believe the obvious:

1. Those aspects of sexuality that are called gender are primarily culturally determined; that is, learned postnatally. This learning process starts at birth, though only with gradually increasing ego development are its effects made manifest in the infant. This cultural process springs from one's society, but a sense of this is funneled through the mother, so that what actually impinges upon her infant is her own idiosyncratic version of society's attitudes. Later, the infant's father, siblings, friends, and then gradually the whole of society present upon his developing identity.

2. If the first main finding of this work is that gender identity is primarily learned, the second is that there are biological forces that contribute to this. I feel that the development of gender is augmented, or interfered with, by certain biological forces. To many people, this is so self-evident that it seems not to need discussion. However, as one reviews much of the literature, especially the psychoanalytic, concerning this issue, one finds that what is taken for granted has often been taken for granted as an act of faith and that there have been few data to prove the faithfully accepted premise.

The plan of this book is as follows: Representative cases will be presented in which certain variables are held constant and others are modified by genetic or constitutional abnormalities or by abnormal interpersonal relationships. We shall look first at biologically neuter people and then at people one aspect of whose (biological) sex is absent or abnormal, and see how, if at all, this modification of biology changes gender. Finally, we shall look at biologically normal people who have had things done to them in infancy and childhood by other people, with profound disturbances in gender identity resulting.

This book will not be a survey of sexuality, on most aspects of which I am not expert. I shall not attempt scholarly reviews of areas in which I myself have not worked; such reviews are available to the reader if he wishes to consult them. Only when it is necessary to the argument will there be a short summary of the amassed knowledge on a subject. In this way it is hoped that the reader will focus on the reports of observed data relating to gender identity.

I might say a few words about the goals of this research. First, and maybe least, is the desire to study these esoteric clinical states in depth and over indefinite stretches of time in the hope of revealing more clearly their manifestations and dynamics. In order to do this properly, a second goal, which may have value beyond the study of these patients, has become apparent: to develop methods of observation that will minimize the biases that distort one's view of what one might observe, and at the same time sufficiently to order the data that we do not miss seeing too much of what *is* there. Third, I hope to learn how better to treat such patients. Fourth is the desire to learn more about the roots of gender identity and behavior, and especially to investigate the gender aspects of that old and intriguing problem of the interrelationships between biological and psychological causes. Fifth, I want to learn more about an aspect of personality development—identification—and especially to see how it works in non-traumatic, nonconflictual situations; for, while I believe that much of the development of character structure is the result of conflict, I do not believe, as some analysts seem to have believed, that most or all of character structure is the result of conflict. Last, and most general of all, it is hoped that this work will bring further information to the study of the mother-infant symbiosis and, to a lesser extent, father-infant and sibling relationships to see how these influences contribute to identity development.

It has taken all these years just to discover that the areas described above are what I want to study.

One crucial warning to the reader—and to myself: This research lacks controls from other cultures. My patients have been primarily white, middle-class Americans. I plan to correct this flaw in the future.

Contents

PART III
ASPECTS OF TREATMENT

Introduction

When the present book was written, there was no plan for a second. Volume I said all I wanted—or had—to say. But in the seven years separating the two volumes, the same thing happened as in the ten years of work that preceded the first: ideas and data accumulated, and what had seemed to be mere isolated studies on masculinity and femininity turned out to have been connected by underlying themes, present but unrecognized. In each instance, once the connection became conscious, the pieces fell in place, and a unified presentation surfaced.

It is clear now that these books, *Sex and Gender*, Volumes I and II, and the other books—written and being written—are one continuous work and that they amount to a progression through the subject, not reports of definitive discovery. They reveal an idiosyncratic approach to the inquiry that cannot be defended as scientifically sophisticated. Each day's activities are determined by what I shall enjoy, not what a proper researcher should do. So I more or less meander, focusing for a few years on the biologically intersexed, then transsexuals, then those with gender perversions, then the parents of children with gender disorders and, impending, the perversions at large. Such an approach suggests important areas may be missed or not studied in enough depth.

And—as gradually became clear—all these scattered episodes of investigation impel toward learning more eventually about the ordinary (often referred to as "the normal"); that emerged as the first theme that has underlain this study in past years and guides it for the future.

The second factor is that psychoanalysis is the perspective used to unify the collecting of data. I prefer to spend the day solely in clinical practice, not laboratory work, and defend that preference with the belief there is still no better way to find out what goes on in the mind (as differentiated from the brain) than by working psychoanalytically. So, due to preference, rather than scientific conviction, in order to study masculinity and femininity I can be found either psychoanalyzing patients or using the closest approach to it that circumstances permit.

The third generalization is that, in trying to understand the origins and nature of masculinity and femininity, I do not believe psychoanalysis, as method or theory, and for all its power, gives all the answers. That is why throughout this investigation one senses the opinion that masculinity and femininity can be understood only if one knows about the interplay of the data and concepts of the biologist, the learning theorist, and the psychoanalyst. Each alone can be so biased and wrong. And although trying to synthesize the three can cause inner friction (not to mention the stubborn discrepancies between the disciplines), the omissions and excesses of each demand a synthesis, if one is to use what is demonstrable in each.

In summary, then, Volume II continues the task begun in Volume I. My impression persists that, in humans (no body of contradictory data having been presented by others), the greater part of masculinity and femininity in either sex is the product of postnatal interpersonal and intrapsychic experiences and is best, though not exclusively, studied as an aspect of the mind.

Part I

Patients with
Biological Abnormalities

CHAPTER 1

Biological Substrates of Sexual Behavior

While the practice of sex has a venerable past, a more systematic understanding of its biology is still beyond us. Recently, however, and with increasing momentum, the study of biological aspects of this phenomenon is permitting us to see at least the dim outlines of the answers we shall be finding in the next years. This will permit us to take over a subject formerly the prerogative of philosophers, whose freedom from the responsibility of proof permitted them the assurance of certainty.

It is obvious that so many disciplines of biological research are now involved in studying problems of sex (for example, genetics, endocrinology, embryology, comparative anatomy, physiology) that in a short chapter one can only indicate some of the major areas in which significant investigations are taking place, and attempt to suggest the richness and promise of the field.

Forsaking the luxury of expressing all my confusions as to fundamentals, I should like to mention one: I do not know how to define the term "sexual behavior" or the related and even more frequently used term "sexuality." One of the great contributors to (though undoubtedly one of the complicators of) the subject was Sigmund Freud, who in 1905 pointed out that significant parts of human behavior that seemed to common sense to be quite unrelated to sexual behavior, are in fact found, when one traces the thread out adequately, to derive from clearly sexual origins.[1] It was Freud's underlining the point that there is far more to sex than the coming together of a male genital and a female genital that put us in our present predicament of not being sure what should be termed *sexuality* or *sexual behavior*. This discussion, however, will restrict the meaning of these terms to that *whose function is directly a prototype of, leads to, or accompanies either procreative behavior or that which is clearly a substitute for procreative behavior.*

We know that reproduction is the fundamental purpose behind sexual behavior.* In the most primitive living creatures, reproduction occurs simply by binary fission, with the genetic makeup of the individual organism being identically reproduced. However, when one gets beyond the simplest organisms one finds techniques for combining genetic material in new combinations. Let us skip across the millennia of evolution and pause a moment with *amphibia*. At this level of evolution, we have long since passed the state of development in which sexual intercourse between males and females has first been introduced for reproduction. These creatures have both external and internal genital organs. The amphibian larva has an indifferent gonad made up of two parts: a medulla, which, if it develops, can only become a testis, and a cortex, which, if it develops, can only become an ovary. In the normal creature, gonadal differentiation is controlled by the sex chromosomes, which cause the opposite-sex cells in the indifferent gonad to melt away. Yet, though advanced and differentiated, the gonads of many amphibia are easily reversible: regardless of the genetic makeup (and on this level of development sex chromosomes are determining the sex of the creature), the genotypic female can be converted to a phenotypic male by suppressing

---

*Though less and less clearly so the higher the organism, until in humans we find that sexual behavior may also have psychological purposes very distinct from procreation.[2]

development of the gonadal cortex and promoting medullary growth. If the experiment is carried out in embryological life, the destined female will become an anatomically normal male, having a completely male, sperm-producing testis, despite the fact that had the individual not been tampered with, it would have developed into a completely normal female. This can be accomplished by even such unrelated experimental modes as temperature extremes, castration, or gonadal grafts.[3]

Such experiments are increasingly difficult to produce as one gets higher in the evolutionary scale, but there may be certain degrees of gonad reversibility possible in humans (difficult not only for the obvious reason that we must not do such experiments but also because we have no evidence from "natural experiments" that such reversibility occurs, unless the "true" hermaphrodite is such a case).

Let us stay with mammals, upon which and whom within the last five or six years there has occurred an explosion of fine research related to neurohumoral mechanisms influencing sexual behavior. Two areas especially have been investigated. The first has been the effect of prenatal hormones on postnatal sexual behavior. What one does, in essence, is to give male or female hormones in varying doses to pregnant animals or to newborns.[4] If one does this, for example, to female offspring, not only do they become (anatomically) pseudohermaphroditic if one gives male hormones but also there are apparently central nervous system changes as well: These females shift both their normal childhood sexual behavior and their adult sexual behavior in the direction of markedly increased male behavior. Especially interesting has been the discovery of critical periods: If these sex hormones are given only during very limited periods in fetal development, the reversals in childhood and adult sexual behavior occur, but if one gives the hormones before or after the critical period, then the same aberrant behavior will not develop.[5]

The second area of investigation has been the use of implants of hormones directly into those parts of the animals' hypothalamus that directly affect sexual behavior. Sexual behavior and sexual drive can be influenced in direct relationship either to the cells that have the hormone implant in their immediate neighborhood or to the quantity of the implant.[6] From these studies emerges the very provocative thesis that in each animal there are both male and female CNS subsystems for the regulation of sexual behavior.* According to Young and co-workers,[7] in the normal animal genetic control leads to fetal anatomical-biochemical development causing one system to become dominant, so that, in a male animal, for example, that system which controls male behavior becomes dominant while the second system with its potential for female behavior plays a far lesser role. When the normal development of the animal is distorted by the experimental use of sex hormones, the normally secondary system becomes increasingly predominant. As yet there is no *histological* evidence that such subsystems exist, but the experiments to date seem to demand such an explanation. Certainly it has been described for many years, especially by Ford and Beach,[10] that the higher mammals show degrees of both masculine and feminine behavior in any individual, and there is much evidence that there is no such thing as an exclusively masculine or exclusively feminine mammal.

It will be helpful in our future discussions if we have available to us a very short review of embryological developments of the sexual apparatus in the male and female. It is interesting to note—and to note it can open up some rich fields for speculation[11]—that in most mammals, but especially in humans, the resting baseline of the sexual tissues is female. That is to say, if something else is not added to the tissue, whether the embryo be genetically male or genetically female, no masculinization will occur. Masculinization, when it does occur results in a penis of normal size, with the urethra running through it and a urethral meatus opening at its end, with fusion of the scrotal skin, and with testes within the scrotal sac. When this masculinization does not occur one has a bifid scrotum, which is in fact external lips, a clitoris with the urethra opening below it and no external gonads. In those individuals who instead of having the normal two sex chromosomes (XX or XY), have only one (XO), the external

*This may blunt the effects of Rado's attack[8] on Freud's belief in a biological bisexuality as one root of psychological bisexuality.[9]

genitalia are female, and although the internal reproductive system does not finish its development, there is a tendency for the tissues to move in the direction of developing into female organs. It seems that by the third month in the male fetus' existence a masculinizing substance begins to be secreted in a few sexual cells, this process being initiated in some unknown way under the control of the Y sex chromosome. Once this masculinizing substance begins to be produced even in minute amounts, it influences more cells in that area to become masculinized so that they produce more of this substance so that more cells get masculinized so that more of the substance gets produced and so on, thus starting the process of the masculinizing of these and mort distant tissues until the final normal male sexual anatomy results that is found at birth.

Now to shift to a whole different discipline, *ethology*, a special aspect of the study of animal learning behavior and a radically different methodology of research. From this treasure house of data, I shall take only one popular example. Lorenz, as is well known, has made himself available to greylag geese at certain critical times in their infancy, times when in the birds' natural state the mother would be with them. Under these unusual conditions, in infancy the birds attach themselves to Lorenz; then throughout their growing period they follow and respond to him as if he were their mother. On reaching sexual maturity, their sexual drives are directed exclusively toward him and other humans and not toward their own species.[12] Many species, it is postulated, are genetically endowed so that certain systems of the brain will respond to certain stimuli in the outside world and not to others, and so that the animal is receptive to being permanently influenced by these stimuli only (or at least especially) at certain circumscribed periods in its development—the critical periods. This process, called *imprinting*, is found in different degrees in many species of birds and mammals and is now being investigated biochemically and neurophysiologically.[13] In grossest form, we might say that we humans are able to respond sexually to humans, rather than to other animals or inanimate objects, in part because of certain not yet discovered central nervous system

"states of readiness" that are produced by our having been imprinted by human mothers rather than by, say, monkeys or
lizards.

Work has been under way recently to determine to what
extent these imprinting mechanisms play a part in human infants,
but the impossibilities of controlled experiments and the difficulties
of interpreting mother-newborn interrelationships make this still
a wide open field. A number of workers feel that some sort of
imprinting does take place in human infants.[14] Of interest to us
now is the fact that at this level of theorizing one comes upon the
impossibility of separating out the biological from the psychological; at this point, one recognizes that the two words *biological*
and *psychological* only represent two conceptual schemes for looking at the identical data.*

We can summarize our knowledge of sexual behavior in
animals by saying that, as with other behavior, the lower in the
evolutionary scale, the more bound the animal is by fixed responses
either to the suitable external stimuli or to the internal nervous
and chemical systems. The more complex the animal, the more
variability in response is provided by these systems, until imper-
ceptibly one enters a sphere in which, first, learned (postnatal)
behavior becomes prominent and, finally, in which conscious
choice plays a part. The higher the animal, the more difficult it
is to trace the course of a piece of behavior from its biological
origins to its ultimate action.

We must be careful: Extrapolation from lower animals to
humans is exhilarating but dangerous. The mechanisms involved
are often too complex to permit this. Nonetheless, we must not
be too insensitive to comparative physiology. It can serve us well
if we discipline ourselves to separate demonstrable data from
our speculations; we must learn to accept the data and to enjoy
the speculations.

This brings us to humans. And here great problems confront
us. To what extent do biological forces play a part in a piece

*I leave out the important writings of learning theorists, and especially the
fascinating work of Harlow, because these studies are not as immediately "biological" as those reviewed above.

of sexual behavior? How much of an individual's sexual behavior and preferences is thrust upon him by predetermined biological forces, to what extent are these biological forces influenced by learning experiences, and to what extent are pieces of behavior primarily psychological (that is, culturally determined)? These questions cannot be answered yet, but we have clues, a few of which I shall try to indicate.

It will help our discussion of these problems to distinguish two different orders of data: sex and gender.

As mentioned earlier, I prefer to restrict the term *sex* to a biological connotation. Thus, with few exceptions, there are two sexes, male and female. To determine sex, one must assay the following physical conditions: chromosomes, external genitalia, internal genitalia (e.g., uterus, prostate), gonads, hormonal states, and secondary sex characteristics.[15] (It seems likely that in the future another criterion will be added: brain systems.) One's sex, then, is determined by an algebraic sum of all these qualities, and, as is obvious, most people fall under one of two separate bell curves, the one of which is called "male," the other "female." It is well known that there is a certain amount of overlapping in all humans, and in some unusual cases the overlapping is considerable, as in certain hermaphrodites. There are also, genetically speaking, other sexes; thus, in addition to the XX female and the XY male, there are individuals (XO, XXY, XXXY, etc.) who have a mixing of some of their biological attributes of sex. Such people are often anatomically intersexed as well.*

Gender is a term that has psychological or cultural rather than biological connotations. If the proper terms for sex are "male" and "female," the corresponding terms for gender are "masculine" and "feminine"; these latter may be quite independent of (biological) sex. Gender is the amount of masculinity or femininity found in a person, and, obviously, while there are mixtures of both in many humans, the normal male has a preponderance of masculinity and the normal female a preponderance of femi-

*While the term *intersexed* has occasionally been used in the past to refer to people with gender problems without genetic or anatomical defects, everyone today, I believe, uses it to mean only those with pronounced biological defects.

ninity. *Gender identity* starts with the knowledge and awareness, whether conscious or unconscious, that one belongs to one sex and not the other, though as one develops, gender identity becomes much more complicated, so that, for example, one may sense himself as not only a male but a masculine man or an effeminate man or even a man who fantasies being a woman. *Gender role* is the overt behavior one displays in society, the role which he plays, especially with other people, to establish his position with them insofar as his and their evaluation of his gender is concerned. While gender, gender identity, and gender role are almost synonymous in the usual person, in certain abnormal cases they are at variance. One problem that arises to complicate our work is that gender behavior, which is for the greatest part learned from birth on, plays an essential part in sexual behavior, which is markedly biological, and at times it is very difficult to separate aspects of gender and sex from a particular piece of behavior.

Let us look now at some of the biological aspects of human sexual and gender behavior. This discussion will not review the physiology of sexual excitement, orgasm, and like subjects. While these have been studied in great detail (by far the most important work being that of Masters and Johnson[16] and the excellent review by Sherfey[17]), I am here more concerned with central than with (anatomically) peripheral mechanisms. Nor will the biology of the anatomic development of one's primary and secondary sexual characteristics be considered further here. As with the material I sketched in on lower animals, it is possible only to sample representative work in humans in order to give an impression of the information presently becoming available.

First, from the work of geneticists: While many of us are still awaiting definitive information about the contributions that chromosomes and genes make to sex and gender behavior, there are geneticists who might consider that our waiting shows undue skepticism. Certainly there have been exciting discoveries in the genetic laboratories in the last decade or so. The discovery by Barr and Bertram of nuclear sex chromatin material in mammalian,[18] including human,[19] cells has given us a simple, rapid, and highly accurate screening test for genetic sex. Also, new techniques for visualizing chromosomes have revealed to us both the normal complement of 46 chromosomes to the human cell and the presence and morphology of the sex chromosomes. This immediately made possible some clarification of the contribution of chromosomes to intersexuality (e.g., the XO Turner's Syndrome of ovarian agenesis or the XXY of the typical Klinefelter's Syndrome). In addition, decades of speculations regarding the alleged role of gross chromosomal anomalies in perversion with gender abnormality were put to rest when it was shown that no such defects were demonstrable—for example, in homosexuality or transvestism.[20]

At this stage in the development of the science of genetics, I can only take the position of a layman, consider the arguments inconclusive, and await more compelling facts.

Now some endocrinological data: As is well known, castration of the male produces changes in sexual behavior. If the testes are removed before puberty, not only are the secondary sex characteristics unable to develop, but also genital sexuality in the adult is almost nonexistent. Castration following puberty results in marked diminution of sexual activity; the speed and completeness with which this destruction of sexual behavior occurs varies with the individual. Castration in females does not produce the same effects. Prepubertal girls who are ovariectomized can, as adults, experience normal sexual excitement and orgasm. Likewise, removal of the ovaries in the adult woman will not diminish her sexual needs or pleasures per se. Some recent findings strongly suggest that sexual libido is dependent on androgens in both men and women;[21] libido is clearly not dependent on estrogens in women[22] but is probably the result of the minute amounts of androgens normally produced in the adrenals, for adrenalectomy in women severely diminishes if it does not destroy their libido.[23] The administration of estrogens to men, on the other hand, does not affect their libido unless the amounts are large enough to suppress testosterone production. Castrated men can maintain sexual vigor if given testosterone. Women given androgens, with or without their ovaries removed, routinely have an upsurge of libido. However, it is important to remember that when hormones are added or subtracted in these ways, the direction of the libido is not changed. Thus, the addition of testosterone does not make women develop masculine tastes in sex, and giving testosterone to effeminate homosexuals does not make them any less effeminate but just increases their need for more homosexual relations.

We also know that frequency of sexual desire and sexual pleasure in women is not curtailed with menopause, except in those women who expect that it will be. On the other hand, with the gradual decrease in testosterone production in the aging male, there is a gradual diminution in sexual vigor, though we know to what advanced age sexual activity can persist.

Still another area of research is that reviewed by Parkes and Bruce,[24] who report that females are much more susceptible to odors than are males. They summarize the literature demonstrating this in lower animals, and show that the same occurs in humans: The lower the estrogen levels, the less acute the sense of smell, with acuity varying through the menstrual cycle. How this affects sexual behavior is still to be investigated.

While everyone is familiar with Freud's discoveries of the tremendous influence of postnatal effects on personality development and on the development of sexuality, it sometimes comes as a surprise to those not familiar with his works to discover that from the beginning of his career until the very end, Freud incessantly repeated his belief that there were biological substrates to behavior. However, because of the inadequacy of the laboratory sciences of his day, he recognized that he was forced to put aside any hope of proving that such substrates exist, maintaining that the future would bring the proof he needed. Nonetheless, in his study of infant and child libidinal development he felt he could find evidence of a biological undercurrent upon which floated the postnatal, learned behavior. It was his feeling that libidinal development (the progression of erotic and nonerotic charging of oral, anal and urethral, and phallic areas with compelling significance as the personality develops) was controlled by a biological clock, ultimately genetically controlled. He felt (and subsequent observers have demonstrated) that there is a gradual maturation of many complicated neuromuscular systems before a new part of the body comes into focus, that is, becomes highly libidinized.

This reminds us of the work on critical periods being done on lower animals; at any rate it is the case in human development that certain orifices—those with mucous membranes—become highly sensitive and highly charged emotionally only after certain amounts of time and biological development have preceded. Thus, for example, only after the neuromuscular systems related to bowel control have sufficiently developed—when the small child is really biologically prepared for toilet training—can such training proceed without damage, and it follows that premature attempts to force such training may have great psychological significance. Another example of probable biological control over the erotization of various parts of the body is found in the work of Spitz:[25] He has determined that while there is in little boys a casual awareness of and playing with the penis, starting around eight to ten months of age, this organ is not selected any more frequently than are other parts of the body, until after a gradual heightening of erotic sensation over many months, when the time and interest spent in genital manipulation increase. By the time of the phallic phase, occurring in both boys and girls at around three to five, there is a very concentrated interest in one's penis or clitoris—in other words, easily recognized masturbation.

Other clinical researchers are making fundamental contributions. One technique for demonstrating the presence of biological forces is the minute observation of newborn behavior. One must be very careful in such research, for the effects of learning begin manifesting themselves at a remarkably early age, some as early as the first few days of life.[26] Nevertheless, evidence is beginning to gather that there are not only biological substrates for behavior in general but there also seem to be behavioral sex differences at birth. Call[27] has discovered a distinct difference between newborn boys and newborn girls: Boys are more restless before feeding and become more tranquil or fall asleep more readily after feeding, whereas the reverse is the fact with girls. In a completely different study, Schaeffer and Bayley[28] have noted that the amount of activity seen in boys in the first few months of life is directly dependent on the way their mothers deal with them, but that, regardless of how the mother treats the infant girl, she proceeds in her development (in regard to amount of activity) independently of her mother's treatment.

It is well known that by far the greatest part of sexual customs in humans is culturally determined, that is, learned after birth rather than biologically determined. These customs include not only formal activities, like ritual dances, but also what a culture has defined for itself as properly masculine or feminine behavior. Generally, regardless of the state of biological determinants of sex present, one becomes a member of that sex to which one is assigned. Money and the Hampsons[29] have shown that in intersexed patients, if the patient is raised as a girl, she feels herself to be a girl even if many of her anatomical attributes are primarily male. However, this does not necessarily disprove the presence of diffuse biological forces influencing gender behavior; it may be that the effects of rearing overwhelm and therefore hide the weaker biological qualities, rather than that the latter do not exist.

An intriguing bit of evidence helps confirm this. In certain of these intersexed "natural experiments," there is an odd turn to the development of their gender identities. As different from what happens in normals and even in many intersexed patients, these people grow up convinced that they belong to the gender opposite to that in which they have been unequivocally raised. For example, an infant who was apparently an anatomically unremarkable girl was raised as a girl by her unsuspecting parents, who wanted a girl. To the bitter dismay of her feminine mother, the child from birth on acted as though she were convinced she should be a boy. All the effects of learning of gender, so crucial in almost all instances, left this child untouched. Then, at puberty, physical examination revealed she was a male with a penis the size of a clitoris, bifid scrotum and cryptorchid testes (all of which had given her at birth the appearance of a normal female). The child had been right all along: his gender identity had been male in the face of all of society's pressures to act like a female.[30] (See Chap. 7.) There are enough other cases so that one can presume these are not merely coincidences but rather exemplifying cases in which biological forces become, as they almost never do in the normal, the most powerful effect in producing gender identity.

A crucial matrix binding all sexual behavior is, obviously, sexual pleasure, in itself a complex mixture of tension, anticipation, physical sensations, and gratification. Following especially upon the work of Olds with rats,[31] studies in the last ten years concerned with discovering in the brain the centers and pathways of pleasure have begun revealing the complex mechanisms underlying this quality of experience. Chronic implanted electrodes in man have confirmed findings in animals, with the great enhancement that humans give subjective reports. An essential input for this pleasure is provided in the limbic system, and most specifically the septal region, of the brain. Heath[32] reports on patients with chronic implanted electrodes who could deliver electrical current to several discrete areas of their own brain by pressing a button. "The patient, in explaining why he pressed the septal button with such frequency, stated that the feeling was 'good'; it was as if he were building up to a sexual orgasm." Of another patient, Heath says, "The patient most consistently reported pleasurable feelings with stimulation to two electrodes in the septal region and one in the mesencephalic tegmentum. With the pleasurable response to septal stimuli, he frequently produced associations in the sexual area. Actual content varied considerably, but, regardless of his baseline emotional state and the subject under discussion in the room, the stimulation was accompanied by the patient's introduction of a sexual subject, usually with a broad grin. When questioned about this, he would say, 'I don't know why that came to mind—I just happened to think of it.'"

Finally, as an example of how a number of different findings can be fitted to create a new understanding of an aspect of sexuality, we can turn to a recent report by Fisher, Gross, and Zuch.[33] They studied the phenomenon of penile erections during sleep, reporting that full or partial erections were found 95 per cent of the time that men are in dreaming (Rapid Eye Movement) sleep, and that these erections start and end synchronously with the REM and do not occur during nondreaming sleep. As reported

by Fisher and co-workers, there is evidence of a primitive mechanism "pulsing" in the brain, starting in prenatal life[34] and continuing throughout life. After a few months of age, when it
"pulses," it is invariably accompanied by dreaming, and in both
infants[35] and adult men, as these workers have now shown, it is
also accompanied by erections. Dreaming sleep is controlled by
a different part of the brain than nondreaming sleep, a part of
the brain which has important connections with the limbic system, stimulation of which may produce erection.[36]

The implication is that there is built into certain primitive parts of the human brain a type of functioning which controls such apparently disparate activities as dreaming sleep and
the production of penile erections. Thus, all dreaming and sexuality may be linked neurophysiologically.

Obviously, we do not have all the pieces, and yet there are
good clues. We know these investigators are on the track of
important discoveries, of syntheses of as yet unrelated data. We
can see now that comparative and human neurophysiology will
be coupled with the discoveries of psychologists and psychoanalysts to increase our understanding of these mechanisms.

This sketch, then, suggests the directions that our present
search for knowledge has taken in this area of substrates of sexual
behavior. But this is only the beginning; our understanding of
sexuality is as nothing if this is all we know, for in this most
intense of all human communications, we must study the signals
that pass between people, and also what memories, fantasies, and
wishes are stirred up in the individual. In other words, we must
turn to *psychology* as an essential methodology in our understanding of sexuality.

CHAPTER 2

The Intersexed Patient
with Normal Gender Identity

Now let us start changing variables. The first case is a person as biologically neuter as a human can be: chromosomally XO, with the resultant anatomic-physiologic neuterness to be described below.

And yet, when she was first seen at age 18 at the Medical Center she was quite unremarkably feminine in her behavior, dress, social and sexual desires, and fantasies, indistinguishable in these regards from other girls in Southern California.

There was one troubling condition that made her less than average. Her breasts had not begun to develop by the time she was eighteen, nor had menstruation started. After talking with her older sisters about this, and after some months' delay while hoping maturation would show itself, she came for medical (not psychiatric) consultation.

Physical examination revealed a good-sized girl (140 pounds, 5′ 5½″) with no unusual findings other than no breast development or areolar pigmentation and sparse pubic hair present only on the labia. Labia and clitoris appeared normal. Introitius was virginal. Uterus and adnexae could not be palpated per rectum. There was little axillary and no obvious leg or body hair. Pertinent laboratory studies were as follows: 17 ketosteroids—9.1 mg/24 hours; FSH—greater than 80; buccal smear chromatin stain—negative (male pattern); vaginal smear—very low (atrophic) estrogenic activity.

She received a laparotomy, the operation record of which states in part:

Examination under anesthesia: The external genitalia had the gross appearance of a female, the clitoris is slightly small. The urethral meatus is located below the clitoris and in approximately the normal location. The remainder of the vestibule is small and flat and no vaginal orifice or pouch could be found. Rectal examination revealed no palpable pelvic organs.

Findings at operation: There is noted a complete lack of uterus. It appears bilaterally that vessels emerged from the side wall of the pelvis in the area of the infundibulopelvic ligament laterally. Structures on each side resembling round ligaments (only much smaller in diameter) are seen and these structures can be seen to exit from the peritoneal cavity in a rather normal fashion. An inguinal canal can be palpated from inside the peritoneal cavity on the left. A less definite inguinal canal is evident on the right, but a clamp can be inserted down the length of the canal from its intraperitoneal origin to the external inguinal ring. There was no evidence of gonadal tissue of either sex. No adrenal hypertrophy was noted. . . .

In brief, the contents of the abdominal cavity were neuter (with the tendency toward female anatomy that occurs with neuterness in humans).

She was placed on stilbestrol (3 mg daily indefinitely) and told that she was sterile due to an anatomical defect, and that she had an anatomical immaturity of the vagina that could be surgically corrected when she was ready to be married.

The day after the operation, on being told that she was sterile the patient began to cry and continued to grieve openly for several days. During the psychiatric treatment that began on the day she was informed of her sterility* (and which continued for three years), the pain that this unavoidable revelation caused was more carefully studied. Probing this pain revealed the presence of three trends rooted in feminine identifications, and indistinguishable in broad outline from the response that would be found in a genetically normal-sexed young woman. The first trend was her desire to marry and to have children; the second, concern regarding the appearance and function of her genitalia; and the third, her feminine interests (in appearance, games, use of leisure, sexual relations, etc.).

In what ways did she express her desire for children before learning that this must be frustrated? (Our information comes not only from the patient but also from an older sister.) According to her sister, "She had a doll that she got when she was eight, and she always said that she was going to save it to give to her little girl after she got married. She still has that doll and it's in perfect condition. . . . She was nine years old when my son was born, and she always loved to take care of him and was very, very good at handling him. . . . You can't kid her about not having children."

As for the patient herself, the following quotes give the flavor of her feelings regarding wanting children. When asked at the beginning of psychotherapy what brought her to the hospital, she began to cry and said, "I wonder what my kids would have looked like?" A couple of months later she was asked if she could recall any dreams from any time in her life. The only one recalled was from one or two years before (when she was worried because her menses had not yet begun): "I was getting married. I had to marry the fellow because I was pregnant."

Regarding the second factor, her concern over the appear-

---

* In order not to disturb her unquestioning sense of being a young woman, I had to approach tactfully any chance of meeting her. Had there been no proper psychiatric reason, I would not have been able to work with her, but since she was so miserable in her knowledge that she could never bear a child, she was glad to have a physician with whom she could talk. As we became more friendly, we decided I should treat her for a minor neurotic symptom not related to her gender identity.

ance and function of her external and internal genitalia surfaced, naturally enough, only after some months of treatment. It was precipitated by two events, which occurred within two months: First, the marriage of a sister 18 months older, who in childhood had built up a pseudo twinship with the patient, and who after her marriage revealed to her sister (the patient) that there had been premarital relations; second, learning that a newly acquired best friend had had sexual relations with a boy the patient herself had previously dated. These disclosures led the patient into a storm of insight—that girls with whom she had identified were compelled by their bodies (especially the genitalia) to search for sexual satisfaction, and that her identification with them had played her false: she had mistakenly believed these girls felt as she herself consciously did, that they did not want and would not indulge in sexual relations before marriage. There was then added to the knowledge that she would not have children the knowledge that neither could she have intercouse, even if she wished to, unless she had a vaginoplasty. So she *knew* that not only were her internal reproductive organs—tht fundamentals of motherhood—defective but so also was the source of her sexual pleasure, her external genitalia. This latter knowledge was more galling than the sadness caused by the former.

Now, at the same time that this patient fully confronted herself with the idea that sex excites girls, she became ashamed of her incomplete genitalia. After her laparotomy, as she watched her girl friends growing up and becoming sexually active, she became increasingly disturbed because she did not have a normal vagina. Primarily, this was not because she was unable to feel the specific genital sexual sensations that she knew other girls were enjoying, but rather that she did not possess that essential insignia of femaleness, a normal vagina. While she was able to reach an orgasm by masturbation of the normally developed external parts of her genitalia, and while she knew she was a female and a woman, she could not consider herself to be in the same category of femaleness as were her girl friends. More important to her than erotic pleasure was her desire to sense herself as a female; the maintenance of gender identity was more crucial for her by far than sexual satisfaction. With other patients we have seen with anatomical defects in their genitalia, *as well as with anatomically normal people*, it is clear that sexual satisfaction serves to establish and maintain one's gender identity.[1]

The patient's family was against her having a vaginoplasty, for they felt that if she did so she would begin having sexual relations before she was married. The patient was of course very anxious for the corrective surgery, and finally the surgeons recommended to the family that she be permitted to have the operation so that she would not feel herself to be so different from her girl friends. Following surgery, the patient was very happy, and at no time subsequently has she regretted the vaginoplasty. As the family feared, it was not many months later that the patient began having intercourse with her boyfriend. She eventually married and has remained married to the present time.

The patient has been seen intermittently in the six years since treatment ended. These follow-ups and her reports of her developing adult life as a married woman present nothing worth reporting in detail, simply because her life as a female, as a woman, and as a young wife is like that of innumerable biologically normal women.

It can be noted that she has been taking estrogens regularly for eight years (since the exploratory laparotomy), and that these have produced breasts and have maintained the soft and feminine subcutaneous fat distribution that the patient had since her teens. She reports sexual excitement and gratification with intercourse, though sexual sensation is restricted, as it was before, to the superficial genital tissues, the vagina being without erotic sensation.

What about the third factor, her feminine interests and her feminine role? Her oldest sister says that the patient was a pretty girl, interested in dresses, dolls, and in putting on cosmetics to play at being grownup. On her dates, every Friday and Saturday night, she liked to go dancing, bowling, or to the movies. Her greatest interest has always been stylish clothes, on which she would spend all her spare money. When in her late teens she first went to work, she did so only to have extra money for clothes. In school, she did best in "homemaking" because she liked to cook and sew.

She does little reading, and that exclusively movie and romance magazines. Her daydreams have the same content as her reading— a concentration on feminine ways.

This is certainly not a list of activities that strikes one as unique, bizarre, carefully thought out, or as evidence worthy of report, were it not that it is my design to underline the unspecialness, the *naturalness* of this patient's identity.

DISCUSSION

The conclusion I draw from our first patient is this: Her feeling of being a female, even if a defective one, is clear-cut; she does not consider herself a male or a hermaphrodite. She knows herself only as a female and as a woman. Her gender identity is not based on some simple biological given, such as endocrine state. It comes from the fact that she looked like a girl when she was born, and that nothing appeared on her body sufficient to disprove this at any time in her life. These were the anatomical prerequisites to the development of her femininity. Given these, it was possible for the attitudes of her family, and later of society, to set in motion the complicated process that results in gender identity. Nothing occurred in the feelings of anyone in the family that the patient would have sensed as an unsureness about the sex to which she rightfully belonged. The question of "rightfully" did not occur to any of the family, since her feminine gender was taken for granted. While one's biology and one's society demand that there be stages in the development of gender identity, some of these stages clearly marked with ceremony, the fundamental ascription of sex (hence also of gender, because of the prevailing belief in a one-to-one relation between the two) is granted instantly and permanently.

When given in this unequivocal manner, such ascription cannot be taken away. It can be weakened by the silent intrapsychic and intrafamilial warfare that leads toward homosexuality, transvestism, and other perversions. Yet people with these disorders, as with normals and neurotics with latent weaknesses in gender identity, know somewhere within themselves to which sex they belong. They may dream or act as if there were fragments of the other sex imbedded in them. But these are wishes, and to go through the activity of creating a wish and the even more complicated process of gratifying it, there must be a part of oneself that knows it is only a wish.

If from the start, the child's elders are not sure enough, because the child is anatomically ambiguous or because the parents are delusional, then a defect in character structure can develop in which the patient knows only the gender identity of a hermaphrodite. The hermaphroditic identity is a rare psychological state, by no means found in all intersexed patients. (See Chap. 4.) As different from the clear-cut gender identity present in the patient described above, the hermaphroditic identity requires (1) anatomically ambiguous external genitalia from birth on, causing (2) confusion in the parents' minds as to the child's proper anatomic sex, leading to (3) ambiguous ways of dealing with the child, which, in turn, result in (4) defects in the process of incorporating parents and their attitudes, and thus (5) incongruous gender identifications that can never be corrected in reality, because the ultimate test of reality, perception, continuously demonstrates (1) anatomically ambiguous external genitalia.

Our present patient, then, demonstrates the thesis that postnatal, nonbiological experiences are crucial in the development and fixing of gender identity, since her femininity and sense of being a young woman have ripened unimpeded despite the absence of anatomical or endocrinological primary or secondary sex characteristics. However, she does not necessarily exemplify the belief that biological forces do not play such a role in most people, but only that gender identity may develop even in the absence of such forces. We shall look later (Chap. 7) at cases that strongly suggest that biological forces can powerfully influence gender identity in rare cases. Granting these rare exceptions, my operating principle (to be discarded only if data are uncovered to disprove it) is that postnatal psychological forces play the most powerful and obvious part in creating gender identity, with genetically controlled biological forces silently augmenting this process.

Before we explore this further, let us see what happens when the person over age 2–4 with normal gender identity is suddenly told that the sex and gender ascribed to him or her are the wrong ones.

CHAPTER 3

The Disruption of
Established Gender Identity

What happens when a person with no real question about her gender identity is suddenly robbed of that certainty? The history of this next patient is useful for such an exposition. Like the young woman described in the preceding chapter, her gender identity was intactly female and feminine despite the fact that she also was biologically neuter. Then, in her teens, she was told for the first time that her sex was genetically and anatomically incorrect.

When I first saw this patient, she was an 18-year-old girl who had been referred to the Gender Identity Research Clinic as a schizophrenic; she had been in treatment at two other clinics for the previous two years. She had gradually become psychotic, starting at age 14, when she was told by a gynecologist that she "might be a boy." She had been brought for that physical examination because her breasts had not started to develop and her periods had not yet begun. Though she was concerned about this, she had no question about her proper sex. She was then examined gynecologically and found to be neuter.* The physician who did the examination talked with her and her mother, making every attempt to be honest, yet tactful. As many enlightened physicians do, he subscribed to the thesis that this information would not be disturbing, and that, with proper explanations, no psychological damage would result. So the child and her mother were told that she had no functioning ovaries and therefore no periods or completed secondary sex characteristics, but especially that her chromatin staining showed a male pattern and that her chromosomes were XO. To the patient, despite all accompanying explanations, this meant that she was genetically, and therefore in the *most* biological sense, no longer a female but a freak, with both male and female qualities. From the day of that pronouncement, she began ruminating on whether she was a female or a male; this rumination and her unsuccessful attempts to reestablish a fixed gender identity led to her gradually thinking and reacting in a more and more bizarre manner—the psychosis.

As soon as she was first brought for psychiatric treatment at

*The report of her physical status at that time stated in part: "She was first seen by us for evaluation of primary amenorrhea. On physical examination, she was found to be short in stature for her age, without axillary hair, but with sparse pubic hair. There was absolutely no mammary development. There was a suggestion of webbing of the neck, with broadened chest cage and scattered nevi across the back and chest. On vaginal examination, the vulva and vagina were found to be immature, with conglutination of the lower edges of the labia majora. No organs were palpable on rectal examination. The vagina was sounded to 2½ inches.

"The following are the results of workup at that time. X-rays revealed a normal bone age. Vaginal smear for estrogen effect was very low. Pituitary gonadotrophins, greater than 100 MUU. 17 ketosteroids 8.9 mg. Buccal smear for sex chromatin reported as male. This latter was repeated three times more with vaginal and buccal smears. We have two reports of female chromatin seen and two reports of no female chromatin seen. . . . On vaginal examination, an immature cervix was visualized. The uterine corpus could not be outlined, and no adnexal masses were palpable. Vaginal canal was completely separate from the urethra and bladder.

"A diagnosis of gonadal dysgenesis was made on this patient, and she was placed on a combination of Estinyl, Estradiol, and Norethynodrel. On this medication she has developed her secondary sex characteristics. Her vagina has matured, with good estrogen effect visible on the mucosa. When medication is taken in cycles, she has withdrawal bleeding. The uterine corpus can now be outlined. It is small and mobile . . ."

age 16, after two years of developing bizarreness, she was diagnosed as schizophrenic; two years later she was still considered psychotic.* Her first therapist described her as follows:

> Frequently her manner and behavior seem bizarre. Often she appears disheveled in dress and hairdo. Her problems are rather clearly expressed through body language and verbalizations. She has often verbalized her suspiciousness of me. In the early interviews, her arms were frequently held back of her, constantly swinging of legs, looking away to the side, and sneaking glances at the worker. As she talked, she would giggle, laugh loudly, cry, pound on the desk or put her head down. There was great vacillation in moods, that seemed either manic or depressed. Her voice would vary from an inaudible whisper to a loud shout.

She was referred to me because she was still psychotic and because I was interested in seeing intersexed patients.

The following quotations are taken from several different periods in the first months of her treatment with me. They exemplify the kind of material that was reported by the other clinics and suggest the moderate psychosis (with hysterical features of hopeful prognostic significance) that was present for the four years from the time she was told of her sexual abnormality until the psychosis died away some months after being in treatment in the Gender Identity Research Clinic.

> As soon as they found out about my condition, I should have been left to die. I am no good to society. I am abnormal. I am different. That is what has always been done since time immemorial. No one can reach me. Not even you. I have to kill myself because society didn't. I am trash of the earth. Not fit to live. The population is cluttered with people like me. Only the tall and the handsome shall live. Little puny people like me shall die. I am God. Did you know

---

* I report the evidences of her psychosis not because they are unusual—they are not—but to permit the reader to be assured that a real psychosis followed the revelation of her sexual neuterness. The term "psychosis" is used; it means just that—not latent or borderline or potential—and is without any esoteric or idiosyncratic connotation.

I am God? I told you I would have delusions of grandeur. And since I am God I shall kill you. You don't deserve to live either, since you are helping me. I will contaminate you with my disease. Keep away from me. Don't touch me. Don't hurt me. Don't let me go! Don't kill me—save me. . . . I am a destructive God. Only I can destroy anything I don't like. I have power over everyone in the world.

As she began feeling better, she described some of her feelings of confused gender identity:

I had fears of being male. I was acting like a little girl partly because of this and partly because I felt I just wouldn't prove to be a female if I acted like one, and I was terrified of having to face that. One day I had a very vivid picture of my pelvis as being all female like I was told it was, but I thought of one place where I would possibly have a male organ and it seemed quite logical to me, because that was the place I was missing the female one and I didn't know for sure. I finally got up enough courage to ask the doctor. She told me I had nothing but fibers there. She told me I was an it, only I didn't have to look [like] or be one because of my medication. She also told me it was possible that if anything had been there, the other chromosomes—it possibly might have been the Y one. All this was terribly hard to take and digest and I guess I still haven't digested it. . . .
I don't want to be a girl. I wish I were a boy. I like being a girl sometimes when men pay attention to me, but I feel I would be more wanted by my parents. My breasts aren't real. Only my vagina is, because it was there before. That is what I meant by my sex feelings originate in only one place like a man's instead of two like a woman's. My breasts were given to me for a time. Who knows when they will be taken away? That is my fear. My terrible fear. Not to be like a woman. . . . I must learn appropriate ways to show emotion. It just builds up in me and then I have to escape. All of a sudden I feel very womanly. From way inside of me at the center and at the core. The externals don't matter to me. . . . I feel like my personality is unique, like no other girl's. No man can touch me. He will never know my inner self, my personality, because I don't have one. It is too odd. He won't understand.

Following some months of treatment aimed at her finding her

sense of femaleness again, and that she truly was a young woman, the psychosis disappeared. What has lingered, but with diminishing intensity, are ruminations about whether a particular thought or act is masculine or feminine. (For example: "You will never know what it is like to pass a rest room marked 'Boys' and wonder if you should go into that one instead of the women's. It's terrible. I was always afraid I would make this mistake sometime and go in the wrong one." "Where do I fit in? If I go to school and work, does it mean I am not a woman? If I am forward at the dances does it mean I am not a woman, or do I have to wait to be asked?") While there was a special intensity in her voice when she discussed such problems, the content is not very different from what we hear in some of our anatomically normal patients.

While I realize that one case, sketchily reported and without any statistical controls, proves nothing, I nevertheless hope that it may serve as a caution to those who optimistically believe that one's gender identity is so unstable that it can be easily dispensed with and a new one created at will.

CHAPTER 4

The Hermaphroditic Identity
of Hermaphrodites

It is rarely questioned that there are only two biologic sexes, male and female, with two resultant genders, masculine and feminine. The evidence for biologic or psychologic bisexuality does not contradict this division, but only demonstrates that within the two sexes there are degrees of maleness and femaleness (*sex*) and of masculinity and femininity (*gender*). Thus, there is ascribed to each person at birth an absolute position as a member of one sex or the other, so that one develops a sense of belonging to only one gender. It is obvious that proper ascription of sex is extremely important; in those infants in whom ambiguous-appearing genitalia at birth make sex assignment uncertain, the proper sex must be diagnosed as soon as possible. Only by careful and rapid diagnosis can future emotional problems be avoided.

Almost everyone starts to develop from birth on a fundamental sense of belonging to one sex. The child's awareness—"I am a male" or "I am a female"—is visible to an observer in the first year or so of life. This aspect of one's over-all sense of identity can be conceptualized as a *core gender identity*, produced by the

29

infant-parents relationship, by the child's perception of its external genitalia, and by a biologic force that springs from the biologic variables of sex. (See Chaps. 5 and 6 for further discussion of core gender identity.) The first two factors are almost always crucial in determining the ultimate gender identity.[1]

While the process of developing gender identity goes on intensively until at least the end of adolescence, the *core* gender identity is fully established before the fully developed phallic stage. This is not to say that castration anxiety or penis envy are not essential parts of the development of gender identity, but rather that these latter conflicts occur after core gender identity is well established.

To take an example: Transvestite men may try to be very feminine when dressed in women's clothes. Yet they do not truly feel that they are females. They *wish* they were (at least to the extent of being a woman with a penis) and their transvestism is an acting out of this wish, but *they know they are not*. Their core gender identity is male; that is, they know their bodies are male, that they have been assigned since birth to the male sex, that they were reared as males, and that all the world unequivocally considers them to be and always to have been males. Only later, as the personality develops, will this male core gender identity be overlaid by the gender identity with feminine elements.

Even when an individual has been reared in the gender opposite to the biological sex, a clear-cut core gender identity develops wherein the person unquestionably feels that he or she is a member of the assigned sex, if no one raising the person questions it either. Money and the Hampsons reported a large series in which this was so, and demonstrated the validity of such a concept as that of a core gender identity by their finding that beyond the age of about two and a half it becomes increasingly difficult or impossible for most people unequivocally raised to change gender.[2]

Following the clinical data, however, one comes upon a curious fact. There are certain rare people who, late in childhood, in adolescence, or in maturity, are able to change their gender successfully and without great internal shock. The following material from a representative case shows how this can happen.

This person is an example of a "woman"* who did not have the opportunity to develop a clear-cut core gender identity. The patient, a skilled technician in his mid-forties, reported this dream, while struggling to change from a woman to a man: "I am working, designing something. I woke up and thought, Wow, why hasn't that ever been made! A measuring mechanism with several screw adjustments on it. There was one on the market; I'd never seen one or heard of it. It was pertinent to the work I was doing." The following summary of his life presents associations for the above dream; in fact, it was while reminiscing about his life and treatment many months after the end of the latter that he recalled having had this dream several years before.

He had had from birth, and was always aware of having had, an "enlarged clitoris" (actually, a bound-down, short penis with hypospadias and no vagina). The enlarged phallus was apparent to his parents from birth, but the doctor who delivered the baby declared him to be female, and it is so stated on the birth certificate with no qualifications. The parents were troubled by and influenced in their behavior toward their "daughter" because of the abnormal external genitalia. An example of the way they responded to this is clearly described by the patient: "I am getting chewed out about not being ladylike or something. I stood up at the dinner table, choked with tears, and practically shouted at my father and mother, 'Well, what am I anyway, a boy or a girl?' My father rises from the other end of the table very red in the face—from the neck up just flaming—and sort of raised his hands and shouted back to me, 'That is something we do not talk about —now shut up and sit down and eat your dinner.' That was the end of it right there."

Memories go back to the age of two, of following Father around the farm, playing at helping with the chores, of dressing

*I shall use the pronoun appropriate to the moment as I write; that is, when the patient was living in a female role, she will be "she" and when male, "he." Apropos of this, I have noticed that people who are disgusted by patients who have successfully passed as members of the opposite sex, insist on denying the patient the use of the pronoun the patients wants. This is rationalized as being a necessary confrontation with reality that shows the patient that he isn't fooling anyone.

in Father's clothes, and of active, intrusive games. This behavior was approved by the parents. As the years passed, she became aware of being different from others. A few childhood sexual experiences, consisting of looking at and touching genitalia with a boy, convinced her of this. By the time she was in high school, gym classes became unbearably humiliating. Despite her athletic excellence, she was not fully accepted by the homosexual girls on the teams; although having no facial or body hair, she was very tall, had no breasts, and had the noticeable "enlarged clitoris."

At eighteen, the patient arranged on her own to have a plastic operation to make the genitalia appear more feminine. At that time, the penis ("clitoris") was removed, leaving only a stump of tissue about three quarters of an inch long when erect. The hypospadiac urethra was left intact so that the patient's need to sit down while urinating remained. Cryptorchid testes were removed, and the bifid scrotum touched up to clarify its appearance as labia. Although the patient now profoundly regrets this operation, at the time she felt very relieved. She said that she knew this operation would help quiet other people's questions about her ambiguous appearance. Even if she still felt separated from both men and women, she was at least free to live unquestioned in an area of female society. And so, until her mid-forties she lived an exclusively "homosexual" life as a "butch," except for one brief episode of falling in love with a man.

After these many years in the homosexual community she came to us. She presented herself as a masculine female. It became apparent that she had distorted by repression her perspective of her earlier life, so that instead of seeing herself as a person who was both a male and a female, she had been able more or less to convince herself that she was a very masculine "butch." Only after much treatment did the "hermaphroditic" identity of childhood reappear. At this point, the patient for the first time permitted a referral for a complete physical workup, which produced the clearcut confirmation of biological maleness. Related to this new awareness, he fell in love with a woman two years older than himself, a forceful person who has mothered, advised, and bullied him through five years of a monogamous relationship, the first either had ever experienced for more than a few weeks.* Gradually the patient dropped away the makeup, the bleached longish-short hairdo, the falsies, the sandals, the handwrought, massive silver jewelry, the high-husky voice, the effeminate mannerisms. His birth certificate and automobile license were changed. He left the homosexual community and changed jobs. He now lives an unexciting, nondangerous life with his wife in an unexceptional middle-class neighborhood. Sexual activity is not intense—he has been castrated for many years and takes no testosterone—and has not changed (oral and manual for both partners) since his "homosexual" days.

On the maternal side, he knows of six other relatives of his generation with the same hermaphroditic abnormality. One is a cousin, who, correctly diagnosed at birth, has grown up to be an unequivocal and fertile man. The patient's "sister," ten years younger, is a heavily bearded (though shaven), muscular "woman" (not castrated) who lives an isolated life, hunting, fishing, farming, and hiding from life, clinging desperately to fragments of a feminine identity.

The patient described above exemplifies what is seen in others who have been raised in an atmosphere of parental doubts caused by ambiguous genitalia. In these unfortunate patients the doubts are not put to rest, because proper diagnosis and treatment of the genital abnormality have not been carried out. And so a most unusual gender identity is produced. Such a person feels that he belongs to neither of the sexes to which everyone else belongs; while he develops aspects of both genders, he exists outside of both in a new category.

As a young child, this patient, although assigned to the female sex, had no chance of developing either a male or female core gender identity. She was born with ambiguous-appearing genitalia, which also produced erectile, intrusion-searching sensations. In the

* It is worth noting that on her birth certificate his wife was given the surname of the person who for several years had been living with her mother; the patient's wife has never known whether this "father" was a female impersonator (a male), a hermaphrodite, or a clearly biological female with masculine qualities.

face of this, she was told she was a girl. Her parents' uncertainty, the weightiest factor in confusing her core gender identity, failed to confirm the concepts produced by the genital sensations. Thus, in childhood, erectile, outward-hanging, and at times thrusting erotic tissue and a masculine neuromuscular system were being asked by the ascriptions of her parents and of society to be female.

The patient lived for years in a homosexual culture, where she was accepted. However, her fantasy life and concept of herself clearly differentiated her from her butch colleagues: She felt she was some sort of hermaphrodite; she knew herself as *both clearly a female and clearly a male*. On the other hand, the butches know they are *clearly only females but identify with males*. This patient's core gender identity was not that of the butches she knew. Until her ambiguity was removed in treatment, she envied her butch friends their sense of belonging, even though she well knew their unhappy lives.

DISCUSSION

The clinical data illustrate that there are people who almost from the beginning of awareness of their own existence do not feel themselves to be members of either one of only two possible sexes. Because of their parents' uncertainty as to their "true" sex, the patients are also uncertain. A sense of body configuration that is in fact different from others will produce a different body ego, and the child's observation that he looks different from other children can only reinforce the uncertainty that his parents have produced. He is in that peculiar position of agreeing with all the world that there are, as it says, only two sexes, while he belongs to neither.

Such a person, then, belongs to an entity that has not previously been distinguished from other identity problems. He is a member of a third gender (a hermaphroditic gender), and the resulting character structure and the special ways he has of managing his life, in our society at least, are evidence of a different core gender identity, and therefore of a different life perspective. Depending on how disturbed his parents are about his ambiguity, he can wait with relative equanimity for the day when he will be fixed so that he can belong; or he does not wait, but bows to his fate of not really belonging to the human race; or he makes the best of both worlds, as seems to occur in those rare hermaphrodites who appear to live comfortably in alternating genders.[3] In any case, such a person has the conviction—as solid as that of a man who feels he is a male or of a woman who feels she is a female— that he is not male or female, but both (or neither).

From the numerous reports in the literature that mention a successful change of gender after infancy, I have chosen a recent one to show how these reports confirm the existence of a third gender without the authors being aware of it. Norris and Keettel[4] describe a child with congenitally anomalous external genitalia, who was considered to be a female at birth. The diagnosis was changed at two months to a male. At 13, the child was revealed to be an almost completely normal female, and so, given the choice, she changed back again to being a female. When seen in psychiatric evaluation some years later, it was noted: "She was an attractive, very feminine woman of 20. Her voice was feminine, as were her actions and dress. She was cooperative and tried her best to be as frank as possible. She described herself as being quite outgoing. She enjoyed parties and people. She did little drinking. She was happily married, and stated that she had a full and complete sexual adjustment (she had a normal vagina and clitoris) and enjoyed being a wife. She looked forward to becoming pregnant and having a child.

"There were no apparent neurotic modes of adjustment, no distortion of personality; she related spontaneously and with warmth. . . .

"We have presented the case of a person who successfully changed sexual roles at a time when it is believed that sexual identification is complete and irreversible. How was this possible?"

The authors go on to say that "her early development was relatively neutral rather than oriented to either sex"; later they reported that she had "a sound personality structure" as an adult. They suggest that "one must look further than the gender role when a sex change is being considered. If a person is laden with neurotic conflict, has difficulty in relationship with the environment, and shows evidence of ego defect, then such a change would indeed be inadvisable. But if the patient does have a well-rounded personality with a strongly developed ego, it is quite possible that he (or she) will be able to adjust to the stress of change adequately, just as he is able to handle other forms of stress. The fact that a gender role has been well established should not deter consideration of a sex change when other factors would indicate it, in the presence of a normal personality."

This paper has been quoted rather fully here, because it expresses clearly what is typical in the literature. To their question, How was this [change] possible? Norris and Keettel answered that it was due to the patient's "sound personality structure." I would not argue that they saw a well-rounded* personality, for the absence of psychotic or neurotic symptomatology is also frequently observed by those who study such patients extensively.[5] The suggestion is put forth here, however, that this is not the essential feature that in the above case made the change possible; rather, the thesis of the present chapter more adequately explains the data: A person who does not have a clear-cut gender identity is able, with the relative ease this patient showed, to shift from one side to the other.†

If the parents and other key people in the child's life are not disturbed by the gender fusion, the child remains calm, as did Norris and Keettel's case. If the parents are shocked and so must deny and be secretive and in this way show they know "something is wrong," then a secretive, denying, and unhappy person results, as is seen in my case presented above. But at either extreme,

---

* "The primeval man was round and had four hands and four feet, back and sides forming a circle, one head with two faces, looking opposite ways, set on a round neck and precisely alike, also four ears, two privy members, and the remainder to correspond."[6]

† As Money clearly puts it, "In general, however, it is very difficult for hermaphrodites with uncorrected, ambiguous-looking genitals to establish a firm gender role and identity. It is from the ranks of this group that are drawn those hermaphrodites who request a reassignment of sex or have an ambisexual role and identity."[7]

whether the person has been in a calm or secretive situation, the change of sex later in life can occur without being sensed as a catastrophe, and treatment is therefore likely to be successful. For these patients, to change sex is not to threaten the sense of one's existence, the core identity. They change sex and they change gender *role*, but they do not change gender *identity*. On the other hand, if a person with a well-fixed, unquestioned gender identity is told—and he knows that the person telling him is correct—that he is really a member of the opposite sex, the effect may be devastating. (See Chap. 3.) I believe that even with treatment, such a person never stops doubting the solidity of his identity.

Thus it is possible to account for the otherwise puzzling fact that some intersexed patients do well when they try to change sex and others do not. It may be said that the ones who do well do so because their gender identity was not well fixed in either the male or female core gender; the ones who do poorly do so because to change their sex is to give up their gender, and for them no longer to belong to their ascribed gender is no longer to belong anywhere; that is, their sense of identity has been shattered.

This chapter is written to dispute the implication that this fundamental aspect of character structure—gender identity—can shift easily. The evidence is quite the reverse. When a male has no question from birth onward that he is a male, he will always think he is a male; when a female has no question from birth onward that she is a female, she will always think she is a female. When a person has no question from birth onward that he is either both male and female or is neither male nor female, he will always think he belongs to a different sort of gender from anyone else in the world. He will then be able to shift rather well from an uncertain role to the role of either of the two usual genders, if assisted in such a shift. This capacity to shift gender role is as much an unalterable part of the patient's identity as is the inability to shift in normals.

A practical conclusion follows from the above. In order properly to treat such people after early childhood, one must accurately determine the patient's core gender identity. If it has become firmly established, as it more or less is beyond two to three years of life, then it should not be changed. If the patient belongs to the third gender, then treatment cannot help but be successful unless grossly mismanaged. Correct diagnosis is essential for successful treatment.

CHAPTER 5

The Sense of Maleness

For most psychoanalysts, it is axiomatic that the development of male sexuality is dependent on how the little boy manages the fantasied dangers and pleasures of having a penis. His pride in the power of his penis and his growing awareness of its value as a source of physical pleasure are threatened by his knowledge that there exist penisless creatures and his fear that he may be made into one. Recently, there has been increasing discussion in the literature, especially by Greenacre,[1] of a period of phallic awareness earlier than the classic phallic stage. It is likely that from birth the infant boy becomes more and more aware of his penis, first by feeling that it is there, and later by endowing it with meaning.

The two theses presented in this chapter are derived from these beginnings of phallic awareness. The first is that the sense of maleness—the person's unquestioned certainty that he belongs to one of only two sexes, the male—is permanently fixed long before the classic phallic stage (age 3 to 5). The second is that although the penis contributes to the sense of maleness, it is not essential. It should be noted that neither of these theses contradicts the importance, as contributions to the boy's developing masculinity, of the phallic stage or the oedipal conflict and its resolution.

By "the sense of maleness" I mean the awareness *I am a male*. This essentially unalterable core of gender identity is to be distinguished from the related but different belief, *I am manly* (or masculine). The latter attitude is a more subtle and complicated development. It emerges only after the child has learned how his parents expect him to express masculinity; that is, to behave as they feel males should. He will also have some idea of what it means to be feminine, to the extent of having such fantasies as "I should like to have a baby" or "I should like to have breasts," the sort of wishes that make up part of the "latent homosexuality" ubiquitous in many cultures. But the knowledge that *I am a male*, with its biological rather than gender implication, starts developing much earlier than either the sense that *I am masculine* or such disturbances in gender identity as *I am feminine; I am like a female*. Such attitudes cover over the core gender identity, but it is nevertheless present behind them. Transvestism is a clear example of this: A man with a sense of being feminine while cross-dressing is excitedly aware of being a male. Essential to his perversion are the two aspects of gender identity: the later one, *I am feminine*, and the earlier core identity, *I am (nonetheless) a male*.

To repeat, the sense of core gender identity (that is, of being male or female) in the normal individual is derived from three sources: the anatomy and physiology of the genitalia; the attitudes of parents, siblings, and peers toward the child's gender role; and a biological force that can more or less modify the attitudinal (environmental) forces. It is not easy to study the relative importance of each of these factors in normals because one factor cannot be dissected from the others. However, certain rare patients provide such an opportunity, as is shown in two boys both born without penises, who yet seem to have matured with no question of their core sense of maleness.

The first patient, genetically normal, was born with no external penis but with bilateral testes in a bifid scrotum that resembled labia majora and labia minora, and with a perineal urethrostomy. He was given a boy's name and reared as a boy.

Severe right hydronephrosis with infection and fever in the first three months of life led to removal of the diseased kidney at ten months. At this time, the perineal urethrostomy was shifted so that the new urethral meatus was approximately where the penis would have been. The bifid scrotum was left unchanged. He has a normal prostate. For four months after surgery he did well, but in his second year, because of recurrent infections, an indwelling catheter was placed in the bladder to preserve the remaining kidney. This instrument has remained almost constantly to the present.

Before he was born, this patient's mother left his father, who dropped completely out of the child's life. Some months later she remarried. The patient and his three-years-older brother now had a stepfather and a stepsister, the patient's age. The stepfather quickly took an active role in the family. A masculine man, he has since served as an excellent object for the child's identification processes. Therefore, in spite of the early dangerous illness, the surgery, the unending medical attention, and the constant presence of the catheter, the patient, now four years old, is considered by both parents to be a psychologically normal boy. They compare him with his seven-year-old brother, whom they consider to be more sensitive, more shy, and a little effeminate. The patient is described as rough, active, and unquestioning in his status as a boy; he enjoys playing football and baseball with his father as well as wrestling with his older brother and sister, these vigorous activities being surprisingly little hampered by the catheter and bottle he carries with him. To quote his mother:

He likes to wrestle and box. He likes all kinds of sports—likes to watch sports on television, and he told me that he wants to be a wrestler—big and fat—when he is big. He plays with dolls, but when he does, he is the father and his sister the mother. He is different altogether than our daughter; she can't occupy her time by herself. You can give him a little stick and send him out to play, and he can make everything out of that stick you can imagine. He doesn't need other people to play with, yet when there are other children he can play with them. They know he has a catheter on. They have seen it and they accepted it and treat him like he was a boy.

At first I was real shook up about all this because I had never heard of anything like it. At the time he was born my first husband and I were on the verge of divorce, and at one time I even thought about giving the baby up for adoption before he was born, but I changed my mind the minute I saw him. He dislikes anything that looks girlish to him—any kind of shirt that even looks like it might belong to a girl—he wants everything boy's. He will play in the den by himself. Sometimes he is Superman. He will mimic quite a bit; in other words, when it comes time to comb his hair, he will comb way back like his father. . . . Someone may hit him hard and really hurt him, and then he will come to me and cry, and I will say, "Go fight your own battle." One day he was mad at his brother for something—let him have it in the stomach and took his breath away. When he gets mad he has a temper, but he treats his sister pretty well; he doesn't fight with her.

His stepfather reports: "He likes to go down to where I work. I think he wants to be like me." Of his catheter and its collecting bag, his mother says, "For a while, I had to talk to him about showing it to everybody. He would lift down his pants and show it to everybody and I had to tell him that you just don't do that. He was proud; to me and everybody else he gave the impression that he was something special because he had this and they didn't. He thinks the tube is part of him. When they took the tube out for four months, he missed it. I think he missed it because it was part of him. He wasn't uncomfortable. After they took it off, they also took his bottle off. Every night he would go to bed and would want to take that bottle to bed with him even though the tube was not actually in."

The patient loves to imitate his stepfather, who has a gun collection; the little boy imitates him with his own toy guns. His stepfather manages a gas station; the child's favorite game is "Gas Station," digging in the dirt, building a station with blocks, or using the cat's tail as a gasoline pump. Obviously, this interest is overdetermined, being influenced not only by his stepfather's business but also by the tremendous interest and concern with his own "gas pump."

The parents are convinced that he would not wish to be changed to a girl. Some months before I saw him, a urologist suggested that perhaps he should henceforth be raised as a girl. His sister was present during the discussion. The patient's mother later heard her telling him that he was now going to be a girl, to which he responded, very vehemently, "No!" His mother told him to pay no attention to her. He has never mentioned the episode since.

In summary, the parents clearly describe a little boy with a masculine identity, shown in his relation with his mother and stepfather. Father and mother appear to have no significant problems in their own gender roles. The appearance of the child corroborates all the information the parents give. He is an alert, friendly, intelligent, warm, and unafraid child, so openly likable that one cannot adequately account for his obvious ego strength in the face of the continually traumatic medical experiences except by attributing his excellent mental health to his good luck in the parents he has. He talks easily of the games he likes to play—baseball, hunting; of his toys—trucks and toy gas stations; his relationship with his sister and brother—the games of house, in which he says he always plays the part of the father; his sister, the mother; and his older brother, the policeman. He talks a great deal and with great pleasure about his dog, his puppies, his cat, and his chicken. In appearance, mannerisms, and expression of interests, he leaves no doubt that his gender identity is well formed and that he is unquestionably masculine.

When asked why he was in the hospital, he picked up his tube and held it out to be seen. When asked why he had the catheter, he replied, "Because I was born . . . in October." Thus, he revealed not only his knowledge but also his manner of dealing with it and of trying to get it out of his mind. It is impressive that this child who has been severely handicapped anatomically, who has been subjected to many medical and surgical experiences, who knows he is abnormal and ill, whose mother was divorced early in his life, has nonetheless progressed in a remarkably normal manner in his general psychological development and, more specifically, in his development as a boy with masculine identifications. It is a tribute to his mother and his stepfather that all this has been accomplished in the face of such great obstacles.

Some experts in the Medical Center recommended that the child be converted to a girl, and that the parents' efforts be devoted to assisting him to transform himself into a woman as the years pass. This recommendation was made because of all the surgery required to construct an adequate penis which, even so, could never have a sexual function. However, because he was so clearly masculine, because it was believed that his gender role could not be shifted by means of psychotherapy or other learning, and because his life span will not be very long because of the disease in the remaining kidney, the psychiatric recommendation was that he continue to be a boy. The parents were relieved by this recommendation, which has been followed by the attending physicians.

The second boy, first seen when fifteen, was also born a genetically and anatomically normal male except for having no penis and a perineal urethrostomy. Both testes lay within a normal scrotum. He is the youngest of four children, the oldest a mongoloid, the others a normal girl and boy. Before the patient was born, his mother was no longer interested in having more children. Given the proper assignment of sex at birth, he was raised as a boy without question by a relatively uninterested mother and a natty, bejeweled father who was a perfume salesman.

Beginning at one and a half years, this patient was in the hospital six times in five years—the last time, for three years unrelieved by a single visit home. His many operations, a laparotomy followed by repeated plastic procedures, resulted in a phallus which a urologist has recently described as "a monstrosity of unearthly appearance." It is not surprising that in adolescence his behavior became a problem at school and in his neighborhood. He has also created a fantasy life which in times of stress spills over into real life in a paranoid manner. "I am the grandson of God and maybe I am the Messiah," he said in white-faced, fear-ridden rage during a critical moment in treatment.

Out of a mass of clinical data related to the development of this boy's gender identity, only two observations directly pertinent to a sense of maleness will be discussed. The first of these is concerned with the patient's "homosexuality." Since the age of seven he has played with neighborhood boys sexual games that have evolved into ceremonies with rules that must be maintained. For example, in one called "the Pull," each of the two partners pulls forward on the other's penis in order to produce pain. The first to cry out in pain loses and must do to the other whatever he asks. Although the patient, with his skin pedicle, feels no pain, at times he cries out. Both children know this is a false cry, but neither ever admits it. In the mutual masturbation that follows, the patient usually permits his partner only a few minutes—timed by the watch—for he does not want his partner to have an orgasm. After this, the partner has to do exactly the same for the patient (except with anal intercourse, which the patient cannot perform because the skin pedicle has no erectile ability). It is clear from his descriptions that a main purpose of these activities is to force the partner to treat him as if his "penis" were as good as one that works (a mechanism of "proving" the penis that seems related to the dynamics of exhibitionism). Besides using homosexuality in this successful defense against loss of the sense of maleness, these activities, plus a peculiar form of masturbation (described below), are also the patient's sexual life. He scarcely dares to contemplate heterosexuality, though he is friendly with girls. He gets some instinctual gratification from these games, though it it scarcely direct, for he has never been able to have an orgasm. He has no genital, perineal, oral, or anal sexual sensations analogous to the genital sexual excitement of normal men; he simply feels an increased body tenseness that gradually exhausts itself. Almost every night he has a "fight," a hypnagogic masturbatory writhing with a blanket between his legs, during which he has only homosexual fantasies of being a ruler over a man, such as a movie star, and commanding this man to play the "games." The patient has never fantasied having an erection or an orgasm. After the "fight" he wets the bed while asleep. This is accompanied by dreams of the same activities he has fantasied or has actually performed. The elements of these dreams make little recognizable use of such dream mechanisms as condensation and displacement.

There is a second factor in this patient's life that he uses to augment gender identity: knives. This is not simply the interest in knives seen in so many boys; although it has the same psycho-dynamic meaning, it is more intense and concrete. Much of the child's personality is expressed through knives. Each has a name, a different function, and a different hiding place in his room. All, of course, are used as a language of aggression. For example, the knife "Uncle Eddie" is always placed in a special pocket of a special knapsack. When the patient is angry at home, he takes the knapsack from a shelf and rides off on his bicycle. He rides once around the block; if he then throws knapsack and knife on the lawn, he is only moderately angry; if he rides off with knapsack and knife, he is very angry and will be gone for an indefinite number of hours in an unknown place; if he throws the bare knife on the lawn, serious trouble lies ahead.

Obviously, he is a very disturbed child. Nonetheless, for all his disturbances in ego functions and problems with formation of an identity, his core gender identity is intact. He has no question that he is a male. For him, the critical issue is that although he is a male, he is a very defective one. Both his normal development and his psychopathology are aimed at repairing the psychological damage or learning to live with it, not in becoming a female. He does not offer himself as a female to his sexual partners, nor is he feminine in appearance or action. His "homosexual" activities are, rather, a pathetic and grandoise attempt to insist to other males that his "penis" is as good as theirs. He of course does not really believe this, but in the real-life fantasy of these sexual games there is at least the momentary belief that he is intact.

DISCUSSION

These two cases are presented as evidence to support two theses, that the sense of maleness (or core gender identity) is present and permanent from earliest life, and that the penis is not essential to this sense of maleness. A variety of psychological and biological forces causes the male child to develop from birth an increasing awareness that he is himself. This "himself" includes an awareness that he belongs to a gender, and early in life he recognizes that not everyone belongs to this gender. Later he learns that not everyone possesses the prime insignia of this gender—the male external genitalia—a disturbing discovery. By this time, he knows he is a male (whether a masculine one or not). Normally, the male external genitalia are a sign to the individual and to society that this is a male, but they are not essential to producing the sense of maleness.

It follows from this argument that clinical states in which there are fantasies and behavior of a feminine sort—both in normals and in those who develop perversions—are not evidence that the core gender identity, the sense of maleness, has been made uncertain, but rather that these fantasies and their behavior overlie and hide the core gender identity. For example, behind Schreber's delusion that he can give birth as a woman to God's children is that unalterable knowledge against which, in part, he raises the delusion as a defense, his awareness that he is a male.

The four-year-old boy shows us that the sense of maleness is established before the fully developed phallic stage. His parents report that his behavior well before the age of four was decidedly masculine. It is apparent that the child is not simply normally masculine, but has also had to exaggerate his masculinity because of his parents' fears that he might not be sufficiently so, as well as his own independent discoveries of his defectiveness. Nonetheless, although the expressions of his masculinity are intensified, his sense of maleness is unquestioned. Establishing a sense of maleness seems to be more difficult without the proper genitalia, but obviously it can be done. However, it is not necessary to turn to this boy to demonstrate the thesis, for observation of any normal child of either sex of one and a half or two years shows that clear distinctions are established very early between the gender roles of the two sexes. The second thesis, that the penis is not necessary for a sense of maleness, is demonstrated by each of the boys described, for neither doubts that he is a male.

We have said that the core gender identity is produced in the normal by the anatomy and physiology of the genitalia, by attitudes of parents, siblings, and peers, and by a biological force. These three sources re-enforce one another; to speak teleologically, their redundancy may serve the purpose of more securely guaranteeing the masculinity that will be required for procreation.

Be that as it may, the cases presented show that these three factors are not all essential. In our two cases, inadequacy of the external genitalia did not destroy the capacity for a clear-cut core gender identity to develop so long as the parents felt unquestioningly that their child was male.

One question must be raised, although it cannot be answered. Though the penis played no part in these boys' gender identities, may not the testes and scrotum have done so? Most theorizing on male sexuality by analysts takes into account only the penis. Bell,[2] in papers not concerned with the problems of identity considered here, stresses the need to consider all the external male genitalia, not the penis alone, in order to understand castration anxiety. We may ask, Is not the sense of maleness created solely by scrotum and testes when there is no penis? I do not think so, though they undoubtedly contribute, at least by confirming to the parents that the ascription of maleness is proper. But this opinion requires support from clinical evidence—the study, for example, of persons without penis, testes, or scrotum who are nonetheless raised from birth as males. I believe such studies would support an even broader thesis than the one I have stated, namely, that although the external genitalia (penis, testes, scrotum) contribute to the sense of maleness, no one of them is essential for it, nor even all of them together. In the absence of complete evidence, I agree in general with Money and the Hampsons,[3] who show in their large series of intersexed patients that gender role is determined by postnatal psychological forces, regardless of the anatomy and physiology of the external genitalia.*

It is interesting that both the little boy with kidney disease and the older boy with the long period of hospitalization in childhood have, in a psychological sense, created a penis that has the same symbolic, aggressive, and intrusive meaning as in normal males. For the first child, it is his catheter and collecting bottle; for the second, it is his knives. Whether there is a primitive biological (instinctive) need for a penis that tends to compel these

*I would make the exception that the biological forces may at times play a significant role, even outweighing the kind of rearing the child is given. This matter will be considered at greater length in Chapter 7.

children to invent the organ if they cannot grow one, or whether such invention is due to psychological pressures or results from a combination of the biological and environmental, cannot be answered by the data. However, these two cases at least suggest that when a little boy knows he is a male, he creates a penis that functions symbolically the same as those of boys with normal penises.

CHAPTER 6

The Sense of Femaleness

The conclusions drawn in the last chapter regarding the sense of maleness apply as well to the development of the sense of femaleness. The first awareness of the sex to which she belongs develops in the infant girl from birth on, and, while having its biological sources (especially sensory perceptions of the genitalia), this awareness is the result primarily of parental confirmation—a fancy term for the myriad of expressions regarding her sex and gender that the girl senses from her parents from birth on. This is a nontraumatic learning experience in the beginning, as taken for granted by the infant as her learning that she has only one head, two eyes, a mouth, and so on.

The equivalent of the little boys who are born without penises, but recognized at birth to be males, are little girls who are genetically, anatomically, and physiologically normal except for being born without vaginas. While such a defect may cause a girl or woman great pain when it is discovered, I have not seen or heard of any such woman who had a disturbance in core gender identity—that is, a fundamental uncertainty as to whether she is a female or a male. Gynecologists, with much more extensive experience with these women, concur; they do not find severe gender defects. These women do not seek to have their bodies masculinized; rather, they press the surgeons for immediate vaginoplasty.

Such an anatomical defect may make a woman feel flawed; she may question whether she is feminine enough without it, or she may dwell on the thought that the vagina the surgeons gave her is not the real thing, but she does *not* think she is a male, and she does *not* wish to be converted into a male.* It may be taken as evidence that they feel themselves to be truly female that these women seek to have a vagina constructed and then use it enthusiastically; Masters and Johnson report that when these women have had an artificial vagina created, it is not only physiologically and biochemically essentially normal, despite the fact that its "mucosa" is created from a skin graft, but these women have demonstrable evidence of orgasms which are physiologically indistinguishable from those of women with natural vaginas.[1] I think it can be shown that the sense of being a female develops out of the same roots (parental attitudes and ascription of sex, genitalia, and a biological force) as that of being a male, and that this core gender identity persists throughout life as unalterably in women as in men.

If this is correct, there is good reason to question Freud's remark about women: "Their sexual life is regularly divided into two phases, of which the first has a masculine character, while only the second is specifically feminine" (p. 228).[2] In fact, an important reason for writing this chapter is to join with those who have questioned whether Freud may not have distorted his whole description of the development of "sexuality" in both boys and girls by his insistence on beginning the story in certain regards only after the child was two or three years old (the onset of the phallic phase). While he gradually came to see the tremendous

---

*If Freud had worked with a woman without a vagina, I think he would have seen that the only thing a woman wants more than a penis is a vagina. It is only when a woman has normal genitalia that she can afford the luxury of wishing she had a penis.

significance of the preoedipal relationships, and especially the great importance that mothers hold for their developing children, his discussion of sexuality (by which he seems to have meant both the development of the capacity for eroticism and the related, but still rather different quality, gender) is quite distorted. There is evidence that what Freud considers the first phase of gender development in a little girl is in fact a secondary phase, the result of defense against a growing awareness that there are people whom the little girl feels are better off, and whom she recognizes as belonging to the classification "male."

This was an issue raised a long time ago, most clearly by Horney[3] and Jones[4] in the 1920s and thirties and most appealingly, in 1944, by Zilboorg.[5] These three anticipated others* in stating that Freud was bringing a personal bias to bear on his theory regarding masculinity and femininity. Because it also exemplifies the feelings of Horney and Jones, the following is quoted from Zilboorg's work:

"Clinical findings forced attention to be concentrated on what is designated as the phallic phase of development. The empirical weight of the phenomenon left little doubt as to its dynamic role both in man and woman. However, when this phenomenon had to be assigned a genetic place in psychoanalytic psychology, two conjectures were made which were both intimately interdependent: first, that both boys and girls go through a preliminary period during which no psychosexual differentiation between them seems to exist; and second, that both boys and girls then enter the phallic phase.

"It is on this point that disagreement began to be voiced; Jones summarized the situation most succinctly when he said: 'In Freud's description of the phallic phase the essential feature common to both sexes was the belief that only one kind of genital organ exists in the world—a male one.'

"Freud insisted on this point to the last, equating clitoris with penis and assuming definitely that vaginal libidinization does not

---

*I cannot refrain from at least footnoting here the impressive work by Bettelheim, *Symbolic Wounds*, which reviews anthropological data demonstrating men's envy and fear of women's femaleness.[6]

take place until the girl has extricated herself from the vicissitudes into which the phallic phase leads and keeps her via the
oedipus complex.

"A few years before Jones considered specifically the phallic
phase, he had suggested that 'the phallic phase in the development
of female sexuality represented a secondary solution of psychical
conflict, of a defensive nature, rather than a simple and direct
developmental process.'

"As early as 1924 Karen Horney pointed out that

The conclusion so far drawn from the investigations—amounting
as it does to an assertion that one half of the human race is dis-
contented with the sex assigned to it and can overcome this discontent
only in favourable circumstances—is decidedly unsatisfying, not only
to feminine narcissism but also to biological science;

and two years later, in 1926, she added:

From beginning to end my experience has proved to me with
unchanging clearness that the oedipus complex in women leads (not
only in extreme cases where the subject has come to grief, but
regularly) to a regression to penis-envy.

"Jones pithily summarized the problem by stating:

There is a healthy suspicion growing that men analysts have been
led to adopt an unduly phallocentric view of the problems in question, the importance of the female organs being correspondingly
underestimated.

"Here one has the first definite suggestion that the feminine
castration complex, in its milder form of penis envy as well as in
its more intense form of castrative hate of man, might be a secondary development, a by-product of an earlier phase which is
distinctly feminine and based perhaps on vaginal uterine libido-
reactions. In short, one might say that the woman is naturally and
primarily a woman with maternal drives, and that only the flight
from womanhood created by certain factors forces her into a
masculine role. . . .

"The point at issue at first appears rather trivial, and yet it is fundamental, for it involves the question of whether femininity is primary in the civilized human female, or secondary and subsequent to the rudimentary masculinity. It is a question of whether the vagina is the primary libidinous pathway in the woman, or the clitoris. . . .

"It does seem that androcentric bias interferes with recognizing some fundamental error. Should one admit that he has been in error, he will be confronted with the necessity of recognizing woman's biopsychological independence, so to speak—the equality of the sexes in the scheme of things. One wonders then whether this suggestion might not be resisted rather sternly, for fear that the genetic theory of sex which was formulated by psychoanalysis might then have to fall by the wayside, and with it perhaps the whole structure of psychoanalysis. That this eventuality is totally improbable even if the sexes be granted full psychoanalytic equality is not at first clear; it is quite possible that it is one's cultural lag which makes it extremely difficult to give up the androcentric bias to which one still unwittingly but sternly adheres and which interferes with serene consideration of the problem. That the issues debated reflect a true protest against the androcentric bias, which in psychoanalysis appears as the phallocentric one, can be easily observed from the major trend of the debate from its very beginning. Karen Horney stated this issue clearly and with utmost candor:

I, as a woman, ask in amazement, And what about motherhood? And the blissful consciousness of bearing a new life within oneself? And the ineffable happiness of the increasing expectation of the appearance of this new being? And the joy when it finally makes its appearance and one holds it for the first time in one's arms? And the deep pleasurable feeling of satisfaction in suckling it and the happiness of the whole period when the infant needs her care?

"There is no denying that there is more than a merely personal psychological credo in this query of Karen Horney's. It deals with a fundamental biological issue which cannot be brushed aside. Later on, Horney called attention to frequent fantasies of rape which occur in women before coitus and long before puberty, and she concludes: 'I can see no possible way of accounting for the origin and content of these phantasies, if we are to assume the non-existence of vaginal sexuality.' "

Throughout this paper, Zilboorg argues eruditely—and, to me, convincingly—for the proposition that there is a primary femininity. However—an issue with which I disagree—a critical part of his argument depends on his first accepting a tenet of Freud's, that the clitoris is masculine, the vagina feminine, the clitoris active, the vagina passive. He says: "It is a question of whether the vagina is the primary libidinous pathway in the woman, or the clitoris" (p. 272).

To me, one cannot *prove* that the clitoris is simply a little penis and is thus masculine or more active than the vagina (though it can have phallic meaning to a woman). More important, I think there is clinical evidence that the sense of being a female and even of feeling feminine (which is really an algebraic sum made up of so many different separate parts) is independent of the female genitalia. The purpose of this chapter is to present evidence for this.

CASE MATERIAL

If we were to design an experiment to help us understand the development of the sense of femaleness, we would wish to study several types of patients: (1) females without vaginas but otherwise biologically normal; (2) females who are biologically neuter, but whose external genitalia at birth looked normal so that no doubt was raised in their parents' minds as to the sex of the infant; (3) females, biologically normal except for masculinization of their external genitalia (but with vaginas), who were raised unequivocally as *girls*; (4) females, biologically normal except for masculinization of their external genitalia (but with vaginas), who were raised unequivocally as *boys*; (5) females who are biologically normal but without a clitoris.

The first category is one familiar to gynecologists. Its outcome is a sense of femaleness with an accompanying femininity that leads as frequently as it does in anatomically normal women to women's tasks and pleasures, including marriage, vaginal inter-course (in the artificial vagina) with orgasm, childbearing (when a uterus is present), and appropriate mothering. The following case illustrates this.

The patient is a 17-year-old, feminine, attractive, intelligent girl who appeared anatomically completely normal at birth, but behind whose external genitalia there was no vagina or uterus. Her parents, having no doubts, raised her as a girl, and female and feminine is what she feels she is. Breasts, pubic hair, and feminine subcutaneous fat distribution began developing at age ten (since she has normal, ovulating ovaries); although she had bouts of monthly abdominal pain, there was no menstruation. At age fourteen, a routine physical examination—but for the first time including examination of the genitalia—revealed she had no vagina. Subsequent workup demonstrated that the uterus was also missing, although the ovaries were present and functioning normally. She was told these findings. "What shocked me most," she recalled, "was I wanted to have kids . . . and I wanted a vagina. I wanted to feel like everybody else. I wanted to use mine. I mean, when the time came around I wanted to use it. I didn't want to feel different from anybody . . . which I did . . . and still do now."

When given the opportunity for a vaginoplasty, she insisted on it instantly. Afterward when asked how she felt about now having a vagina, she said, "It's different; it's better; it's a step further. I feel like anybody else now." This is not literally true. At another time she makes it clear that she feels almost like other girls and that this is deeply gratifying, but she cannot escape her awareness that her vagina is not one she was born with.

Her reaction was what we would expect of a female who had no question as to her sex and who had the desires and fantasies (hopes) of a feminine woman. The absence of vagina and uterus had not damaged her sense of being a female, though since age fourteen the knowledge of this absence had made her feel like a defective female. She never felt she was a boy or ever wanted to be a male.

The second case, described in Chapter 2, is represented by the chromosomally XO girl without gonads or any physiologically significant levels of female hormones. You will recall that she is feminine, wants to be, and works at being, attractive in the ways that other girls do; she wants marriage, intercourse, and babies. While she knows she is anatomically defective, as with the non-neuter woman in the first case in this chapter, she does not question that she is female.

Subjects in the third (masculinized females raised as girls) and fourth (masculinized females raised as boys) categories have been of key importance in the work of Money and the Hampsons.[7] They studied differences in gender identity that arose in infants with the same defect—adrenogenital syndrome. In this condition, the external genitalia of the otherwise normally sexed female infant have been masculinized *in utero* by excessive adrenal androgens. They describe two such children, both biologically normal females, genetically and in their internal sexual anatomy and physiology, but with masculinized external genitalia. The proper diagnosis having been made, one child was raised unequivocally as a female (category three); she turned out to be as feminine as other little girls. The other, not recognized to be female, was raised without question as a male (category four) and became an unremarkably masculine little boy.

In the fifth category is the female normal in all respects, except for the congenital absence of a clitoris. While never having seen such a case, I guess that such a child would have no question that she is a female; hence, during infancy and childhood she would develop an essentially intact sense of femaleness, although, like the girl without a vagina, the part of this sense that would have resulted from the body sensations of that part of the anatomy would be missing. Beyond such speculation, we do have a clue in regard to such people. It is the practice in certain parts of the Moslem world to excise the clitoris of every female—some in infancy, some not until years later. Despite the fact that there are today millions of such women, they do not fail to develop or ever lose their sense of being females; nor do they or their men report that their femininity is reduced.

DISCUSSION

Except in the very rare situation where the parents are uncertain from birth on whether they have a boy or a girl, whatever complicated feelings they may have about having a daughter, they will not doubt that she is a female. And, barring some fanciful explanation—such as that she has an inherited racial unconscious awareness of creatures who have penises—the infant will unquestioningly develop her sense of the dimensions and sensations of her body from her own sensory experiences, which confirm for her, her parents' conviction she is female. In this way, an unquestioned sense of belonging to the female sex develops. As with males, this sense of gender is fixed in the first few years of life and is a piece of identity so firm that almost no vicissitudes of living can destroy it. Even a severe psychosis or the deterioration of organic brain disease will not loosen the core gender identity. While other aspects of gender identity may be severely distorted in the symptomatology of such illnesses, the severe disruptions of gender identity we often see in psychotics (Schreber is an example of a marked case) are not evidence that the sense of maleness or femaleness has been destroyed. The patient still knows his sex, and in unguarded moments behaves appropriately for his sex, though his delusions and hallucinations reveal the force of his *wish* to be a member of the opposite sex.

It seems to be well established that the vagina is sensed, though probably not erotized, in little girls, yet I believe that it is not the essential source of femininity. Just as with little boys, in whom the presence of a penis greatly augments the sense of maleness but is not a *sine qua non*, little girls without vaginas develop an unquestioned sense of femaleness. They do so because their parents have no doubt they are females. I presume that an awareness of their biological femaleness coursing below the surface of consciousness augments their development, but, as we have seen (Chap. 2), even in its absence in the neuter (XO) child, a feminine gender identity develops if the infant is unquestioningly assigned to the female sex.

Having committed himself to the position that little girls believe themselves to be castrated boys,* Freud is out on a limb,

*Freud's transsexual theory of female sexuality: Psychologically, women believe themselves to be males trapped in a female body (castrated) and yearn only to have their bodies transformed by adding on to it a penis.

with the faulty premise leading to unwarranted conclusions.* For instance, he says that "the first steps towards definitive femininity" (p. 232) occur only after following a "very circuitous path" (p. 230),[8] by which he means that no *first* definitive femininity has appeared before the phallic stage (age 3 to 5), a statement which simple observation contradicts; that working out the rage produced by penis envy on one's first husband is the reason that "as a rule, second marriages turn out much better" (p. 234),[9] an opinion that we would be hard to prove to be a rule; and—the famous one —that as a result of the anatomical distinction between the sexes, he, (Freud) "cannot evade the notion (though I hesitate to give it expression) that for women the level of what is ethically normal is different from what it is in men. Their super-ego is never so inexorable, so impersonal, so independent of its emotional origins as we require it to be in men. Character-traits which critics of every epoch have brought up against women—that they show less sense of justice than men, that they are less ready to submit to the great exigencies of life, that they are more often influenced in their judgments by their feelings of affection or hostility—all these would be amply accounted for by the modification in the formation of their super-ego which we have inferred above. We must not allow ourselves to be deflected from such conclusions by the denials of the feminists, who are anxious to force us to regard the two sexes as completely equal in position and worth . . ." (pp. 257–258).[10]†

*See Zilboorg ("Masculine and Feminine," p. 268): "All agree that in the examination of natural phenomena the introduction of values is perilous to truth. I am inclined to believe that it is the introduction of the concept of the superiority of man in the psychoanalytic theory of sexual development—a concept of values—that is responsible for the general lack of clarity."

†Professor Henry Higgins maintains the same position:
  "Women are irrational, that's all there is to that!
  Their heads are full of cotton, hay, and rags.
  They're nothing but exasperating, irritating,
  Vacillating, calculating, agitating,
  Maddening, and infuriating hags! . . .
  Why can't a woman be more like a man?
  Men are so honest, so thoroughly square;
  Eternally noble, historically fair;

One gets the impression from observing little girls—and I cannot believe you have not seen the same—that they show definitive signs of femininity long before the phallic and oedipal phases and that one can trace these early traits of femininity from at least the first year or so of life, not ever seeing them disappear as the little girl grows up and becomes mature. If the observation is correct, then this fundamental building block in Freud's theory of the development of femininity—penis envy and castration complex—becomes only one aspect of this development rather than the origin of it, and opinions like those of Freud quoted above must stand or fall on demonstrable evidence, no longer buttressed by the theory that women are by nature inferior to men, their personalities simply variants on the theme of their being castrated males.

It would seem that for Freud there is no such thing as a woman with aspects of femininity that are primary and not just the result of resolution of conflict, of coming to terms with disappointment, of renunciation—as if the history of femininity in a girl starts in mid-childhood, by which time she begins to react with troubled affect, restitutive fantasies, and changes in her character structure to what she imagines to be her missing penis, and, in our culture, the disadvantages that come with being in the category "female." Such an approach fails to take into account the long period of time when the infant girl would have no more reason to complain about her femaleness than she would about any other part of her body.

However, for the girl born without a vagina or uterus, described first in this chapter, since sensed representation of these parts could not exist even dimly, her sense of femaleness could

---

Who when you win will always give your back a pat
Why can't a woman be like that?
Why does ev'ryone do what the others do?
Can't a woman learn to use her head?
Why do they do everything their mothers do?
Why don't they grow up like their father instead?
Why can't a woman take after a man?
Men are so pleasant, so easy to please;
Whenever you're with them, you're always at ease . . ."11

not be exactly the same as that of anatomically normal girls.* I am not alleging that the body ego of this girl is the same as that of an anatomically normal female, for she has not had that vaginal awareness which is dimly present in anatomically normal little girls. I presume that with the latter there is a sense of space within, of indefinite dimensions but definite significance, produced especially by the vagina and even more vaguely by the uterus, this sense being brought in time by use more clearly into the sensed body ego, in a way comparable to the building up of the infant's body ego by the felt use of the various parts of its body.

Let her words indicate how, despite her femininity and her unquestioned sense of being female, that part of her core gender identity produced by body sensations was formed a bit differently from the anatomically normal girl:

"We were taught in school about menstruation [at age 10, four years before she was told she had no vagina or uterus]. I never understood it at all. I even read the books, and I still didn't understand it. I just didn't figure . . . nothing fit in. My mind was just a blank to it. Then in the 8th grade, I recognized more—that there was a vagina. Yet I still never knew what was intercourse. I didn't know I was different from other people."

I then asked her if, after the school lectures describing the vagina and uterus, she became aware that she was lacking. "No, in fact you may think it a little ridiculous, but I'll tell you how I thought girls menstruated—from the breasts. But they *had* explained how menstruation really occurred. I don't know *how* I thought that."

She says she looked as normal as other girls she saw nude; however, when her girl friends began talking about their first sexual experiences in adolescence and she began picturing more

---

*I am certainly not trying to say that all women have the identical sense of femaleness but only that one anatomically normal girl whose parents do not question her sex assignment will have just about the same core gender identity as another—and that these girls have a very different core gender identity from those raised as boys or as hermaphrodites and not much different from those with absent vaginas but with sureness of sex assignment.

clearly what a vagina was, she does not recall exploring for hers, although she was now masturbating.

Then, still before being told she had no vagina and with still no conscious thought that she might not have one: "I'll tell you what happened the first time when I realized something must be wrong. This boy tried to rape me. He had me down and there was nothing I could do. He started to have intercourse with me—and he just stopped. I thought maybe he was just stopping because he felt bad. Then [much later], for some reason or another, I came out and told somebody I thought I was never going to have kids—and yet I still did not know anything [about the abnormality] and I've never been able to explain that. I felt I couldn't have kids and I wanted kids and I felt I couldn't and yet I don't know what gave me those feelings. *I did not know a thing*" [her emphasis].

In other words, a girl's conviction that she is a female comes from her parents' conviction,* but that part of her awareness of being a female that comes from her sensing her genitalia will vary according to the anatomy and physiology of these tissues (without varying so much that she does not believe herself to be female).

As with little boys, in time the increasingly complicated structure of the personality will overlay the core gender identity with complications and subtleties of gender which are not to be our concern now. I am referring to the varying degrees of masculinity that can be found in little girls: the identifications with their fathers and brothers and the development of masculine traits; fantasies of being like boys; envy of the masculine role and of the prized insignia of that role, a penis; disturbances in resolving the oedipal situation; and so on. However, as with the clearly masculine behavior of little boys, one can see evidence of gratifying, unquestioned femininity in little girls, often by the time they

---

*I do not mean that parents' attitudes are all that is necessary psychologically to produce a core gender identity. They are a *sine qua non*, but all the richness and uniqueness of identity development that goes on *within* the individual will fill out the dimensions and qualities of the identity. However, I shall not be discussing these intrapsychic events; the psychoanalytic literature has been concerned with this for years.

begin to walk. These vary from culture to culture (and from family to family), but even though learned, by this early age they are nonetheless already rather firm parts of the child's identity.

These ideas may have some relevance for treatment. It is possible that the analyst's view of a successful analysis may be skewed if he feels that he has reached the core of a woman's femininity when he has been able to get her to share with equanimity his belief that she is really an inferior form of male.

CONCLUSION

Freud says: "We have found the same libidinal forces at work in it [female sexuality] as in the male child and we have been able to convince ourselves that for a period of time these forces follow the same course and have the same outcome in each.

"Biological factors subsequently deflect these libidinal forces [in the girl's case] from their original aims and conduct even active and in every sense masculine trends into feminine channels" (p. 240).[12]

Strangely, in the face of what they must have observed daily in their own small children, there are still analysts who are committed to this attitude of Freud's. Yet it is hard to believe that a marvelous observer like Freud could have really believed that the development of masculinity and femininity is the same in boys as in girls until the phallic phase. It may be that having committed himself to this theory ("We have been able to convince ourselves") Freud tended to ignore his observations. There are hints that he was aware of an earlier phase before the little girl discovers penises, a phase before femaleness has been depreciated:

When the little girl discovers her own deficiency, from seeing a male genital, *it is only with hesitation and reluctance that she accepts the unwelcome knowledge.* As we have seen, she clings obstinately to the expectation of one day having a genital of the same kind too, and her wish for it survives long after her hope has expired. The child invariably regards castration in the first instance as a misfortune peculiar to herself; only later does she realize that it extends to certain other children and lastly to certain grown-ups. When she comes to understand the general nature of this characteristic, it follows that femaleness—and with it, of course, her mother—suffers a great *depreciation* in her eyes (p. 233).[13]

I have italicized some of this quotation, for therein Freud indicates the earlier phase of primary femininity. "When" means that time has already passed and that there was a time before "the little girl discovers her own deficiency"; the word "depreciation" indicates a process that started at a higher point and then retreated.

Therefore, I think that Freud also knew of a time in the little girl's life when she did not feel depreciated, but rather accepted herself unquestioningly as a female.

CHAPTER 7

A Biological Force
in Gender Identity?

The cases discussed so far confirm that gender identity is created postnatally as a result of psychological influences: First, the anatomy and physiology of the external genitalia, by which is meant the appearance of and sensation from the visible and/or palpable genitalia, and second, the attitudinal forces of the parents, siblings, and peers. This chapter will look more closely at a third possible determinant, a biological force, which, though hidden from conscious awareness, nonetheless seems to provide some of the drive energy for gender identity.

I have now seen seven cases in which a biological abnormality of one of the criteria for determining sex was present but unknown to the patient, and yet the patient's gender identity was like that of a person raised in the opposite sex. The question arises in these patients whether the abnormality of sex influenced gender behavior in a biological manner or whether the observed effects were psychologically produced.

By a "biological force," I mean *energy from biological sources* (such as endocrine or CNS systems), *which influences gender identity formation and behavior.* We will look at these seven cases to see what clues we can find and also what questions can be asked that may jeopardize a proposition that a biological force plays a part in the development of gender identity.

The strongest argument in favor of a biological force is the work on lower mammals that was briefly noted in Chapter 1. This work indicates that single doses of sex hormones during the animal's critical period, just before or just after birth, depending on the species, can organize as yet unknown parts of the brain so that for the rest of the animal's existence, it is fixed in its gender and sexual behavior as if it were in some regards a member of the opposite sex. However, this is of limited help to us at this date in understanding humans; similar experimental studies being impossible, we have had to turn to clinical cases for hints. There is no need to stress that these cases do not *prove* anything.

Throughout his writings Freud[1] never abandoned the position that biological forces are an essential though unmeasurable part of the development of sexuality, including masculinity and femininity. He was not able, however, to investigate these forces further because the patients with whom he worked were not appropriate. The present chapter is an attempt to reopen this issue by means of clinical data (though it has long since been studied by other methods, as reviewed in Chap. 1). It may be possible to gain insight into these forces by clinical examination of certain patients who demonstrate their influence with unusual clarity.

We have seen that most intersexed patients develop the gender identity appropriate to the sex that is ascribed to them at birth. Thus, if the parents are not aware of the intersexuality and bring the child up as a boy, he will feel himself to be a boy, regardless of his biological status. There is no acceptable evidence in the reported cases in the literature that the latent genetic and biological forces exert any measurable influence; the processes of psychological childhood development seem to suffice to explain the resulting gender identity. However, among the intersexed patients I have seen are rare individuals in whom neither the external genitalia nor the gender role assignment and attitudes of the parents primarily determined the individual's gender identity; in these people, some other factor seemed to be of decisive importance, since it overrode these primary influences.

This other factor, assumed to be biological, will be indicated in the reports of seven such "experiments" that follow. These patients were trying to maintain that they possessed a certain gender, despite the fact that everyone disputed this claim. The patients in question had arrived at a gender identity in a way opposed to that which is general in society. For example, although they had the external genitalia of one sex and the upbringing appropriate to that sex, they still felt certain that they belonged to the other sex. This certainty was not for the purpose of enjoying sexuality; they were not primarily interested in obtaining sexual gratification, nor did they come for treatment because of inability to obtain it. They wanted help because of their impelling desire to be granted the right to belong to the sex they felt was theirs. They were remarkable in that their speech, posture, gestures, walk, and other behavioral evidences of gender identity were in accord with their own psychological conception of their identity, though in flagrant contradiction to their anatomical structure. It was clear to all who observed them that these patients had the capacity to behave as we ordinarily expect a masculine man or a feminine woman to behave.

CLINICAL MATERIAL

Case One: The first patient to be described is a child who at birth was found to be an apparently normal female and so was brought up as a girl for fourteen years. When the child was born, the external genitalia seemed to be in keeping with what is expected of a normal girl. There was not even the appearance of an enlarged clitoris, a common enough normal variation in females. The physician and parents had no hesitation in considering the child a girl, and she was so named and brought up. Within a few months of her birth, however, her mother was already having difficulty. The baby was active and forceful, whereas her mother, a graceful, feminine, neurotically masochistic "perfect lady," increasingly despaired because her daughter was so lacking in gentleness and so much in opposition to many of the feminine qualities the mother wished to bring forth in her daughter.

The mother talked of her daughter's infancy and childhood:

> The child ate so fast. It wasn't like a little girl, but at least it wasn't a big fuss over every meal. There was no colic. As a tiny baby she moved too fast. She did everything crash! bang! nothing gentle, yet because she ate well and slept well she was a good baby. But there was still the feeling in me—no one else. They all thought I was just very young, that I was worried for nothing. She didn't rebel about eating, but that seemed rather gluttonous to me, like a little animal just eating—and *playing wildly*. I don't recall her ever sitting down with a book, except to take a magazine and fling it over the floor and look in the pages and page through and tear it—*violently*. Not to hold the book as if it was something beautiful to see, but as if it was something to destroy or throw away. The bicycle seemed not a thing of pleasure but something to get as far and as fast as possible.
>
> [Q. When you use the word "violent," how far back in her life do you feel that it applies?] About one. When she was put out to play on the sidewalk with the other children, she played with a neighbor boy and they played very much alike. So I thought, well, here is a fellow human being. It dissatisfied me. I wanted a *girl*—but here she was a—I never figured out if I was hostile to her or she was hostile to me. There was just nothing.
>
> [Q. What didn't she give you?] She seemed to take the food and go to bed. I couldn't play with her. That's what I was crying about the day I was looking at her, as a tiny baby. I was trying to play games and sing songs. There was nothing I could do for her. It was just as if I wasn't even necessary to her.

Thus it can be seen that from the very first, something was going wrong between mother and child. The rest of the child's development proceeded as if according to plan, but not the mother's plan. In all games with other children the child seemed to take male roles. Her bicycle was her pride and joy and was constantly kept polished. She could scarcely be forced into girls' clothes. The family finally compromised and permitted her to dress as a cowboy or in jeans and T shirt, except on rare occasions such as Christmas or Easter, when she grudgingly consented to wear dresses. Her companions were boys, with whom she played boys' games—hiking, jumping, exploring, football. In the course of these she was bruised and cut, continually tearing her clothes but never complaining, enjoying the roughness and tension of these games. She did average work throughout school, but well below what psychological tests had measured as her potential.

As the years passed, her mother bribed, threatened, and, when allowed by her, loved her in continuing attempts to get the child to dress, walk, sit, talk, think, feel, and otherwise act as a feminine girl. The great effort failed. The hopelessness produced was only partly eased by three subsequent babies, two boys and a girl, all of whom had intact gender identities.

When adolescence approached and her girl schoolmates began to sprout, she became quiet. At this time she developed a cold with a hoarseness that persisted. Because of this change in voice she withdrew in great embarrassment from all social contacts and wanted to drop out of school. A physical examination made at this time raised doubts shortly to be confirmed at the Medical Center. When the inquiry was completed, it was revealed that although the external genitalia looked the same as those of a normal girl of her age, she was in fact a chromosomally normal male with a fully erectile tiny penis of clitoral size, hypospadias, bilateral cryptorchidism, bifid scrotum, and normal prostate. Just before the final confirmation by the urologist and by the chromatin staining techniques, the child was first seen in psychiatric consultation. In her bandana and dress, she looked grotesque, and yet this was her usual appearance, for she had been told for fourteen years that she was a girl.

Since she was so obviously miserable when dressed as a girl, since she had such a tremendous desire to be considered a boy, and since the anatomical and laboratory tests indicated that she was unequivocally a male, it was decided to tell her she was a boy. While this was done with some trepidation, there seemed to be more danger in not telling her. So she was informed of her proper sex in a straightforward manner. It had been expected that she would react to this information with great intensity, and so the lack of impact the information seemed to have on her was striking. It must be stressed, on the other hand, that neither was there any pathological absence of affect. She acted as though she were being told something of which she had always been dimly aware, of which she had no doubt. She did not show the sense of relief of someone who has struggled to prove a point, or the sense of triumph of one who has won after strenuous opposition, or the sense of shock of one given some astonishing information. Rather, her attitude was as if to say, "Yes. Very good. Thank you. I am not surprised."

This poised and well-integrated reaction was confirmed by the patient's subsequent behavior. She went home, took off her girl's clothing, and became a boy, immediately beginning to behave like other boys in the community. This was confirmed when the child was seen a few days later, and in the six years that have followed there has been no reason to change this opinion.

The family, foreseeing some of the complications that might arise for them in the community, moved to another neighborhood, where they were unknown. Their boy was accepted fully at a new school, where his past history was not known. He now takes part in sports as an equal with other boys, has close friends among boys who have no doubt that he is a boy and about whose own masculinity no doubts have been raised. He goes on dates with girls; he is attractive to girls; he is attracted to girls; he has no difficulty in getting dates; he is capable of intense sexual feelings toward girls; he has orgasms with ejaculation either from wet dreams or genital masturbation, in both of which his sexual objects are females (as they were before he was told he was a boy). He has the typical concerns, pleasures, and interests that are found in young men who have been brought up without any ambiguity about their gender identity. He is tall, well built, good-looking, with no effeminate mannerisms or vocal expressions, and with no hypertrophied masculinity either. Significantly, he has passed from being a mediocre to an excellent student. For example, he came to be among the first in his class in mathematics, a subject in which he had done very poorly when he thought he was a girl. He developed for the first time an affectionate and understanding relationship with his mother, and for several years treated his father openly as a rival. Parenthetically, it may be remarked that this had some interesting repercussions on the family, but that is not the province of this chapter.

An area of great concern was his embarrassment in undressing in the presence of other boys because of the absence of a penis. He has undergone several surgical procedures to bring the testes into the scrotum and especially to attempt to construct a penis. These operations, which he accepted stoically because of his high motivation, did not succeed in producing a very successful penis.

Despite the very severe disturbance in mutuality from birth onward, not only is the young man not psychotic but he is remarkably free from neurotic signs and symptoms. During his first fourteen years—living as a girl—he (she) gave the distinct appearance of being severely maladjusted in certain important areas of his (her) life, but within no clear-cut diagnostic category. This disappeared instantly with the change from being a girl to being a boy, and it must be considered to have been, not an inner conflict, but a reaction against a reality situation. This child, who dealt with the world as though he were a boy, though apparently in a female body and treated by everyone as a girl, reacted "neurotically" to this external pressure. Before the change, the child was shy, had few friends, and was chronically moody, irritable, and somewhat depressed. However, when told that she was a boy, the symptoms of the supposed neurosis completely disappeared. It might be expected that such a momentous change in the life of a child would have led to psychological reverberations; however, it has not been possible, despite the many hours spent with him, his father, or his mother, to discover any neurotic symptoms beyond the range of the normal emotional variations of healthy people in our society. It appears that what was momentous for the investigators was not so for the child. Somehow, preconsciously, the "girl" must always have known his true gender identity. Being told he was a male only confirmed to him that now the world was no longer opposing something in him. Thus there were no reaction formations, denials, ruminations, or the excessive doubting that one would expect in a person in conflict about his identity. He only reacted as though the world had come to its senses. Although he would seem to fit into the category of those rare people who have no difficulty in shifting their gender identity from one sex to the other, this of course is not so. He never did shift his identity from female to male; he simply had his right of maleness confirmed by society.

DISCUSSION

In order to understand better the development of such patients and their remarkable ability to maintain a fundamental sense of maleness in the face of overwhelming pressures from their anatomical structure and from the meaningful environment, it would be well to put aside the clinical data for the moment and consider further elements which go to form gender identity. Most discussions of this problem concern themselves with the consequences of castration anxiety and penis envy. Essential as these are for understanding some of those patients who later in childhood develop internal conflicts about their gender identity, such problems as castration fear and penis envy are not, in my opinion, relevant to the discussion of what contributes to the formation of the earliest aspects of gender identity. By the time of the phallic stage, an unalterable sense of gender identity—the core gender identity ("I am male"; "I am female")—has already been established in the normal person.

While later, as a result of conflict, the boy may have doubts about his maleness, or may even say, "I wish I were female," this still implies that he knows he is male but would rather it were otherwise. Thus we can say that the *core* gender identity remains unchanged throughout life; this is not to say that gender identity is not constantly developing and being modified, but only that at the core the awareness of being either a male or female remains constant. It has already been noted that this core gender identity is produced, starting at birth, by three components. The first of these is the contribution made by the *anatomy of the external genitalia*. By their "natural" appearance, the external genitalia serve as a *sign* to parents that the ascription of one sex rather than the other at birth was correct. Then too, by the production of sensation, the genitalia, primarily from external structures but in females additionally and dimly from the vagina, contribute to a part of the primitive body ego, the sense of self, and the awareness of gender. The second component, the *infant-parent relationships*, is made up of the parents' expectations of the child's gender identity, their own gender identities, the child's identifications with both sexes, libidinal gratifications and frustrations between child and parents, and the many other psychological aspects of preoedipal and oedipal development. The third component is the postulated *biological force*.

On turning attention back to the patient described above, we find that much of the previous discussion of the sources of the sense of gender identity does not apply. First, the child's anatomy did not give the visual confirmation of maleness, nor was there a penis or a scrotum with testes to produce genital sensation. Second, the child's development defied the parental attitudes. Additionally, the effects of excessive physical closeness between mother and infant, a factor that will interest us when we consider transsexualism, was not present. Yet *there was an overpowering drive unalterably and continuously thrusting this child toward maleness.* While it is true that problems may arise in certain people, postponing the development of core gender identity, or leading to grave problems or doubts about their gender identity, this child practically from birth on gave unmistakable indications of a force at work that was powerful enough to contradict his anatomy and environment. It was of such magnitude that even the absence of male genitalia did not raise significant doubt in his unconscious mind as to his maleness. This force was also strong enough for him successfully to withstand the "temptation" to submit to the entreaties and seductions of his parents to adopt a feminine attitude.

There appears, then, to be evidence in support of the theory of a third component producing gender identity, a force which, variably powerful in most humans, is usually hidden silently behind the effects of postnatal psychological influences. This force has as yet not been demonstrated by endocrinological or neurophysiological studies, though musculoskeletal development, height-weight ratios, and so forth, in children may be part of the biological base of such gender differences.[2] It may in part be made up of interrelated hormonal thrusts such as occur in the fetus to differentiate the Wolffian (male) from the original Mullerian (female) structures found indistinguishably at first in *both* sexes.[3] Some day, such a force may be found to be the algebraic sum of the activities of a number of neuroanatomical centers and hierarchies of neurophysiological functions. At present we cannot be so specific.

This concept of a biological force would seem to be controversial. Although many analysts accept a constitutional biological factor in all sexuality, libidinal development, and personality development, it is not likely that they would have accepted a thesis that in certain patients this biological force is the decisive factor, that in fact it can even override anatomy and the parental influences. However, if this thesis is correct, then the normal development of gender identity may be as follows:

A sex-linked genetic biological tendency toward masculinity in males and femininity in females works silently but effectively from fetal existence on, being overlaid after birth by the effects of environment, the biological and environmental influences working more or less in harmony to produce a preponderance of masculinity in men and of femininity in women. In some, the biological is stronger and in others weaker. The case that has been discussed would fall in the former category. Had he been born with normal-appearing external genitalia, he would have grown up unnoticed as a masculine boy. This line of reasoning tends to confirm what many have suggested, that some effeminate men and masculine women are the result of an unhappy combination of a weaker biological push toward proper gender plus noxious effects of environment (e.g., a special type of pathological mother-infant relationship).

This is a heavy burden of speculation to hang on a single case. So it may be well to indicate with brief summaries of other patients that, although rare, more people do exist in whom a need to belong to the gender opposite to the only acceptable one was substantiated by biological criteria.*

*When the material in this chapter was first published, a second case, a genetic male with testicular feminization syndrome, was briefly described, in order also to exemplify the presence of this biological force. A more complete report on this patient now appears in Chapter 11; as the reader will see, this case at the very least indicates some of the excitement and some of the pitfalls in doing clinical research into the psychodynamics of identity development.

*Case Two:** This patient is a 28-year-old genetically normal male, now living as a woman, who throughout childhood was considered to be a normal male.

Certainly he was male in anatomical appearance. However, as far back as memory goes, he was extremely feminine. By means of reports from numerous institutions in which he lived, we have been able to trace back to age four clear-cut evidence of his very feminine appearance and behavior. While he would dress in women's clothes whenever possible, he was never sexually excited by the clothes; rather he put them on in order to make believe that he really was a female, which he wanted to be. As the years passed, he learned more and more how to appear like a female; by the end of his teens he was able to pass successfully as a woman. Among other jobs, she worked as a stripper in a night club; she could do this because in her late teens she had developed normal-appearing female breasts, had very scant body hair, and had the appearance when nude of a normally well-rounded woman, though hiding from view normal-appearing testes and penis. She also would have sexual relations with men who knew her to be a male, but, as with transsexuals, would not have intercourse with any man who was interested in her penis. Occasionally during such relations, and also with masturbation, she had orgasms but reports being disgusted by her penis, wanting to be solely female.

She came to the attention of medical experts by chance. Hospitalized as a result of hepatitis, she was discovered to be genetically and anatomically male, except for the secondary sex characteristics already described. However, biopsy of her testes revealed them to be markedly atrophic, with germinal aplasia; a diagnosis of Sertoli Cell Only Syndrome was made. Examination of seminal ejaculate showed a total absence of sperm. (This much of her history has already been reported.[5]) Having been completely worked up and diagnosed at one medical center, the patient was then transferred to UCLA, where the workup was repeated and the same diagnosis made independently.

*Howard J. Baker, M.D., helped me with the evaluation of this patient and was also responsible for the patient's treatment. Dr. Baker and I have subsequently reported on the patients described in this chapter.[4]

After some months of evaluation and treatment, she revealed that *after* her breasts developed in her late teens, she had begun taking estrogens fairly regularly for a few months to make them even larger. Since this did not work, she stopped taking the hormones. Each endocrinologist we consulted said that the picture of Sertoli Cell Only Syndrome seen in her testes could not have been simulated by these exogenous estrogens. It is interesting that although she said she did not take estrogens in the years afterward, the feminine appearance of her body maintained itself. Even before she told us she had taken estrogens in the past, we felt we should rule out her being simply a transsexual with no endocrinologic defect; so, during the four months we kept her hospitalized, she was under close surveillance. She did not take estrogens. Nevertheless, she did not have any involution of her secondary sex characteristics, nor did she develop a menopausal syndrome as should have occurred had she been taking estrogens up to that point.

Eventually, her penis and testes were removed and a vagina was created. The testes were again carefully examined and again the diagnosis of Sertoli Cell Only Syndrome was made.* She now lives as a woman.

Not having information about his relationship with his mother from birth on, one cannot be sure that this person is not a transsexual who coincidentally has an endocrine disorder. We only know that because of normal male appearance at birth, the doctor said he was a boy. With this ascription he quite properly became a male in the eyes of his mother, father, brother, peers, society—of everyone except himself. Then, just as the transsexual male does, he lived in his feminine manner, eventually learning to pass successfully as a woman.

The history of developing clearly female secondary sex characteristics at first made us think of a biological force at work

*There is uncertainty in the literature and among the experts with whom we have talked as to whether testes with the abnormality that has been seen in this patient's case can produce excessive amount of estrogens. Some experts say that this does occur, while others say that they do not believe it can occur, though they cannot be positive it does not. For whatever it is worth in our understanding, Sertoli Cell *tumors* in dogs always feminize.

from infancy on as a cause of this femininity. Then the secret she revealed of taking estrogens in her teens made us doubt for a while that any such innate biological force was at work; but again our stand was changed when the endocrinologists stated that the testicular defect could not be produced by any amounts of exogenous estrogens. We remain cautious, however, for these opinions are tempered in our minds by the memory of our having been fooled in a similar case (see Chap. 11). Throwing onto the scales the disagreement among experts as to whether the testes in Sertoli Cell Only Syndrome produce estrogens, the reader can see how one can finally work his way from the warm nest created by the certainty of a theory into the more trying, yet more exhilarating world of uncertainty.

Still, cases such as this should not be brushed aside at this stage of our lack of knowledge, but should be kept in our bellies to give us just a touch of indigestion.

Case Three: This patient, now 30 years old, was born an apparently normal male, because of unexceptionally normal male genitalia. However, from earliest childhood, the little boy insisted on dressing in girls' clothes, putting on girls' jewelry, walking and talking like a girl, playing only with girls, and being interested only in girls' activities. When dressing in girls' clothes, the child never became sexually excited. This activity was seen by the child's grandmother (who substituted from birth on as the child's mother, since for ten years the real mother was hospitalized with tuberculosis). His father was enraged the first time he saw his son dressed like a girl, and he positively forbade such activity whenever he got any hint of it. At the same time, the grandmother was permitting it.

In adolescence, the boy's body became feminized: female subcutaneous fat distribution, small but feminine breasts, and well-developed nipples. Facial hair, which did not appear till his mid-twenties, is still very sparse. There is no body hair other than pubic and axillary, and limb hair is very sparse. Dressing and passing as a young woman, she would go out on dates, and in her twenties became engaged to a man. However, she never really became sexually excited, although on one or two occasions, developed a partial erection. She denies ever masturbating or having an orgasm.

She was referred to me because she was in trouble with the police for refusing to dress or live any longer as a man. In addition to her feminine ways and her feminized body, the penis was normal-sized, but with very small testes. Chromosomes were XXY. A diagnosis of Klinefelter's Syndrome was made and confirmed by testicular biopsy and endocrine studies.

She now lives as a woman, following removal of her penis and testes. (This patient has been reported in greater detail elsewhere.[6])

Case Four: This patient, first seen at age 17 in the Medical Center, came, shortly after birth, to the people who raised him; his natural parents are unknown. His "mother," the woman who raised him, had died just before he came to us and so was not available to describe his infancy. His "father," however, said the child was a completely normal-appearing male infant, and that no question was raised then or at any other time as to whether or not he was a male.

However, from at least age 4, according to his father, he had long hair and wore women's clothes whenever possible; when required to dress like a boy, he still wore effeminate-looking clothes. His foster parents apparently went along with his femininity, for he did most of the domestic chores around the house and was permitted to do so in feminine clothes. All his mannerisms and fantasies from earliest childhood reflected his desire to be a girl. He says that he has always felt that he was a girl. Just before coming to the hospital, having quit school because they insisted on treating him as a boy, and following the death of his foster mother, he had taken over as the "woman" in the family, cooking and keeping house for his foster father.

He denied ever taking estrogens, denied masturbation, overt homosexuality, heterosexuality, and ever having had erections or wet dreams. He said that around age 13 his breasts began to enlarge.

Physical examination revealed a male with normal male hair

distribution, musculature, stature, and penis size. However, he had minute, barely palpable, very soft testes that were obviously nonfunctional. In addition, he was found to have a mass of hard tissue about 2 centimeters in diameter beneath each nipple, with the rest of each breast obviously enlarged. He appeared feminine in his speech and gestures; this was enhanced by his long hair, long nails, feminine gait, and artificially high voice. Following complete laboratory studies, the patient was diagnosed as suffering from testicular failure of unknown etiology (chromosomes were XY).

Once again, then, we have an example of a normal-appearing male who nonetheless feels himself to be a female and whose development from puberty on confirms this feeling. Once again, also, we cannot rule out the possibility that his earliest experiences with his foster mother and father had caused his femininity, and that the biological abnormality is coincidental. At the same time, we are struck by the number of people we are seeing who have such biological abnormalities and who also have severe aberrations of gender identity.

*Case Five:** This 24-year-old pretty, delicate, graceful, quietly stylish woman was born an apparently normal male and, like the other cases of gonadal failure I am reporting, said that she felt herself from earliest childhood to be very feminine, wished she were a girl, and developed the feeling that she was somehow female, though not denying the maleness of her anatomy.

Her fantasy life, games, dress, and other activity all reflected the markedly feminine gender identity. She reports—and we cannot possibly confirm—that in puberty her breasts enlarged. We can, however, confirm her claim that she did not develop facial, body, or limb hair in the amount or distribution that males normally do. At 17, she stopped living as a male, and has passed undetected as a female since that time. As in the other cases, her sexual fantasies and actual choice of sexual objects has always been heterosexual, if we measure this quality by the

*Dr. Baker has been responsible for this patient's treatment since my first evaluation.

standard of one's core gender identity and not simply by one's anatomy.

Her report that she had small testes could not at first be confirmed, for she had been castrated several years before; the circumstances were apparently clouded, for the physician who performed the operation has refused to give us any information. However, her eunuchoid body build, the softness of her skin, and her female hair-distribution would seem to be the result of some disturbance in testicular function. Then we learned from one of our urologists that he had seen her years before, finding hermaphroditic genitalia and very small testes. The endocrinologist diagnosed the patient as a "chromatin negative Klinefelter's Syndrome."

*Case Six:** This 42-year-old man had felt as though he were a girl as far back as he can remember. He has memories of around age 3 of dressing in girls' clothes and playing with girls' toys, doing this because he only felt comfortable in girls' clothes. He received no sexual pleasure from this.

Until he was 19, he had no body hair, spoke in a very high-pitched voice, and was very thin and short. Although he married at age 18, he had never had an ejaculation with intercourse. At age 20, he was diagnosed as having some form of hypogonadism, possibly Klinefelter's: bilateral testicular tubular atrophy, increased interstitial ground substance, thickened and hyalinized tubular basement membrane, tubules lined with Sertoli cells, a few spermatogenia and primary spermatocytes, but with little if any spermatogenesis. Leydig cells were virtually absent. Because of this, he was placed on testosterone, grew four inches in height, was able to ejaculate, developed body hair, had some mild deepening of his voice; despite all this, he continued to feel as though he were a woman.

Then, at age 24, he was switched to another form of testosterone and began to feel less like a woman. He gradually gave up cross-dressing, went through a period when he felt he belonged

*Once again, I am indebted to Dr. Baker, who has provided all the above information on this patient, whom he is treating.

to neither sex, and then began consciously to feel more and more like a man. At the present time he feels himself to be a male and a man, though a passive one with many interests and fantasies of a female nature. In his dreams, he appears as neither male nor female but rather as an "it."

Case Seven: This is a 40-year-old genetically normal male who nonetheless has a number of anatomical defects of his primary and secondary sex characteristics. Physical examination showed him to be beardless and without body hair, with a high-pitched voice that sounded normal for a woman, prominent and female-appearing breasts, small testes, a small penis, and a female escutcheon. He has always wanted to be a girl, has always chosen men as his sexual objects, in childhood in fantasy and in adult life in his affectionate behavior. However, he denies erections or masturbation or overt genital sexual experiences with others. He has lived intermittently undetected as a woman for months at a time, and would prefer to do this permanently if permitted.

MORE DISCUSSION

Let us summarize. All seven of these people had no visible anatomical flaw at birth or until puberty. All were raised as anatomically normal members of their assigned sex. Nevertheless, all felt in some way that they belonged to the opposite sex. Then, at puberty, all developed some sort of cross-sex change of their body, in effect confirming their earlier gender wishes. A biological force—e.g., a hidden hormonal or CNS aberration—exerting its effect upon gender identity development from infancy on suggests itself as an explanation.

What have other workers seen? The literature on intersexuality, although huge, is in many ways inadequate for our present study, since most authors do not discuss their patients' masculinity and femininity, or when they do so, they say nothing about the parents' attitudes when rearing the child. However, a review of more than one hundred articles on male hypogonadism alone*

*I am indebted to Dr. Baker for having done this task.

clearly revealed a pertinent clue, suggesting that the biological force that we are postulating may have been seen in other cases besides ours: In those cases of testicular failure, especially Kline-felter's Syndrome, in which manifestations of gender identity were discussed, and where the patients all appeared to be ana-tomically normal males at birth, only later being diagnosed as having Klinefelter's Syndrome, a disproportionately large number* cross-dressed, were homosexuals, and/or had other sexual per-versions. These aberrations, to judge from the literature, occur far more frequently in patients with Klinefelter's Syndrome (and other probably related syndromes with hypogonadism, such as Sertoli Cell Only Syndrome) than in the anatomically and hor-monally normal population. (However, many patients with hypo-gonadism have no disturbances in gender identity.)

Since it is impossible to summarize the entire review here, we can give only representative examples.† There are eleven previ-ously reported cases of Klinefelter's Syndrome who cross-dressed.[8] Of these, at least eight are definitely described as having felt as though they were a woman or desired to become one. Specific information in this area is lacking in the remaining three.

Money and Pollitt reported on sixteen cases of Klinefelter's Syndrome.[9] Two of these cross-dressed, one of them saying that he felt he was a woman and wanted sex transformation surgery. Two were homosexuals. Eleven others were described as having a weak sexual drive, homosexual experiences, or no heterosexual experiences. Only one was married, and he had had no intercourse in twenty years of marriage. In other words, all sixteen of these

---

*There is no point in attempting a pseudo-statistical analysis of this number. It is a strong impression we have, nothing more. In order to give this impression validity, we would need information on the many cases in the literature where no information at all is reported regarding gender identity. What has struck us is that where such information is given, cross-gender behavior and fantasies are so often reported. Still, it may be that the absence of such cross-gender activity is just the reason that gender material is not reported. At least we can say that there seem to be a lot more people with gonadal failure who have overt and severe cross-gender problems than are found in the anatomically normal popu-lation.

†The interested reader will find further information in the works listed in the References for this chapter[7] and more fully cited in the Bibliography.

people had either obvious cross-gender manifestations, or at the very least no heterosexual desires.

Kvale and Fishman, after psychologically testing 12 Kline-felter patients, reported feminine identification and homosexuality in all the subjects.[10] Benjamin found that 28 of 91 male trans-sexuals demonstrated a more or less distinct immaturity and hypo-gonadism to the point of eunuchoidism.[11] Lief and co-workers reported on a male who experienced cyclical alterations of gender identity in association with demonstrable variations in hormonal output.[12] Hoaken and co-workers reported on two Klinefelter's who were pedophiliacs, one of whom desired to become a woman.[13]

Is it really necessary to invoke a "biological force" to explain the data? At the present time, I do not know. My bias is that there *is* such a force, for, being a biologist, I cannot believe that biological substrates are as powerless as some learning theorists seem to believe. However, my disagreement with them is a matter of degree only, for certainly insofar as the development of gender identity is concerned in almost all humans, by far the most power-ful effect comes from postnatal psychodynamic factors. As the patients described throughout this work demonstrate, one can remove the effects of the external genitalia and still get an intact gender identity, and in almost all people, regardless of chromo-somes, endocrine states, and other sources of a biological force, the gender identity that results can be accounted for without having to postulate such a force. However, it seems logical that the effects of rearing are silently augmented by congruence with one's biology.

The cases reported in this chapter therefore introduce an intriguing note, for they suggest that the effects of rearing may very rarely be overturned by something else. Since each of these patients has a defect in a major criterion determining his sex, one can surmise that these patients are impelled by an overpoweringly strong biological force to insist in their thinking, fantasy life, and behavior that they are members of the opposite sex.

Unfortunately, these data do not prove the case; in fact, sev-eral important questions are left unanswered. When this subject of the biological force was first described in 1964,[14] there were

several major errors in my thinking. The first was that one of
the two cases used to demonstrate the point does no such thing.
This patient, by revealing a secret which she had kept from me
for years, has shown that she does not exemplify the presence of
an endogenous biological force but rather the effects of rearing
(see Chap. 11).

The second error was that at that time I had not discovered
that the mother-infant relationship can produce a boy who from
earliest life shows in his behavior his conviction that he is a female
trapped in a male body. At that time I had mistakenly said, "Nonetheless, while these parental attitudes are known to be important
in producing homosexuality and other perversions, they do not
produce an intact core identity that contradicts the evidence
of genital anatomy, so that in the face of all apparent evidence
to the contrary, a child would *know* (rather than only wish) that
she is a he. One or both parents may wish consciously or unconsciously for a child to be of the opposite sex. When this attitude
is expressed pathologically, the parents may permanently damage
the gender identity of their child. The child that results, however,
does not have the unequivocal, solid, unimpaired gender identity
that this child has. Transvestites that claim to be females trapped
in male bodies are common enough, but their core identities have
so many openly bisexual components that these people clinically
look very different from the patients here discussed."[15] Having
by now seen many more patients, and having studied them and
their families in much greater detail, I know that the above statement is not correct. (See Chaps. 8–11.)

A third error, though of no great concern in this immediate
discussion, was that I believed that to produce such a profound
disturbance in gender identity that a child acts as though he were
a member of the opposite sex, the mother would have had such
a generalized noxious effect that many other aspects of the child's
ego development would be badly damaged. Since it was hard to
imagine a mother who would create such havoc in gender identity
not causing much other damage, I could not account for the fact
that an individual such as our first case in this chapter could
lose her neurotic signs and symptoms as soon as she was told she

was actually a male. However, there is now evidence (see Chaps. 8–11) that it is possible for children to be severely damaged in the development of their gender identity and still remain quite intact in other aspects of identity development and ego functions.

The first question, therefore, is whether these presently reported cases are anything more than just further examples of the effects of mother-infant and later intrapsychic and interpersonal relations rather than examples of a biological force.* Since there is no detailed information regarding the ways the mothers treated these infants and the ways the infants responded, except in the first case, we are not in a safe position to say that these people may not just coincidentally possess an abnormality of their sex. This question could be resolved if we had a significantly large number of cases and controls and could thereby answer the question by statistical means. Being so far from this ideal, I can only report these seven thought-provoking cases. It seems unlikely to be coincidental that, in the intersexed patients I have studied, seven apparently transsexual people would appear who also had biological abnormalities of the sorts here described.

Others who believe there is such a thing as a biological force take it to be the main cause of transsexualism. Benjamin[16] reports that about 30 per cent of the transsexuals he has seen have some sort of sexual biological abnormality. Unfortunately, the statement is not confirmed with precise clinical material; we are not sure what the nature of these biological abnormalities are in each case.

So, we must leave this subject without any sense of its having been settled. I hope this material will help keep the door of uncertainty open against those who might close it too soon, and that it will be difficult for anyone without more complete data to decide this issue now. It may also help to encourage the study of further cases in greater detail, so as to give us truer clues.

---

*At least we know they are not examples of a hermaphroditic identity, for in none was there any abnormality of the external genitalia that would make sex assignment uncertain at birth.

Part II

Patients Without
Biological Abnormalities

CHAPTER 8

Male Childhood Transsexualism

So far, all of our "natural experiments" have been intersexed patients, with biological abnormalities being the changed variables. Now I want to shift to people who have no biological abnormalities of sex (so far as any present-day tests can reveal), but with whom life has experimented by changing certain psychological variables that play a part in creating gender identity.

To most readers, there can be few individuals more outlandish than those who insist that their sex is wrong, that they (that is, their sense of identity) are trapped in the wrong body by some grotesque trick of fate, and that the world should permit and even assist them to become members of the opposite sex. Since these persons—transsexuals—are usually quite sane, their claim is more disturbing to the normal members of society whose struggles regarding gender identity are much less intense, more secret, and more or less unconscious. Yet these rare people have brought insights to understanding some of the origins of gender identity that I had not been able to find in more normal people.

Transsexualism is the conviction in a biologically normal

person of being a member of the opposite sex; in adults, this belief
is these days accompanied by requests for surgical and endocrinological procedures that change anatomical appearance to that of
the opposite sex.

The purpose of this chapter is to describe male childhood
transsexualism, a clear-cut, potentially malignant personality disorder which has not previously been identified, although it has
undoubtedly been observed. The boys to be described are anatomically normal; at birth, they were unequivocally assigned to
the male sex. No one has ever questioned that biological state.*
Nonetheless, one boy at age 1 and the others at age 2 were
dressing in women's† clothes whenever they had the opportunity
—at home, when visiting neighbors, or, later, at nursery school.
When no women's clothes were easily available, they improvised,
making dresses out of towels, blankets, or any other suitable material. As part of their cross-dressing, they used jewelry, cosmetics,
women's hats and shoes, and women's underwear. Gestures, walk,
posture in repose, inflection of voice, vocabulary, and subject
matter of conversation were feminine, though only when they
were dressed as or taking on the role of women. Games were
played almost exclusively with girls, with the boys taking girls'
parts, such as mother, sister, nurse, actress. They always sat to
urinate.

This behavior was not casually indulged in, but was insistent,
occurring each day for at least a few hours. The mothers considered this as "cute," though at times they feared it was occupying
too much of the boys' attention—"Darling, why don't you put
that away for a little while? Won't you, please?"—while never,
until treatment started, discouraging the behavior for more than
brief periods. The mothers did not say their boys were girls,
consciously wish they were girls, or give them girls' names.
Nonetheless, they thought the boys beautiful, encouraged them in

* For the sake of completeness, in studying transsexuals I have run a chromosomal analysis on a randomly selected adult, adolescent, and child male transsexual. The results confirmed the findings of all other workers: The chromosomes
are normal; the sex chromosomes in particular are normal XY.

†The term "women" will frequently be used from here on to include both
women and girls.

feminine behavior, and at times consciously daydreamed what their sons might look like as adult women.

On occasion, the boys said they were girls and that they would be women when they grew up. They thought of changing their sex, as was indicated by their asking their mothers if their breasts would grow and why their penises could not be removed.

The reader should realize that the above findings are not the usual evidences of cross-gender identifications so familiar to the child psychiatrist, inferred from so many children's dreams, stories, or games played in therapy. What is seen in these transsexual boys is a blatant and continuously compelling preoccupation.

Green and Money[1] have reported their findings on effeminate boys, as has Bakwin[2] on cross-dressing in children. However, it is unclear from their data whether any or all of these children properly belong in the category of childhood transsexualism to be described. M. Sperling[3] has described the simultaneous treatment of mothers and their little boys who dress in women's clothes. It is likely, to judge from her description of the members of the families in which these boys develop, that she has been treating transsexual boys, but one cannot be certain from the descriptions. Francis[4] describes passivity and homosexual predisposition in latency boys, and again the description may well be that of the infantile transsexual, but since these are older boys, and since data concerning the mother-infant relationship and the time when the cross-dressing activity began are not given, one does not know whether these boys were also infant transsexuals. Bender,[5] in a discussion of homosexuality in children, discusses fifteen boys and girls—"children with difficulties in psychosexual identification." One group of these children comprises those who "identified themselves with the parent of the opposite sex, when the parent of the same sex was hated or feared, was ineffectual, or was entirely absent." Among the cases reported is a six-year-old boy who "expressed a desire to have breasts like his mother and to urinate like her. He wanted to be a girl and have his penis taken off"; he committed suicide as a young adult, as so many transsexuals threaten to do if the world will not accept them as mem-

bers of the opposite sex. While each of these children had a severe
disturbance in gender identity, none but this boy fits the criterion
for transsexualism to be discussed below: a fixed belief that one is
a member of the opposite sex and will grow up and develop the
anatomical characteristics of the opposite sex. In addition, no detailed descriptions of the mother-infant relationships are given for
these cases, nor is there a discussion about etiology. A paper by
Charatan and Galef[6] describes a boy who is probably a transsexual
and whose parents are like those to be discussed here.

Adult male transsexualism is a rare condition[7] in which a
man who has been very feminine all his life feels he is truly a
woman (a *role* and an *identity*) and a female (a *biological state*),
and wishes his body to be "corrected" so that it anatomically ap-
proximates a female's. He is different from the typical transvestite,
a fetishist who uses women's garments for sexual pleasure and who
considers himself a male wanting intermittently to take a woman's
role; or an effeminate homosexual (e.g., a "drag queen"), who does
not get excited by women's clothes and who does not feel himself
to be a woman or a female, but rather thinks of himself as a male
homosexual who likes to dress in women's clothes to mimic and
make fun of women.

The little boy who is transsexual, like the adult, is fully identified with the woman's role, has as many feminine mannerisms,
interests, and fantasies as a little girl his age, and openly expresses
wishes to have his body turn into a female's.

CLINICAL DATA*

This report summarizes findings on three little boys and their
families. These three were the only cases of childhood transsexualism seen in the first ten years of this research project concerned with the development of gender identity. Our having seen
so few probably indicates that this is a very rare condition; however, we can not even guess at its incidence. Moreover, it will

*Material gathered during the psychoanalysis of one of these mothers will
be reported in the next chapter. Greenson has reported more fully on one of
these boys.[8]

take more cases before it will be known whether the findings are significant.

Sons: This condition is called childhood transsexualism because its most obvious manifestation is the boy's feeling that he is a girl; it starts in infancy with the full-blown picture obvious by age 2 to 3. All the findings can be placed under the rubric of *identification with females.* Because of the tremendous pressure of this identification, once these little boys have started feeling like women, the progress they make in cross-dressing and acting like women is limited only by the availability of the clothes and the cooperation of the family in permitting the child to behave in a feminine manner.

Although their ego development is incomplete and their life experience meager, these little boys learn with remarkable rapidity and are encouraged by their mothers to dress themselves in a stylish manner so that they do not look grotesque in the clothes even when they are only two or three years old. They also pick up feminine gestures, posture, ways of walking, and so on that continuously astonish (and, unfortunately, please) their mothers. Members of the family, friends, or other observers get the impression that this behavior must be biologically determined because these children learn it so spontaneously that it does not seem possible that it is not "natural," that is, biological. Each mother has repeatedly noticed that her son will invent a piece of appropriately feminine behavior without having seen it before in a woman. The children are possessed by a never-ending urge to watch their mothers dress, put on makeup, fix their hair, choose clothes and jewelry, and otherwise display femininity. All the mothers comment that at two or three, these little boys were talking with them as equals concerning feminine matters, and were already well on their way to a later-developed impeccable feminine taste.

As these boys grow, they unswervingly express femininity in their play and fantasies. They take only female role in games, never playing with boys unless they can do so as "girls"; they are completely accepted by little girls as equals and quickly take the lead in setting up the games: what the subject matter and plot will be, who will take which parts, and so on. This pressure of feminine fantasying is seen clearly when they become involved in play therapy.

It is interesting to note that all three of these boys are considered to be extremely creative by their families, teachers, and other observers. All have a remarkable precocity with regard to painting, dancing, costumes, designing of clothes, acting, hairdressing, story-telling, and love of music. None is psychotic. None denies he has a penis but all nonetheless expect to be women when they grow up.

Each of these boys was first brought for psychiatric evaluation between the ages of 4 and 5, although each had manifested the gross signs of this condition from age 2 or earlier. In each case, the child was brought in only because some outsider had insisted to the mother that there might be something abnormal about him. In the case of the first child seen, his cross-dressing began a day or so after he first walked, at which time he put on his mother's shoes and with great skill maneuvered around the house as though he had been accustomed to walking in high-heeled shoes. This boy had actually shown manifestations of femininity which his mother recognized were unusual when he was less than a year old; sitting on her lap, he would look at magazines with her and stop her whenever there was a photograph of a beautiful woman, expressing intense pleasure with loud cooing sounds. For the other two boys, the obvious signs may not have begun until the age of 2, though it is quite possible that when their mothers have been observed longer by us, we may find that the earliest signs began sooner.

Mothers: The family constellations from which this condition arose in these boys are strikingly similar. This fact can best be illustrated by first describing the mothers, then the fathers.

While there are obvious differences in these mothers' personalities, two similarities dominate the data. The first is an almost identical way of expressing bisexuality. The mothers are all feminine in the same boyish manner. They wear their hair short but stylishly so, use very little makeup, prefer suits or sweaters and skirts, and all find it inconceivable to wear frilly, fluffy, or ribbony-and-bowed dresses. All three have a conscious sense of being neuter over which they feel they erect a feminine façade. This is not, however, an accurate description of the way they reveal themselves in treatment; rather, it is the way they sense their gender identity consciously. Beneath this neuterness all three can more dimly feel a mild depressive quality that is a constant part of their lives, and treatment reveals a more profound depression that would seriously disrupt them without the overlying defenses just described. One of these women, up to the time of her analysis, had had only one gratifying relationship with another person, and this was with another woman. The second mother has had no affectionate relationship with any adults, but her best friend in high school was an overt homosexual. Not enough is known yet about the third mother in this regard. Heterosexuality does not arouse much enthusiasm in them. All married in their late twenties; all were virgins when they married (and by easy choice); all have been faithful to their husbands; none willingly has sexual relations with her husband more than once a month, often less; and none feels any real satisfaction in her sexual relations (though all can have orgasms). None considers that her marriage is happy or that any affection or real communication passes between her husband and herself, but all three have persisted in their marriages for years. Before treatment, none was aware of desire for other men, and none constructed daydreams of romantic affairs with other men.

All three mothers dressed in boys' clothes throughout latency. (This finding is more significant for these women, who were girls a generation or more ago when this was considered unusual by their parents and peers, than it might be for younger women). They also chose to be almost exclusively with boys, as equals in sports, in fights, and in excluding girls other than themselves from the group. Each mother says that as a child she looked and acted like a boy and had wishes to become male, but, as different from transsexual females, none felt that she was somehow a male or

would grow up to be a man. Each gave up such behavior completely and permanently with the onset of the body changes of
puberty. None now appears like a masculine woman.

The second quality common to the three women is a deep
sense of emptiness, or incompleteness. In the one mother who has
been psychoanalyzed, this characteristic was found to be related
to her relationship with her own "empty" mother, by her acute
fall at age 6 from her position as her father's beloved when her
sister was born, and by a sense of anatomical incompleteness
produced especially by living in a very close relationship with two
masculine, stalwart brothers. While the other two women have
not yet been studied in enough depth to make clear the dynamics
of their sense of emptiness, it has the same quality clinically as
with the first. All have a bright, brittle veneer through which a
gentle, hurt hopelessness shows. All busy themselves through the
day with housewifely activities which they feel are necessary but
meaningless. All feel they do not know themselves but presume
they have no worth. For example, one left high school though
first in her class. Years later, she finished her high school require-
ments, but did not return to school for her final examination
grades because she felt (consciously) that she had "flunked."
Months later she learned that she had received the highest grades.
The other two women have similar attitudes toward their potentials.

Fathers: All three men, dissimilar in many aspects of their personalities as were the mothers, nonetheless share certain essential
qualities. All three clearly are considered by their families and
themselves to be husband and father, yet they are literally almost
completely physically absent from their families. When their
children were infants, these men were out of the house before
the babies awoke and returned home in the evening after the
babies were in bed. Even when the boys were older, they usually
did not even see their fathers throughout the week except at dinner, at which time these silent men hardly communicated with
either words or gestures. The meal over, one man would shut himself in a separate room to work; the other two left the house to

occupy themselves with their hobbies. Even on weekends, they were absent most of the time for the same reasons. As their boys' cross-dressing appeared and then increased in its manifestations, none of these fathers voiced any forceful concern or insisted that such femininity was so unusual that it must be changed.

For that matter, when the mothers finally thought the family should look for help, all three fathers balked. In other words, these men are "dynamically" absent—their absence is a most living, tantalizing one—as compared to the "static" absence of a dead or divorced father. There is reason to guess that, while unseen, these fathers may not just be permitting the mothers to feminize their sons; they may very subtly be pushing their sons back upon the mothers' bodies. However, the evidence will need several years' more gathering before it can be fully reported. None of these men is psychotic or even schizoid. To oversimplify the complexities of their personalities, one has a passive-aggressive personality, one is an alcoholic, and one has an obsessive-compulsive personality.

Psychodynamics and Etiology: These boys do not only wish at times that they were girls, or fantasy themselves as girls. This latter is common, consciously and frequently, in effeminate boys, less frequent and unconscious in more masculine boys; yet none of these effeminate or more normal boys thinks he is a female. What, then, makes these little males maintain, in the face of the anatomic reality to the contrary, that they are nonetheless females?

On the basis of what has been observed so far, one can see certain common factors at work. In each case, the essential psychodynamic process seems to be excessive identification with their mothers, caused by the inability of these mothers to permit their sons to separate from their mothers' bodies. Although the normal infant's increasing capacity to move into and deal with reality is matched by his mother's ability to let him farther out on his tether before she has to rescue him, these mothers cannot permit such freedom. In many essential ways, they treat the infant as if he were part of their own body and therefore part of their own identity.

The most fundamental way in which these mothers produce this blurring of ego boundaries between themselves and their infant son is by literally keeping the child up against their bodies for far more hours of the day and night than occurs in normal mother-infant relationships. These mothers do not even emphasize that amount of separation that clothes would produce within the microenvironment in which the infant lives, for there is more intimacy with infant and mother nude than usually occurs. The mother holding the child is consciously filled with great love and with an almost insupportably intense desire to mother and gratify the infant. These women surround these babies with their flesh, their breath, their cooing voices, and their enveloping movements. Other loving mothers may do this also, but not, I believe, for as many hours a day. Then, at a time when the normal separation of mother and infant is accelerating, these mothers are still nestling the boys in upon their bodies as much as when they were defenseless infants—and it is this delay in permitting the boys to be free of their mothers' bodies, of their constant cuddling and following eyes, that I feel may be the primary pathology.

The problem appears to be not that the baby is held but *how* he is held, how *long* he is held, and the accompanying feelings of overflowing love and concern interwoven (with no reality cause for the concern) that bathe him day and night. One of these mothers says that she kept her child against her body all the time because he had congenital dislocation of the hips; another says she did it because her own mother was so empty and uninterested in her that she herself was never going to do the same to her child; the third did it consciously explaining to herself that she was sad and wanted the comfort of her child against her.

Whatever the reason, these infants are given the most gratifying experience, as closely reproducing intrauterine life as the exigencies of extrauterine life permit. In an atmosphere of permissiveness and love, these infants have their every need gratified instantly by these tremendously solicitous mothers. This means that every sensation the mother tries to produce upon her infant's body is pleasurable or pain- and tension-reducing. It does not deny that

this mother may be struggling to deny hatred of her child's maleness (evidence for hatred of males in one of these mothers, and
its sources in her own childhood, is presented in the next chapter).
It implies only that the impingement of the *effects* of his mother's
feelings upon his body does not produce pain or tension in the
child. Such gratifying ministrations might not be too pathological
in the first months of life, but their persistence for four or five
years becomes a grotesque aberration. These children are not
weaned, toilet-trained, physically punished, or emotionally abused;
whatever their demands, they are gratified. Whenever such a
mother talks about her son, one does not sense that she sees the
boy as separate from herself. Everything is "we": "We sat down
together and talked it over and we decided that it would be best
if we did such and such." These mothers feel no need for privacy
in order to separate themselves from their children, so the boys are
free to join them in the bath or at toilet. Because each of the
boys is the youngest child, the mothers were able to keep the boys
close longer than if another child had been born to interrupt this
symbiosis.

There appears to be a biologically regulated pace for separation in every species, ranging from the newborn who is immediately on its own to the lengthy separation process in humans. H.
and M. Harlow[9] describe three stages of development of socializa-
tion (separation) in monkeys: (1) Mother gives absolute love and
protection; (2) infant begins to want and be able to separate from
mother, and mother encourages this when it is appropriate and
safe; (3) play with peers is sought by infant and encouraged by
mother and other adults.*

We have all seen this process in humans as well. While we

*To quote the Harlows: "The maternal affectional system in the rhesus
macaque, and presumably in all the *Anthropoidea*—monkeys, apes, and men—
goes through at least three basic developmental stages: (1) the stage of maternal
attachment and protection; (2) the transitional or ambivalence stage, which
might also be described as the disattachment stage; and (3) the stage of maternal
separation or rejection. These stages proceed about twice as rapidly in monkeys
as in anthropoid apes and about twice as rapidly in anthropoid apes as in human
beings."

have heard of the pathology resulting from premature separation of infants and mothers, we are less familiar with what would happen with too much bliss.

There may be confusion if the reader feels, because I use the word "symbiosis," that *this* rare kind of symbiosis resembles other mother-infant relationships for which the same term is used. Obviously, using the same term does not necessarily make the living, real relationship the same, for example, in the mother-schizophrenic child symbiosis as what would be seen by an observer in a mother–transsexual boy symbiosis. The latter is blissful: skin-to-skin closeness, no frustrations of sensual pleasures by his mother (no weaning, toilet-training, restriction of masturbation, restriction from playing with and on the mother's body, and so on), no torment, no double bind, no pushing away to provoke separation— and all this continuing uninterrupted for four or five years. Certainly the symbioses that result in normal children or psychotic children are not like that.

The implication in the above discussion is not that close body contact between mother and infant is pathogenic in itself, but rather that it is the vehicle by which certain subtle communications pass from the mother to the infant. Perhaps what is felt by the transsexual-to-be infant is no more than constant pleasure or absence of tension, an ambiance that makes it unnecessary for the child to sense clearly the limits of his own body dimensions and the beginnings of another's body. Thus, one would not expect that in cultures where babies are carried all day by their mothers, there need be an increase in childhood transsexualism if these babies are carried by more disinterested mothers, for the latter mothers are not concentrated on their infants and on vigilantly maintaining the body contact between the infant and mother. Nor, I suppose, did Indian mothers fail to hit or hiss at their papooses if the babies irritated them. In contrast, the mothers described herein do not even have the capacity to recognize anger they might feel toward their babies.

So much has been said, from Freud's earliest papers on, about the crucial effects of fear of castration on the little boy's growing masculinity that the reader may wonder how one can discuss extreme femininity in little boys without relating it to castration anxiety. Most of us, for instance, have seen effeminate boys who have sacrificed some of their masculinity to save their maleness (penis). Are not these transsexual boys the same? The answer suggested is that these little boys are clinically quite different in appearance and have different past histories. It is hard to believe that this femininity, which is observable in these children long before the classically described phallic phase—in one case by age 1—is the result of the kinds of castration fears that are known to be fully developed only years later. Also, it seems very unlikely that the blissful state of closeness that such a mother produces can cause the boy so much fear of his penis being cut off that he pleads to have it cut off, and that he can preserve his sense of maleness by becoming a female.

It may be worth noting that castration anxiety, phallic behavior and fantasies, and neurotic (defensive) reactions have in fact appeared in the one boy treated successfully so far. However, they were not present when he was permitted to be transsexual; they only occurred after many months of treatment, and only when his femininity had died down and he began to enjoy being a male and being masculine. It was when he came to feel that having a penis was worth while that he became concerned about losing it.*

The three boys are physically fearless, possibly because being extensions of their mothers they feel that they can do anything she can. However, with the start of treatment and its forcing a wedge into the symbiosis, the boys become phobic. For example, one boy in the first week of treatment said for the first time, "Mother, will you ever die?" After his mother replied that she would, he said "When you die, then I want to be put in the coffin with you even if I haven't died yet myself, and then we can still be together."† These children show their inability to separate from their mothers in many different ways. For example, before treatment, they are often unable to leave her side and when they are in the same room, even at age 5 they go only a few feet

*Reported by R. R. Greenson, M.D.
†Reported by A. C. Rosen, Ph.D.

from her, then run back and touch her or hold her hand. One of the boys was able to attend nursery school even when his mother was not with him, but could do so only because it was "Mommy's school" (a cooperative school where she occasionally worked).

Lest one think these children are psychotic because they so flagrantly insist they are what they are not, let me mention that they are intelligent, charming, creative children with no difficulty in establishing warm relationships with people of both sexes, their peers, and their elders. Their feeling that they were assigned to the wrong sex is wrong, but it is not a delusion if a delusion is a fantasy constructed and believed in to protect oneself from one's unconscious knowledge of an opposing, unacceptable idea. These children have not developed the idea that they are females as a result of a traumatic situation. Instead, their belief is based on their having been exposed to their mothers' bodies and attitudes for too long and in too gratifying a manner. Since neither of their parents ever adequately contradicts their sense of femaleness, it is constantly and powerfully reinforced. Obviously, not all beliefs that are contradicted by reality are delusions.

To summarize what seem to be the main causes: These mothers do not permit normal separation to occur, as a result of which the infant cannot adequately tell where his mother ends and he begins. Then, with his father not there, he not only does not have a man present as an object for identification, but he is also left unshielded from the malignant effect of his mother's excessive closeness.

The findings in these boys suggest that something similar happens when a more normal personality is formed: that much of normal development can be nontraumatic, pleasurable, not the result of defense. However, in our psychoanalytic work we may take for granted, as givens, immense sweeps of personality that, being neither the result of conflict nor presently conflictual, do not surface.

It is my impression that for most analysts, as for Kris,[10] psychoanalysis is "the science of human behavior viewed as conflict." However, Hartmann's work on conflict-free areas of the ego, the work of the ethologists, Piaget, some of the academic psychologists, and many others should make us more curious about nonconflictual, pleasurable accretions to personality formation.* The whole subject of the creation of conflict-free identifications produced by a conflict-free process of identification should be studied more by analysts.†

DIFFERENTIAL DIAGNOSIS

The differential diagnosis of male transsexualism includes all states in which feminine identification in males is expressed by cross-dressing: occasional transvestic behavior in little boys and men who are not transvestites, effeminate homosexuality, transvestism, transsexualism, and childhood transsexualism. Confusion in and out of the literature is caused if all people who cross-dress are called "transvestites," for this ignores major differences clinically, psychodynamically, and etiologically. Likewise, to call all men with excessive feminine identification "homosexuals" or "latent homosexuals" is to blur meanings unnecessarily, leading to faults in treatment as well as in theory.

The clinical and psychodynamic differences in each of these conditions can only be most briefly discussed now, but these will be looked at again in later chapters.

First, what is the difference between transvestism and child-

*Many readers may regret my not dealing with these challenges of ego psychology. I avoid doing so because it would require too much theorizing—prematurely—to attempt such a synthesis with my data.

† And in addition to these probably immutable, primitive, solid, helpful identifications there is the whole area of probably immutable, primitive, more destructive identifications and deformations. In a book review,[11] Loewald writes of this: "Since the authors pay much attention to the impact the structural theory has had on clinical problems of psychoanalysis, it is regrettable that so little is said about the importance the issue of identification has come to assume in clinical analysis. The role of defense and conflict is justifiably a center of attention in any psychoanalytic consideration, theoretical as well as clinical. But the more we advance in our understanding of psychoanalytic problems, the more, I believe, we become impressed with the importance of the deeper problems of deficiency and deformation of the psychic structures themselves, over and above the problems of conflict between the structures and defenses against it. If the authors had taken these issues more fully into consideration—and the structural theory in good part is both the result of and a guide to a clearer understanding of just these issues—they would have done more justice to the 'superiority' of the structural theory; and they probably would have written a vastly different chapter on the psychopathology of the psychoses in that case (p. 435)."

hood transsexualism? Transvestism may manifest itself in childhood but does not in infancy; at its earliest, I believe it appears
only after masculinity has developed in the little boy. For the
moment, I shall not describe the transvestite (see Chap. 16 for a
fuller description) except to say that he has a fetishistic attachment
to women's clothes, which causes him to put them on intermittently, although at no time does he forget that he is a male, the
possessor of that grand device, a penis.

Second, childhood transsexualism should be differentiated
from the casual transvestic behavior so common in little boys.
Before the process of finding his masculinity is complete, a little
boy may put on a piece of his mother's or sister's apparel and
enjoy strutting around in it for awhile until either he becomes
tired of it or someone in the family stops him. Some boys will do
this more, some less, but such play is usually not evidence of
pathology of gender identity.

The third condition to be considered is adult male transsexualism, wherein a male hopes, by means of sex transformation
procedures, to convert his normal male body to that of a female.
As with our little transsexual boys, he feels he is essentially female, though with a male body. He learns to pass successfully as a
woman, not even known by friends or fellow workers to be a
male. He does not alternate between a masculine and a feminine
role, as does the transvestite; he is not secretly thrilled with the
thought of having a penis secreted beneath his dress; he gets no
real sexual pleasure from his penis, and does not maintain, or wish
to maintain, a sense of masculinity by knowing it is part of his
body ego. If he succeeds in having his penis removed, he does not
regret it.

I believe that childhood transsexuals may become adult transsexuals.

CONCLUSION

This is a very rare condition, one that most practitioners will
not see in their lifetime, and one can argue therefore that it is
quite insignificant. Certainly in this regard it is. However, it is
from a study of a condition like this that one gets an especially

clear view of a special type of mother-infant symbiosis, and also of the process of identification and its bearing upon the development of gender identity. These pathological cases, then, may lead to further understanding of normal gender identity development and of pathological states of feminization in males.

A word about the specificity of etiology in character disorders. It is suggested that in order to define a specific character type, one should be able to distinguish it from all other types by demonstrating (not only theorizing about):

1. *Differences in signs and symptoms:* Childhood transsexualism can be clearly differentiated clinically from all other character disorders in which cross-dressing occurs (except adult transsexualism). In none other does a biologically normal male display his femininity so "successfully," profoundly, and uncompromisingly.

2. *Differences in psychodynamics:* This is the only condition in which little boys feel themselves consciously to be females in the face of demonstrable male anatomy, have no desire to preserve their penis, and suffer none of the usual masculine vicissitudes of castration anxiety.

3. *Differences in etiology:* In no other condition is the nature of the disturbance in mother-infant separation the same, and in no other condition is the mother-infant symbiosis so complete. Etiological in these mothers' personality is a special kind of bisexualness. All try to cure a sense of emptiness by holding their babies against their bodies too much over too many months. To this is added the special role that the fathers play in permitting this grotesque expression of femininity in their sons to be displayed.

Finally, let us note an area where future research should take us. It is not enough to use such general terms as I have done, terms such as "overflowing love and concern," for there probably are an infinite variety of forms of overflowing love, and each will impinge differently upon an infant. I believe that when one of these bisexual mothers expresses her love, she does not keep out of her ministrations her bisexuality and its components of identification with males and envy of males. What her behavior actually delivers upon her infant's body may be nontraumatic; that is, it causes neither physical discomfort nor painful affects, such as anxiety. Nonetheless, I think it will shape his destiny.

But "I think," "I believe," "it seems," "it appears," "surely" (which always means "possibly") are the marks left by our lack of precise observations—and these phrases dominate our literature. We need to develop methods of observing the actual behavior—all that is manifest, no matter how subliminal. I expect (I think, I believe, surely) that when we have discovered such exact ways for observing (and which still do not harm or distort the mother-infant relationship), we shall have the same exciting propects as did the earliest microscopists or psychoanalysts.

This thought provides the opportunity for speculation in an area of important uncertainty. Take the problem of controls in behaviorial research on the importance of childhood experiences in shaping personality. It is necessary to match subjects—children and parents—in regard to age, income, education, etc., etc.; but suppose, as analysts have powerful reasons to believe, that character structure is indeed in part formed in infancy and childhood by a subtle but measurable interplay between parents and children. Then all the controls for gross social factors will provide no assurance that the microenvironment the mother provides is or is not significant.

I do not know how else to confront the challenge created by certain anthropological data. Muensterberger[12] reports his own observations and reviews those of others of prolonged gratification of infants in some primitive societies. Mother and infant are in a happy, skin-to-skin contact for many hours of the day and night, and for years, even to the extent that the child urinates and defecates unmolested on its mother's body; weaning and urinary and toilet training occur very late and atraumatically. Yet the reports fail to mention that these customs, which sound the same as what is seen in our transsexual boys, cause excessive identification with mother.

Very important! And I do not have the data to deal with this exciting complication. Only direct observation and comparison of the subtle ways in which white, middle-class American mothers versus these primitive mothers handle, breathe upon, coo over, nestle, hover over, ignore, look at, and otherwise impinge upon their infants can make true controls out of otherwise too gross observations.

For the moment, I believe that our transsexual boys' mothers create a different, more intense symbiosis than do primitive mothers and that our fathers are absent in a very special way that will not be found in the fathers of Muensterberger's subjects. Also, our subjects are isolated inside a house; in those primitive societies, they are in the midst of the bustle of the community life.

But, to repeat—in order to be vehement—no amount of arguing or citing of authorities can resolve the problem. Only dependable data can do that.

CHAPTER 9

The Mother's Contribution to Boyhood Transsexualism

We shall now look more closely at a family in which a transsexual boy was created, and in a more detailed way see some of the forces that possessed these people.

Almost all psychoanalytic studies concerned with the causes of marked cross-gender behavior in males (e.g.[1]) have been based on the analyses of adult transvestites. Until that of M. Sperling,[2] none had been published on children, though recently there have been some nonanalytic reports.[3] Despite the surge of papers in the literature concerning the influence of parents (especially mothers) on their children's perversions,[4] only Sperling[5] has reported at length on the analysis of such a patient.

Feeling that it might help us understand the genesis of cross-gender identity problems, we arranged in our research team to analyze the mother and son in such a family.* (See also Sperling.[6]) The data from this mother's analysis confirm the work of Greenacre, Khan, Sperling, and others[7] regarding the effects of a

*After almost three years, we were finally able to get the father to come in once a week to see one of our analyst team members.

108

mother's unconscious wishes on the infant who is later to become perverse.* By the time he was a year old, this boy's gender needs already mirrored those his mother unconsciously wished upon him: *His marked femininity was caused primarily by his mother's wishes.*

We shall be interested to examine in more detail than in the last chapter the needs of a woman who can do this so successfully and to so young a boy. We shall be especially concerned with her problem of separating himself from her son. I shall try to indicate where this process was pathological and how it contributed to the boy's distorted sense of identity.

In this chapter, it will be necessary to omit an adequate description of the analytic process itself and instead to concentrate on the data collected that bear on how this woman feminized her son. In order to keep our focus limited to what went on inside this woman vis-à-vis her male infant, much material on how her personality was formed will either have to be omitted or dealt with in a very cursory fashion.

CASE MATERIAL: MOTHER

The patient, married, in her forties, with an 11-year-old daughter and a 5-year-old son, was a perky, charming, and sharply alert person; she appeared younger than her age and looked like one of the flippant, intelligent movie stars who in the last generation have portrayed a boyish femininity in which soft sweetness covers a capacity to outdo the masculine bluster of men. She would not have come to analysis had she not been told to, and in coming she had doubts about whether she could be helped because she was "nothing," a "cipher," a "mirage." Her son had been cross-dressing since at least the age of about 11 months. However, neither the patient nor her husband had considered this odd until a few months before she was first seen, when the patient was scolded by a neighbor for allowing the boy to walk about in his sister's clothes. Subsequent quizzical looks and comments by others caused the patient to bring the child for con-

*After studying transsexuals, I am much less certain what the word "perverse" means.

sultation, but still without her consciously feeling that his behavior was strange. She explained this aberrance of hers by saying that she had though this was not unusual because other children dress up—she herself had frequently done it as a child.

As a result of her analysis, what sources of her son's distorted, feminine identity have become known to her?

Cloth and Clothes: A very specific contribution to her son's cross-dressing is this mother's special interest in cloth and clothes. This is far more intense than the normal heightened interest in clothes expected of a woman in our society. It would not be proper to call this fetishism on her part, since, rather, it is a sensual pleasure approaching voluptuousness in the feel of cloth.* She continuously plays with and strokes her clothes (this is not a stroking of her body).

Her father was noted for his beautiful needlework and weaving. Her maternal grandmother and great-grandmother were prize-winning lace makers. The patient herself was a very creative dress designer before marriage, and still works daily designing and making all her own clothes. Clothes and fabrics appear frequently in her dreams. The first dream she had in analysis—I shall avoid the temptation to comment on it further—illustrates the importance of cloth for her:

There were two of me—an amazing, unpleasant feeling. One was standing facing one way, the other another way—backward. The latter was holding a lot of cloth and moving backward toward something dark. It was like a study in perspective in painting, like a dark tunnel. I felt myself to be the one who was looking at myself—the other one, going backwards. The look on that one's face—the one going backwards—was sly. She had taken the cloth.†

In many ways, her relationship to cloth and clothes is as to a transitional object, in this case the primary object being skin.

---

* In both the patient and her son there is a generalized heightened awareness of a pleasure in many types of perception. Both are almost overwhelmed with pleasure from music, from harmonious nonmusical sounds, from colors, from the tactile quality of objects; both are potentially very creative and artistic.

†Throughout her childhood, the patient had wanted to be a nun ("none").

Skin: excessive mutual identification: A second contribution to her son's cross-dressing was her creating a merging of their identities so that each identified extensively with the other. Throughout many months in the first phase of analysis, she never talked about him as though she was a mother talking about her son. When she described a conversation they had had, it always sounded as though two equals had been conversing in a sensitive, imaginative, understanding and giving way.

There has been excessive sharing of each other's anatomy by identification, made possible by continuous skin contact all through the day. The mood for this mutual identification was additionally set by her feeling that penises are ugly, but that he (her phallus) was beautiful and that his penis was also; and also by her permitting her children to be with her whenever she was nude, to a degree quite unusual in our culture. "This morning I was in the bathroom undressed. He came in while I was facing backward and didn't know he was there and slapped me on the fanny and said with a laugh, 'What a lovely butt.' I laughed and told him how cute he was."

He had sat or lain enfolded in her body for much of the first year of his life, and later, as he became mobile, he was permitted to share her body with her as though it was his own. This was not experienced by either as heterosexual, but was rather the same sort of unself-conscious freedom one has with one's own body, unencumbered by excitement, curiosity, hostility, or shame. "When he was an infant, if he was restless or had the hiccups, I'd roll up my pajama top, roll down his diapers and lay him on my abdomen. It always quieted him."

She always knew she was much more alert to his moods than to her daughter's, and he played on her correspondingly because he knew she was so much in tune with him. This had begun at birth. From then until he was two, whether awake or asleep, he was always with her. She could not stand hearing him cry; so, while awake, he was never separated from the sight of her for more than a few minutes. Since he never slept more than an hour and a half at a time during the first year, her nights were spent in exhaustedly patting him, feeding him, or singing him back to sleep. The following associations and dream fragment show her awareness of this mutual identification and her awareness of how she used it to shape his gender identity. "Last night I was looking at a photograph of when I was twelve. I looked just like a boy. Here is a dream I had last night. I am radioactive. At that point I was awakened because Lance [her son] was shaking me. In my first waking moment I thought: He mustn't touch me; now he is contaminated too." Her empathy for his feelings since birth was profound and instantaneous. As treatment began to separate them into two entities, this formerly fearless child became phobic.

Bisexuality: Another prime factor is a disturbance in gender identity, her bisexuality.*

The first aspect of her bisexuality was her appearance. She always dressed either in suits or a skirt and blouse; she wore only tailored blouses or shirts so that her slim body looked boyish in them. Her hair was tousled and kept fairly short, though in an appropriately smart style. Her voice was low and husky. Nonetheless, there was no harsh "butch" quality about her because of the obvious femininity also present in her appearance and behavior.

The over-all effect on her of this complex mixing of masculine and feminine qualities was a sense of having been essentially without gender since latency. She would take pride in photographs of herself in her early teens in which she appeared to be a boy. At every opportunity for masquerading (as, at Halloween), she would dress up and pass unrecognized as a boy. She was constantly getting groups of children together to put on little shows, in which she would take male or female parts with equal success. Of this she said, "When you take off your own clothes and put on different clothes, you can be anyone."

The second aspect now to be stressed is a phase of strongly transsexual wishes that lasted throughout latency until adolescence. During these years, she competed with boys on equal terms in organized athletics, at school, and in games; she felt that the same

---

*By which is here meant a heavy proportion of sensed and observable thoughts, feelings, and behavior reflecting both masculine and feminine identifications.

standards in appearance and in competitive performance should hold for her as for boys. Underlying this behavior were powerful wishes for her body to become male, and, this not being likely, for it to be somehow neuter. The onset of her periods and the growth of breasts were very traumatic and ended her hopes for maleness. From then on, she turned to cultivating the appearance of femininity.

What are some of the causes of her bisexuality? First in importance is her mother, an empty woman who, as a model for identification, not surprisingly gave the patient a profound sense of emptiness. (It is not possible now to describe the quality of emptiness in the patient's mother, the way it was transmitted to the patient, nor the envy, rage, and guilt it provoked, but the situation is suggested in the following dream which the patient recalled from childhood: "I had died and was now dead. But my mother kept sending me to the store on errands because she hadn't even paid enough attention to know it.")

Her father, an alcoholic, was a man who displayed two distinct personalities, the one a happy, humorous, singing, very affectionate father; the other, a man of terrifying violence and scarcely veiled sexuality during the frequent times he was drunk. Driven from any satisfying closeness with her mother, the patient found comfort in her father during her first six years. He took over much of her mother's role in her upbringing. It was he who comforted the patient when she was sick and took her to the doctor, he who took her to sporting events (to which her brothers were not taken), and it was he who bought all her clothes. The damage to the development of a normal gender identity provoked by her empty mother produced a vacuum which was more than filled by her father. Despite his unpredictable moods, she was clearly his favorite until her sister, six years younger, was born. Then, with a feeling of profound disappointment, she changed this relationship with her father until by adolescence she was continually fighting with him. She left home at sixteen, almost never seeing her father again until he died years later.

A dream exemplifies her relationship with her father: "I am sitting with another girl younger than myself in an open field at night, when we suddenly see a wild, frenzied stallion charging down the road. As it approaches, I notice that instead of eyes, it has burning holes showing its red-hot interior. It is not running at us on purpose, but still it is coming directly at us. Just as it is about to trample us, it is turned aside by a fence railing, a railing which in fact had fronted our house in childhood."*

The next source for the masculine defect in her gender identity was the maleness of the two older of her three brothers. Her brothers were 2 years older, 3 years younger, and 13 years younger than herself. The two older ones were vigorous boys, who, in the rather cramped living conditions of her childhood, gave her more than ample opportunity to compare differences in the anatomy of the sexes. In addition, the cultural tradition of this family was that males are very superior and females very inferior. Again, part of a dream illustrates: "I came out upon a parking lot, looking for my car. There I saw my oldest brother in the center of a group of boys. He was the leader of this group and they were listening with fascination as he was telling dirty jokes. I looked and saw my car at the other end of the parking lot. The blue paint had been scraped off the side and the radiator in front had been smashed in."

We have now looked, at least sketchily, at the patient's bisexuality, wherein, because of frustration and an overpowering sense of loss due to her mother's emptiness, her father's acceptance of her as a tomboy, her father's violent masculinity, and the clear preference shown to her penis-possessing brothers, the patient had a significant streak of masculinity built into her. This contributed to a conscious feeling of being of neuter gender without any denial that she was anatomically a female.†

* That the fence railing stood for her mother's protection was an indication that the prognosis was better than if her mother had truly been as empty as the patient had felt her to be for a long time in analysis.

† A highly important aspect of the patient's personality must be omitted: The hostility which lay beneath her sense of emptiness and beneath her sense of absence of gender. The prognosis would have been very poor were not the hostility there as witness to the rage and hope for fulfillment of certain inner needs. Thus, her emptiness was not only the product of identification with an empty mother and with an awareness of being bisexual; it also served as a defense—neuterness hurts less than frustrated hope.

Emptiness: For a long time, the patient presented herself as an empty person. She had wanted to become a nun, thought of her gender as neuter, presented the appearance of a distinct personality only when play-acting, and denied in the transference all feelings of anger, replacing them with charm, obsequiousness, and coyness. She could talk for a full hour and give no information about her life in reality, her affects, or her fantasies. She was often like a cloud that had wafted into the office, hovered, and then drifted out.

This emptiness had a number of sources. First, her empty, perfunctory mother was hardly an adequate woman from whom the patient could learn femininity. (Dream: "I was in a room trying to reach some wooden milk bottles—like children's toys—on a shelf.") Second, her disappointment and rage had to be denied, and emptiness did this so well for her. Third, emptiness was a camouflage that permitted her bisexuality to persist. Fourth, a marked object-hunger (manifested in her play-acting as a child and her play-acting relationships in adulthood with all those she sought out as co-actors) could be made less frustrating if supplanted by a sense of emptiness.

However, this feeling of emptiness could be removed by her son. Her pregnancies were a joy for her, but the "cure" of emptiness came only when she had a son, and to maintain the sense of well-being within her body, she held him to her, not allowing the normal process of mother-infant separation to progress. She was "addicted" to him, using him as a substance to be taken in to restore tranquility. In this way he was used as a transitional object, keeping her from having to separate from her own mother.

Penis envy and revenge: As a result of the barren, frustrating, perfunctory care given her by her mother, not having a penis and not having the attributes of masculinity caused a sense of emptiness, and, much more painful, resulted in intense penis envy. This penis envy made her have to identify with her brothers, to compete against them, and to overcome them and their influences. Thus we find, as would be expected, a great nucleus of revenge as a source of her bisexuality. The second dream in her analysis was as follows: "Lance had gotten into my drawer, and took something valuable. He was with some man I didn't know, a doctor or something. I was enraged." As is well known, such a woman says, in effect: "I do not need a penis for myself and I only admire those people who, like me, do not possess a penis; people with penises are really inferior." She has consciously felt that all penises are ugly except her son's, which to her is beautiful, an aspect of the mutual identification already discussed.

Her hatred of her husband, often manifested by chair-throwing rages, was interrupted only by periods of apathy with him. This contrasts with the obsequiousness that dominates her relations to all men in authority.

Family history of acceptance of cross-dressing: Another contribution to her son's femininity is her knowledge of her family's having accepted such behavior in herself and her youngest brother. On occasion, as far back as she can remember, she would dress in her brothers' clothes, especially in plays she produced with the neighborhood children. This went on for years; there was nothing covert about it. The patient's special skill in being able to imitate boys when she was dressed as one was a matter for praise rather than concern. The patient says about transvestic tendencies in childhood: "All children do it." This is partly true, for such tendencies are frequently seen and are not necessarily of prognostic significance.* In addition, a brother thirteen years younger had shown transvestic tendencies in childhood without anyone in the family showing concern.

Her son's beauty and creativity: The child's physical beauty and artistic abilities made his mother's "task" of creating a transsexual easier. Since his infancy, strangers had stopped her on the street to

*On the other hand, it is to be kept clearly in mind that in this chapter we are not talking about a child with mild cross-dressing tendencies but a child with an almost overpoweringly compulsive need to be female, the restriction of which produces severe anxiety and frustration, whereas the commonly seen cross-dressing tendencies of children do not have this quality and do not significantly invade the gender identity.

comment on how remarkably pretty he was. In his first months of life, she was already thinking how beautiful he might be as a girl, and at the beginning of analysis she was still thrilled when she considered what a beautiful woman he could make when he grew up. Observers of the research team who have seen the boy all agree that he is indeed a lovely-looking child, though none shared his mother's feeling that he was like a beautiful girl. There is no question, however, that his beauty has fitted into her needs to feminize him. (While this is probably not an infrequent situation in some boys who develop transvestic or other effeminate mannerisms, it is contributory rather than essential, for unbeautiful little boys are also "successfully" feminized by their mother's wishes.)

What seems inherent artistic creativity has played a similar contributory rather than essential role in the development of the child's femininity. His remarkable sensitivity, intelligence, and capacity to express himself, either in play by himself or with other children or adults, by means of colors, textures, materials, play-acting, painting, and so on have been conceded by many observers since at least his first year. At his school his capacity for body expression was considered so great that a professional movie was made of his improvised dancing. At the age of two he would sit raptly listening to Gregorian chants with his mother, and for the past year he has been singing by heart, in Latin, all of both the male and female parts of Orff's "Carmina Burana." He is not an autistic child.

Patient's husband: Her choice of a husband was still another of the patient's indirect contributions to her son's feminization. The father is a man whose emptiness equals if it does not surpass the patient's. This quality will not be discussed here except to mention that what developed was, in effect, a conspiracy between husband and wife, since he has never interfered with his wife's feminizing the little boy; and at times has encouraged it. When at home, which is infrequent, he scarcely communicates with his family. He is not schizophrenic. His similarity to her mother, with whom he gets along beautifully, is not coincidental. Interestingly, his type of emptiness and passivity does not occur in an effeminate man. His appearance and interests are unremarkably masculine, though he is quite passive.

CASE MATERIAL: SON

Lance* is now six years old. There is unanimous agreement among everyone who has seen him that he is a lovely-looking, charming, witty, brilliant, warm, sensitive, altogether winning child. He is described by his parents as having been a beautiful child at birth and in infancy, and indeed is so now.

He was a planned baby. At the time of conception, his mother's hatred of her husband was long since fully developed, but, "I had to have a baby." There was no thought of using the baby to save the marriage; she had never felt a desire to separate from or divorce her husband. The proper balance in the marriage for both was a mixed sense of emptiness and hatred.

Although breast-feeding was attempted for three weeks after his birth, almost no milk was produced; thus, the infant was on a bottle from birth with no evident feeding difficulties. From birth to the present, he has been a "prodigious eater" but has never been fat. Within a few months, as soon as he was sufficiently coordinated, he refused to let his mother feed him, holding his own bottle while she held him. Soon after, he was using utensils very skillfully for eating solids, again refusing from the very first day to let her help him. Long before he was able to walk, he was trying to do so without help, pushing his mother away.

All this independence was expressed without rancor. It persisted, so that up until a few months after beginning his own treatment, he was considered by his parents and others as almost without fear of physical danger. This was not preceded by any overt period of fear and was not used for self-aggrandizement. It did not have the history or appearance of a counterphobic state. For the present, until more data become available, I shall assume that his ability to learn these skills is the result of his capacity for intense identification with his mother; the first operational stage

*I have chosen a name with the same masculine implications and exotic, heroic qualities as the child's real name.

in this identification process is probably imitiation of mother's behavior. Then too, in view of the marked identification with his mother, he may also have felt himself to have incorporated her adultness (i.e., omnipotence).

In his first year of life he never slept more than an hour and a half before awakening famished. His mother says she never had more than three hours uninterrupted sleep until he was more than three years old. She says, "He overdid everything. He cried louder, laughed louder, ate more, got more angry, and had less sleep than any baby I have ever heard of." Since he began to crawl, he has been voraciously curious, a quality which has not only impressed his mother and his teachers but also has them at their wits' end.

He was more than five years old before giving up a night bottle. "It was life and death to him. I told him that when he was five he should be thinking seriously of getting rid of it. We talked it over many times; we tried many nights, but he would get hysterical without it. When he finally gave it up, he and I had a big celebration. I gave him a pound box of chocolates."

When Lance was between 8 months and a year old (his mother cannot recall exactly), his mother remembers him sitting on the floor with her, looking at magazines. As she turned the pages, he would stop her whenever there were photographs of women cooking or of well-dressed, beautiful women, and though he could not talk, he would coo with deepest pleasure. Then, when he was not quite one year old, overt cross-dressing began for him in the first few days after he began to walk. He put on a pair of his mother's high-heeled shoes and not only successfully walked in them but also climbed a flight of stairs. His mother was quite astonished at his skill and—indicating an attitude very much a contributing part of his excessive feminization—was thrilled. From then on, his life focused on cross-dressing. He turned to both his mother's and sister's clothes, feeling compelled to dress up for part of each day. This need was fierce when it possessed him; it should not be confused with the mildly pleasurable occasional cross-dressing seen in so many children of both sexes. This behavior was observed and continuously admired by both parents.

Bak[8] and Greenacre[9] suggest that there is a close relationship between a transitional object[10] and fetishism. This seems true for this child's cross-dressing too: A quilt was used from the age of about 6 months to 3½ years, when it was displaced by his mother's bedjacket. "He took it and still has it [age 6]. I didn't give it to him but after dragging it around for a few weeks, it was such a mess, I let him have it." Again one sees the excessive permissiveness that helped corrupt the child.

There was a very marked difference between this boy and an adult transvestite: Lance was not a fetishist; he was not genitally sexually excited by female clothes. The latter state may be dependent on resolution (however faulty) of the oedipal situation.[11]

The presentation has concentrated on the earliest effects on Lance of his mother's unconscious wishes. This, of course, is not the whole story in the development of the boy's feminine identity, for as his character structure formed, more and more secondary, defensive qualities were woven into it. What at first had been for him a passive and pleasant experience, became contaminated by elements of rage, frustration, depression, and the like. Now, as he was exposed to the rigors of the phallic stage and the onset of the oedipal situation, his femininity began to be used to protect him against these painful aspects. But this cannot be reported now.

DISCUSSION

Let us review what has happened in this particular case. A strongly bisexual woman, with severe penis envy derived from her father and older brothers, in its turn the result of a sense of emptiness produced by her mother, married an empty man and had a son. On the one hand, the boy was (the phallus) of her flesh; on the other, he was clearly a male and no longer of her flesh. He was therefore both to be kept as a part of herself, by identification, and treated as an object whom she would feminize. *He was his mother's feminized phallus.**

---

*This is not the same as being her substitute little girl. Occasionally (but by no means even in most cases), the parents will say that they wanted a girl and that they treated their son as though he were a female because they were so disappointed in not getting a girl. This is a rationalization used in those cases

The child's cross-dressing cannot be explained on the basis of castration anxiety occurring at the height of the phallic stage or distorted resolution of the oedipal situation by a faulty identificatory process. Understanding of marked femininity in very young boys obviously demands consideration of events that occurred long before the phallic and oedipal phases. It will require more data to show to what extent similar dynamics have been present in the mother-infant relationship of those who develop perversions of gender (e.g., typical transvestism) later than this child did. At any rate, one cannot consider this child's perversion to be a penis-preserving, potency-preserving "classical" perversion.

The study of the atmosphere with which a mother's personality surrounds her infant has been among the great accomplishments of recent years in psychoanalysis. Of many invaluable papers in this area, it is possible to deal with only a very few. From Greenacre's essential contributions, I regretfully restrict myself to the following: ". . . is there already at the phallic phase a weakness in the pregenital structure with a rift in early ego development definitely forecast or present, which sharpens the castration problem and draws the primitive form of denial mechanism so readily into its service? I incline to this . . . view. A review of the actual cases suggests that there are two main eras of disturbances; namely, those of the first eighteen months or so, and those occurring at three to four years of age. In considering the disrupting influences of the first era, we may again group them into early physical disturbances causing marked sudden fluctuations in body image or subjective feelings of this nature; disturbances of mother-child relationship which affect the sense of the infant's own body and leave an imprint on the early emerging ego; and third, the effect of early primary identifications. . . ."[12]

Lichtenstein, talking about the development of identity, has said (p. 202): "I am inclined to see in the early mother-child unit,

---

where there is a mother's strong need to feminize her son. Her true motivation is not to make up for not having a daughter; rather, it is the above-described overpowering need to revenge herself on males. Certainly most women who have a son after wanting a daughter do not feminize the infant; they do not need the revenge.

and not in its breaking up, the primary condition for identity in man . . . the very extremeness of the symbiotic relation of the human child to his mother . . . becomes the very source of the emergence of *human* identity . . . thus the maternal ` Umwelt` (which includes the unconscious of the mother) ordains an organ-function to the child, and it is this primary function in which I see the nucleus of the emerging human identity. . . . [and later, p. 204] I suggest the use of the well-known concept of 'imprinting' for the description of certain aspects of early infant-mother interaction. . . . The imprinting stimulus combination would be the individual and unique unconscious wishes, the unconscious needs of the mother with regard to her child."[13]

The juxtaposition of Greenacre's and Lichtenstein's observations reveals two rather different views of the symbiotic mother-infant unit. Greenacre implies a disruption of what otherwise would have been a rather smooth process. Lichtenstein implies that even the smooth enough process shapes the infant's identity. In a related way, Winnicott writes of a "normal illness"[14] at the end of pregnancy and on into the first weeks after the infant is born, in which the normal mother is in a preoccupied, "devoted" state of sensitivity to her infant.

We are more used to hearing of specific impingements by a mother's pathology, impingements which break the relatively smooth process. Greenacre's "focal symbiosis,"[15] Khan's "cumulative trauma"[16] and "symbiotic omnipotence,"[17] Kris's "strain,"[18] and even Shield's "too-good mother"[19] imply, as Khan has said, *breaches* in the protective-shield[20] role of the mother. Greenacre's and Lichtenstein's perspectives are, of course, not contradictory; each is applicable to greater or lesser degree with every mother-infant unit. Certainly, even when holding, loving, and "good enough care"[21] are abundantly present—they were for Lance—the mother's personality may still gently coerce the infant into a perverse identity without the infant very actively cooperating in it or defending himself against his mother in the earliest stages of this process. Khan[22] has given us a study of such a breach, describing how a mother's depression produced changes in her child that in adult life led to the daughter's homosexuality. Khan says, "One reason this sort of child colludes so much with the mother's 'organized defense' is because of the absolute necessity of the relationship for the child. The child is totally dependent on the parent's livingness and, therefore, has to sponsor all the defenses that enable the mother to live." However, what is felt as trauma for the *child* may be no more sensed by the *infant* than the air he breathes; he may not sponsor his mother's defense in infancy because he may not be able to tell the difference between his mother's defenses and "good enough care."

In a recent paper, Khan[23] discusses a special mother-infant relationship ("symbiotic omnipotence") which is pertinent to our case, though the patients he describes were not cross-dressers. He notes:

Relatively little has been written about the mother's task as the provider of phase-adequate aggressive experiences. This function of the mother derives from her capacity to tolerate aggression and hate in herself, and in relation to the child. Where this capacity is lacking in the mother, exaggeration of positiveness interferes with the meaning of the mother for the child and thus leads to a failure to enable the child to distance itself from the mother. It is the peculiarity of these mothers that they shirked every type of aggressive confrontation with the child.

Lance's mother bent her son to her wishes, but she did this in a warm, loving, concerned, overprotective atmosphere in which was invisibly mixed her need to ruin his masculinity. So rather than a breach being formed in the protective shield, the shield itself bent him—"imprinted"* him. Such imprinting may also be the case in more normal development, which would then depend for its normalcy on the normalcy of the mother, at least insofar as her relation to her infant is concerned. In both the normal and the pathological situation, the child may respond fully and willingly to what the mother is doing.

*I use the term with hesitation since the ethological connotation of a critical time and CNS change of function has not been demonstrated. Probably I am here approaching conceptually some of the thinking of behaviorists and other learning theorists.

It is of interest to speculate momentarily on another meaning that women's clothes may have for the feminized male who cross-dresses, besides those usually described (women's clothes = vagina or womb; women's clothes = phallus). As Bak[24] has noted, these data include a more primitive dynamic: *women's clothes = mother's skin.* If this is so, then the transvestite, the fetishist, the adult transsexual, or a boy like Lance not only facilitates the repeated process of identifying with his mother by trying to appear like a woman, but he may also be trying to recapture the primitive sensuality of having her skin applied against his. I think therefore that the equations stating that women's clothes equal either the male or female genital come later in development and are less elemental than this equation: *clothes = mother.**

I should like now to note briefly another possibility suggested by this case: *the infant (child) as transitional object for its mother.* As a result of her own empty and therefore frustrating mother, Lance's mother suffered from a sense of emptiness, as we have already indicated. It is my thesis that Lance was developed into a bisexual object by his mother so that she could keep herself from feeling her chronic awful sense of emptiness. As with other women, she was faced with the task of separating herself from her child, and as with other mothers, the success or failure of this intricate process was considerably dependent on her relationship with her own mother. Suffering from a profound sense of deprivation from her mother, she felt she must spare her son such pain, but in addition, I feel he was to serve as the gratification so long waited for from her mother. She felt she must let him have all pleasures possible, so that he (and by identification with him, she) would not feel deprived and empty. To do this, she kept him so close, literally, to her own body that he was a transitional object, in two senses. First he was a part of her own body suspended in transition toward becoming a separate object, and, second, he was a transitional object in Winni-

*Dr. Frederic G. Worden has suggested that the penis may not only indicate to the transsexual his maleness, but may also represent a wedge driven into the blissful mother-infant symbiosis. If he wants his penis removed, it may not be only to make him into a female, but also to restore the blissful lost closeness with his mother, which putting on women's clothes can only partly do.

cott's sense, in that he bridged the incompleted separation between herself and her own mother.

While she was able to permit Lance some chance of separating, she greatly slowed the process down, a fixation produced especially by the primordial joys of the continuous skin-to-skin contact and by her feeling she must not abandon him to frustration. This enhanced in him an overidentification with his mother, a smudging of ego boundaries, and therefore of gender identity.

CONCLUSION

After many months of analysis a new clue emerged: *The patient had done this before to another infant.* She had mentioned in passing early in her analysis that her brother, 13 years younger than she, had been a cross-dresser. Now, when she talked of this again, there was an essential difference in the story: *It was she, not her mother, who had brought the baby up,* their empty, withdrawn mother supplying only perfunctory nursing care. This little boy's cross-dressing had not been produced by the patient's mother but by the patient herself. At the end of this hour, she told me for the first time her brother's name: *Lance.*

So, it may be that we have come upon some of the specific causes for Lance's gender identity. A bisexual mother with severe envy of, and anger toward, males promotes an excessive symbiosis, producing a pathological identification between herself and her son (her phallus) by means of unlimited physical contact and other intimacy in the first months of his life. The main purpose of her identification with her son (her inability to help him separate from her physically or to permit him to differentiate his own clear identity) is her need for him to "cure" her of the emptiness she received from her own mother. It is this need which lies behind the bisexuality and the penis envy which so dominated her life. Thus, unfortunately, are the dimensions of his body ego, such a crucial element in gender identity, opened to include her—her body and her bisexually distorted femininity—as part of himself. When the boy's father does not put an end to this process of two people of opposite sexes devouring each other's gender, the boy who feels he is a girl may be produced.

CHAPTER 10

Artistic Ability
and Boyhood Femininity

The thesis that artistic ability or interest is linked in men to identification with their mothers is a familiar one to analysts. In this brief chapter, observations gathered from our three little transsexual boys will be presented that support data found in the analyses of adults. While three cases do not prove a theory, they permit one to remain attached to that theory while awaiting the certainty provided by more cases.

You recall that our three boys manifested overt transsexual behavior by age 2–3 at the latest, wanting to be girls and to have the bodies of females. They were not simply indulging in the occasional, experimental, low-voltage cross-dressing seen in many little boys but rather were expressing a passionate need to put on as much of women's (girls') apparel as could be managed, a fascination with playing exclusively with female dolls and with daydreams of being a girl, and a frankly stated wish to become a girl ("I want to be a girl. Why wasn't I born a girl? Aren't I really a girl? Can I be a woman when I grow up?"). This remarkable identification with women was found in these little boys to be associated with (1) mothers who acted and dressed like boys until adolescence; (2) fathers who were almost literally absent from the home, day or night, weekdays or weekends; (3) the parents' excessive permissiveness, so that the developing femininity was openly encouraged by allowing the boys to dress as girls whenever they chose ("He's so beautiful; wouldn't he look lovely as a girl?"); and especially by (4) excessive and intimate body contact for many hours, day and night, from birth to the time they were seen at age 4-5, this delay in mother-infant separation perpetuated by the little boys' constant touching of their mothers' nude bodies and clothes.

The artistic ability (creativity) all three showed became apparent to their mothers by age three and was immediately discovered by their teachers as soon as they entered nursery school. The following are reported by these mothers (and confirmed by others).*

Heightened sensitivity to perception: Each boy has been entranced with sight (colors, patterns, painted pictures); hearing (music and other harmonious or rhythmical sounds); and touch (by the feeling of materials, especially cloth textures, but including other touching and handling of animate and inanimate objects). In addition, all are reported to respond intensely to sounds and smells that are not even noticed by others.

Painting: All have shown precocious ability with paints and other coloring materials, not only in the flamboyant use of colors but also in imaginative, well-formed objects expansively placed on the paper and telling an understandable story.

Dancing and mime: All improvise graceful dances to music, in one case performed before audiences; in addition, they enjoy making light, tender, and feminine gestures during play to enhance the reality of the make-believe.

"Creative writing": In the years before they have learned to write, these children are nonetheless telling original stories to audiences and creating plays, which they also produce and direct with siblings and friends before audiences.

*While one of the mothers has similar artistic potential, the other two do not.

Acting: This is not merely imitative (though imitation is keenly developed) but, like the dancing, skillfully and enthusiastically improvised.

"Designing" of clothes, jewelry, hair styles, makeup: While these talents are rudimentary, the ardor with which the children watch and critically evaluate related displays of their mothers' femininity have astonished (and, unfortunately, thrilled) all three mothers. The boys are constantly giving their mothers advice, and the mothers consider their sons' taste better than many adults', and comment on the originality of the boys' suggestions for modish style.

Increased curiosity and activity: The three boys have impressed their families, teachers, and our research team with their constant, active searching of the environment, asking questions about the world they encounter, enthusiasm, and heightened motor activity, as compared with siblings and friends—an insatiable taking in of stimuli. Two of the three are so active that for several years their mothers despaired of being able to keep up with them; the third is "merely" vigorous. There is no frantic quality in all this, as reported by the mothers or watched by us, but rather an intense alertness and activity not dispelled by pauses of quietness or contemplation. In the two boys who are the most active this is accompanied by marked accident-proneness.

DISCUSSION

Many children are expressive and creative until the ego strengths of latency mute their imagination. However, this is not a report on three such children: The qualities *these* boys express, taken en masse, seem to be beyond the powers of most normal children. In each case, the boy has been singled out at school as artistically superior to the other children; the observations of our research team confirm this (e.g., when we look at the children's paintings). We cannot tell if time or treatment will remove this lovely sign of nonetheless severe psychopathology, but at present, these children are remarkably creative.

One cannot, however, be sure that such boys will become artistic adults, even though many of their interests are the ones that become the professions of some effeminate men (hairdressers, choreographers, clothes designers, actors, etc.). No adult transsexual has ever been reported to be an artist (although I know of one professional artist who was enough tinged with a transsexual urge that he created for himself a good-sized "vagina" by gradually digging out his penile urethra where it joins the perineum; he never consciously thought he was a female or wanted to be rid of his penis, however).

It is not surprising that the artistic interests of these little boys are those our Western society considers more feminine than masculine, for while these boys are intelligent, active, curious, and original, their creativity is sensual, not intellectual. They touch, stroke, smell, hear, look, and taste—they create to please their senses. They are not interested in mathematics, the function of machines, construction, or logic—precisions of the mind. These observations are in keeping with similar findings in adult men, in whom one also much more frequently finds severe disturbances in gender identity among creative artists than with creative theoretical and applied scientists.

The most imaginative part of this thesis that creativity may be related to identification with mother is the familiar analytic idea that creativity is thwarted procreativity. While this intuitively sounds right, we cannot presume because it is illuminating that it is a true or sufficient explanation. The need to create could have other sources (even beyond the often-mentioned, surmised constitutional ones) than the unconscious desire to have a baby. For example, one could speculate that artistic creativity is also inspired by a fear of death, fear of death being here considered as fear of absolute dissolution of identity—which brings us back to the yearning for his mother, the separation anxiety, and the prolonged and excessive mother-infant symbiosis which has so blurred the formation of normal gender identity.

CONCLUSION

We have observed no more than this: Excessive feminine identification and unusual artistic ability exist together in three very young transsexual boys. From this point on, we must leave our data behind and join with others who have predicted from the findings of analyzed adults that creativity in men is energized by their identifying with their mothers in childhood. However, the observations referred to in this chapter seem to improve this theory's chances a bit, for they show that boys who have so identified with their mothers that they violently wish to be females are unusually artistic; they are stirred deeply and pleasurably by external sensations, are curious and restless, and take the fantasies that result from their feminine identification to realize new and artistic creations.*

*In the Appendix are some quotations which exemplify the raw material from which these opinions regarding the boys' creativity are derived.

CHAPTER 11

Etiological Factors in Adult Male Transsexualism

Even having seen the three little transsexuals, it did not at first dawn on me that these little boys might be the adult transsexuals of future years. In attempting to write up the first case, I found myself, on calling the child an "infantile transvestite," continuously having to explain that although he cross-dressed, he did not have essential qualities of the adolescent or adult male transvestite (e.g., love of and anxious regard for his penis). While thinking of this, it suddenly became apparent to me that these little boys did, however, seem to have the essential stigmata in character structure and psychodynamics of the adult transsexual; if these boys are the transsexuals of the future, it would be necessary either to follow them without treatment until they grew up or to find cases who would fill in the gap between these little boys and adult transsexuals. If this could be done, we would go a long way toward understanding some of the specific etiologies of an adult psychiatric condition.

The literature on transsexualism is a meager one, for the condition, named in 1949,[1] was scarcely recognized as a clearly

distinguishable one before 1953.[2] Since that time it has been studied
by several workers, but the number of patients with this condition are very few,[3] and it is even uncertain which people with
problems in gender identity should be considered under this diagnosis. Despite speculations regarding etiology, I believe it would
be fair to summarize the literature by saying that the etiology to
date has been unknown.

The most likely cause of this condition has been considered
to be some biological force which produces considerable reversal
of gender in the absence of any demonstrable biological abnormalities of sex. The astonishingly strong identification with members
of the opposite sex, and the capacity to live permanently and
undetected as a member of the opposite sex to which the person
belongs biologically, have led observers to feel that such powerful,
profound, and successful identification with the opposite sex could
not be simply a "learned," that is, psychological, phenomenon.
This had been my feeling also, from the time that I first saw such
a patient in 1957 until these past years, when the impact of
clinical data changed my opinion.

Before discussing these data, it is best that a few terms be
clarified further. First, what is meant by "transsexual"? This term
has generally been defined, unfortunately, by a criterion which
is an inadequate one for defining a personality type; in this condition, the criterion listed by most authors has been that the patient
earnestly seeks out sex-transformation procedures (alterations of
genitalia, hormones to change secondary sex characteristics, etc.).
It is more logical to try to define a character type by how the
character structure is manifested rather than by the type of treatment the person seeks. Transsexualism should be defined in more
characterological terms: In an oversimplified way, I consider a
transsexual to be a person who feels himself (consciously and unconsciously) to belong to the opposite sex while not denying his
sexual anatomy. He is to be differentiated—and can easily be
clinically differentiated—from the great masses of people who have
identifications with members of the opposite sex and who reveal
these identifications in, for example, their dreams, and even in
isolated areas of behavior, but who do not so unequivocally believe
themselves to be members of the opposite sex (see Chap. 16).

To return to the argument, there are the little boys, and there are adult transsexuals. Are the two related?

The next clue came from the work of Green and Money, who for eight years have been following a series of very effeminate little boys.[4] Recently, when talking with Green, I asked him whether these boys, some of whom were as young as three when first seen, had continued over these years to maintain their extreme femininity and the belief that they are really female. He reported that this was the case in a few of his subjects. His data strongly indicate that these little boys were on their way to being transsexuals, and so we now had some rather precise coverage from birth through to early adolescence (though, of course, not in one continuously observed case).

The missing link was an adult transsexual (and—one must be precise—not just a person seeking sex-transformation procedures, but a person who would fit more rigorous criteria for defining transsexualism as a character disorder), who would not only be able to give rather good historical information leading back into childhood but who would also permit us to interview her mother; by this time we had the suspicion, from the work with the little boys, that the adult transsexuals' mothers might, at times, be crucial contributors to the causes of the condition. I have recently had the opportunity to do this and in the embarrassing episode to be reported below, had data thrust upon me that may help close the gap between the information learned from the cases of the infant transsexuals and the adult transsexuals.

Eight years ago, a patient was seen who was found to be a unique type of a most rare disorder: testicular feminization syndrome, a condition in which it is felt that the testes are producing estrogens in sufficient amount that the genetically male fetus fails to be masculinized and so develops female genitalia, and in puberty female secondary sex characteristics. This particular case was unique in that the patient was completely feminized in her secondary sex characteristics (breasts and other subcutaneous fat distribution; absence of body, facial, and limb hair; feminization of the pelvic girdle; and very feminine and soft skin), with a nonetheless normal-sized penis and testes. Abdominal contents were normal male. Following extensive workup, including examination of testicular tissue by microscope, it was decided that the findings were compatible with estrogen production by the testes; a report of these findings was published.[5] At the time of this workup the patient was nineteen years old and had been living undetected as a young woman for about two years. As far back as her memory reached, she had wanted to be a girl and had felt herself to be a girl, though she was fully aware that she was anatomically a male and was treated by her family and by society as a boy. Consideration was given to the possibility that she had been taking estrogens on her own, but it was finally decided that this was not the case, for the following reasons: (1) She very clearly denied taking such estrogens at the time that she revealed many other parts of her past history which would seem to be equally embarrassing to reveal; (2) even after successfully getting the operation she wanted, she still denied taking estrogens; (3) in order to have effected the biological changes found on physical examination and laboratory tests, she would have had to take just the right drug in just the right amounts starting at just the right time at puberty in order to have converted her body to the state in which it was found at age nineteen, and it was felt that this amount of information about endocrinology and sophistication about womanhood was beyond the possibilities of this person when 12 years old. (There are no cases in the endocrinological literature of a male taking massive doses of estrogens exogenously from puberty on); (4) she was closely observed during hospitalization preoperatively and her belongings searched; no estrogens were found; shortly after the testes were removed, she developed a menopause, which was considered good evidence that the testes were the source of estrogens; (5) when the testes were examined microscopically and sent to experts in other medical centers for confirmation, the tissue was considered as capable of producing testicular feminization syndrome; (6) the testes, examined postoperatively, were found to contain over twice as much estradiol as is present in the normal adult male.

Not being considered a transsexual, her genitalia were surgically transformed so that she now had the penis and testes removed and an artificial vagina constructed from the skin of the penis.

She subsequently married, moved away, and lived a very full life as a woman. She remained in contact over the years, and infrequently I would have a chance to talk to her and find out how her life was going.

Five years later she returned. She had now been passing successfully as a woman, had been working as a woman, and had been leading a very active, sexually gratifying life as a beautiful and popular young woman. Over the years, she had carefully observed the behavior of her women friends and had learned all the fine details of the expressions of femininity of a woman of her social class and age. Bit by bit, she had reassured herself on any of the possible defects in her femininity, the most important confirmations coming from the men who made love to her, none of whom complained that her anatomy was in the slightest bit suspicious. However, she still was not certain that her vagina was normal enough, and so I arranged for her to see a urologist who, because of his reputation, was in an outstanding position to speak to her as an authority; he told her unequivocally that her genitalia were quite beyond suspicion. This reassurance was the final stage in her feeling safe in her role as a woman; so, with her having successfully established herself in the world as a woman, and with her having developed a trusting and warm relationship with me over the years, a great weight was lifted from her.

During the hour following the welcome news given her by the urologist, she told me something with the greatest casualness, in mid-sentence, after having kept it from me for eight years and without giving the slightest warning it was coming. She suddenly revealed that she had never had a biological defect that had feminized her, but that she had been taking estrogens since age twelve. In earlier years when talking to me, she had not only said that she had always hoped and expected that when she grew up she would grow into a woman's body but also that, starting in puberty, this had *spontaneously*, gradually, but unwaveringly taken place. In contrast, she now revealed that just as puberty began, at the time her voice started to lower and she developed pubic hair, she began stealing Stilbestrol from her mother, who was taking it on prescription following a panhysterectomy. The child then began filling the prescription on her own, telling the pharmacist that she was picking up the hormone for her mother and paying for it with money taken from her mother's purse. She did not know what the effects would be, only that this was a female substance; she had no idea how much to take, but more or less tried to follow the amounts her mother took. She kept this up continuously throughout adolescence, and because by chance she had picked just the right time to start taking the hormone, she was able to prevent the development of all secondary sex characteristics that might have been produced by androgens, and to substitute instead those produced by estrogens. Nonetheless, the androgens continued to be produced, enough that a normal-sized adult penis developed with capacity for erection and orgasm until sexual excitability was suppressed at age fifteen by the massive doses of estrogens. Thus, she became a lovely-looking young "woman," though with a normal-sized penis. In other words, she is not an example of a "biological force" that subtly and inevitably influences gender identity, as I had reported;[6] rather, she is a transsexual.

My chagrin at learning this was matched by my amusement that she had pulled off this coup with such skill. Now able to deal openly with me, for the first time she reported much that was new about her childhood and permitted me to talk with her mother, something that had been forbidden for those eight years. The following data relating to transsexualism are derived from interviews with the patient and her mother subsequent to the revelation.

The patient was born the last of four children. Before her mother had married, she had wanted to have two girls and two boys, and this in fact is what she had, first two girls and then two boys. There was no doubt in anyone's mind that this last-born infant was a boy, and it was appropriately named. The patient cannot remember anything of the first two years of her life, and her mother, from the memories that still remain after almost thirty years, does not remember as much as one would like of details that can enrich the history regarding the development of the infant's gender identity. However, her mother does recall that the child, while robust, was gentle and delicate in his movements. The mother says that she let her infant's hair grow long for two years, specifically because the child looked so beautiful and was "so much like a girl."* In addition, the baby was dressed in girls' clothes. The father did not interfere with this process except that at age two he said that the boy's hair should be cut, and so it was. Around this time, the father, who had long since withdrawn himself from the family (this being the war, he was working at night and sleeping during the daytime), developed narcolepsy. And so, throughout the patient's infancy and childhood, almost the only times he saw his father were when his father was either asleep or falling asleep. When the patient was eight or nine her father died.

The mother remembers that beginning around age 2 and until age 8, she and her little son played a nighttime game, which the patient also vividly recalls. This game was "mother hen and baby chick." Every night they both went to bed together at the same time, and the mother would curl herself up in such a way that she completely surrounded the little boy within the curve produced by her bent head, her torso, her arms, and her curled-up thighs and legs. Only when both were molded into this position did they fall asleep. This extrauterine "womb" was invariably established each night, and the power of the mother's need to do this was so strong that although the child wet the bed almost every night during this period, his mother still slept with him curled up within her embrace. If such intimacy persisted for those six years, it may be that there were earlier forms of intense symbiosis that are now lost to us; the mother recalls none.

In addition, this mother permitted her child complete freedom to share her privacy. There was no locking of doors, worry about nudity, bathroom secrecy, or any other attempts to separate the mother's body from the child's touch or vision.

Thus, we have the two very specific, crucial ingredients that

*To what extent do the infants themselves "contribute" their share to this condition by in fact being especially lovely-looking or more cuddly and responsive than the usual male infant? I do not know. As noted earlier, not all boys feminized by their mothers start out beautiful.

were found in the transsexual little boys: too much contact with
the mother's body for too long and a father who is psychologically
absent and so does not interrupt the process of the son's
feminization.

What do we know about this mother? She describes her own
mother as a quiet, withdrawn woman who was overburdened by
the housework, a woman without any joy and without any
warmth for her children. Our patient's mother felt herself to be
a dutiful daughter whose task in life was to take over the household
chores for her mother. She had the feeling with her own children
that she was going to make up to them for the emptiness of her
own childhood with her mother. Her relationship with her father
was considerably better, for she was able to establish a warmer
relationship with him, but he died when she was eight.

Around that time, she began thinking of herself as though
she were a boy. To be exact, she did not think she was a male,
she did not think she was a boy like the other boys, but nonetheless all of her interests were those of a boy. She was excellent in
sports and played with the boys as an equal. She was not interested in girl friends, in playing with dolls, or in all the other
play activities that little girls indulge in to prepare themselves for
marriage and motherhood. She dressed in boys' clothes. This does
not mean that she dressed like a boy; it means that she dressed
in boys' clothes. She did not consider herself to be a tomboy,
as were some of her friends, but rather that she was dressed as
were boys, was thinking and fantasying like a boy, and interested
in boys' things, though never doubting that she was a girl. She
did not believe that she would grow up to become a male or to
live as a man. Her menses began at age 15, and when her breasts
started to develop, she immediately put aside all of her boys' activities, dressed and acted in a feminine manner, went out on dates,
though she did not indulge in any sexual activities more intense
than permitting good-night kisses. The first man she went with
for any length of time, she married.

In other words, in this essential regard, already described for
the mothers of the little boy transsexuals (i.e., the special kind of
bisexuality), this woman is the same as they.

It is interesting to note that, as with the little boys' mothers, this woman was very active in the neighborhood as a child in putting on plays which she "wrote," directed, produced, and played leading parts in. She played male and female roles equally.

We thus find, in the first adult transsexual with whom there was an opportunity to get fairly detailed information about infancy, childhood, and the personalities of the parents, that the identical findings are present as were found in the little boys. The suspicion thus becomes strong that the little boys we have been observing are the adult transsexuals of the future, and some of the etiological factors in certain male transsexuals are becoming more visible.*

It must be clearly understood that I know that the above factors are not found in every male seeking sex transformation (see Chap. 14), nor even in those who we all would agree are transsexuals. However, I would guess that other workers will find these factors in some of their patients, that such findings will show up in the most feminine of all males, and that these will be the ones who have been most driven to pass as women, who pass the most successfully, have no desire for excitement and notoriety, and have had the least sexual relations when still known to be males. (Note: I have just evaluated a 14-year-old male transsexual, the first adolescent transsexual studied in this research. During the child's infancy, his father left the house every weekday before

---

*These findings and speculations do not completely exclude the possibility that some biological force plays a role. For instance, these mothers might not have wished to "over-love" infants who struggled away from their excessive body contact. It is also possible that there are families in which the mother and father are like those I have just described and that, although the infant is held excessively, he still does not come to think he is female. In such a case, we could speculate that something was biologically different in the boy who was feminized from the one who was not.

In addition, we cannot be sure that a boy as feminized as these might not "spontaneously" become more masculine without treatment. To make such a discovery, we would have to be sure not to treat him after evaluating him and his family—and this will happen only if the family refuses treatment. We would then nonetheless have to maintain good enough contact with them to be allowed to reevaluate them as the years pass. (Does such evaluation in itself serve as treatment, and so save the child while spoiling the "experiment"?)

the baby was awake and usually returned after bedtime; this went on for several years. The child's mother, who until puberty dressed as a boy, wanted to be a boy, and was a fine athlete competing with boys, held the baby against her body all night during ages 10 to 16 months as a cure for colic.)

CONCLUSION

We can now see the outlines of some possible causes of the most advanced degrees of male transsexualism. We also have presumptive evidence that what we are seeing in the little children is the same as what was done to some adults who are transsexuals. The data suggest that in some cases, advanced transsexualism is a condition whose causes occur in earliest childhood, with the parent of the opposite sex playing the essential role in the metamorphosis of gender identity to the opposite sex.

Fortunately, adult transsexualism, which is a malignant condition irreversible by psychological methods, may be treatable and reversible in the small child.[7] It seems important, therefore, that the diagnosis be properly made, that this condition in childhood be separated from the less severe problems in gender identity, and that treatment be immediately instituted so that a more normal gender identity can be developed.

CHAPTER 12

The Transsexual's Denial
of Homosexuality

It is frustrating but not unpleasant, having studied patients with severe problems in gender identity, to find myself unable to answer so many important questions. Of these, few have more theoretical or practical interest than the problem of homosexuality, an issue that needs to be faced when one is trying to understand these people who, with their marked cross-gender behavior, are attracted to people of their own sex.

As early as 1905, Freud[1] put us on notice that it is too naïve to think that homosexuality can be defined as simply sexual relations between two people of the same sex, for that avoids taking into account what people do in fantasies, both conscious and unconscious. Homosexual impulses, especially unconscious ones, play a tremendous part in Freud's theories. Originally, under the influence of Fleiss, Freud developed a theory that personality, arising out of a biological bisexual matrix, is an interplay of heterosexual and homosexual impulses, the resulting psychological bisexuality essentially influencing both normal and abnormal development.

However, while indicating that homosexual impulses are far more frequent than had previously been recognized, Freud left us many problems. For instance, we observe a piece of behavior, or listen to a patient telling us about a dream or fantasy or event in real life, in which no overt sexual need for a person of the same sex is expressed. For certain reasons, we judge that hidden from sight is a homosexual impulse, but since it is hidden—and especially if it is hidden from the subject—we call it latent. Difficulties arise.

First, when the observer says it is there but hidden, what is his evidence for the inference? Is it built from observations or from theory?

Second, if X is a manifestation of latent homosexuality and it is found in everyone, is everyone a homosexual? What is a homosexual impulse? What is homosexuality? What is a homosexual? If everyone has latent homosexual impulses, who is not a homosexual and why not?

These questions lead to others inherited from Freud that cluster around the problem of the difference between concomitance and etiology. If one finds evidence that there are conscious and unconscious homosexual impulses in, say, paranoid people, does this mean that these impulses cause paranoidness, as Freud and many later psychoanalytic authors feel; or, since such impulses are universal (Freud's theory of universal innate bisexuality), has one only discovered an essential attribute of all mankind and not just of paranoids?* There are ways out of this predicament, some suggested by Freud himself. One might determine how strongly the impulse passes toward consciousness and will therefore influence behavior (including defensive reactions against the impulse). Or, one can look from the point of view of ego functions, character structure, and/or identity, and decide how, under what circumstances, and with what skill and style a person deals with homosexual impulses. Freud warned Abraham in 1915:

---

*Bychowski,[3] who feels that "bisexuality" (i.e., repressed homosexuality) causes paranoid schizophrenia, lists authors, with whom he agrees, who feel that "bisexuality" is at the root of the etiology of other conditions: melancholia (Abraham), alcoholism (Abraham), alcoholic psychoses (Kielholz), cocaine addiction (Hartmann), and bulimia (Bychowski).

"Although you are correct . . . you pass by the real explanation. Anal-eroticism, castration complexes, etc. [I would add 'bisexuality' to the 'etc.'] are ubiquitous sources of excitation which must have their share in *every* clinical picture. One time *this* is made from them, another time *that*. Naturally we have the task of ascertaining what is made from them, but the explanation of the disorder can only be found in the mechanism considered dynamically, topographically, and economically."[2]

Take another example: Don Juanism. It is well known that compulsive promiscuity in a man may be a technique used to tell himself that he does not have homosexual impulses. But we throw away so much information about such a man if we brush off the complexity of his personality by considering him "just another homosexual." We would like to know more about him. Does he consciously consider himself a homosexual and has he decided to use promiscuity as a façade specifically planned to keep his homosexuality from being detected? Or, far more common, is he unable to accept the inner condemnation and so is not consciously aware of homosexual impulses? Does he fear that he loves men, or is it that he fears not being manly? (To love men is, in our society, not to be manly, but there are other sources for nonmanly feelings.) What experiences in his life, especially in his relationships with his mother and father, led to his using promiscuity as the defense against homosexual impulses rather than, say, using alcohol or jewelry designing? Granting that such a man has sexual relations with women for primarily nonsexual reasons (he hates and envies them, hopes to ruin them, and gets little sensation of pleasure during sexual activities), still, how does he manage to have an erection whenever needed, as different from a man who admits to being a homosexual and loathes a woman's body too much even to approach it?* It seems illogical to me—or

---

*This is partly answered by Weissman,[4] who points out how a bisexual man may approximate heterosexuality by means of a fetish (either an inanimate object or a part of a person used as if not human—that is, as if not a person): "Fetishism aids the homosexual to overcome his identification with the phallic woman and thus enables him to accept the woman's vagina in the act of sexual intercourse." However, only with extremely precise clinical data can we understand how one man has enough ego capacities to invent fetishism whereas another cannot be potent even with such a crutch.

at least terribly incomplete—to say he is a homosexual (though he has homosexual impulses that must be kept from consciousness); more important, such bland diagnosticating indicates a lack of interest in the great differences in character structure between a man who can manage only by being a Don Juan and one who can do so only if he is admittedly a homosexual. Some (e.g., Marmor[5]) have wondered whether we might not return to the less complicated definition of homosexuality as that state in which sexual practices are performed by preference in conscious fantasy or in reality with a person of the same sex. In this way, while we limit the meaning greatly, we might also avoid complications that have not been as fruitful as it was once thought they were.

But if it is troublesome to arbitrate what shall be called homosexuality, how much more difficult it is to say who is a homosexual; the latter word represents a commitment, a conviction, an identity. In our culture, to admit that one is *a* homosexual—which is more absolute than to say one is homosexual (an adjective implying that he has a considerable weight of homosexual impulses) or that one practices homosexuality—is to commit oneself to a great deal. It may be more useful—though seemingly naïve— to reserve the term "a homosexual" for a person who *admits to himself* that he is a homosexual. One implication of this is that while homosexual impulses are frequently found (in people who are homosexuals and in people who are not), the sense of identity— "I am a homosexual"—will be much rarer. (This still does not solve the problem of the person who is not yet prepared to admit to this identity, but who grows into it in time, this being a frequent story told by some less than "absolute" homosexuals.) Possibly, by this much more restrictive use of the term "a homosexual" we shall be more ready to look at the ego functions and character structures present in those people who are drawn toward sexual relations with people of the same sex, but who raise such vigorous defenses against these activities, for it is in the strengths of drives and the qualities of defenses against drives that one finds the qualities that make one person different from another.

Greenson, in conversation and in a paper,[6] has emphasized the difference between wanting to possess another person and wanting to be that person—"I want to have" versus "I want to be."* This may be an important clue in our attempts nowadays to describe as precisely as possible what we all mean by "homosexual" and "homosexuality."

Let us see—in a most tentative summarizing—what are some of the different conditions which have been called homosexuality (for simplicity, discussed in men only):

  1. *Sexual:*   "I, a male, want to have him."
     a. *Overt homosexuality:* sexual relations between people of the same sex—facultative and obligatory.[7]
     b. *Conscious fantasies* of sexual relations with a person of the same sex:
        (1) experimental ("I wonder what it would be like to . . .")
        (2) self-accusatory ("I hate to think it but maybe I am . . .")
        (3) erotic ("I want him.")
     c. *The observed manifestation of unconscious fantasies* of sexual relations with a person of the same sex:
        (1) character disorders (e.g., Don Juanism, hysterical personality)
        (2) dreams, artistic productions
        (3) certain paranoid hallucinations
        (4) friendship
        (5) etc., etc.
  2. *Gender:*   "I, a male, want to be her."
     a. *Heterosexual effeminacy* in a man who enjoys and prefers making love to a woman; while identifying with certain aspects of womanliness, the aspects identified with (e.g., women's creativity) and the degree are less than his pleasure in having women as objects to have and hold. "I want to be like her in certain nonerotic ways, but even more so, I want to have her."
     b. *Homosexual effeminacy* in a man who enjoys and

---

*This has been discussed in the past in terms of blurring of ego boundaries, oceanic feelings, etc., as seen in such states as infancy, psychosis, love, artistic creativity, and religious ecstacy.

prefers making love to a man; he has identified with the erotic as well as nonerotic aspects of a woman and additionally hates women (in part for having captured him, as his identifying with them keeps indicating to him?), while also preserving his sense of maleness. "I want to be like her, but I hate her for this—and I prefer to be a male."

c. *Transvestism;* 'I want to be a woman, and at the same time I do not want to stop being me, a male. If I am to have her, I can only do it via the disguise of being one of her type (cross-dressing) or by making love to a substitute for her (fetishism)."

d. *Transsexualism;* "I, a male, am her."

This categorizing leaves much to be desired; however, it may suggest that some workers by calling all these manifestations "homosexual" are trying to cover too many syndromes, too many manifestations, with the word. In the literature at present, the term used for a man who wants other men is "homosexual," and for a man who is effeminate, the term is also "homosexual." Would it not be clearer *not* to use the same word for these two classes, which, while related,* certainly also cover different realms of behavior, fantasies, convictions regarding gender, and early life experiences?

Of course, these conditions are all related, the common denominator being identification with women. As long ago as 1910, Freud, talking of homosexuals, described what has been consistently confirmed. My only modification is that he is talking about men's identification with women, of which homosexuality is a major, but not the only, aspect. He says: "In all our male homosexual cases the subjects had had a very intense erotic attachment to a female person, as a rule their mother, during the first period of childhood, which is afterwards forgotten; this attachment was evoked or encouraged by too much tenderness on the part of the mother herself, and further reinforced by the small

---

*E.g., if part of the effeminacy of a man is the result of his identifying with women's sexual role, he will want men sexually; the gender and sexual aspects would be inextricably related. If he identifies with nonsexual aspects, they will not be so related.

part played by the father during their childhood. Sadger emphasizes the fact that the mothers of his homosexual patients were
frequently masculine women, women with energetic traits of
character, who were able to push the father out of his proper
place. I have occasionally seen the same thing, but I was more
strongly impressed by cases in which the father was absent from
the beginning or left the scene at an early date, so that the boy
found himself left entirely under feminine influence. Indeed, it
almost seems as though the presence of a strong father would
ensure that the son made the correct decision in his choice of
object, namely someone of the opposite sex (p. 99)."[8]

As usual, Freud says it in the simplest and most accurate
manner.

I would ask, however, that we look at the details within the
above generalization, for in these details—such as the differences
in styles of rearing between one mother and another, how much
hatred of maleness does one have as compared to another, and
how and when is it made manifest; to what degree can she love
her infant as her own flesh, and to what degree and when and
how can she let him leave her body and become himself—will
we find some of the origins of the different ways in which men
express or repress their feminine identifications later in life.

This above discussion can be applied to transvestites and even
more so to transsexuals. To dismiss transvestites and transsexuals
as being just "homosexuals" is to minimize their catastrophic
aberrations in gender identity and to throw away the chance to
study the differences that exist between them, admitted homosexuals, and people without such abnormalities. Thus, for example,
in the process of making ourselves look more closely at and
describe transsexuals more accurately, we may be able to study
better how they develop identifications with the people of the
opposite sex in infancy and early childhood, and to study the
intrapsychic forces that make transsexuals preserve these identifications permanently. Doing this, we might see better why these
people insist, in the face of all common sense, that they are not
homosexuals.* They realize that what they are doing sexually

*To say that they are simply rationalizing also seems too glib and another
case of throwing away an opportunity to learn more.

is homosexual by everyone's definition but their own. They recognize that they are trapped and forced to maneuver, in a way that sounds almost delusional, between their humiliation at the contrast between being considered madmen for denying that they are homosexual and their inner sense of belonging to the opposite sex.

Those of us who have worked with these patients have been struck by the fact that all transsexuals and many transvestites (but by no means all) insist that they are not homosexuals. Homosexuals do not insist that they are not homosexuals. How do these classes of people differ? The answer, which I do not have but shall be studying more in the next several years, may lie in an understanding of the formation of, and the later struggle to maintain, a gender identity. Still, in one group of patients—the little boy transsexuals—the answer seems fairly clear: They atraumatically come to consider themselves girls, encouraged in many ways to do so as are normal little girls, and so if as adults they should maintain that they are not homosexuals, such insistence might come from an inner nonconflict-created sense of conviction of being females that transcends all evidence of their anatomy. However, even with this conviction, they have a decided disadvantage as compared to the rest of us. Living in our society, they come to see that the discrepancy between their sex and gender does not make sense. They cannot avoid their own suspicion that they must be homosexual, since they are exclusively attracted to someone of the same sex. And yet they do not *feel* homosexual, nor is their gender identity primarily the result of defenses against conflict, as it is, for instance in certain Muscle-Beach types of hypermasculine men.

As different from homosexuals, adult transsexuals in their sexual practices do not exalt their own primary and secondary sex characteristics and demean those of the opposite sex. As with healthy heterosexuals, they truly appreciate the sexual attributes of both sexes, those of one sex to be parts of their own bodies and those of the other to be used as objects of their excitement. And so, if males, they get excited by men's bodies (like homosexuals) and want the anatomy of females (not like homosexuals).

(Again, I want to stress that this is quantitatively very different from, and arises from a matrix of personality very different from, the wishes we analysts commonly hear expressed in our typical patients—for example, women's penis envy or men's breast envy.)

Yet, logical or not to us outside observers, they feel themselves more driven by the logic of their gender identity than by the visible logic of their bodies. Let a brief vignette illustrate this.

The patient, now in her forties, is a female who for many years has dressed and acted in a very masculine way. She knew she was born a female and was destined to be a woman, but she has always felt diffusely male. She described an odd condition: She had gradually come to believe, over many months' time, that she was growing a penis in her abdomen. While she knew that this was highly unlikely, she was not so sophisticated that she could feel this, at least consciously, to be impossible. Since she had always wanted to be a male, she was deeply gratified that her wish might be coming true. She had a friend whose hermaphroditism had been diagnosed at UCLA, and she hoped that the same diagnosis could be made for herself.

She described the "penis" as follows. It usually lay transversely across the lower abdomen, a tubular "organ" about the size of a penis and barely palpable in its resting state. However, there were two times when it changed its position and enlarged. The first occurred when she would awake in the morning with a full bladder, the second when she was sexually aroused. In both situations, the "penis" seemed to grow larger—to about six inches in length—was much easier to feel beneath the abdominal wall and moved from its transverse position to a vertical one. When in this latter position, its form could be distinguished on the abdominal wall. It was movable, but at its base was apparently attached to some part of the pelvic contents. When in this "erect" state, it was used by the patient as a sexual organ; she would mount her partner and slide the protrusion up and down on her partner's vulva until both had orgasms. The patient's orgasm was described as both abdominal and genital. Her partner, a woman with whom she had lived monogamously for over ten years, confirmed the story in every detail. Neither of the two were hallucinatory or delusional. I was unable to sense any suggestion that either was psychotic, so little so that their demeanor impressed me that they were right, despite my telling myself the story was absurd.

Physical examination revealed the presence of the abdominal structure exactly as the patient had described it, while demonstrating that she was biologically a completely normal female. The patient was advised to have an exploratory laparotomy, but she refused because of fear that the doctors would rob her of her "penis." When she was told that she might have an abdominal cancer she still refused, since this would mean that there really was no penis and she would prefer to die of cancer than face the certainty of not being in any way male. (We have seen this reaction before, that death by disease is preferred to a threat to gender identity.) However, great pressures were put on her by all of us, which in effect forced her to submit to surgery. A uterine fibroid was found and removed that exactly fitted her own description of her "penis." With a full bladder, the whole uterus, and therefore the tumor, was displaced upward, this apparently also occurring with uterine movement during sexual excitement.

From the day she left the hospital after surgery, she broke off all contact with me for a year. Then she and her friend came back for treatment spontaneously, because the patient had become very depressed. This reaction had started on the day of surgery when she had been told the findings of the laparotomy. To her, the meaning was terribly clear: If I have no penis, then I am a homosexual woman. She had stopped her sexual relations instantly and completely following surgery. She has not had and cannot have sexual relations ever again unless her dread that she is a homosexual can be overcome.

The contrast between her and her partner, a formerly married woman with a child, is provocative. We do not yet know why the patient cannot go on in life if her identity is that of a homosexual, whereas her partner is quite unconcerned about this. Is it that transsexuals, "normals," neurotic or psychotic people, the perverse, and people with syndromes (e.g., nymphomania and Don Juanism) directed very specifically against their "dreadful" homosexuality are so frightened because they have each internalized society's fearful hatred of homosexuality? We cannot yet describe specifically what happens in the above people to make them dread homosexuality, but which has not yet happened in small children, the polymorphous perverse, and many homosexuals, that they can live at ease within themselves in regard to their sexual desires for others of the same sex.

It is my impression, based especially on the analysis of "normal" women (i.e., not subjects in this research) that homosexual experiences in nonhomosexuals are rather less threatening to women than to men. I would speculate that this is because women do not need to go through as marked a process of separation from their mothers' bodies in order to learn their femininity, while men must successfully accomplish such a separation to become masculine.

Perhaps this patient senses that her masculinity depends on her being able to separate herself from her mother, and that if she felt herself to be a woman loving a woman's body the separation would be less complete and thus threaten her sense of self ("identity diffusion").

Beyond what is known about society's attitudes, I can think of one small clue. First of all, we may be too imprecise when we use the term "dread of homosexuality." We may really mean "dread of turning into the opposite sex." It is a feared loss of gender identity that is involved.[9] However, this brings us no closer to answering why some people do not feel that sexual and affectionate relations with a member of the same sex are a threat to their gender identity. An adequate answer would require the unlikely: the psychoanalyses of people with aberrances of gender who do not feel a need to be psychoanalyzed, because they are sufficiently comfortable with their cross-gender impulses (one of the big methodological problems of our research).

At this point, I should like to speculate about our patient. While we have no detailed history from the patient's infancy and childhood, suppose her transsexualism were due to forces comparable to those discovered in the three little boys, or even to some biological effect. This would mean that her belief in her essential maleness was produced in some manner during infancy, primarily by effects other than psychic conflict (that is, by the nonconflictual kinds of forces that in part produce normal and appropriate gender identity). If so, her belief in her maleness was not originally a defense but was accepted matter of factly, as is our own. She would then feel her sexual relationship with her friend to be heterosexual (though she would not deny that the outside world would call it homosexual since there are two anatomical females living together). However, when her acceptance of her maleness was taken from her by the unimpeachable authority of the medical profession, she was in something of the same predicament as the girl described in Chapter 3, who on being told at age 14 that she was biologically neuter rather being than a normal female, became psychotic.

To carry our speculation further, as Greenson has done,[10] this suggests that the fear of being a homosexual might be partly* an elaborated explanation of a more primitive fear: loss of gender identity. Possibly the fear of being homosexual may at times be not so much a fear produced by the castration conflicts of the height of the oedipal phase (around age 6 or 7) as the much more primitive fear of merging with someone of the opposite sex and losing one's identity in this way. Maybe Freud's speculations in the Schreber case are incomplete, when he says that the paranoid psychosis was a defense against Schreber's fear of admitting his homosexual desires. Macalpine and Hunter,[11] for instance, feel that behind Schreber's fantasies of being feminized were asexual procreation fantasies and identifications with his mother, material of a much more primitive nature than Freud was concerned with in his discussion of Schreber's pathological relationship to his father and the inverted oedipal complex which Freud felt produced Schreber's unacceptable wishes for intercourse with God. Klein[12] and some of her followers, especially Rosenfeld,[13] feel that the classical analytic formulation may reverse the true situation; they feel that homosexuality is a defense against, not the cause of, infantile terrors (postulated as "the paranoid position").

The whole formula that paranoidness is a defense against

---

*The psychoanalytic reader will, I hope, forgive me if I do not try to review the massive literature on homosexuality that describes so many other sources of such fear.

loving someone of the same sex might be modified to read that the desire by a man to love such a person is felt by him to be an indication that he may not be a man, but may be becoming a woman. Castration anxiety in all men might then mean that one does not so much fear losing his organ as that by losing the organ that is usually the only truly distinguishing feature of maleness in a boy, he might lose his sense of maleness, his identity.* For some men who have more severe flaws in their gender identity, it may be that the fear is not only of turning into a woman but of becoming feminized to the point of being a female.

Greenson has suggested that homosexual men are less threatened by homosexuality than are other men because somehow they have become convinced that homosexual practices do not make one a woman or a female. Accordingly, they feel that they can afford to be homosexuals, safe from any such threat to the stability of their identity.

*The boys born without penises (Chap. 5) are an exception to this since in reality they have been reassured from birth on, by their parents' attitudes, that they are males, even if the usual prime insignia is missing.

CHAPTER 13

Identity, Homosexuality, and Paranoidness

It is well known that the man who is unable to permit himself to become aware of desires for sexual relations with other men may, in the struggle against such awareness, become paranoid. There is no need to review the theories and the observations that have become so commonplace since Freud's great insights into the Schreber case. While probably only a few diehards would still maintain that the struggle against the awareness of homosexual impulses is *the* etiology in the paranoid psychoses, most experienced psychiatrists will on occasion have seen patients who became grossly paranoid in the midst of such a struggle.

One can scarcely be satisfied with the explanation that it is the awareness of social disapproval of homosexuality in our society that produces the paranoid reaction. Certainly there are other desires that a human can have that are as socially disapproved as homosexuality, and yet these other desires are not considered to cause paranoidness. In addition—the issue we were worrying in the last chapter—one is still left with the question of how most homosexuals manage to be so very unpsychotic; that is, how do they come to terms with this allegedly overwhelming social stigma? It seems to me that it is not simply internalized social disapproval that can make the threat of succumbing to homosexual pleasure so disrupting to some people, but rather that something more profound than social disapproval is threatening the person. I think that that threat is not that of being a homosexual, though that is what the patient tells us. Maybe it is the threat that one will no longer be himself; that is, that he feels he is losing his identity.

Unfortunately, to introduce the term "identity" or any of its semantic relatives, such as "self," "self-representation," "personality," "character structure," or even "ego," is to try to assign a word to a quality, a feeling, a sense, for which no adequate word has yet been hammered out. Proper concern has been expressed many time that the word "identity" is so diffuse and so metapsychologically uncertain that one has trouble knowing what an author means when he uses the word, and the question may quite properly be raised whether there is such a thing as "identity" if one can neither define it nor even describe it.* Certainly, I am in the same predicament, and use the term more as an act of faith that there is a real "thing" behind the word than from ability to prove that the "thing" exists. Nonetheless, I can see in others and sense in myself clusters of fantasies, feelings, beliefs—whatever you wish—that make me aware that I exist and that I can find myself to be distinctly different from all other people in certain pretty clear-cut ways. The structural concepts of ego, superego, and id are very helpful in mapping out these ways in which I recognize my similarities and differences from other people and things, but none of these structural terms covers the clinical data that one senses must be covered in the concept "identity." Therefore, even though the term can be misused and is not yet adequately defined, I believe it still says more than if it were fragmented metapsychologically into structural parts.

It seems apparent that a main factor in causing anxiety to

*Leites[1] has reviewed the literature on identity and has been unable to find a logically intact definition. Whenever the word appears, he feels that a simpler word can be substituted (e.g., "conviction," "belief," "self") which in no way alters the meaning of the sentence in which the word "identity" appears.

rise to the surface of consciousness is a threat to one's identity. We see this in such nongender areas as the clinging to orthodoxy and philosophies, in resistances met in treatment, in masochism, and in other ritualized ways of doing things. Oversimplified and incompletely, one could say that anxiety may result when there is a shift from the status quo, when homeostasis is threatened. That such shifts may also be accomplished by exhilaration, by sense of purpose, feeling of mastery, and other pleasant affects (much of which is as essential for normal life as it is for certain types of character disorders) of course does not deny their origins in anxiety.

For the man whose core gender identity is male and whose gender identity is essentially masculine, the threat of his succumbing to homosexual impulses is not simply that he will meet social disapproval, and not even only that he will be attacked by the forces of his superego, but also that his feeling of being himself, a lover of females and a member of that class—males—is being jeopardized (though masculine homosexual men are an exception I cannot discuss since I do not yet understand them). There may be a clue in this as to why most homosexuals do not become psychotic.* If homosexuals are not psychotic or barely keeping themselves from being overtly psychotic, then one cannot force one's theories by saying that the threat or the presence of homosexual pleasures can in itself produce paranoidness. We may be able to understand the fact that most homosexuals are not really in any danger of psychosis by noting that to them homosexuality is not a great threat. Perhaps homosexual desires are not as threatening to homosexuals because their identity is different from that of "healthy heterosexuals"[3]: The homosexual, if he has stronger

---

*It seems to me apparent by now that the argument that homosexuality covers over a psychosis, or that all homosexuals are very emotionally disturbed, is one that has been severely undercut by well-documented data (e.g., Hooker[2]). This is not to say that homosexuality is not made up, in part, of defensive maneuvers raised against certain unconscious conflicts. But the fact is that no one has even demonstrated that statistically significant numbers of people who prefer to practice their sexual relations on members of the same sex are as a group "sicker" (whatever that means) than a control group of those who prefer to practice their sexual relations with members of the opposite sex.

and more primitive identifications with women, may not so profoundly threaten his sense of masculinity when he loves a man. Having once established his identity—even if by a conflict-laden route—he may be doing what comes naturally, not just doing it defensively (though in most adult homosexual behavior there is probably an admixture of defense and of nondefensive pleasurable behavior). In other words, one can have the rather comfortable identity of being a homosexual (even in the many cases where this is the end-product of a stormy, neurotic personality development), just as one can have the rather comfortable identity of being a heterosexual; in both cases, the relatively stable identity will make the development of paranoidness less likely. For that person who wants to consider himself heterosexual but whose gender identity is less firmly fixed, the shift in status quo that the threat of homosexual pleasure poses becomes a threat to his sense of identity. I am reminded at this time of an analogous situation, the hermaphroditic identity, which, we saw, may develop in hermaphrodites who from birth on are considered by their parents not clearly to belong to one sex or the other. Such people usually are made aware from birth on that although their sex is uncertain they might as well consider themselves to be either a boy or a girl, but the very uncertainty of that message helps create the hermaphroditic identity. When these people are eventually told, as is sometimes the case, that they really belong to the opposite sex from the one in which they have lived, they shift over without severe distress. However, when the hermaphroditism is not diagnosed at birth and the child raised unquestioningly in one sex, a clear-cut gender identity appropriate to that sex develops; if a physician makes the proper diagnosis of sex later in life and tells this person that he or she really belongs in the opposite sex, severe disruption of identity ensues.

I would like to review now some material on a homosexual young man of twenty. He was referred to me because he had been insisting that he could no longer stand living with his male body and was searching out ways to obtain a sex transformation operation. It became apparent in the first interview we had that he did not have a transsexual character structure, though his demands for sexual transformation were nonetheless insistent and powerful. I am sure that had he had the money or had such an operation been available to him, he would have willingly sought it.

A few events from his past are pertinent here. His father had been chronically hospitalized starting about two years after the patient was born, and the little boy had just enough time to spend intermittently with his father to develop a love that became passionate because of the poignant interruptions for further hospitalization. He was raised by his angry, powerful, bitter, lonely, burdened mother. When the little boy was about six, his father died, the boy's growing effeminacy now increasing more rapidly. By adolescence he was wishing that he had been born a girl, was secretly wearing makeup and plucking his eyebrows, and was having sexual fantasies exclusively of being made love to by muscular men with large penises, in which circumstances he would imagine himself being a beautiful woman. Within a few months of first learning that sex-transformation operations exist, he became inflamed with the idea of undergoing such an operation.

His past history was not that of a transsexual but seemed much more typically that of an effeminate homosexual; his appearance was not that of any transsexuals I have seen. The latter all have a quality that must be called feminine, not effeminate; transsexuals do not have the hostile, mimicking quality connoted by the word "effeminate." (Note the homosexual argot term "camp," meaning to overdo one's hostile effeminate mimicry.) In addition, though he was slim, delicate, and a little mincing, there was a masculine quality interwoven into his movements. His voice was also undisguisedly appropriately masculine (with me, though not with certain of his acquaintances). Because of many distressing symptoms associated with an obsessive-compulsive personality, we both felt that he should start in psychotherapy, though I told him very quickly that I not only could not arrange for any sex-transformation procedures but I was not impressed that he was the kind of person who usually seeks them out. He did not argue this point violently with me, but, on the other hand, I did not feel at the beginning that he had changed his feelings about trying to get such an operation.

What is important for this discussion is that long before he knew the word "homosexual," he knew himself to be one; he knew that his romantic and sexual feelings were directed toward males and that he admired and wanted to emulate females. However, his effeminacy was not produced from birth on by excessive intimate contact with his mother's female body and her femininity, as is the femininity of the transsexual, but only began to develop several years later, as a result, first, of the suppression of his independence and masculinity by his angry, overpowering mother, and, second, of his yearning to be loved by his lost father. At no time did he think that he was a female, that he had any female organs or juices, or that as he would grow he would develop more biologically female qualities. In other words, he always knew himself to be a male without any question (core gender identity), although his identifications with women caused him at times to behave, talk and sound, and fantasy sexual relations with men as though he were a woman. This particular mixture of qualities is not one which indicates transsexualism, but rather a somewhat less advanced degree of identification with females which in the adult shows itself as effeminate homosexuality, which is accompanied by varying degrees of transvestic behavior (that is, trying on women's garments) but is neither transvestism nor transsexualism.

To state this briefly in identity terms, as has been described earlier, I believe the transvestite (which by no means includes everybody who puts on clothes of the opposite sex) feels himself to be a male (*sex*) and intermittently likes to have the feeling of being a woman (*gender role*) coursing through him; the true transsexual (that is, when the term is not simply used as a diagnosis for every person who requests sex-transformation procedures whatever the nature of his character structure) feels himself to be both a female and a woman; the homosexual, regardless of the degree of his effeminacy, considers himself to be a male and a man, though he clearly identifies himself as being a man of a particular class: homosexual.

In summing up the manifold expressions of this patient's gender identity, one would consider him more effeminate than a great many homosexuals and far less so than many who still do not have fantasies of being a woman. In addition, this patient did have transsexual fantasies; for example, when he would think of having intercourse, it was with him having the body of a woman. This is by no means found in all effeminate homosexuals and certainly not as their exclusive fantasy. So, if one were adding up the myriad of gender qualities observed in him, one would have to say that he had some transsexual tendencies, but that these were nowhere near the degree of reaching into the depths of his personality that one sees in the transsexual.

He grew older, having started treatment at age 17, and over the next three years he no longer had any fixed desire to be sexually transformed; his sexual fantasies began to be increasingly intermingled with fantasies of himself as a male having clearly admitted homosexual relations, though the transsexual fantasies occasionally returned. He became increasingly masculine, even to the extent of experimenting with a series of beards and crew haircuts, though continuing to let his fingernails grow long as a clear indicator to himself of some remaining fantasies of being a woman. His withdrawn and lonely life changed into one in which he had friends, and he was now able to travel in homosexual circles, clearly identifying himself as a homosexual, even having a few sexual experiences. These changes were accompanied by a great decrease in his obsessive-compulsivity and an increasing warmth with people of both sexes.

As is conceded for even the most formidably homosexual of men, there are certain potentials for heterosexuality; in this patient, these gradually became more manifest in three years of psychotherapy. This increasing heterosexuality reached a point where the patient became interested in a young woman he had known for many years. Where in the past he had been friendly because he identified with her, he now developed an interest in her as a separate person of the opposite sex. That is to say, while for many years he had enjoyed being with her, had admired her, had emulated her, and in his fantasies had conceived of himself as a female in her image (a process not so different from that followed by teen-age girls with older women), he now looked on her body as a separate object that he desired to *possess* rather than to *be* (Greenson).[4]

This emergence of heterosexual feelings into his consciousness suddenly accelerated one day when she was even able to cause in him some distinct flutters of sexual excitement, an intensity of feelings that finally led him to admit that he loved her. A week later, now even more vulnerable, he allowed another girl to coerce him into being a passive partner in some sexual play (though not intercourse).

He recognized that both these relationships, with their strong heterosexual overtones, were the results of increasing pressure that had been put on him in the months immediately prior by my interpretations regarding his heterosexual potential. Over these months, I had pointed to changes in his dreams, shifts in his fantasies, his increasingly masculine appearance, his acceptance by acquaintances as a more masculine person; especially he had had to listen to my constructions using information he had given me about his relationship with his mother in his childhood and his feelings about his father's illness and death. In all this psychotherapeutic work, he had complained of the pressure under which I was putting him, and especially he had complained that I did not understand that he really was a homosexual. (Everyone who has treated homosexuals is familiar with the great resistance such patients have to giving up not only their safe sexual objects but also their sense of being homosexuals. And this is also true whenever one works with a patient on trying to shift a character structure. So much of the tenacity that analysts have considered to be repetition compulsion that is beyond the pleasure principle may be no more "beyond the pleasure principle" than is the grip of a drowning man on a floating piece of wood.)

A few days after these heterosexual events, he became angry and suspicious toward me; he found himself ruminating about our last treatment hour, and it occurred to him that he had been wrong over the past three years in thinking I had been honest with him and committed to helping him. (This change in his attitude is not to be considered delusional; it may well have been based on his realization that I really did have wishes that he could become heterosexual, and that, to the extent that I had not expressed these wishes overtly and vociferously, he would feel that I was dishonest. The fact is, I would certainly wish for him happiness in his homosexuality as preferable to his having had a "sex transformation," but my bias is that in our world heterosexuality still has greater potentials for pleasure and happiness.)

However, his anger and suspiciousness had a sharp, bizarre edge, a quiet, controlled rage that astonished me. He was now convinced that in the previous treatment hour I had openly admitted to him that I was a liar and that "you said you would use any trick you could think of to force me to become heterosexual." During this present hour, in which he expressed these revelations with suppressed rage, I found myself for the first time frequently unable to follow his train of thought. He had never before expressed suspiciousness or rage or any disorder in his thinking processes. This episode was actually astonishing and confusing to me, for he was completely different in affect than ever before; this plus his intense suspiciousness and rambling, disordered associations, left me rather worried. However, these symptoms passed, for in the next hour he was warmer and more comfortable with me than ever before.

In certain men who cannot accept the presence of emerging homosexual desires, it may not be homosexuality per se that produces paranoidness; rather, for them homosexuality threatens their sense of identity. The present case comes upon this issue from the opposite direction: People who have anchored their identity in a conviction of being homosexual may be threatened by the emergence of their heterosexual feelings. The common denominator in each instance is the threatened loss of the familiar desired identity. Of course, this is not to say that all "functional" psychoses are produced in this way, but rather that in certain people who already have significant fracture lines in their character structure, as this man had with his obsessive-compulsivity, the threat to the integrity of a not too stable identity can produce a sense of panic which may then proceed to expand into a mild or severe state of paranoidness.

CHAPTER 14

A Feminine Man: a Control Case

A single case certainly cannot be used convincingly as a control unless one has assurance that the single case represents a whole class. I want to do something of that sort now, to compare one class—the extreme form of transsexualism that the three little boys and the adult transsexuals described represent—with another class: all males who want sex-transformation procedures, but who are less totally feminine. If the "experiment" is successful, then it will be found that transsexuals—adult and child, who are extremely feminine, who are nonfetishistic, who started their feminine behavior before age three, and who are not by choice intermittently masculine—have mothers and fathers like the ones our little boys have.

On the other hand, if a male requesting sex transformation is less totally feminine, his parents will not fit the described picture. To stick my neck out well beyond where the data should encourage dangerous living, I will predict that if this person is fetishistic (i.e., gets an erection from women's clothes), if he has lived intermittently as a man and during this time was not considered feminine or even effeminate, if he has ever been married, if he has had children, if he has ever appreciated having a penis, if he would not go through great hardship to get his operation, if he is uncertain whether he is ready for it if the opportunity is offered to him, if he willingly permits another man to handle his penis, if he does not recall being feminine as far back as his memory reaches, if he publicizes before or after the operation the fact that he was born a male, if he calmly settles for less in the way of medical procedures than he has heard is technically possible, then he will not have the kind of parents the little boys have—and, depending on how many of the above points characterize him, the more likely he will be to have postoperative emotional difficulties, up to and including psychosis.

Some psychiatrists might maintain that effeminate boys and tomboyish girls, who are familiar enough, are essentially the same in their gender identities as the transsexual children being described in this work and yet have very different parents and infancies. If they were the same, then much of what I am saying would not be very significant, for then all sorts of different parents would be producing the same types of children.

On the other hand, it might be maintained that psychiatrists dealing with other than transsexual children *have* seen parents who would fit the descriptions I have given for the three transsexual boys. It has been said, for instance, that stressing the symbiotic relationship between the mother and infant in the etiology of childhood transsexualism raises serious questions, for is not symbiosis also discussed in the etiology of some schizophrenics? Of course. The answer obviously is that there are all sorts of symbiotic relations and to have called something "symbiosis" tells very little about its qualities. We need precise descriptions of the mothers' personalities and what they literally did upon their infants' bodies before we know what form of symbiosis a worker is considering.

I believe it is the custom in the psychiatric world to speak too much in generalities. It could be that many of the attacks on psychodynamic formulations found in the psychological and medical literature arise because we analysts at times use generalizations instead of giving detailed information. Otherwise, all overprotective mothers would be the same, whereas in fact the degree and quality of such behavior is tremendously different from mother to mother. It is in the moment by moment, hour by hour, day by day, and year by year living that mothers or fathers stamp their effects upon their infants.*

CASE MATERIAL

The patient who is to be described now will represent a *control* against whom we can compare more typical transsexuals. This is a man with a marked degree of femininity, so great that he sought help in getting a sex-transformation operation. If the sole criterion for diagnosis of transsexualism were that one intensely desires such an operation, then this patient would be called a transsexual (and in fact such patients usually are in the literature). However, as has been noted earlier, I feel that we are on safer ground if we more completely describe the gender identity, recognizing that not all people requesting sex-transformation procedures have the same disturbances in gender identity. It is my thesis that differences in gender identity are almost always produced by differences in infant rearing,† and this patient exemplifies this.

*A problem so far insoluble in the reporting of much clinical data in the psychological "sciences" is that papers must be read quickly, and with half the time taken up with reviews of the literature, discussions, and theoretical formulations, practically no time is available for the data, and so data are almost never presented but rather abstracts of data. This same reporting would be completely unacceptable anywhere else in the scientific world, and, in fact, ours often smacks of the propagandizing techniques of advertising, which can also give a scientific gloss to generalizations. The only way to know what a histologist has seen is to look through his microscope with him or look at photographs that perfectly reproduce what he has seen. For many good reasons, we cannot do the same with the data we are collecting in psychiatry, and this methodological problem still seems insoluble. In certain areas of our work, where they do not interfere, audiovisual recording techniques can remedy this deficit. However, even when these are used, they cannot serve to communicate to mass audiences as can books or journal articles. Unable to solve this problem in this work I have tried at least to summarize accurately what actually was said by patients, so that one is less at my mercy if I say, for example, that a mother is overprotective.

†"Rearing" is an inadequate term used to cover a tremendously complicated continuing experience wherein the psychodynamics at work within the parents interplay with the developing, increasingly complex psychodynamics of

When first seen, the patient was in his late thirties. On the telephone, he had sounded unremarkably like a man and when seen in person gave the same impression. He was tall, erect, and masculine in his walk and bearing, had no effeminate mannerisms or inflections, wore his hair appropriately cut for a man, showed no hint of makeup, and was wearing a conservative masculine-looking suit. His manly appearance was confirmed by his statements that he has been able to live completely accepted as a man throughout his adult life, with no one ever questioning his masculinity so long as he appeared this way. However, on and off since his teens and until recent years, he had spent months at a time passing undetected as a woman.

In his late teens he had married and had had intercourse regularly with his wife, with three children resulting. When he had intercourse he had no difficulty getting excited, having erections, maintaining erections, or having orgasms with a strong erotic sensation at ejaculation, assisted occasionally by fantasies during intercourse of being a woman. He had known since earliest childhood that he also had strongly feminine tendencies and had dressed in girls' clothes intermittently in childhood and quite regularly in adolescence, finally learning on his own how to dress as a woman so well that he could live as a woman. I have considered the pathognomonic sign of transvestism to be the capacity for sexual excitement precipitated by clothing of the opposite sex; using that criterion, this patient was not a transvestite, because never in his life had he been excited by *women's* apparel. However, he was a fetishist. He had discovered at puberty that rubber was exciting to him, and from that time to the present has become very excited with rubber garments, which he is able to purchase from firms specializing in supplying such fetishists.

In addition, a factor rather different from many but by no means all transvestites, was that he considered himself to be a

their infant, with all its fantasies as to who its parents are and who it is. I do not mean here that the child's gender identity develops passively, at the mercy of what the parents do, though I do believe that in the beginning of life this is essentially the case (plus unknown biological factors). Then, as the child's personality develops, his own independent fantasy life and other ego functions help shape his gender identity—as has been described by many workers from Freud on.

homosexual. On the other hand, as with transsexuals, he would not have relations with men who were interested in his penis. When having homosexual relations, which were anal, he would assume a woman's position, wear something that would hide his genitalia, fantasy himself a woman with a vagina, and would then have a completely different feeling of orgasm than when he was having heterosexual relations. When fantasying himself a woman during intercourse with a man, he had no sexual sensation in his penis, though he could feel the semen being ejaculated; his sense of orgasm was abdominal.

His reason for seeking a psychiatric consultation was that he felt in himself very strongly these two opposing senses of gender, which had so openly expressed themselves in his behavior—the one a clear feeling of comfortable masculinity; the other, a clear sense of femininity, with a capacity to turn from one to the other almost at will. He knew he was a male; while he did not think he was a female trapped in a male body, he would have preferred to be a female, but he recognized the great difficulty in attempting such a change. So he came seeking advice as to whether it was worth going through the expense and pain to get a sex-conversion operation. The very fact that he was uncertain and seeking advice makes him different from the extreme transsexuals I have seen; the latter are willing to put up with anything in order to get the operation; they ask for no one's opinion as to whether it would be helpful for them. However, he is like a lot of men who are not so intensely transsexual, but who have transsexual tendencies without a fixed feminine gender identity.

We would predict, then, that his parents' personalities and the way they treated him from birth on would be different from what has been described earlier for the transsexual boys. This was the case.

The information was given by both the patient and his mother. His mother's appearance was different from that of the mothers of marked transsexuals in that she was dressed in a more showy, feminine manner. Although almost seventy years old, she was dressed in the style of a woman in her twenties, with a florid print dress and a lace-ruffled bib around her neck. She was in stylish high heels that were surprisingly young-looking and would seem to have put her at a certain risk to balance upon them. There was no indication in her dress or her subsequent behavior of the special bisexuality that appeared in the mothers of the transsexuals described in earlier chapters.

Because of the birth of a sibling within two years after the patient was born, his mother did not have the opportunity for prolonged and uninterrupted preoccupation with her son which we found in the mothers of our little boys. In fact, she did not desire this; however, the child burned his ankle badly between age 2 and 3 and had to be carried for about six months. It is impossible to know if this contributed in any way to his femininity. At any rate, his mother had not wished to do this but had it forced on her; as she described the casual manner in which she lugged her baby around, it did not sound at all like the excessive body contact found in the histories of the marked trans-sexuals. On the other hand, she did not say there was not *any* contact, but gave a clear picture of the kind of handling of an infant or small child that is frequently found when there are not disturbances in gender identity (picking the child up and hugging him when he hurt himself, holding him for feeding, and the like). The baby was weaned at about a year and a half and toilet-trained at two years. There was no question in his mother's mind that these demands had to be made on the child, and there were no particular problems associated with treating him firmly. She denied any history of lengthy exposure to her nude body either during the day or at night; she did not take her baby to bed with her, for she shared the bed nightly with the patient's father. There is no evidence (the mother specifically denies it) that she saw her son dressing in women's clothes at any time during childhood, and in fact she now is made miserable by his femininity. Such rearing has none of the excessive permissiveness found in the transsexual boys.

She does not recall his attachment to a blanket or any other cloth object, nor does he, but both are familiar with this as a common practice of children. In addition, neither describes him as having a special interest in the texture of cloth, though he becomes preoccupied with the feel of soft rubber garments.

Both give a description of his father that is in no way like that of the fathers of transsexuals. A man of military bearing, he was very active in the upbringing of all his children, forceful, and clearly the man of the family, apparently too much so in the sense that he created with his alternating fierce punishments and enveloping love a most ambivalent family atmosphere. His interests were masculine (if not hypermasculine) and, while much of his displayed gender behavior may have been overcompensation for hidden problems in this regard, nonetheless what the family had to live with every day was completely different behavior from that of the absent, empty fathers of the transsexuals.

CONCLUSION

In short, this patient can look and act more masculine than do transsexuals when he chooses, has different sexual desires from those of transsexuals, considers himself to be a homosexual male who would like a female body, in contrast to the belief of transsexuals that they are females trapped in males' bodies, and is uncertain if and when he wants to have a sex-transformation operation. One would conjecture from this present picture that his parents had treated him differently in childhood than the transsexuals' parents were treating them. This was the case. His father was not a distant, empty, somewhat effeminate man who paid little attention to his son and did nothing to stop his feminine behavior. His mother is not one of those specially bisexual women previously described, who has an empty, unchanging relationship with a husband and can indefinitely maintain the status quo in order to preserve an empty, oppressive marriage; she did not interfere with the separation of the infant from her body in the way that transsexuals' mothers do with their sons.

What caused this man's marked disturbance in gender identity is unknown; I believe that events occurred in his earliest childhood about which we can learn nothing, but which played a part in creating his feminine tendencies and his fetishism. However, while we do not know what has caused his pathology, we do know that it was not caused by the same forces that are found in the histories of the extremely transsexual people I have seen.

CHAPTER 15

A Bisexual Mother:
a Control Case

None of the data presented in earlier chapters on the causes of transsexualism in boys *proves* anything. We must always remember that while they help us to make a logical argument, they are not firsthand observations of the special mother-infant relationship which I am stating may at times lead to transsexualism. Until we are able to observe a mother and infant from the latter's birth on in a relationship that results in, creates, transsexualism, we do not have reliable data (yet the reader undoubtedly realizes that if we could simply stand around and observe such a process, our presence would itself probably radically change the mother-infant relationship). So for the present, our answers lie where we are unable to look—in the moment-by-moment, day in-day out physical contact of mother and infant and in the exact way in which the mother is felt by the infant's sensory apparatus and what these sensations come to mean as communications of affects: the warm, moist, peaceful respiration of a mother who loves and needs the infant to be enfolded by her (and how long does she do this today, and is "today" every day, and is "every day" extended for several years?); the tense mother whose stiff muscles, less pillowy skin, and jerky respirations thrust the baby away prematurely; and so on over the infinite range of mothering styles.

But we do not have these data. So we must infer what was likely from what we see and hear now as these mothers tell us what they felt then and what they feel now about their sons.

This is the thesis. A transsexual boy is most likely to be produced when these factors are present: (1) His mother, motivated in part by transsexual tendencies in herself that are repressed in adolescence, (2) and in part by a conscious desire to prevent her son from suffering by the absence of loving mothering that she suffered from her own mother, (3) lovingly and intensely holds her infant son against her body for too long, (4) while there is no man (father) present either to stop the mother from encouraging the process of feminization or to serve as a manly person from whom the boy can learn to be masculine.

Postulate: the more these factors are present, the more likely is an infant male to develop into a transsexual; change or remove some and the boy is less transsexual. Thus, I would predict that excessive body contact alone would not produce a feminized boy; the body contact would have to be done by a mother who has enough disturbance in her gender identity that she can let (wish?) bisexuality grow in her son, and/or it would have to be done by a mother who holds the boy against her too much in her attempt to "cure" vicariously her own depression and sense of emptiness. Or: it could not be done, no matter what the mother's personality, if there was a masculine father present. Or: a mother with transsexual tendencies will still not make her boy transsexual if she does not transmit onto the boy's body (senses) her own transsexual feelings, especially by holding him too much.

In this regard, I presume that mothers—all mothers—begin to indicate to their infants their criteria for masculinity and femininity from birth on. They can do this, for example, by encouraging certain types of behavior and discouraging others. This learning process uses the same sorts of gross and microscopic, conscious and unconscious communications of approval and dislike that help build certain other personality characteristics.*

One of the most startling observations I made in this search for causes of transsexualism was the marked and very special bisexuality of the mothers. Each spontaneously mentioned and stressed the quality of boyishness that had been present in her until adolescence and which had then been replaced, at least on the surface, by an exclusively heterosexual role that culminated in (empty) marriage and children. What was especially impressive was the vividness of these mothers' description of their boyishness, with their conscious desires to be so male-like, the dressing in boys' clothes, the choice of boys as preferred playmates, and the intense drive for success in athletics that made them the equal of or superior to boys in the neighborhood.

Listening to these mothers talking of this quality gave an impression of something more than tomboyishness. They went through a phase that was filled with conscious transsexual desires (though less intense than in truly transsexual females). (See Chaps. 12 and 17.) Unlike transsexual females, they do not express these desires from infancy on, or try more and more to act like boys, eventually to pass in the world as men, nor do they seek out sex-transformation procedures. However, neither are they simply tomboys, who, for instance, at the end of a day of horseback riding and mutual sharing with girl friends of hatred of the boys they envy. get dressed up in their most feminine clothes and talk about hair styles, cosmetics, and their concerns and hopes about oncoming changes in secondary sex characteristics.

As has been described, these mothers made me wonder whether their transsexual tendencies, now pretty much unconscious, might not be the crucial element in damaging their sons'

*I noted the following in a pet store. A mother and her little son were watching a fish tank in which piranhas were being fed a live goldfish.
    Son: I want one (pointing to a piranha).
    Mother: (to shopkeeper) See, he likes the goldfish.
    Son: No! The other ones!
    Mother: He doesn't really like those [piranhas]. He's really a goldfish himself (loving smile).
    I doubt if Coriolanus' mother would have treated her son like this.

gender identity. However, a moment's thought reminded me that it is not the mother's personality that is the final pathway in modifying her child but the activities in the three-dimensional world that this personality produces and that literally touch her child's various senses.

A test of the thesis comes when one searches for mothers who have a history of this sort of bisexuality but whose sons are not transsexual. The woman to be discussed now provides such a test. Married, in her thirties, a housewife, and with two preadolescent sons, this woman has, and has had since childhood, strong transsexual tendencies without being a transsexual. Her sons, while they certainly have their problems, are masculine. How can we account for this?

First, let us pause and see exactly how she describes her transsexual tendencies. She says:

I can remember as a small child wanting desperately to be a boy. My mother usually dressed me in boy's clothing and I behaved as much like a boy as I could. I played with boys and worked hard to be the strongest, toughest, and to be the best in sports.

I remember taping one of my baby brother's baby bottle nipples to my pubic area and pretending I had a penis. I often stood up to urinate like my brothers. I thought that if I acted enough like a boy I might grow up to be a man. I often examined my vagina, hoping to find a penis growing. Whenever I had the opportunity I would examine my little sister or little girls to see if I was built the same or was actually growing the penis I wanted. When I began to masturbate I would find an implement that had the appearance of a penis. I would insert the end of it in my vagina and grasp it as if it were a penis, and by moving my hand up and down on it I would have an orgasm.

I had my first homosexual experience when I was thirteen years old. I lay on top of another girl and simulated intercourse. I had an orgasm and felt I was really being a boy. As I grew older I had many sexual experiences with both men and women. I never felt masculine while having sexual relations with a man. I had a very satisfying time sexually with men and still do.

When I'm having sexual relations with a woman I can feel completely masculine, as long as she doesn't touch me in the pubic area. No matter what sexual activity I'm engaged in with a woman I always have an orgasm when she has one, and this can occur without my genitals having been touched. During my sexual relationship with a woman I actually feel as though I have a penis. I feel totally masculine and superior to the female I'm with. When I experience an orgasm I feel that I ejaculate. It's difficult to explain. My orgasm is not a single feeling but more of a spasmodic sensation. I can have sexual relations with a woman, have one orgasm and be completely satisfied. When I have intercourse with a man I have to have several orgasms before I can relax and feel satisfied.

When I want to stimulate myself sexually I imagine myself as a man with a woman in various sexual situations.

And yet this woman's sons (whom I have observed since early childhood) are not transsexual. She said, "I've got good boys; I really have . . . and yet I am so screwed up. I don't understand how it could have happened that they are okay. I guess maybe it's because I was always conscious of these feelings [of wanting to be male], and still am. And so I always made sure to keep all these feelings away whenever I was with my babies. When I was with them, it was like when I am with a man. I don't have these feelings at that time. I am just a woman then."

Of course, here again our problem in methodology arises. If we are not there to observe her with her infant son, we cannot be sure that her conscious efforts to keep her needs to be male out of her mothering did in fact protect her sons, though it is quite possible. At any rate, in this regard she differs from the mothers of the transsexual boys, none of whom continued after puberty to sense their previous transsexual drives. We can wonder whether, in the mothers of the transsexual boys, these drives, now subjected to repression and distortion, were not therefore left free to play upon their sons, while the present patient, still conscious of their presence, was better able to control them.

In addition, she did not use her sons in the same way the other mothers did, to fill up an emptiness produced in childhood by the mother's own empty mother; while feeling wonderfully fulfilled during her pregnancies, deliveries, and early mothering of her infants, she did not hold them against her body excessively. However, she had that same emptiness, having been in effect abandoned by her mother. For example, when a teen-ager, her mother had her held by juvenile authorities after an episode of delinquent behavior; when the authorities then contacted her mother and said that the girl could return home, her mother refused to let her do so, and so the child was sent instead to an institution and kept there for months while the authorities tried to find a place for her. There were other similar episodes. (This woman's treatment revolved primarily around her sense of abandonment by her own mother.)

The factor of father's absence was also a part of her sons' childhood. The boys had different fathers, each man being divorced from this mother and disappearing from the scene while each boy was an infant. Yet, probably because she was not feminizing them (she was not wishing it of them, holding them too much, or encouraging feminine behavior when it appeared, as were the mothers of the transsexual boys), the absence of a father—whatever damage it did—did not have the destructive effects to gender identity that it did in the transsexual boys.

In summary, then, we see in this family that even if certain of the important factors producing transsexualism in little boys are present, the distorted gender identity may not develop if other factors are not present. In this case, a mother with transsexual tendencies and with a sense of emptiness produced by her own empty mother did *not* produce a transsexual son, even though there was not a man consistently present in the child's childhood, because the mother did not "wish" the transsexualism upon her child and did not interfere with the process of differentiation from her own body.

CHAPTER 16

Differential Diagnosis: Transvestism and Transsexualism

Transvestism and transsexualism are each severe disturbances in gender identity sharing two features so distinctive and bizarre that the conditions are often taken to be the same: first, an abnormally strong identification with women, and second (resulting from the first), cross-dressing. Since homosexuals (both "masculine" and "effeminate") also have abnormally strong identifications with certain aspects of femininity, many psychiatrists mistakenly consider transvestism and transsexualism to be simply homosexual variants.

It will be the purpose of this chapter more carefully to describe and thus distinguish these conditions from each other.

TRANSVESTISM

Let us define adult male *transvestism* as completely pleasurable; it is fetishistic, intermittent cross-dressing in a biologically normal man who does not question that he is a male—that is, the possessor of a penis.

Within this definition there are two common forms (and a

176

number of infrequent variants). Probably the most frequent is that of the man who, in addition to the above criteria, has learned a woman's role so well that he can or wishes to successfully pass undetected in society as a woman; when he does so, the activity alternates with living most of his life in a man's role. While his transvestism started in childhood or adolescence with sexual excitement precipitously provoked by a single garment, there is gradual emergence over the years of a nonerotic desire to sense himself intermittently as a woman (with a penis) and to pass as one.

He is exhibitionistic in this in that he is constantly aware of the penis under his women's clothes, and, when it is not dangerous to do so, gets great pleasure in revealing that he is a male-woman. This is not, however, the perversion exhibitionism, which is very rare in transvestites. The pleasure in tricking the unsuspecting into thinking he is a woman, and then revealing his maleness (e.g., by suddenly dropping his voice) is not so much erotic as it is a proof that there is such a thing as a woman with a penis. He has identified with a "phallic" woman (mother) and consciously senses himself to be a phallic "woman." He therefore can tell himself that he is, or with practice will become, a better woman than a biological female if he chooses to do so.

He stresses that he prefers sexual relations only with women and is not effeminate when not dressed as a woman.

The second type is the intermittent cross-dresser who considers himself a transvestite but who emphasizes the point that he is always masculine, even when indulging in his fetishism, which is with individual pieces of women's garments; he does not wish to look like a woman, feel like a woman, or pass as a woman. He simply considers himself to be a man who gets sexually excited by his fetish.*

Other less common variants are the fetishistic cross-dressers

---

*These men consider themselves to be tranvestites, and feel that those who want to pass as women are putting on an act and faking their need to appear feminine. I believe both types are quite real and distinct.

In this work, I shall be considering only those men who wish to pass, for they are the ones with the more marked disturbance in gender identity.

who enjoy homosexual relations, the ones who enjoy being bound and humiliated, those who like the women's clothes to be made of rubber, and other modifications. As the modifications come to dominate, one is less sure if the person should be considered "simply" a transvestite.

It is my working premise that these variations are not of mysterious origin, and that if we were able to learn the exact details of the infantile relationships these men had with their mothers and fathers (as we have begun to do with the transsexual boys), we could find the reasons why these variants are chosen.

In any case, the transvestite is not a heterosexual man with rarely expressed transvestic tendencies, an effeminate heterosexual, effeminate homosexual, homosexual "queen," or transsexual.

Differentiating these last-named syndromes is not simply a matter of splitting hairs; while each may share a common piece of behavior—(putting on women's clothes), or a common psychodynamic feature (e.g., cross-gender identifications) or a common fantasy (e.g., conscious or unconscious desires for sexual relations with a person of the same sex), the differences in gender identity are too profound to be ignored. Confusion in and out of the literature is caused if all people who cross-dress are called "transvestites," for this disregards major differences clinically, psychodynamically, and etiologically. Likewise, to call all men with excessive feminine identification "homosexuals" or "latent homosexuals" is to blur meanings unnecessarily, leading to faults in treatment as well as theory. Let us briefly differentiate these groups from the patients who fall within the above definition of transvestism. One essential difference is the quantitative one, the matter of degree. The men with a relatively intact gender identity may be interested in cross-dressing enough to enjoy it as a joke when it is presented in a comedy and, with embarrassed pleasure, may even dress up in women's clothes under certain carnival conditions; such a man in psychoanalysis would show evidence for the underlying cross-gender identifications, but the strength behind the resultant wishes is rather weak. He may be able to enjoy heterosexual relations without falling back on perverse techniques to fortify his potency.

The effeminate heterosexual may have an effeminate manner in his behavior and speech, may be an overly loving and "maternal" father when his children are small, and may be oversolicitous to other people and thrillingly responsive to the universe of art—may even have a considerable uneasiness regarding homosexual matters, and still can spend his intimate life comfortably only with a woman.

An effeminate homosexual, in addition to his effeminate behavior and his preference for homosexual intercourse may show transvestic tendencies (e.g., wearing jewelry, using cosmetics, and choosing clothes designed for males but commonly recognized as effeminate) and will still not have a fetishistic relationship to clothes or an acted-out desire to appear as a woman.

A homosexual "queen" also does not use clothes fetishistically. Some grotesquely parody women; others who can even pass successfully cannot hide their disdain for women as sexual creatures. By their raging preoccupation with overt homosexual relations, they show that their interest is not in appearing like a normal woman. While an occasional transvestite may indulge himself in a homosexual "experiment," he is not often homosexually promiscuous. "Queens" do not try to consider themselves to be "women" with a penis; they simply take themselves to be effeminate homosexual men.

The next condition to be considered is adult transsexualism. The adult transexual is a male who hopes, by means of sex-transformation procedures, to convert his normal male body to female. He feels he is essentially female though with a male body. He learns to pass successfully as a woman, not even known by friends or fellow workers to be a male. He does not alternate between a masculine and a feminine role, as does the transvestite; he is not secretly thrilled with the thought of having a penis secreted beneath his dress, he gets no real sexual pleasure from his penis, and does not maintain—or wish to maintain—a sense of masculinity by knowing it is part of his body ego. If he succeeds in having his penis removed, he does not regret it.

On the other hand, in tranvestism, the man has no question that he is a male and that he wants to remain a male. He alternates periods of comfortable masculinity with episodes of feminine behavior in which the cross-dressing occurs. An essential part of his pleasure is to know that while dressed as a woman he has a penis, sometimes to think of himself as a phallic "woman," and to reveal himself to others (when it is not too dangerous) as a male. He would never sacrifice his penis in order to become a "female." He is also a fetishist; due to a feeling that women and their bodies are dangerous, his sexual excitement is to a greater or lesser degree dependent on his having an inanimate substitute for a human sexual object; in this condition the fetishes are women's apparel. His primary sexual object is generally a woman (though conscious urges for men are occasionally seen, and unconscious homosexual urges are more nearly emergent than in men with less strong feminine identification). Tranvestism is in great part a defensive structure raised to protect a threatened but desired sense of masculinity and maleness, and the corollary, to preserve a badly threatened potency. One should not be fooled by the apparent paradox that he does this via the detour of dressing like a woman.

A few words are indicated regarding the differential in children. There are two significant observable manifestations that mark the underlying differences in identity between transvestite and transsexual children. One, only the transvestite boys are fetishistic, that is, have erections due to women's clothes. Two, transvestism often makes its first appearance in childhood but does so only after clear-cut masculinity has already developed in the boy. Transsexualism, however, starts earlier and may even reveal itself by the end of the first year; it more completely possesses the boy's gender, controlling his behavior as early as any kind of gender role has begun to evolve.

Childhood transsexualism, as has been noted, should also be differentiated from the casual transvestic behavior so common in little boys. Before the process of finding his masculinity is complete, a little boy may put on a piece of his mother's or sister's apparel and enjoy strutting around in it for awhile until he either becomes tired of it or someone in the family stops him. Some boys will do this more, some less, but such play is not evidence of pathology of gender identity.

Let one case of transvestism, even in its brevity, stand for a generality of others.

This man enjoys dressing in women's clothes, wants to appear like a woman, becomes sexually excited by handling and putting on women's clothes, but knows without question that he is a male —that is, the possessor of a penis. His excitement comes in part from his constant awareness that he is a phallic "woman"; he knows that beneath his woman's underwear, dress, makeup, wig, and feminine behavior there always exists a penis.

For the first three years of his life, his masculinity was more or less that of other boys his age. Then it was his bad fortune, because of a prolonged and eventually fatal illness of his mother, to fall into the hands of his aunt and her daughter. These women hated males. For the first time, both of them were provided with a defenseless male on whom they could expend their rage and envy. The little boy became theirs, with his mother hospitalized and his father not interested in bringing him up. They let his hair grow long, and they designed, cut, and sewed for him new and effeminate clothes. They kept him this way for three years. One day, shortly before she died, his mother came home on a visit from the hospital. The two women had a clever idea: They dressed this by-now feminized little boy as a little girl, introduced the little "girl" to the visiting mother, who never learned the child was her son, and a snapshot was taken to commemorate the occasion of the vicious joke.

A couple of years later, his father showed up to claim him again. By this time the child's mother had died and his father had remarried. At age 6 appears his first memory: he has been "bad" because he dripped wax on his stepmother's sister's stockings. With the uncannny sense of destruction that some women have when in the exciting presence of little boys, she chose what she felt was the perfect punishment, and forced him to put on the stockings.* He dates his transvestism from this point, and for him transvestism means *pleasure* in cross-dressing. From then on, what

*His half brother, this woman's nephew, was dressed as a girl by our subject's stepmother; the family was proud that the little boy then looked like Shirley Temple. The patient and his wife feel they have "read" this half brother and from various clues are convinced he is now a transvestite.

had been the passively endured experience of being a living puppet for his aunt and older cousin was transformed into an active experience colored by sexual excitement. Now what had been traumatic was mastered, becoming his greatest pleasure. In this way the victim has his own sort of triumph.

Dressing in little girls' clothes continued throughout his childhood. These episodes were thrilling and accompanied by erections. Orgasms began in adolescence, the first following his putting on an aunt's underpants. From that day on, there was a progression in the use of single pieces of women's clothes for masturbation, with underwear, shoes, stockings, dresses, each in their turn, serving for months as the sole object of his excitement. Built into each such experience was the memory of the passively endured traumatic humiliation of being dressed by the two mother substitutes. Though he has never remembered those events before age six,* he nonetheless carries their (unconscious) memory with him into each of his dressing experiences.

In his teens he began going out on dates with girls, indulging in sexual relations with pleasure and success, keeping from all the girls the facts of his transvestism. When he eventually began going with the woman he was later to marry, he told her of his perversion. She was interested but not shocked, and so they married, eventually to have children.

In order for him to get sexual pleasure or even to retain his potency, he must introduce his transvestism into his intimate relations with his wife. Thus, he will dress up, put on makeup, and expect her to talk to him as though he were a woman if he is to enjoy intercourse fully. However, his fantasy is not that he is an anatomically normal woman; he is aware that he is a "woman" with a penis. While this is scarcely normal heterosexual behavior, and while his excessive identification with women is obvious enough, it would be grossly oversimplified to call this "homosexual" behavior. There are strongly homosexual overtones to his sexual behavior, but he has never had homosexual relations and is repelled by them in the same manner and by the same kinds of

*He has been told about them and has shown me photographs in the family album showing him dressed as a girl, holding his dying mother's hand.

defenses (other than transvestism) as are used by most men commonly considered heterosexual.

ETIOLOGICAL FACTORS IN TRANSVESTISM

a. *Genetic, constitutional, biochemical, etc.* To date, there is no acceptable evidence that in the vast majority of cases of transvestism there is any genetic, constitutional, or biochemical abnormality (e.g., no known laboratory method of assaying male and female hormones has revealed disturbances in these transvestites).*

b. *Mother's unconscious wishes.* Whatever the genetic, constitutional, or otherwise biological features that may in the future be discovered to contribute to the causes of transvestism, there is one consistent factor in the history of adult male transvestites. This is the mothers't need to feminize their little boys. These mothers have an unusually strong envy of males which expresses itself in this rather subtle way. There are rare mothers who kill their sons, there are many more who in their hatred of their sons help produce many different neurotic and occasionally psychotic states, and there are some who produce passivity and ineffectualness. The mother of the transvestite shares with these other mothers the need to damage her son, but her technique is different: In order to humiliate him, she makes a little "girl" of him *on occasion.* By "on occasion" I mean that she lets him know that he is a boy (that is, the possessor of a penis and a member of the class "male"), but she very specifically and precisely introduces occasions on which the child is to be like a girl; that is, when she dresses him in girl's clothes or otherwise expresses her wish that he be a girl.

I presume that many such women, unable to find their way to being "butch" homosexuals, must settle for living among men and boys—including their own—filled with envy and rage, sensing their own blighted femininity and hating themselves for the defect.

*Some very rare conditions with associated cross-dressing have been reported, with specific hormonal shifts, tumors, or abnormal central nervous system electrical activity (e.g.,[1]).

†Occasionally, it is not a mother but another girl or woman who, by means of her age and size (i.e., power), in some way, on occasion or continuously, substitutes for the boy's mother.

If this be true, then, since they cannot arrive at successful femininity either, they make a parody of it by dressing up their sons. Whether on a deeper level they believe there are such creatures as phallic "women," and are trying to prove they exist by creating one could only be answered if such a mother were analyzed. I know of no such case, and so can only surmise that the transvestite is partly the creation of his mother's unconscious wish and not only the product of his own defenses, as Fenichel[2] sees it.

c. *Father: the co-conspirator.* But much as the boy's mother may wish to damage him in this way, she cannot succeed without her husband's connivance. It is astonishing to discover how often the fathers, knowing that their wives are dressing their sons in girls' clothes, do not put a stop to it. These men are usually hardly members of the family in that they are scarcely ever home, or if they are home, they are silent and passive. There is a different kind of father, however, who may also be secretly (unconsciously) conspiring with the mother. This is the less obviously passive father who nonetheless chooses not to see the evidence that is clear enough, until finally one day he is forced to discover his son dressed as a girl. His method of dealing with this is to punish the child by making his son dress even more completely as a girl; in this way he manages to get across a message to the child that works opposite to what the father said he wished: Many transvestites date their overt transvestism from the time of their fathers' punishment.

Not infrequently in the history of male transvestites, one finds that the father was not a co-conspirator, but was literally not there. Widows and divorced women who need to create their son's transvestism will obviously be able to manage this much more easily if there is no man around the house.

I do not know whether transvestites' fathers who are absent from the family are of the same sort as those of the transsexual boys, not yet having studied such a father in depth. Certainly, from the superficial descriptions that are the best I can yet give, one cannot distinguish the fathers of some transvestites from the fathers of the boy transsexuals.

d. *Castration anxiety.* One fact becomes obvious to little

boys: The clearest sign that they are males is their penis. It therefore is what stands between them and a dreadful sense of inferiority and damage. In addition, penile sensations make it a highly valued organ for pleasure. Its loss would be awful for most little boys. And yet, it is just the future transvestite who feels so threatened with this loss because of his feminine wishes. He handles this danger by the thought that if females are evidence of a state of penislessness, the cause is not hopeless if there are women with penises. What better proof can there be of this than if one is such a creature oneself? Thus, in fantasy does the transvestite make himself into a phallic "woman."[3]

e. *Wives and girl friends.* While not a cause of transvestism, a factor that is essential for "successful" transvestism is the cooperation of the women who later fill the transvestite's life. In their adolescence, many transvestites will begin to use female clothes fetishistically: A particular article of women's apparel will produce sexual excitement. However, as time passes, the transvestite is interested in more and more clothes and in his appearance of being a woman. Thus, what started simply as fetishism gradually becomes a desire to pass as a woman. Practically none is very successful in this; most are grotesque caricatures of women. However, the "fortunate" ones eventually meet women who become their girl friends or wives. Such a woman takes it upon herself to make the transvestite look more like a woman. We shall look at these women further (in Chap. 18); for now, suffice it to say that they are similar to the transvestites' mothers described above in their secret (and often unconscious) need to humiliate males by feminizing them. The fact that some transvestites eventually learn to pass successfully as women is almost invariably due to the great effort that their wives or girl friends exert to teach them how to dress properly, use cosmetics properly, and develop mannerisms of their body and voices that are so feminine that no one could recognize that this was a biological male. Thus, in his adult life the transvestite finds a woman who in many ways is the same as his mother, and so he triumphs over the original traumatic situation by now having a woman with whom he can have sexual relations who nonetheless treats him as his mother did.

f. *The fear of being homosexual.*[4] What the mothers (and mother-surrogates) of transvestites do to their little boys from birth on is pathologically to accelerate and exaggerate the normal process of feminine identification that occurs to a much lesser extent in all little boys. The result of this is a problem in identity, built into the process of identity formation early in life: the future transvestite will be less than sure of what he is (insofar as *gender* is concerned, although he knows his *sex* is male). The attempts to fight off the threat of being swamped by one's feminine desires take many forms in many men, such as hypermasculinity, marked aggressiveness, hatred of homosexuals, or paranoidness. The form which interests us in this chapter is transvestism. It is interesting how many transvestites insist that they are not homosexual, that they have no such desires whatsoever. The whole complex psychological system that we call transvestism is a rather efficient method of handling very strong feminine identifications without the patient having to succumb to the feeling that his sense of masculinity is being submerged by feminine wishes. The transvestite fights this battle against being destroyed by his feminine desires, first, by alternating his masculinity with the feminine behavior, and thus reassuring himself even when feminine that it isn't permanent; and, second, by being always aware even at the height of the feminine behavior—when he is fully dressed in women's clothes—that he has the absolute insignia of maleness, a penis. And there is no more acute awareness of its presence than when he is reassuringly experiencing it with an erection.

g. *Social.* In the last decade or so there has been an increasing awareness and acceptance in our culture of transvestic behavior. Jokes, songs, movies, plays, photographs, newspaper stories, and scientific interest have all seized on the subject. The laws and society's religious and moral stands are being questioned. Socially sanctioned transvestic behavior is frequent—at carnival times, at masquerade parties, and the like.

In addition, organizations for people with impulse disorders, such as alcoholics, drug addicts, gamblers, and homosexuals, have developed, giving their members a sense of belonging, of cause, and of social action. This also has begun with transvestites, some of whom are now developing their own quasi organizations ("sororities").

TRANSSEXUALISM

Now let us compare transvestism and transsexualism. A *transsexual* is a person who feels himself consciously and unconsciously to belong to the opposite sex while not denying his sexual anatomy. The transsexual male (like the transvestite, a biologically normal male by all present-day tests) is a person who consciously and insistently seeks out sex-transformation procedures. In the transsexual male, these include complete removal of the penis and testes with the construction of a normal-appearing vulva and an artificially constructed vagina. In addition, secondary sex characteristics are shifted so that breasts are produced (usually by estrogens), subcutaneous fat distribution is modified (also by estrogens), and facial and body hair are removed by electrolysis. Also, more easily changed and nonanatomical qualities are modified, as in the transvestite, by the use of such aids as cosmetics and wearing apparel.

Certain implications that help to define the condition follow from these transformation procedures. First, since the male external genitalia have been removed, the transsexual demonstrates his ability to do without penile sexual gratification. Being very uncertain that he will be able to achieve any other kind of direct sexual gratification, he is nonetheless willing to sacrifice this critically important sexual organ. In addition, by ridding himself of his penis, he removes the outstanding insignia of his maleness.

It is especially around the differences in gender identity, manifested by the overwhelming desire to transform the external genitalia, that the differentiation between transvestism and transsexualism can be made. The transvestite definitely does not wish to sacrifice his external genitalia. In the first place they are the main source of sexual gratification for him, as they are in the normal or the homosexual male; he has no more desire to lose this great pleasure than has any other male, except the transsexual. The transsexual, on the other hand, by the simple fact that he has an erection is disgusted and deeply distressed. Erections force a sense of maleness upon him so that what should be felt as pleasure becomes unpleasure, and the more intensely excited the organ is the more his need to be rid of it. In the second place, the transvestite needs his penis as an insignia of maleness. We already know that it is essential for the transvestite to be fully conscious of the fact that he is a phallic "woman" during the times when he is dressed as a woman. He does not desire to be a biological woman; to him, this is an inferior condition which he quite consciously feels he can surpass. One cannot be a male transvestite without knowing, loving, and magnificently expanding the importance of one's own phallus. It is quite the reverse for the transsexual. The insignia of maleness is what causes his despair. He does not wish to be a phallic "woman"; he wishes to be a biologically normal woman. All of his actions are directed toward correcting what he feels to be a genetic mistake that has tragically trapped a female psyche in a male body. He more than gladly will sacrifice any direct sexual pleasure for the opportunity to live permanently in the gender role of a woman. The need for alternating between a sense of masculinity and a sense of femininity so essential to the transvestite is meaningless to the transsexual. He wishes to become and permanently remain a woman. As a result of this, he subjects himself to great distress and pain, stoically experiencing the necessary surgical procedures and the many social humiliations necessary to achieve this artificial anatomical femaleness.

The transsexual is not a fetishist with regard to women's clothes. I have never talked with a transvestite who did not openly describe his fetishism or with a transsexual who admitted to such an interest.

Transvestites typically have transsexual fantasies at times and some have other more or less overt transsexual tendencies. It is not unusual for some transvestites to attempt anatomically to modify certain secondary sex characteristics. Some take estrogens, not only because they can then feel that they are carrying a female substance within them but also to get some breast development, some softness of subcutaneous tissue, some possible decrease in facial and body hair. However, they unquestioningly draw the line about modifying their penises. This is a *sine qua non* of the transvestite as opposed to the transsexual. Many transvestites at one time or another have contemplated sex-transformation operations. Those who were old enough were shaken by the publicity and revelations of Christine Jorgenson, and some report that for a few days they were in a turmoil as to whether to get such operations or not. None proceeded further than fantasying, because as they permitted their daydreams to spin out they became aware of the fact that they were not about to sacrifice their penises.

However, the definition of a transsexual should not be made simply on the grounds that the patient insists on and succeeds in having the sex-transformation operations, or does not. In those countries in which it is relatively easy to arrange such procedures, and in which social disapproval is not very strong, a fair number of males who do not fulfill the criteria for transsexualism described above have undergone this operation. These people have been female impersonators and they have found it helpful in their professions, especially those who are strippers, to complete their body transformation. Their scarcely disguised interest in having the operation seems especially to be an attempt at promiscuity (though this is not to deny their marked feminine identification). They function as prostitutes following successful surgery. Their desire to live simply as women seems to be rather weak; they do not try secretly to pass as normal women; instead, they want to be publicly known as homosexual men who have now been transformed into the appearance of women but neither they or their partners feel that they *are* women, but rather simulated women. However, a much smaller number of patients who have received sex-transformation operations are markedly transsexual in that they feel themselves to be females and desire only to do away with their undesired maleness. They live in anonymity in a nonpromiscuous, nonprostitution, nonexhibitionistic relationship with a man.

Another feature distinguishing the transvestite from the transsexual is sexual object choice. The transvestite usually prides himself on his heterosexuality. Very frequently he is married and has had children. Most of the time he has had as infrequent overt homosexual relations as the "normal" heterosexual, and it is possible that he has had even less. While there is little question that he is constantly preoccupied with worrying about whether he is a homosexual and more or less preoccupied with conscious (and very unwelcome) homosexual desires, he maintains a vigilant guard against such feelings. Most transvestites who have homosexual relations consider these relations to be homosexual, whereas transsexuals say such experiences are not homosexual since they occur between a male and "a female trapped in a male body." The transsexual is completely taken up with his interests in men. His day is spent in fantasies of having become a normal woman who is married to a normal man. It would seem that the transvestite comes to terms with his homosexual needs while maintaining a certain amount of heterosexuality, made possible by his transvestism, while the transsexual avoids the accusation of being homosexual by telling himself that he is in fact a woman and that it is normal for him to desire men.

Let us briefly describe a typical male transsexual.* This patient is twenty-five years old. She is a dyed-blonde, well-rounded "woman" who in none of the ordinary mannerisms of life (smoking cigarettes, walking, crossing her legs, blowing her nose, gesticulating, etc.) in any way reveals she was ever a male. She points out that she had the same mannerisms when living as a male, when she seemed bizarre. She recalls no time in life of not wanting to be a girl, of not feeling extremely feminine, of not having interests and daydreams that seemed to her the same as those of normal girls. Her earliest memories, starting around the age of three, already show this very feminine attitude. As a boy, she was treated with ridicule by the other boys, despite which she maintained her same feminine behavior. When masturbation began in adolescence, her daydreams from the start were that she was a woman being made love to by a man. By fantasying, she would translate the sexual sensations in her penis into the sensations that she imagined would be felt in a vagina, but all attempts at translation of orgasm into a female orgasm were sufficiently unsuccess-

---

*The reader who would like to learn more about the life of transsexuals will find the definitive descriptions as well as considerable discussion on treatment in Benjamin's book.[5] In addition, an outstanding review of 43 cases of transsexualism by Walinder[6] confirms my own impressions of the phenomenology of transsexualism.

ful that very early in adolescence she was already wishing that she had no penis. She hated to masturbate and says she did so only once a year or less, not because of conscious guilt but because it so concretely demonstrated her anatomical maleness. At around this time, the publicity on Christine Jorgenson broke, and so the rather amorphous wishes to be a girl now focused on the hope that this could in fact be accomplished.

She began going out with men and having sexual relations. However, she never permitted a man to touch or see her genitalia, since they were such a source of shame; she defined as normal any man who made no such attempts. If a man should show a specific interest in her external genitalia, she considered him to be homosexual, and since her own gender identity has to be established in part by the man partner's "normalcy," she would never have anything to do with him again. Orgasm occurred in a few instances over the years during the infrequent sexual relations she had with men, always being a spontaneous emission set off by the man's orgasm.

Some months before I first saw her, she made contact with an operated transsexual, who suggested that they live together (not sexually, of course). She did so, and at that point for the first time she went through the preparations that were to lead to her being able to pass successfully as a female. She received intensive training from her transsexual friend in the application of cosmetics, proper wearing of women's clothes, and how to smooth out any coarseness in her feminine mannerisms. The patient was a remarkably apt student and within a short period of time was able to go about in society without being noticed. She was greatly assisted in this by her slim, rather delicate body build; at least, she was slim and delicate for a man. As a woman in heels she appears tall and slightly husky.

She was so successful that she very shortly found herself a job, being hired unsuspectingly as a woman. There she began to meet men and to go out on dates. Since she was now taking estrogens, she quickly grew ample breasts; she went to an electrolysist to remove the rather heavy beard that up to this point she was able to control only by heavy pancake makeup.

Having accomplished this much, she permitted herself to

"neck" with some of her dates and was sufficiently appealing that she received two marriage proposals in a few months' time. She was thrilled with all of this, and was acting like a rather typical hysterical female both in her exhibitionistic dress and in her teasing, sexual manner with men. (Each of the transsexual "women" we have tested psychologically has shown a personality typically found in the tests of hysterical women.*)

She was so successful in her sex transformation that her transsexual friend finally became very envious, forcing the patient to leave the house.

During this period, she was not only managing her female role in society and her performance as a sexual woman, but she was also successfully managing her family, something which some transsexuals are not able to do. She revealed the whole story to her family who knew her only as a dreadfully effeminate boy, explaining that she was more than that. They have come to accept her in her new role as a woman.

By working very hard, she saved enough money to fly to a foreign country where a sex-transformation procedure was successfully completed: her testes were removed and the scrotum used as external lips; her penis was removed and penile skin invaginated into the artificial vagina to serve as mucosa. As with other male transsexuals, she has orgasms with vaginal intercourse.

The patient has now married and hopes to adopt children.

CONCLUSION

For the first time it is possible in our society for the transvestite to carry his transvestism as far as he wishes without endangering himself. For a very few, the end result might be to live permanently in women's clothes. However, this progression does

---

*Psychological tests have been scandalously inadequate in detecting profound disturbances in gender identity. Unless one writes "Male" or "Female" at the top of the test page, one cannot properly assess the test results. Disturbances in affect, thinking disorders, specific neurotic syndromes, impulsivity, and all the other findings the tests can measure have appeared and are properly evaluated in the patients described in this book, but that most fundamental psychological state—one's *feeling* that he is a male or female—can be detected by only one test: the question, "Are you male or female?"

not lead to a belief he is a female and that his body should be appropriately transformed. The ultimate in transvestism seems to be that the transvestite live permanently as a phallic "woman," with his wife providing him with the sexual gratifications he needs, and—an especially strong aspect of his relationship—the mothering components.

The ultimate progression for the transsexual is very different and has not yet been reached in our society: he would not only like to have his body appear completely female but he would like to have the internal organs so changed (for example, by transplants) that he would now have his own functioning ovaries and uterus, ultimately to bear a child truly his own.

CHAPTER 17

Female (Versus Male)
Transvestism

The purpose of this chapter is to share some impressions to which a group of unusual patients have introduced me. These people, living permanently as unremarkably masculine men, are biologically normal females and were so recognized as children. In the process of passing successfully as men, they dress completely in the same sort of clothes as do normal men. Thus they would seem, from the obvious fact that they always wear men's clothes, to be fine examples of transvestism in females. And yet this chapter is about a condition that may not exist—female transvestism.

No one claims that female transvestism is common. It has rarely been written about,[1] and ideas about its causes are almost as sparse as is interest in it. Still, it is an accepted condition, a form of behavior that implies a specific character structure and psychodynamics. The least sophisticated idea about it (as with male transvestism) is that it is simply a peccadillo indulged in by certain homosexuals with more than their share of gender confusion.

It is possible, however, that if we look more closely at the behavior of women who cross-dress, we may learn more about the subject of gender identity. Proper clinical data can assist one in distinguishing, from what seem to be only semantics, some different personality types who, since they share a common form of exotic behavior, may mistakenly be assumed to have more similar character structures than they really do.

First, the obvious point made earlier: people who have in common a similar psychodynamic quality do not therefore necessarily have a similar personality (e.g., primary process thinking is found in everyone, artistic creativity requires in part primary process thinking, but not everyone is an artist). Transvestic (that is, cross-dressing) tendencies are ubiquitous (at least in latent, subliminal, or vicarious forms), but not all those who cross-dress are transvestites, though they certainly are transvestic. (See Chap. 16.)

And yet many people take it for granted that there are female transvestites. This may be because they confuse transvestic tendencies with transvestism. Certainly in recent years there has been gross permission for normal women in our culture to wear feminized versions of men's clothes or even specifically male clothing. In addition, and more to the point, masculine women dress in decidedly masculine fashion—but they choose their apparel carefully so that they do not look unequivocally male: They are not trying to pass undetected as men.

Nonetheless, there are an extremely rare number of females who dress all the time as men, live as men, work as men—in fact, pass unrecognized in society as men. Are they not transvestites? No—and again one must be careful that one is not merely quibbling with words. These women are transsexuals, quite comparable to male transsexuals. They wish to be males, that is to have a body in every way male, and to live in all ways as a man does. They cannot stomach sexual relations with men; they are aroused only by women. Men's clothes have no erotic value whatsoever; these people have no clothing fetish.

I have never seen or heard of a woman who is a biologically normal female and does not question that she was properly assigned as a female, who is an intermittent, fetishistic cross-dresser.

One might imagine for the female a state analogous to the

male transvestite's sense of being a "woman" with a penis: It would be the penisless "man," a condition approximated by those "butch" or "dike" homosexual women who insist that penises are unnecessary and worthless. But the fact is that even these very tough women are not transvestites. Neither they nor other women have a fetishistic relationship to male apparel: They do not become sexually excited by such objects. Also, they do not attempt to pass undetected as men, but instead flaunt their scorn for them, insisting that men are unnecessary and unwanted; their admiration and envy of men is mostly unconscious.

Measured by the criteria indicated for male transvestism, there is little in the female transsexual that is analogous to the male transvestite. Because their gender identity is not anchored to the preservation of their genitalia as it is in transvestism, these females' cross-dressing, masculine behavior, and masculine fantasies and dreams are permanent, not alternating as in transvestism. While they wish to pass, this passing is not occasional, but leads eventually to an uninterrupted state of living as a man. These females have no need to reveal exhibitionistically their true biological sex to others, as do male transvestites. There is no necessary and exciting constant awareness and reassurance of one's own genitalia. Different from the transvestite, who stresses his sexual relations with the opposite sex, these females never have sexual relations with men if they can avoid it.

The female transsexual earns a living as a man, working with men; for example, among those I know one is an expert machine tool operator, another an engineering draftsman, another a research chemist. Their jobs are quiet, steady, and unspectacular; their work records as men are excellent. They are sociable, not recluses, and have friendships with both men and women. Neither their friends nor their colleagues at work know they are biologically female.

They are not clinically psychotic.

There is no feminine tinge to any aspect of their behavior; nor, on the other hand, are they the tough caricatures of men that "butch" homosexuals are. All shave, because they can convince someone to give them testosterone, and all sooner or later manage to arrange to have their breasts and pelvic organs removed. As preoccupied as the psychoanalysts' women patients can be with penis envy, as much as we find disguised or gross evidence of wishes to possess a penis in such women, if—imagine for a moment—in dead seriousness we should ever offer a penis to any of our women patients who are not transsexual, we would see that she would be horrified. But not the transsexual female. She would be most grateful indeed.

This is not a description of a brilliant masquerade, a trick briefly maintained under circumstances very carefully selected to insure safety from unmasking. Instead, we are looking at a way of life, as unremarkable in its manifestations as is that of the man with a normal gender identity.

Female transsexualism is very rare, estimates running from one-third[2] to one-eighth[3] as common as in males. I do not know why, but wonder if it is related to the fact that almost everyone spends infancy in close contact with a female body (mother) so that if a disturbance in the process of identification should occur, it is more likely in the male child, who must give up or outgrow his identifications with a female, a task not required of female children.

CASE REPORT*

This patient, a biologically normal female, was first seen at age 15. The child at that time, though clothed in a dress, had very short hair and no mannerisms appropriate for a girl. She had always felt like a boy and had always wanted to be a boy; her parents said that even further back than the child's memory can reach, she was very boyish.

A short time before the family came to the Medical Center for consultation, it was discovered that the child had been living a double life for about a year, going to school as a girl and in the evenings and weekends going out with a group of boys, accepted unsuspectingly by them as being a boy. The Medical Center was asked to rule out a biological basis for the child's

*See Chapter 12 for a report on another female transsexual.

behavior, and this having been done, she was referred to the Gender Identity Research Clinic.

The parents, whom I have talked with on many occasions since in the past six years, are a happily married couple, the mother a feminine woman whose interests have always been focused on her husband, her child, and her home. The father is a very masculine man. Being unable to have children of their own, they adopted the patient at birth. The mother happily and maternally took over all the usual chores of caring for the infant, the father hovering in the background until, increasingly between six months and a year, he began playing with his daughter, taking her for walks, and being with her as much as possible. Because of the nature of his work, he had free time available during the day and so spent a great deal of time with his daughter during the first years of her life. They were very close, but in no way was the mother excluded from the relationship.

Here is the transcript of a conference before our research team, this excerpt taken from a few minutes when we are all looking at the family album. All the pictures, after the first series taken in infancy, show the child dressed in boys' costumes, especially cowboy suits. The greatest number of pictures have horses in them.

MOTHER: She was a year old in that picture.

PATIENT: Daddy used to swim with me, and I would hang on his back. [*Picture of patient on horseback at a children's rodeo.*]

MOTHER: Here is when she started going into the costume (cowboy). She must have twenty-five hats—sailors', cowboys', rebel hats, old soldier things.

PATIENT: I used to always want to be a sailor. I liked what they wore. I just always wanted a real good sailor suit. I have always wanted—in fact, I still do—a good holster, because I like to shoot. I can't shoot a pistol very well, but I can shoot a rifle.

MOTHER: When you were small you always had guns strapped around you. . . . On summer vacation, she had a gun—some kind of pistol. What kind was it?

PATIENT: Was that a real one?

MOTHER: Sure it was real.
PATIENT: A thirty-eight.
MOTHER: She slept with that thing under her pillow.
PATIENT: I slept with it because I felt it was real good. I didn't need it, but I liked it a lot; it was real; it was a real gun and lots of kids didn't have them.

. . .

PATIENT: My mother thought I was crazy because she would always want to buy me clothes and stuff and I hated clothes. I loved clothes as a boy. I loved to buy clothes every day as a boy. I like good, nice clothes, but my mother would always want to buy me a dress. We would get in a store, and I would say, "Why don't we look at shirts; I need a shirt for riding." Then we had a big fight. Last Easter she wanted to buy me an Easter dress. I didn't want them to spend their money, because I knew how I felt about it. I said, "Don't spend your money"—so we had a big fight about that. Because I had dresses hanging in the closet that I never wore, except when I had to go to church, and half the time I went to church as a boy. I fought her all the way.

MOTHER: That was Easter this year. She wouldn't *have* that dress. (*to daughter*) Everyone of your friends had an Easter dress; they would drop dead before they would go out in anything from last year, but not you. I couldn't—a girl who didn't want a new outfit for Easter!

DR. G. (*to the mother*): When you talk, you sound strange to me. I feel like correcting you and saying, Why are you talking about "she"—because I have never seen this boy except like this? So to me, when you say, "she," I want to say, "You are making a mistake."

And another time, in another interview:

PATIENT: I enjoy myself as a boy. It seems I have grown just like a boy. It seems to me I started out building planes, riding horses, which is a girl's sport too. Girls do these sports, but they do girls' things too—but I didn't. And so I grew up, and in my mind and everything that worked in me wanted to be a boy. Everything I enjoyed was a boy.

Right now I have to have this because I believe I have grown as a boy. And it is about time I start thinking about girls, which isn't right because of my body, but in my mind it is normal. I don't feel I am abnormal as a boy. Nothing about me seems abnormal, except I have the wrong body. In other words, the head is put on the wrong body. That's the way I figure it. I don't know if it is right; I don't have a medical mind. I figure when I get older, I will grow and think from boyhood into a man. I don't know whether I can be one, but I believe that's the way I am going to think. Your body is just something that holds you together; it's part of you; it's an important part—but your mind is strong; it is your will; your mind is everything. I mean as far as everything you want to be. If you had the body, the hands to play baseball, and it just wasn't in your mind, and it wasn't what you enjoyed, you might go and be a doctor. When all this was going on, I thought of God: Am I doing wrong? God created me as a girl, so maybe I should be. But I couldn't be, and which is more important, your mind or your body? God created my mind too, and if my mind is working this way, He created that. I just couldn't figure it out. I went to the priest; he didn't help me any. He got me all confused. I didn't know what to do. So I just sat down and thought. I used to pray a lot. We studied about God dying on the Cross for us, and I think if He did all that suffering, I can do this suffering for Him, but I can't suffer all my life like this; I would go crazy. I have got to have an out, a way to solve my problem, try to face up to it and solve it. . . . And so far I have solved this much of it.

DR. G.: If you could physically, what would you change?

PATIENT: Of course, my sexual organs to male. And I would like to be five feet eleven inches, and have all my parts correspond to that height, to be normally built with a good build. I wouldn't want to be like those guys you see on the Mr. America things; I don't go for that, but just a normal-looking boy and a fairly good body and with no fat, which is a problem now. I would like to be strong, just pretty strong, and I would not like to be weak, just normal. Maybe I would like to play football. I have played football before, but I doubt if I could play with the rest of the guys twenty feet taller than I. I can play baseball pretty good but can't play football very well. I was good at baseball. I have always thrown right. It would make me mad when we had a girl on our team; she would ruin the whole game. I would hit home runs, just stand up there and wham them over.

At still a different point:

MOTHER: This has evidently been in her for a long time. As a little girl, when I wanted to take her to church on Sunday, I used to have to battle to get a dress on her, because she always wanted to be in blue jeans or some kind of pants. I just figured she would outgrow it.

DR. S.:   How old was she when you first got her?

MOTHER: I waited five months for her to be born, and we didn't know whether it would be a boy or a girl. It didn't matter [*said with emotion*]. The sex of the child makes no difference when you want a baby [*now crying*].

DR. S.:   What was it like when you first brought her home?

MOTHER: (*long pause*): It was wonderful. [*weeping*] She was a beautiful baby, an adorable baby.

DR. S.:   When did you first notice she was tomboyish?

MOTHER: [*still crying*]:   From the time she could walk, I guess. She could ride a bicycle better than any boy around where we lived. She played with boys most of the time as a little girl, for there weren't any girls available. She liked to go out with her daddy. They were very close. They used to walk together all the time. There was a merry-go-round and he would take her over, and that's how she became interested in horses.

DR. R.:   Did she ever play house when she was small? Mother and father games?

MOTHER: She had a million dolls, and she would never pay any attention to them. We still have them—just as good as new . . .

When the children played games, she was the father whenever they played.

Later:

DR. S. (*to patient*):   How did you learn what is required to be a boy?
PATIENT: I don't know—it was always in me. When I was a girl, I had to change. All my life I have always acted like a boy. I didn't like to; as a kid, it didn't matter. There weᵣe tomboys and so I could walk like a boy and dress like a boy all the time.
DR. S.:   You had to "act" like a girl?
PATIENT: *That* was the act and *that* was the hard part. When I was eleven or twelve, I met A and started liking her. After a while we found out that I was wishing more that I was a boy—completely a boy—and wishing that we could go out as boy and girl. We had just gone out with friends as two girls. Then, about two years ago, I thought of a method to go out like a boy. My hair got cut short because that was the style. And then I made up a sort of brace to wear [to flatten out her breasts]. I finally worked it out so that I went out with A as a boy. We went to a drive-in; I didn't know whether it would work, but I had to find out. It worked, and so we went out the very next night. Then I went and got my hair cut at a barbershop. I didn't get it cut very short. I still had it long enough so that I could wear it both ways. And my parents nearly split a gut when I came home. When I was being a girl, I would put on a scarf.

So we can see that this child from the early memories of herself and the remaining memories of her parents was abnormally boyish from earliest childhood. This persisted and grew, and although for a while it did not arouse attention because she could pass as a tomboy, during adolescence when the tomboys became more feminine, this child persisted, more masculine than anyone she knew. By age eleven, she had a girl friend and began having sexual relations with this girl, A. But she quickly became disgusted with A because A, being homosexual, wanted to touch the patient's genitals. The patient, on the other hand, did not consider herself to be homosexual (at that time not even knowing the word), and was horrified that A accepted her as a girl. The relationship broke off. However, it served the function of permitting the patient to have a girl friend and to begin to pass as a boy. This passing increased. The patient, rather brilliantly, considering her age, managed to go to an all-girl school as a girl in the daytime, and in the evenings would go out as a boy, slipping out of the house, not even being caught by her parents. She even went on dates as a boy with girls whom she was seeing every day as a girl in school, and the management of this situation became most intricate indeed.

Eventually the child became desperate, as she wanted to be a boy more and more, but had to pass herself off as a girl at school and with her parents. Finally, she ran away from home and lived for a week with a group of boys who accepted her as one of the boys, not knowing her true sex. The police, called by her parents, finally tracked her down and brought her home; this precipitated the crisis that led to her coming to see us.

Since that time, six years ago, she has lived exclusively as a boy, not known to be a female. The family has moved far from where they lived prior to the time of the first consultation. As a boy, the child, now a young man, has gone to high school and to college, being accepted at both as a boy, the true story known only to the highest authorities in the institutions. For the last few years, he has been employed in an exclusively man's world, living day and night with men.

Up until a year ago, he went out on dates because he has always been possessed of a strong sexual drive. However, he has given up going out with girls, preferring to feel frustrated than to have to suffer the even greater frustration of being able to seduce the girls and then not being able to permit them to learn the structure of his body. He was able to disguise his physical sexual characteristics by inventing and manufacturing for himself a camisole for his chest and an artificial penis which would give the right bulge to his pants. At one point, he was so successful (and had constructed such an excellent "penis") that he had "intercourse" with a girl. For several months she failed to have a period and was fearful that he had gotten her pregnant.

He has masturbated since adolescence, each of these experiences being an agonizing one, because all the fantasying of being a boy having intercourse fails at orgasm since the sensations absolutely define the femaleness of his genitalia for him.

He is unrelenting in his desire to have sex-transformation operations and even managed to arrange, on his own, for a plastic surgeon to remove his breasts. He is awaiting a propitious time when he can have his ovaries and uterus removed and has had lengthy discussions with urologists, trying to determine whether they can make a skin graft which will look at all like a normal penis. He has been taking testosterone since age 16, with the result that he shaves regularly and has a male hair distribution. Also, as another result, his voice has lowered to within a masculine range.

He has not only never been psychotic, but has in fact great ego strengths as well as a driving capacity for warm and close relationships with other people.

I do not know what causes this young person's transsexualism. No evidence of maleness was present in the physical examination or in the laboratory tests. There seem to be no adequate clues in the history as given by the patient and his parents. As the years passed, I have learned more about transsexualism and so have gone back over the early months of the patient's life, asking new questions of these parents as I learned to ask them in my research. They have not as yet revealed an answer.

However, in the past year, from a different case, I received some clues that may bear on the subject of the causes of female transsexualism. I have learned about the family situation of a young girl who is a transsexual. Having to be very vague regarding this case, I can only give a few general remarks. The child is a boy in her interests; she hopes to grow to be a male and has sought out information regarding the medical possibilities of getting a penis. All who have seen her feel her to be far beyond any tomboy they have ever known. (She is even further out at her age than the patient just described was at the same age.)

She has been in far more physical contact since birth with

her father than her mother, who was psychologically absent during her early childhood. In many ways (which cannot be reported), the family situation during her earliest childhood was analogous to that described for the three transsexual boys. This may be a hint that too much father and too little mother masculinizes girls. One might then speculate that transsexualism is much rarer in females than in males because it is much more likely that there will be a mother who is excessively close than a mother who is absent and a father who is excessively close.

To return to our case above, there is no evidence that the patient's mother was psychologically absent during the first six months or year of her life, but rather that she was a very adequate woman in dealing with her infant. On the other hand, there are clues running through many of the interviews that the father, a rather powerful, masculine man, spent a great deal of time with his little girl, taking her for a number of hours a day for walks, rides, to the barbershop with him, and even into the neighborhood bar when he would get a drink. However, this is only a most tentative clue.

Cases like this are the ones that tempt one to postulate a biological force that may contribute to transsexualism. However, the more patients I have seen, and the more detailed information I have gotten about their childhood, the more frequently data was reported that pointed to psychological forces causing their transsexualism.

In summary, it can be said that there are male transvestites and male transsexuals; among women there are female transsexuals but no female transvestites.

CHAPTER 18

Transvestites' Women

In the pornographic literature of transvestism, there is a certain genre of illustration that repeatedly shows cruelly beautiful, monstrous-breasted, stiletto-heeled women, often with phallic-like whips dangling beside their pelves, bullying the poor, pretty, defenseless transvestite.

This chapter will try to analyze such illustrations, using data collected from and about the women of transvestites—their mothers, sisters, girl friends, and wives—in order to show what in this fantasy excites transvestites; in tracing back to the roots of this excitement, we shall come upon the essential role these women play in the cause and maintenance of transvestism. The women studied all share the attribute of taking a conscious and intense pleasure in seeing males dressed as females. All have in common a fear of and a need to ruin masculinity. Very envious of males, such women or girls revenge themselves by either dressing their males in female clothes or encouraging such dressing once it develops "spontaneously." Thus, it is a woman or girl who first dresses many of these men in women's clothes, though the women deny any knowledge that they might have damaged their sons or brothers. However, whatever similarities these women have, it must be emphasized that they are very different in many aspects of their personalities. For example, one is a forceful leader of ladies' clubs; another, a crabbed masochist; a third, a tired, graceful, faceless housewife; a fourth, not clinically psychotic, has truly believed since childhood that she is a witch. And so on.

One can discern two categories of such women:

1. *The malicious male-hater:* There are those who start a boy's cross-dressing activities by themselves putting the clothes on the child without his entering upon the activity spontaneously. As girls and later as women, they are ruthless, angry, competitive, and hating toward all males, whom they humiliate whenever possible. These women do not do this damage to infants but only to boys who have grown enough to have developed a masculine gender identity. *Only after this masculinity has appeared are these females' rage and need for revenge excited.* This same hatred is also found in the mothers of adult tranvestites who say that as boys they were never dressed by their mothers in girls' clothes.

2. *The succorer:* The next group of women do not initiate males into transvestism, but only support it with sympathy and enthusiasm when they come to know a transvestite. Their appearance and manner is much more feminine than the first group's; they are more gentle with men, not openly competitive, not scornful, and are warm and affectionate early in the relationship. Their most conspicuous quality is a pronounced need to succor other creatures. These are the women who marry transvestites knowing of their condition, or who, on discovering it, adjust to it easily. They so encourage their transvestites that, by teaching these men how to dress and behave as women, they convert them from gross parodies of women into completely normal-looking "women" who pass undetected in open society. They do this with an air of innocent enthusiasm, as if the acts of putting lipstick on a man, plucking his eyebrows, or stuffing his brassière were essentially the same action as teaching these artifices to a teen-age girl. It does not appear that their sons become transvestites.

THE MALICIOUS MALE-HATER

Subject 1 (an adult transvestite): To show the malignant effect that a male-hating girl can produce, let us, by returning to the history of the transvestite already described in Chapter 16, look at what one such girl was able to accomplish. Her mother, uncles, and aunts were in a family business, and she, being some years older than her male cousins, was placed in charge of them part of each day. Thus, she had five little boys in her care, whom she dressed in girls' clothes on many occasions. She later said of one, "He was a little beast, but so nice when he was dressed like a girl." While she cannot be found responsible for all of their abnormal gender development, nonetheless it is to be noted that one of these boys has grown up to be an effeminate homosexual; one has a marked interest in cloth and wears somewhat effeminate men's clothes; one has posed for family photographs in women's clothes and is suspected of being a transvestite; the youngest—the one with whom she spent the most time—is an avowed transvestite; no information is available regarding the fifth.

The one known to be a transvestite, our already cited subject, has been fated, both by chance and his inner needs, to live with several women who helped create his transvestic behavior. The first was the above cousin, who, with her own mother, took over the raising of the little boy between ages three and five, because of the illness and eventual death of his mother. You will recall that both these women dressed the boy as a girl on occasion (as revealed in the family photo album, though he has no memory of this). Then his father remarried; we know that his stepmother's sister on occasion, as punishment for minor misdeeds, would dress him in girls' clothes to shame him (though to what extent the little boy maneuvered this himself is unknown). To compound this tangled tale, his half brother was dressed in girls' clothes as a small child by *his* mother, the patient's stepmother, giving joy because he then resembled Shirley Temple.

Finally, our subject married (a succorer). Although he did not know it at the time, his wife came from a family in which cross-dressing in a male already existed. His wife had a half brother, her mother's child. This boy had been dressed by his mother in a fairy costume around age five so he would look like a girl cousin he had envied. In his teens, in preparation for a masquerade, his mother designed, made, and dressed him in his costume: a stuffed brassière, garter belt, nurse's uniform and cap. Under the nurse's cap, his mother attached a wig manufactured from his half sister's (our transvestite's wife-to-be) hair. The two women had had a happy, laughing time as they worked for several days getting this costume ready. His wife also recalls dressing a neighbor boy in girls' clothes many times.

When his wife married our subject, she already knew of his transvestism. She was not dismayed during their courtship when he confessed this need to her, and it was not until years later that she felt surprised that she had reacted so blandly. Her thought at that moment of confession had been that he was "a hurt little boy who needs to be held and loved." She linked this lack of concern to her familiarity with cross-dressing, since she had helped her mother do this to her brother, and also to her awareness that she had been pleased when she learned of his transvestism because it meant that he had a painful weakness that would require her nursing, loving attention. She knew he was in other regards a violent and physically powerful man. So, learning that beneath his violence lay an astonishing weakness—the need to dress like a woman—she felt a warm, soft sweetness come upon her, an awakening of tenderness that masked her sense of triumph. She then eagerly encouraged him in his use of her clothes. As time passed, she bought him women's clothes, applied his makeup, taught him how to behave as a feminine woman, and in so many ways enthusiastically assisted him that they were finally able to go publicly into the world as two women.

Subject 2 (an adult transvestite): "I have pictures of myself dressed as a little girl when I was a small child. My mother thought it was cute. She was right. I was a pretty little girl.

*The reports of Subjects 2 through 6 are from men who were specifically trying to demonstrate that transvestism can be a happy, guiltless state. While these quotations show the part women have played in the subjects' lives, the

"The highlights of my life as a girl came when I was between the ages of ten and seventeen. I had an aunt who was childless and wanted to take me through the steps from childhood to young womanhood. She knew of my desire to be a girl. I would spend every summer at her ranch. The first thing she would do was give me a pixie haircut, which always turned out pretty good since I would avoid getting a haircut for two months before I went to her ranch. She then would take me into the bedroom and show me all my pretty new things she had bought me. The next day, dressed as a girl, we would go to town and shop for a new dress for me. Everyone she met, she would introduce me as her 'niece.' This went on every year until I was thirteen years old. Then she decided I should start my womanhood. I will never forget that summer. When I arrived I got the same pixie haircut as usual, but when we went into the bedroom there, laid out on the bed, was a girdle, a garter belt, and bra—size 32AA—and my first pair of nylons. She then took me over to the new dressing table she had bought me and slid back the top to reveal my very own makeup kit. I was thrilled to death. She said she wanted her 'niece' to start off right, and it was about time I started to develop a bust.

"The next morning I was up early to ready myself for the usual shopping trip to town, only this time it was for a pair of high heels and a new dress. I remember I stuffed my bra with cotton, put on my garter belt and slipped on my nylons with no effort. After all, I became an expert from practice the night before. My aunt applied my lipstick because I was so excited I couldn't get it on straight. Then off to town we went, aunt and 'niece.' What a wonderful day. I shall never forget it."

Subject 3 (an adult transvestite): "At about the age of fourteen, I discovered in my dad's photo album a photo he had taken of me at five and a half, just before having my long

---

painfulness of being made into a "sissy" or worse is either suppressed from the report or repressed from memory. (Note that I presume it must be painful, though, to be more accurate, one must consider the possibility that these subjects never felt humiliated.)

[bobbed] hair cut off. My mother had dressed me in girl's clothes to see what I would have looked like if I had been a daughter, which is what she had wanted first. When I saw the photo I recalled the incident clearly and the sight of the photo thoroughly shook me, for it appeared to be a rather pretty young girl. The emotional result was twofold. It aroused my first interest in girls and also an interest in girls' clothes. I found myself compelled to go back and look at the photos again and again. One winter my wife and I were living alone. Our marital relations were good. We were spending New Year's Eve entirely alone, and for some reason my wife, not knowing of my mere leanings (at the time) toward transvestism (a word I did not know at the time), decided to put one of her dresses on me and make up my face just as a sort of New Year's Eve prank. When she finished we sat around for a while and she asked me how I liked it. When I answered in the affirmative she became resentful and very anxious for me to take off the clothes she had put on me voluntarily.

"I knew that she had a very effeminate male cousin with whom she had spent her childhood. She then told me that when they were little children together he would often play he was a girl when she would put her clothes on him. Although she was on the friendliest of terms with him I got the impression that she at least partly blamed herself for what she called his 'homosexualism,' which to me at that time merely meant effeminism."

Subject 4 (an adult transvestite): "My earliest memories of transvestism go back to when I was six years old. One night, my mother let me try on a one-piece pink foundation garment just for fun. While I had this garment on, I experienced a feeling that I had never felt before, and I liked it. I suppose my mother thought I would forget all about it, but I didn't. One day, while I was in my mother's room dressing up she caught me. I must admit that it was very embarrassing for me standing there in front of her clad in women's clothes. She was very upset over this and that night when my father got home she told him about it. He was also very upset over it, and for punishment he told my mother that as soon as I got home from school in the afternoon I was to get dressed up from the skin out. I was very happy with this decision."

Subject 5 (an adult transvestite): This seven-year-old girl, who lived next door, gave me a complete set of her clothes, and I wore them almost every chance I had until they were outgrown and had worn out. . . . When I was about eight or nine there was a Halloween party in the church and my mother dressed me as a girl. . . . I remember the first winter that I was given ice skates at about nine or ten. They were the old clamp-on style, to put on and off your own boots. Mother gave me her boots as I had none."

THE SUCCORER

Subject 6 (an adult transvestite): "We fell in love and as soon as I felt we could we were married. We have been as happy as two people can be and the best part of it is that she knows all about me, and not only accepts me as I am but assists in my transformation and then admires me." This is the way the relationship looks at first, when the wife is pleased to see her husband's femininity. She does not know yet that as he becomes a more successful transvestite her enthusiasm will wane. Then he will be hurt that she is no longer interested in his dressing up, his sexual needs, his work. The fighting will start; neither will understand what has happened, and they will divorce. I have not seen a transvestite who has been married for years where this did not happen; it happens faster or slower depending on how fast the transvestite becomes successful, either as a transvestite or in the world. His confidence and euphoria destroy the necessary dynamics of the marriage.

Subject 7 (a transvestite's wife): When this woman married, her fiance had already fully informed her of his transvestism.* He

*I have met her cousin, a woman who enjoys dressing men in women's clothes and who had never felt at ease with a man until she began going with transvestites. There is a photograph in the family album of a nephew dressed as a girl.

had been at the lowest point of his life when they met. The son of a socially prominent family, he had just been publicly exposed to great shame when his transvestism, revealed by his previous wife during a divorce trial, made sensational newspaper copy. He was broke, lonely, humiliated—in a most wretched state. She was soon attracted to him, finding his abject condition very appealing, for her life had been dedicated since childhood to the concentration of her attentions on one suffering person or animal after another. They married. Because his skills with feminine ways were still rough, she enthusiastically taught him how to appear more feminine until he could go about undetected in society, passing as a woman. In addition, he also became successful in his role as a man. With her help he developed a business that capitalized on both his previous scientific training and his feminine interests. He brought to full flower his personality as a "woman." As a man, he played an active part in his business and as a "woman" he participated in scientific meetings. His growing success in the world was matched by a reduction in his wife's enthusiasm for him. What I at first took to be a cooling of her interest simply because she was getting tired of the transvestism and disturbed at having sexual relations with a "woman" with a penis, turned out to be more an increasing anger at him because he had first presented himself to her as a weak, helpless, effeminate person, and then, by means of his transvestism, became strong, aggressive, successful, and very interested in having sexual relations with her.*

Finally, with her husband revelling in his success, this woman ended their marriage, for she became convinced her husband was "a con man and the worst kind of criminal." Strangely enough, she was not referring to his transvestism, which in itself still did

---

*We know that many women ("fruit flies") are attracted to effeminate men or men who are otherwise clearly identified as not sexually dangerous (i.e., potent). Those of us who work in Los Angeles are very familiar with the need of many women who live primarily by exhibitionism—movie starlets and models —to go with and marry effeminate and usually overtly homosexual men. These women can relate comfortably with sexually disarmed men, and in this regard they are similar to transvestites' wives. The transvestite's wife mistakenly assumes that her husband will be impotent and dependent upon her, but she soon learns the hard way that perversions function to preserve potency.

not bother her. Instead, her extravagant accusations were that he was a liar and cheat in his financial affairs, opinions to which she monomaniacally clung in the face of incontrovertible evidence that he was not. From her (unconscious) point of view, she was right that he had conned her, for she had found him apparently unmanned and unmanly and seemingly permanently in need of her loving support; then he had tricked her by becoming potent in so much of his life. Not being able to face this need of hers for him to be "castrated" and her rage that he had successfully escaped from this state, she maintained her conscious awareness of having been tricked, but now rationalized it in terms of his being a financial cheat.

DISCUSSION

We can now better understand the picture-fantasy mentioned at the beginning of this chapter. It reminds the transvestite that the sexually important women of his life have the power. They are physically strong; they have beauty's power; they are equipped with those phallically-shaped whips, sharp heels, and boots; they hang those bosom-bombs heavily over his head; they are cruel and haughty; they are sure of themselves; their gigantically voluptuous bodies are strong, hard, slim, long, and smooth, i.e., phallic. Even the most unpsychodynamic person can get a glimmer of what is meant by the fantasy of a "phallic" woman. It takes little imagination to recognize in the transvestite man's erotic daydream the little boy's impression of the woman or older girl, who, in her greater power, so damaged his masculinity. By a remarkable tour de force he takes the original humiliation and converts it into an active process of sexual mastery and pleasure. He thus salvages some sexual potency, power, and masculinity from an originally castrating event.

In addition, he restores his dignity (sense of identity) by finally getting his revenge on women. In the disguise of a woman, he subjects his woman to intercourse, demonstrating to her his triumphant (successfully erect) penis. It is interesting that the women who become the girl friends or wives of adult transvestites are tricked by the disguises of the transvestite into thinking him weak and unmanly. Just as the illustration makes him appear like a poor cowering wretch, the fact is that the man who is excitedly masturbating while looking at such a picture is in fact filled with a sense of triumph as he is successful in producing an erection, excitement, and orgasm.*

In his classic paper on transvestism, Fenichel[1] points to the importance of the concept of the phallic woman as an invention of the transvestite, a fantasy he must create as a protection against his fear of castration during the oedipal phase. I would like to state this a little more fully: The transvestite, his sense of wholeness and worth in himself damaged, often *before* the oedipal phase, by the powerful feminizing effect of the woman who dressed him or who otherwise scorned his maleness, has a disturbance in his sense of identity, in his taken-for-granted feeling of wholeness as a male. Because of this, he senses that that prime *insignia* of maleness, his penis, is in danger. Then, knowing of the biological and social "inferiority" of women, and also knowing that within himself there is a propensity toward being reduced to this "inferior" state, he denies that such creatures exist and invents the "phallic" woman. In a way, he does not have to invent such a person, for the living prototype actually has existed in his life—that is, the fiercely dangerous and powerful woman who already so humiliated him as a child. But he will have his triumph over her and all women, in the process of which he will reestablish his masculinity, the scar of the perversion remaining as a permanent sign of the original traumatic relationship. While it seems paradoxical, this triumph comes when he dresses up as a woman, for then, appearing like a woman, he can nonetheless say that he is a whole person, since he is the living proof that there is such a thing as a woman who has a penis. Transvestites often express this quite conciously in their statement that with a little practice they can get to be a better woman than any woman is, since they possess the best of both man and woman.

*The illustration has another trick built into it. Because in these stories the bullying women force the transvestite to dress in women's clothes, the masturbator can pretend that he himself is not responsible and therefore not guilty for dressing up.

Another confirmation for my belief that a woman's need to feminize a male is an essential factor in these cases of cross-dressing is a most unusual one: a new perversion or at least a new combination of a couple of old ones. The informant in this case is a middle-aged man, a transvestite, who because of the special nature of his work, is able to visit a number of homes each day, thousands in a year. In this way he meets many mothers of young sons. Through a subtle means of questioning these women, he is able to cull from them those few to whom he is able to make the following proposition. Since none is wealthy, he suggests that, having a special source of girls' clothes, he can save the mother money by giving her girls' clothes in which she can then dress her little boy, so as to save wear and tear on the boy's masculine clothes. In this way, he has succeeded in persuading fifteen mothers to convert their little sons into cross-dressers. When he revisits the family and looks upon the success of his efforts he becomes greatly excited, thus gratifying his perversion. He has no question that they sense they are entering into a conspiracy with him to feminize these little boys. In all these cases, the father was missing in essence or in fact.

It should be noted that such a fantasy as the one we are trying to understand has no power to interest the little transsexual boys. For them this whole issue of humiliation converted to mastery has no significance. Their identification with women is much more profound: They do not feel that their gender identity is damaged by femininity, but that they are really females. This is so different from the males who become transvestites later, after a male core gender identity has already been created. The latter never deny that they are males, nor do they wish to become females, whereas these little boys, like adult male transsexuals, have no sense of humiliation about being feminine, but only wish to be even more feminized. Transsexuals who have looked at such pictures derive no sexual excitement from them.

I am reminded that it is the style these days to blame women when weakness, passivity, and effeminacy are found in men, to point especially to mothers as the agents who damage their sons' sense of identity. The above findings do nothing to dispel this impression. However, although not discussed in this chapter, another essential factor plays a part in the feminization of a man. It is the failure of his father to be an adequate model of masculinity with whom the child can identify when he needs to turn to a man, and, even earlier in the boy's existence, the failure of his father to act as a shield protecting his son against the urges to feminize him that his mother or sisters may have. As many workers have noted in cases of markedly feminized men, whether they were transsexuals, transvestites, or effeminate homosexuals, their fathers were either physically absent or practically nonexistent although living in the family. While it is extremely unlikely that a manly man would knowingly marry a woman who has to revenge herself by damaging the masculine gender identity of a little boy, if by mistake such a man should marry such a woman, he would undoubtedly prevent the development of transvestism in his son by not encouraging or permitting the boy's femininity in the manner that the fathers in these cases have done.

CHAPTER 19

Bondage and Cross-Dressing

There is an odd and dangerous perversion that, to judge from the literature, does not often come to the psychiatrist's or psychoanalyst's attention, but which may nonetheless be rather common if one weighs the amount of pornographic books and movies produced on the subject. It consists in tieing up women and torturing them, either in reality or in fantasy.

The literature on this perversion is meager and superficial, usually being simply case histories of the Krafft-Ebing variety.[1] However, I presume there are other references to bondage, possibly in papers about sadomasochism, beating fantasies, and so on. I have been unable to find any studies specifically on bondage in the psychoanalytic literature, presumably because these patients do not seek analytic treatment. However, talking with colleagues has given me the impression that, as with transvestic behavior, binding is much less rare than the literature would suggest.

CASE MATERIAL

The patient, a man in his twenties, manly, vigorous, intelligent, pleased to be married and the father of a little girl, was

218

referred for evaluation by his therapist. The patient was concerned that his perversion might cause him to harm some woman. And though he did not wish to give it up—"It's me; without it, I wouldn't be me"—he did want help.

He knew of no time when he had not been perverse. His memories went back to age three or four when he recalls that he would put on women's stockings and enjoy stroking the material and also the feeling of the stockings clinging to his legs. He remembers at this age tieing up his aunt (his mother's sister) four or five times. He insisted that the memory was real to him, although he said that it could have been a fantasy, since he found it hard to believe that an adult woman would have permitted a child to do this. His recollection was that she would sit in a chair, talking with others and paying no attention to him, while he, with voluptuous concentration, bound her.

Daydreams of binding women go back to age three or four and have continued to the present. He has never had the slightest desire to bind men, nor has he any interest in girls or young women younger than about twenty. Those he desires must be mature, desirable, and feminine. They are to appear pleased with being women, being neither pathetically feminine nor masculine. Those over age 35 to 40 are no longer interesting. If they fit his criteria, he would then like to tie them up, tightly and painfully. His excitement grows only if they are suffering physically and are frightened; the more desperate they are to escape, the more excited he becomes. They can be clothed or unclothed, though he prefers that they wear sexy underwear and extremely flattering stockings. The present feminine style of wearing boots is especially appealing, because it hides ankles (bony and therefore not feminine enough) and emphasizes calves (flesh).

When all is ready in the fantasy, he prefers "normal" intercourse (penis-vagina).

So far, he has not had much opportunity to indulge his perversion in reality. What he has done are the following: put on women's underclothes and stockings; fantasied (since childhood) about binding women (these women are made to be bad, evil, sinful—e.g., prostitutes); used the same fantasies with masturbation (since puberty), accompanied when possible by putting on women's undergarments and binding himself; masturbated while looking at books with pictures of bound women; watched television for hours, looking at old movies for possible scenes of bound women, or roamed the city searching out movies that cater to men with this perversion; tied up his wife and had intercourse with her while she was bound (but without first dressing in women's clothes).

He believes that he has been putting on one or another woman's garment since earliest childhood. Only those that "capture" flesh are interesting to him: girdles, bras, stockings. However, these garments do not *in themselves* excite him as they do the transvestite (who, as different from other men who also cross-dress, gets excited specifically by the clothes he fondles).* Rather, for this patient the anticipation of binding is a pleasure that will lead to erection before he actually binds himself. Nor is this fetishism, although related; in fetishism, the inanimate object stands for a person. In this patient, the clothing does not so much stand for a person as it is part of the anticipation of an action—binding.

When putting on such garments, he is trying to approximate realistically his impossible dream that he, a man, is tieing up and tormenting himself, a woman. However, he never tries to pass as a woman; he has never tried to be feminine, except for a few moments when putting on women's garments before masturbating. He has no interest in dressing completely as a woman, has no interest in makeup, long fingernails, long hair, wigs, etc. He does not follow women's styles or have any feminine interests. That aspect of his identity that is made up of female parts has never coalesced even transiently into a woman's identity.

In itself, this perversion should cause little concern. Unfortunately, there is some question if he can contain it in fantasy or in simply playing it out with his wife. He not only consistently bruises her and gives her rope burns, but at times ties her so tightly and in such grotesque positions that if he did not imme-

---

*This is a fine point but one which I consider of importance because in just such apparently minute details can we hope to track down differences in infantile experience which may help us find different etiologies.

diately release her she would be in agony. More disturbing, one time he trussed himself up, put a rope around his neck, slipped off a stool on which he was standing, and snapped himself into unconsciousness, his life saved only because the rope around his neck broke.* However, most dangerous of all is the sharp flash of excitement that overruns his control when he is alone with a strange woman in her home, a situation to which his work brings him several times a week. On such an occasion, many signals can turn him on, even something as insignificant as seeing a piece of rope lying around. He then feels he must tie the woman up. So far, to prevent this he carries pictures of bound women, goes off and then masturbates so as to spare the endangered woman.

As is the case with wives of transvestites, it takes a very special woman to willingly marry a perverse man and then share his perversion with him. This patient's wife, who appears feminine, warm, open, and intelligent, has known him since adolescence and knew of his sexual needs before they married. In those days, she noted that she became most excited when they would make love in a car, when the restriction imposed by the cramped quarters would greatly increase her excitement. Now she is aware that she becomes excited by being bound, and feels that her own increasing needs may lead to her husband's violence with strange women (she knows of his fantasies toward them).

To get a glimpse of this man's childhood his parents were interviewed. The patient was present and was surprised, he later reported, to learn much of the following history.

Born two years after his brother, the oldest of the siblings in the family, the patient had over a year of development uncomplicated by bad luck. Then, between his first and second years, his father left for military service. This left a household consisting of (besides the two little boys) many women under one roof: the patient's mother, his mother's sister, an adult girl friend of his

---

*Police are familiar with this as the cause of death in perverse men not consciously trying to commit suicide. Bakwin and Bakwin[2] reviewed the literature of suicides in adolescent boys who are found hanging, dressed in women's garments.

mother, intermittently three adult female cousins of his mother, his mother's mother, and (a very peripheral participant) his mother's father. When the patient was two years old, in the midst of developing his masculinity and with unquestionably clear-cut signs of it, his sister was born, to die three weeks later. Within a few weeks his mother and grandmother began putting dresses on him and calling him by his dead sister's name on occasion.

At this point, perhaps it is best to let the parents speak for themselves, the following being direct quotations:

MOTHER: With our older boy, we just figured he's a boy. He wore the sailor suit; he had the baseball cap, and everything. I didn't realize Z [patient] didn't have the same thing. We babied him a little more and he was very pretty as a little boy. We called him "Ann" [his dead sister's name]. That was when he was two years old. He started liking silk stockings. I think it was before you [father] came home from the service. My mother even bought him a little dress. He didn't wear it hardly at all; he had it on a couple of times. He would sit with the long stockings and feel them all the time.

FATHER: He'd sit there by the hour.

MOTHER: Not by the hour; it seemed that to you. It didn't matter to me. I didn't ever think any different. But as I was picking out these pictures [photographs I had requested from the family album—RJS) I thought, What have I done? because in all these pictures, I had babied him and took better care of him and put a scarf on his head if it was cold. But he had more feminine stuff than the older boy. I kept his hair long until he was three or four, not real long, just a little bit—it was cute. He was a very quiet child, no bother. You never knew what he was thinking, whereas the other boy would have his tantrums to get his own way; he was pure masculine. You could tell the difference.

Later on in the interview:

MOTHER: What brought it on—I sort of encouraged—I lost the baby girl. I wanted a girl.

FATHER: Her folks didn't especially want her to have this third child. I was gone in the service. They thought two's enough. They put the pressure on her not to have this child. Naturally, when she had the child and it died, it was quite a shock. She was pretty sick. It made me pretty sick too. Kind of like retribution: That's our punishment. That's why I believe they put so much stress on Z.

MOTHER: I didn't mourn the baby at all. I just figured it was my punishment for trying to do away with her before she was born. I didn't want to do that either, but my mother has a strong personality.

Later on in the interview:

DOCTOR S.: Did he play in girls' clothes?

MOTHER: No. He only had this little dress on two or three times.

DR. S.: He didn't want to put on girls' clothes?

MOTHER: Like I say, he was real easy to get along with. If you'd tell him something he'd do it. He liked it; he liked the long stockings. He didn't care about the dress. He wanted to do what his brother did and they didn't play anything feminine. He has always been rough and ready. He had a rocking horse, trains, cars. . . .

But through all the years, I knew one of them was taking my clothes. I didn't know which one.

Later on in the interview:

MOTHER: He wasn't a baby you could cuddle and hold; he never wanted to be rocked. He was just stiff like a board . . . six months old . . . I couldn't hold him. He didn't want loving. I thought he was a real pretty baby. Very white. Nice-looking baby, curly hair. He was a good baby but never wanted to be held. He would stiffen—always. He was a hard-feeling baby. Girls are soft.

Later on in the interview:

FATHER: After I got home [from the service, when the patient was 2½], I noticed him with nylons on. He'd just sit there. He had his hands on them. [He had put them on himself; no one else had done this.] When he decided he wanted them on, there was no trick to his putting them on. . . . There were an awful lot of women in the house; the place was loaded with women.

MOTHER: I can only remember at our housewarming, he tied up my sister's wrists and maybe her ankles. He was four—she would sit there—and other people—her husband was right there too. I glanced at them. At the time, I thought, That's funny, but that's all—a half hour or so. She was talking to the other adults.

Later on in the interview:

MOTHER: I never pushed any masculine things at him . . . his hair long and everything. It wasn't long, just over his ears, real pretty. His hair was first cut when he was four and even then it wasn't short.

We would call him "Ann"—just a few times, whenever we'd put on this dress. We wouldn't call him that ordinarily. My mother or I put it on him. My mother bought it specially for him.

DISCUSSION

My thesis is this: When a little boy has developed a clear sense of identity as a male and a clear sense of being a masculine male, to then begin treating him like a girl is traumatic and may lead to major pathology in gender identity.

This case seems to fit the thesis. At just the time when his father left the household for military service, the mother and the grandmother of this two-year-old boy substituted him in name and dress for the newborn sister who had just died. Living in the same house during this period were, at various times, from four to seven adult women, none of whom tried to stop the attempted intermittent feminizing of the boy, and the only adult male, a grandfather, played no part in the dynamics of the household. Within a few months after a dress was put on him and he was called by his dead sister's name when so dressed, the boy, aged two, was putting on women's stockings and sitting in them for hours, stroking the material, no one thinking it necessary to stop him, much less wonder what passion had seized him.

The one essential part of the thesis that cannot be confirmed is that this was traumatic—that is, painful—to the child. We know it was done and we know he then began behavior with feminine clothes that has persisted throughout his life. But we can only surmise this pain, for no observers detected it and he cannot remember the events.

It seems a reasonable surmise. Certainly, the threat of being feminized is observably great in older boys. The struggle to be manly is a crucial ingredient of puberty rites and of much of the turmoil of adolescence, and for the adult man, defense of his masculinity often seems even more important than preserving his life. I believe it is the sense of being a male and of having a masculine identity (an achievement that has taken work in the small child, as does most ego development), which makes typical boys and men more or less vulnerable to threats to their manliness. I also believe that such masculinity is rather well-developed by the time a boy is two, and that any observer can see this without difficulty. I therefore presume that the two-year-old, while not sensing as much danger as would, say, an adult man, in being forced into a woman's clothes, nonetheless feels threatened.

The presumption that what was done to this little boy was painful gains credence from the fantasy that the perversion repeatedly plays out in the world. While preserving some affectionate and sexual relationships with females, it also revenges him for what was done to him. So he finds himself unable to enjoy sexual relations in reality or in fantasy unless at the same time he is tormenting women.* While something of this sort can be found in the feelings—sexual and otherwise—that most men have with

*In this, he is probably related to the men who murder women as the precipitant for sexual excitement.

women (having been born, reared, and therefore frustrated by a woman), the intensity of this man's need to harm women suggests that he feels what was done to him was more destructive, and demanding of great revenge. We see a primitiveness in his fantasies that is best accounted for by a very early and very severe trauma.

We do not have specific details to tell us why he chose specifically to build his pleasure around tieing up women. One can wonder, perhaps naïvely, whether he himself was tied up or looked upon certain things that were done to him as being a kind of binding; or, one can speculate that the binding is a more symbolic representation of what was done to him. But in any case, at this point we do not have sufficient data to trace exactly his need for binding. (It is my strong belief that if we had enough data we could explain this specificity without resorting to theoretical, nonspecific explanations.)

We know of other males who are dressed by older women. Such a history is a very frequent finding in adult transvestites, and once again whenever this history is found, (1) the clothes have been put on the passive boy who in the beginning was not seeking such an experience, and (2) it has been done after the boy had already developed clear manifestations of masculinity. I have speculated that it is these masculine manifestations that arouse envy in the women who, to get their revenge, must do this to boys (Chaps. 16 and 18). I do not know why transvestites do not need to torment women as intensely as does this man.

Not having observed the infancy and childhood of the above patient, and not having observed or read anyone else's observations of the infancy and early childhood of a male who is to become a transvestite, I cannot at this point answer the important question why this child did not grow up to be a transvestite. Certainly he is a cross-dresser; that is, he puts on garments of the opposite sex for pleasure. However, as different from the transvestite, he does not get an erection from the garments themselves but rather from the anticipation of the fantasy of tieing up women. He also has no desire to pass as a woman, as do many transvestites. So it would seem that he is in the general family of cross-dressers, but is neither a transsexual, a transvestite who would like intermittently to pass as a woman, or one of the more limited forms of transvestites who have fetishistic needs for women's clothing but do not wish to be intermittently feminine or pass as a women.

It is worth noting that some transvestites do enjoy binding others (either women or other transvestites) or being bound themselves. Obviously, all these people are related in some ways, but we should also differentiate these clinical states as carefully as we can.

Part III

Aspects of Treatment

CHAPTER 20

Treatment of Patients with Biological Abnormalities of Sex

The attention that has recently been focused on intersexed patients in the literature has helped alert medical practitioners to this rare but delicate problem. The surgical, endocrinological, genetic, and other physical aspects have been dealt with skillfully and thoughtfully in other places (see, e.g., Jones and Scott[1]); I shall therefore restrict my discussion to certain problems of psychiatric management.

The term "intersexed patient," as we know, includes a heterogeneous group of people with ambiguities of the external or internal genitalia and gonads, or conflict between the apparance of the external genitalia and secondary sex characteristics. When the genitalia appear normal, no doubt is placed in the parents' minds, and the upbringing of the child will then follow the course to which it was destined, just as occurs with every child in every family. Sex definition is conferred at birth, and conformity within the limits permitted by each culture is impressed on the child. This proceeds subtly and without stirring much conscious awareness of the process so long as there is acquiescence to the parents' wishes. However, if the child deviates from the norm in his behavior, the parents' anxiety may be stirred. This, converted into anger, embarrassment, tense coercion, or the like, signals the child that to proceed further with that particular bit of behavior will threaten him with loss of parental esteem. Thus, this gyroscope, the parents' attitudes toward their child's gender identity, guides the child's development.

Regardless, then, of genetic sex, gonads, or internal genitalia, an infant appearing to belong to one sex can expect to be appropriately named, dressed, reacted to, and molded. Should there be some anatomically hidden form of intersexuality present, it will remain hidden, usually until adolescence if not for the whole of one's life.

Before the discussion becomes more specific, let us consider typical approaches to treatment that have been used within the last century. Krafft-Ebing[2] who postulated a central nervous system center to control gender behavior for each sex, left us with the problem of what to do until we could find such a center and learn ways to influence it. Pennington[3] said she solved this by correcting "the biochemical malfunctioning in the center of bisexual development" (!) by phrenotropic agents. In the last generation, easy decisions with minimal stress for the physician were made possible by the rule held to by Young,[4] that when the gonadal sex was determined, the patient had no choice but to change roles, if necessary, to that sex. More recently, Cappon and co-workers[5] devised a mathematical formula for weighing the components of somatic and psychological sex, and concluded that the correct gender role is calculated by algebraically summing those components. They state that this summing always demonstrates that gender role follows somatic sex, and that change to the sex as thus determined can be safely undertaken at any time in life. In the last decade, Money and the Hampsons[6] have expressed the view with which I agree: Gender identity is more or less fixed by primordial experiences, especially in the first eighteen months of life; they cite many cases to show that, generally, successful crossing to the opposite sex is rare after early childhood.

If one has determined that the patient is comfortable and fixed in a gender role, to me the management of the patient is clear: Any effort at changing this role, even if it is in opposition to some aspect of the sex, is likely to be unsuccessful; and if the therapist should begin to give the patient insight into his complicated biology, a psychological disaster may result. This is true except in young children; in them, the gender identity gradually becomes fixed at around two and a half years. Change of sex and gender can be successful at this stage, but only heroic efforts in subsequent years can shift it, given parents who have a clear-cut sense of their child's sex.

It is of the greatest importance that the physician who has contact with newborn infants remember that the possibility exists, even though it is rare, that wrong clues may be given by the appearance of the external genitalia. If he is alert to this possibility, then when he is confronted with an infant with ambiguous genitalia, he will be in a position in most cases to determine the proper sex. It is important that such a decision be made as quickly as possible, since for some parents lengthy indecision makes it more difficult for them finally to feel comfortably certain of their child's sex, an indecision that may produce a hermaphroditic identity. On the other hand, every care must be taken to diagnose the condition clearly, and the physician must not be rushed into a premature diagnosis. The work of Money and the Hampsons noted earlier indicates that, should an incorrect ascription of sex have been made, the error can be corrected without significant damage to the child's ultimate gender role if the change can be accomplished not later than about two and a half years. After this time, permanent character structures relating to gender identity have been formed and can change only with difficulty.

Now let us consider some of the problems found in older intersexed patients. At this point, the reader should be warned that this is ι ot the place for—nor am I the author to write—a knowledgeable text of psychotherapy. So there will be no mention of the subtleties of empathy and intuition, timing or tact, skill in detecting unconscious mechanisms and symbolic meanings, capacity for reconstructing events of infancy from adult memories, dreams, transference manifestations, or styles of acting-out. Such qualities are needed to treat these patients, but the following discussion shall be restricted to more practical issues that pertain especially to gender identity patients.

More generalities are in order before taking up specific cases:

First, in what may be the making of a virtue out of a necessity, it is my opinion that the treatment of the patients reported herein benefited because they were also research patients. In this way, a crucially supportive note was introduced into the treatment; namely, their feeling that even if the results to themselves might be limited, they were contributing to the understanding and treatment of future patients. In addition, my desire to know everything possible about them stimulated a desire in them to want to know more about themselves. So all have willingly joined in a contract: I treat them and they inform me.

Second, one becomes aware of the severe reality problems in the lives of intersexed patients at soon as he begins treating them. In this respect, then, dealing with these patients is like dealing with other people with severe anatomical defects. The therapist can probably work more fully and skillfully if these patients do not threaten his own sense of body integrity. Then he can quietly express his regret at the patient's bad luck, and neither hold himself stiffly at a distance, playing at being the doctor, nor dissolve into a corrupting, stifling sympathy. For many of these patients, the task with them is too important to allow for the doctor's untamed sympathy. Also, it is the doctor's job to cut down on the exhausting fantasies in which these patients indulge themselves; for example, of the sort wherein they constantly imagine themselves whole, thus tantalizing themselves with hope. Where there is no hope of anatomical wholeness, it is important to bring this out with the patient; when this insight is followed by a sense of anger, frustration, and then loss, it can become grieving, wherein, as with normal grief, anticipation of regaining the lost part is given up, and the patient accepts the fact that the past loss cannot ever be fully replaced.

A third factor in treating these patients is a therapist who can empathize with them, yet not be himself threatened by their problems. Unless he can accept with equanimity the cross-gender identifications and behavior in which one is constantly immersed with these patients, he may become moralistic, anxious, bored, depressed, vindictive, sarcastic, or will otherwise harm the patient with his own defensive maneuvers.* The researcher really selfish in his search for information cannot afford such attitudes, not only because they bias what he hears (this is easy enough to do under the best of circumstances), but they also prevent the patient from trusting the therapist, ruining both treatment and research.

Fourth, the therapist is greatly benefited if he is not only intuitive, open-minded, and curious but also has his feet somehow planted on reality. The problems that these patients have to face in the real world are great; if one floats in unconscious processes and symbolic meanings, as he must do in the analysis of normal neurotics, he may not adequately balance the strength of certain unconscious forces, which may be present but minimal, against the reality forces. Most of us know how blessed is the therapist who knows how *not* to use certain information he has.

It may be best now to talk of specific cases rather than to generalize further. In this way, some of the more obvious methods used in the managing of intersexed patients will emerge.

Case One: What does one do psychiatrically with the intersexed patient who has no disturbance in gender identity but has anatomical and endocrinological defects that need correction? As close to nothing as possible.

Our patient in Chapter 2 exemplifies this. While she knew she was a female and was a feminine young woman, she had come to realize more and more strongly during adolescence that something was wrong, because she had not grown breasts and was not menstruating. I believe the gynecologists dealt with her

*A minor point that can exemplify this: I quickly measure the strength of a patient's gender identity by the pronouns I find myself automatically using. For example, if, regardless of a patient's being a biologically normal male, I use "she" unthinkingly, the patient has a strong, nonhostile, feminine identification. When I cannot feel comfortable with either pronoun, then I expect to find that the patient's gender identity has strong, visible masculine and feminine components.

in the most therapeutic manner by telling her that she had a condition manifested by several defects, all related, all correctable
except for her infertility, and none raising any question as to her
being a female. (I saw her in treatment, not because there was
any problem in gender identity, but because of a specific
neurotic symptom.)

All the surgical and endocrinological procedures were successful and without psychological complications. My only interven-
tion was to talk her family into permitting her a vagina before
she was engaged. As with most intersexed patients, her motivation
for being anatomically more normal was so high that she was
most stoical in the face of great physical pain.

Case Two: This is the girl who at age 14 was told that she
was an XO intersexed and who then developed a psychosis (Chap.
3). The first essential point in her treatment was probably a
proper evaluation of her psychosis. For example, for one therapist the psychosis might have meant "schizophrenia," which he
was trained to consider an essentially hopeless organic brain
disease; for another, "schizophrenia" caused by the insupportable
agony of a conflict over forbidden homosexual wishes. The one
might have treated her with EST, the other might have enlarged
her awareness of an unacceptable interest in women.

The essence of what I did came from having seen in the
shambles of her psychosis some undamaged femininity and respond-
ing to its presence, thus pointing it up for her. Having no question in my mind as to whether she was feminine and had a
female core gender identity, it was easy for me to answer all
questions she asked about her sex and gender, probably supporting
her since I was unafraid that her gender identity was irreparably
damaged, as she had believed. Therefore, the support given her
did not come from a person who felt trapped into having to
invent optimistic lies. As she came to trust me, she came also to
trust my opinions, and with this the psychosis disappeared (and
has not returned in the last three years).

Case Three: This child, one of the boys born without a penis
(Chap. 5) was first seen in his early teens when he was rather

weird and mildly psychotic, with strange behavior and thinking mixed in with a lot of normal behavior. That he was so damaged psychologically is not surprising because for much of the first five years of his life, he had been hospitalized for innumerable operations for the purpose of attempting to build for him an artificial penis. During this time he was abandoned by his parents, but became the pet of the hospital authorities. Because of this, his psychotherapy was opened up to include our whole Medical Center and its volunteer workers, secretaries, interns, residents, and professors. He became well known throughout the hospital, all of the facilities of which were made available to his needs. In other words, his transference was to the hospital and its personnel, just as in his infancy and childhood his "parents" had been a hospital and its personnel. Since his core gender identity was intact, the treatment was aimed at improving his anatomical state and in making him feel that he could rejoin the human race via warm and friendly acceptance of him by the hospital personnel. This was not easy, for when angry he would seriously threaten us with murder. When everyone stood firm, he came to trust us. The psychosis passed several years ago, and his treatment now is concerned with helping him to keep a job (his parents do not see or assist him) so that he can attend college.

Case Four: Since it was impossible to provide the other little penisless boy (Chap. 5) with a functioning penis, some of the pediatricians and surgeons felt that it would be much easier to convert his body in a female direction. While this is surgically and endocrinologically sound, it was obvious on observing the child that he was firmly masculine and had no question that he was a male. Accordingly, to have told him that he was now going to become a female would, I believe, have been perma- nently damaging psychologically. Had it been possible to make the decision when he was born, it would have been wiser (so long as he was not Catholic, in which case it would be immoral by definition to change his sex) for him to be brought up as a female (because the surgical results would be so much better). However, at age four, he felt securely that he was a boy. So it was decided that he would be less harmed by knowing himself to be anatomically defective as a male, than by telling him he should learn to be a girl. Being psychologically sound, he required no psychiatric treatment, except insofar as one might consider a consultation that would preserve his gender from the effects of medical tampering to be treatment.

Case Five: The management of this child contrasts with that of the last boy. This child, brought up without question as a boy, was first seen at age six, at which time he was diagnosed as being a normal female except for external genitalia that looked like a boy's, the effects of adrenogenital syndrome. Because of the onset of precocious puberty (a special complication of this condition), his voice was deep, body and facial hair had begun to appear, his phallus was enlarging steadily, and—dreadful complication—he was imminently to begin menstruation, because of the normal ovulating ovaries, uterus, and vagina hidden behind his masculine external genitalia.

He could have been managed by removing his ovaries, uterus, and vagina, in which case he would have still needed medical treatment, but his sense of identity would have been left intact. However, sufficient pressure was exerted by medical authorities (for moralistic reasons) that his "penis" was amputated, and his "scrotal sac" was split and recreated as the external lips they were originally meant to be anatomically; then the child was told that he was a she. The subsequent psychiatric treatment that was attempted resulted after several years in a child who was a grotesque caricature of a girl. She is now twelve years old. She says she does not ever want to go out with boys, does not ever want to marry, does not want children, and would like to be a "cowboy or a racer" [of automobiles] when she grows up.

I evaluated but did not treat this child, and could not have treated it because my attitude would have been too inimical to any chance of a child thus successfully switching gender. However, I did have the opportunity to see "her" three times for follow-up over the subsequent six years and thus to witness the failure of this brave attempt.

Case Six: In Chapter 6, we described a 17-year-old girl who was born without a vagina and uterus, but who had no question that she was a female. Because of there being no problem in gender identity, this did not play a part in her life; there is therefore nothing further to be discussed here, unless to mention the obvious that, in such a case, the best psychiatric treatment is not to treat psychiatrically.

Case Seven: This is a little girl of eight who was recently discovered to be a genetic male with cryptorchid testes, a bifid scrotum, severe hypospadias, and a penis the size of a clitoris. She was of course considered a female at birth and was raised as a girl. The main psychiatric maneuver on my part was to see only the parents in consultation, but not the little girl. In the past, not knowing any better, I have seen parents and child; it always raised the problem of what the child thought was the reason for coming to the hospital, when the child had no psychological problems and no awareness of anything being anatomically wrong. These parents were told what anatomical defects needed correction to preserve the femininity of their little girl. They were told that their daughter was truly a girl and that, although sterile, she was as able as any girl to continue to be feminine, to fall in love, marry, enjoy sexual relations, and be motherly to any adopted children.

On occasion, one sees parents who are fully informed of the genetic, anatomical, endocrinological, and even gender identity implications of their child's condition. In such cases, one can only hope that the parents, carrying this secret within themselves, will not inadvertently express it either subtly or grossly at any time in the future.

It may be worth emphasizing that these children exemplify two "truths." One is the genetic, anatomical, endocrinological "truth"; that is, the components that are added up to classify a person as to sex. The second "truth" is that of gender, and, as I hope has been demonstrated in this work, sex and gender are not necessarily always congruent. In these intersexed cases, when one has to choose between "truths," I vote for the truth which describes accurately the patient's sense of gender identity. Unfortunately, in the history of the treatment of such patients, the literature has abounded with statements by authors who insist that the "truth" should be that of the genes or the anatomy, regardless of the psychological state of the child. While this is frequently a good procedure to follow in the newborn, when gender identity has not yet been formed, to insist on this with the older child has the smell of cruelty.

Case Eight: In those patients designated as having a fixed gender identity formed primarily by a biological force, the most crucial step in treatment is the correct evaluation that the identity really is firm. Thus it was with the "girl" (Chap. 7) who for the first fourteen years of her life acted as though she were aware she was a boy, although never denying that she was a girl. The essential finding was that her gender identity was really that of a boy; so it seemed absurd not to break what until then had been an unalterable rule for me: that a person brought up unequivocally in one sex should not be told after the age of two or three that the sexual ascription was wrong. With this "girl," however, every manifestation of gender identity so clearly pointed to a capacity to change successfully that the child was instantly told his proper anatomical diagnosis, and he just as rapidly took on his new, and rightful role as a boy. He has maintained this role to the present, and has needed no psychiatric treatment to help maneuver this potentially treacherous route successfully, although I see him infrequently in order to assist in some of the routine management of changing his life over to what is appropriate for his new sex assignment. However, in this regard, I am functioning as an enlightened friend.

CHAPTER 21

The Treatment of
Transvestism and Transsexualism

There is as yet no adequate treatment for either transvestism or transsexualism; what follows will only emphasize this opinion.

TRANSVESTISM

The transvestite does not often wish to stop being a transvestite. He would like society to change so that he would be safe; this not having happened, he will occasionally seek out a psychiatrist to learn how to avoid the fear, shame, and guilt produced by society's attitudes. Although he may ask the psychiatrist to cure him of the transvestism, what he is really asking is to be cured of his pain. He generally does not consider his transvestism to be painful. Quite the opposite, it is most enjoyable; what it stirs up in others is what leads to the pain.* So when the transvestite

---

*I have been unable to determine, either from the literature or from patients evaluated or seen in research-treatment, to what extent their guilt is an inherent part of the complex psychodynamics at the heart of the condition and to what extent it is the effect of society's fear of and indignation at cross-gender impulses. Practically speaking, the amount of guilt felt by the transvestite is insufficient to galvanize the treatment, once he learns how to deal with society.

discovers that the doctor's goal *really* is the removal of the syn-drome, the patient usually leaves.

There are variations in the above discussion of egosyntonicity. In adolescence, the transvestite will feel evil and a freak, but the pleasure is too intense to be stopped. Later on, the man may have fits of remorse and disgust after orgasm, throw away the clothes, and, if he has been caught at it, come to the psychiatrist filled with strong motivation to change. This almost always passes off after one or two visits. Rarely, a patient will continue in treatment for months or years, but the reports in the literature of extended treatment end with some such statement as: "The patient was improved but moved before treatment ended."

I would consider a transvestite to be cured of transvestism if, without the need for conscious control—inhibition, suppression, denial, avoidance, or courage—he no longer cared to cross-dress, had not substituted barely disguised but similar forms of sexual or gender role behavior, and now potently and pleasurably was using a woman with whom he had an affectionate relationship for his sexual gratification. (This last would be asking a lot of most men, not just transvestites.) In other words, his character struc-ture would have so changed that he now wished to maintain the differences between men and women, no longer needing to merge with women, since his excessive identification with them had withered.

Certainly such changes do not seem impossible. To a lesser degree, they may occur in the normal development of children and adolescents and in the treatment of some effeminate men, whether practicing homosexuals or not. Oddly enough, there is no case reported where one can feel this has occurred with a transvestite.* The few psychoanalytic writings on the subject reveal that the treatment has illuminated the psychodynamics, but in no case where the descriptive material is that of a real trans-vestite is it clear that the patient lost his perversion—either the sexual (fetishist) aspect or the gender (the desire to pass as a

*Although one report, suggesting personality change, is optimistic, the follow-up is superficial.[1]

woman).[2] This holds true for the rest of the psychiatric literature except for a very few recent papers to be discussed.*

The only recently reported treatment for which more than one author shows enthusiasm is that called aversion therapy, conditioning, negative conditioning, or behavior therapy. These reports show a resurgence of interest in the use of repeated applications of pain or vomiting that was in vogue fifty years ago, and sporadically since (e.g., in the treatment of alcoholics). While the theory has become more sophisticated, the techniques have retained their simplicity: painful electric shock to the edge of agony, or monumental bouts of vomiting, these administered while the patient dresses in his favorite garments, looks at photographs, or listens to tapes of himself describing himself as a transvestite, and so on.[4]

I am prejudiced against these techniques,† worried for fear learning theory is being prostituted into a device for flailing at psychoanalytic theory and data, and fearful that such forms of treatment may become facile techniques for cruelty in unscrupulous hands. Still one must be cautious about claiming the only true faith. There are many treatments in medicine which may be brutal for patients, but which when properly used are the best we as yet have to offer (e.g., EST in the psychotic depression). If the goal of the treatment of the transvestite is set as being the removal of cross-dressing, if nothing else has been of use, and if aversion treatment removes the activity, then it should be used—if . . . the next series of "ifs" takes us into an even soggier swamp, the whole issue of who defines what is antisocial and how much does this behavior endanger society or its individuals. How much pain should be inflicted on a patient to make him conform? For the homicidal, a great deal. How much for the transvestite?

*Because this is a biased statement, I should note that there are sporadic reports[3] of patients who are described as better, relieved, improved, etc., but it is not really clear what was done in treatment, why the patient changed, and what were the manifestations of the change, or, in some cases, even whether the patients were transvestites or more simply fetishists.

†So are others.[5] "I submit that electric shocks (faradic aversion treatment) are in the same category as the flogging, ducking, and cannon-firing of the past, and that good intentions do not justify the means employed."[6]

To what extent does society's lenient attitude cause deviant behavior to increase? Does deviant sexual and gender behavior weaken a society? What does "weaken a society" mean? . . . How do we discuss transvestism and its treatment if we haven't the answers to these kinds of questions?

The recent optimistic reports of the aversionists leave a therapist hungry with hope and a skeptic skeptical. If the treatment works and there are patients who want it, the misery should be worth suffering; we must not discard a treatment that is of use simply because it is not the kind we prefer for theoretical, moral, or idiosyncratic, personal reasons. However, so far, the number of successes is very small; the follow-ups, too short; and the method of checking whether the treatment has worked, either skimpily reported or skimpily applied. ("Are you better?" "Yes." Good—the patient is better.)

Let me report briefly a "cure" that I observed but played no significant part in, and as one picks holes in the argument, he can experience the kind of skepticism some of us feel regarding any cures of transvestism ascribed to *any* method of treatment.

I had been seeing this man, a typical transvestite, for about a year. He would not consider himself a patient but rather a research subject, though I was aware that his occasional visits were motivated by more than his willingness to assist in the research. As different from most transvestites, he had a clear though mild paranoid quality, which put him into closer contact with some of his psychodynamics than is seen in the typical transvestite. Sometime before his first visit, he had gotten from some reading the idea that transvestism and homosexuality were connected. To determine if this was true for himself, over a period of several months he talked with homosexuals, visited "gay" bars, and read increasingly about homosexuality. (I take this to be evidence of homosexual desires, still forbidden but nonetheless moving toward conscious gratification.) Along with this interest, he coerced his wife into sexual games in which homosexual qualities were increasingly manifest. This was accompanied by a crescendo of anxiety, irritability, suspiciousness, depressive fits, and hyperactivity, culminating in a paranoid psychosis precipitated by his having his wife, dressed like a prostitute, attach to herself an artificial penis he had made, with which she then performed anal intercourse upon him. Following this dreadful, and finally quite conscious, gratification of his homosexual desires, he became suicidal and homicidal. As we talked throughout the several hours of this emergency, he vividly expressed his opinion, derived possibly in part from his readings, but mainly from his own psychotic thoughts, that his transvestism had been an attempt to keep himself from sensing his homosexual desires. As he absorbed what he was saying, he became calmer. He also stopped his transvestism. Since that moment, a year ago, he has not practiced it again.

A psychodynamic remission. He now has insight, the product of his psychosis and the cause of his remission. Where formerly a potential psychosis was held in check by the complex character structure we have called transvestism, the psychosis is now contained by insight. . . . But is that the answer? Is there proof this is so? Would a recurrence of the psychosis prove the theory wrong?

The patient now says that he no longer has any desire to dress. He has given away the clothes, makeup, wigs, transvestite magazines and books, and the clothes catalogues. When he sees a woman wearing articles of clothes the sight of which (clothes) would formerly have excited him, he feels no lust (nor disgust either). His wife corroborates all this, although, since she cannot climb into his mind and know all he thinks, she still fears it may start up again. (To what extent do her fears that he may again indulge press him toward doing just that?)

Yet it is with as inadequate data as the above that we must judge the results of treatment reported in the literature. In this case, the time of remission has been too short to say that his "self-cure" has worked. Many transvestites are known to have periods of disgust or fear in which they swear off their perversion and get rid of their paraphernalia. Under sufficient provocation—and a terrifying psychosis may be as effective as a course of apomorphine, electric shock, or a jail sentence—transvestites can refrain from months to years.

The point is this: It is too early to be enthusiastic over results of aversion treatment. If it turns out that its users can effect long remissions in many cases, without a high price in substitute symptom formation or overlying crippling inhibitions, then this painful therapy will be valuable. Until then, it cannot be reported that it is the proper treatment for transvestism.*

Another form of treatment that might be considered is castration. Legislation permitting this under certain circumstances for managing "sexual psychopaths" has been enacted in California and in Scandinavia. The loss of testosterone would undoubtedly drastically reduce the number of orgasms the transvestite enjoys from the fetishistic aspect of his perversion; it probably would not affect his desire to pass as a woman. Transvestites who have lived into their sixties and seventies note a decrease in sexual desire, but none in the desire to cross-dress.

Since transvestites do not endanger other people, there is no rationale for forcing them to be castrated.

For the sake of completeness, we can note reports on two other types of treatment. The first[8] is that a borderline patient who was a transvestite gave up his transvestism after receiving nialamid, meprobamate, and chlorpromazine; on maintenance dosage for four years, he is reported as in "good mental health." It is not clear how extensive the follow-up evaluation has been. At any rate, this method has not yet produced a wave of former transvestites successfully treated with phrenotropic drugs.

The second report is that EST made two transvestites feel better.[9]

TRANSSEXUALISM

It is impossible to discuss the treatment of transsexuals without becoming involved in moral issues (see next chapter). The transsexual, unlike the transvestite, does not wish to remain a male,† but wishes to have his body changed so that he becomes as completely female as medical techniques can contrive. In addition, possibly, to threatening the masculinity of the physicians to

*See also Coates[7] for a reasoned display of skepticism.
†For simplicity, I shall discuss this primarily in terms of males.

whom the transsexual makes his request, the patient treads on ancient feelings in society regarding the preservation of fertility. Then too, of a more practical nature, the surgery is extensive and not without danger; being of a completely elective nature—the indications are purely psychological—one hesitates to embark on cosmetic procedures that are so much more intricate and hazardous than fixing a nose.

The most troubling aspect is that the easier it is to have such procedures done, the more patients request them. As the word gets around, as it has in the last decade or so, more and more effeminate men request to be changed. Lumping them all together in one category leads to the implication that anyone making such a request is a transsexual.[10] If it is a surgeon who oversimplifies these differences in gender identity, and there is no one to stay his hand, there will be tragic consequences. For the effeminate homosexual who prizes the pleasures his penis brings with other men or for the transvestite who so enjoys his fetishism and the sense of being a woman with a phallus, the realities of having been castrated can be disastrous. For the patient, this may mean a severe depression or paranoid psychosis, and for the physician the treacherous uncertainties of the medical-legal issues involved, which still have not been clarified by the courts.

The general rule that applies to the treatment of the transsexual is that no matter what one does—including nothing—it will be wrong. First, what happens if the procedures are completed? That many are better adjusted (we won't pause to document that vague term) postoperatively than they were before is a conjecture that can be proven only by having seen transsexuals (not pseudotranssexuals) in intensive follow-up from months to years after they have completed their sex-transformation procedures. Their anguish before the procedures is intense and genuine (one of the many points distinguishing their reactions from pseudotranssexuals). Nonetheless, they are left more or less dissatisfied, feeling that although the necessary procedures have feminized some of their appearance and functions, the results are far from complete. The transsexual will wish to have not only breasts, vagina, and femalelike external genitalia, absent facial and body hair (all of which can be supplied) but also ovaries, uterus, and fertility. So if the surgeon complies with the patient's request, he is likely to be still harassed by the patient, who wants more. Some become sexually promiscuous and some entertainers, capitalizing on their notoriety. In addition, these patients are as exhibitionistic as women with hysterical personalities, and are unreliable in a subtle way I still cannot articulate but the gross manifestations of this in the office are a high rate of missed appointments, lateness, and peculiar distortions of their history even in areas outside that of the development of gender. These qualities make working with such patients distasteful for some physicians.* (It adds nothing to our knowledge to apply the *coup de grâce* by dismissing them with the statement, "They're all psychopaths.") Pauly, in his excellent review of one hundred cases of transsexualism, concludes: "Follow-up studies at the present time indicate some apparent success, but these results must be interpreted with caution."[11]

On the other hand, if one does not assist transsexual patients, they are deeply unhappy. The argument against treating this unhappiness by surgery or hormones is exemplified by the following statement: ". . . if . . . the demand for a change of sex operation is based upon a delusion [*sic*] conviction, then only the treatment of the underlying psychosis or personality disorder is in my view admissible or correct.

"Sometimes such patients are suffering from schizophrenia, and are overtly psychotic; sometimes it is hard to see where, apart from their singular and absolute rejection of their own sexuality, their judgement is in other ways abnormal. In either case only such treatment as will enable them to come to terms with the reality of their condition is open to the psychiatrist to offer or endorse."[12]

One would not provide a throne for a psychotic who delusionally felt he was a king; is it not as irrational to grant the transsexual his request just because he is unhappy? The cases are not

---

*These qualities have not been present in the few transsexual females with whom I have worked. Such patients have been dependable, quietly determined, and without flamboyance. As a result, they became quite successful in living their inconspicuous lives as men.

identical. Psychotics who want thrones do not become less disturbed even when they become kings, but most transsexuals are less depressed and anxious, more sociable and affectionate, and so forth after "the change." Also, very few transsexuals are clinically psychotic. (While I have heard of such, in my limited experience I happen not to have seen one who was, although one or two were a bit frayed at the edges.) Their "delusion" is placed in a setting of intact reality testing. Almost all these patients know that their request is strange; they do not question that society considers them bizarre; there is nothing grandiose or persecutory in their thinking; they are not trying to change the world or to construct a philosophic system to impose on others, etc., etc. I go into this detail only so that we can avoid the simple answers that emerge through using simple words like "psychotic" and "delusion" rather than by describing the data as we observe them.

However, for all this, if there were any psychiatric treatment that was even partly useful, it would probably be better than this disquieting "psychosurgery." It has been suggested that "no psychotherapeutic procedure less than intensive, prolonged, classic psychoanalysis would have any effect. If properly done, it could probably reduce the patient's agitation and the level of his unhappiness. It is not impossible that his major symptoms may decrease in frequency and urgency."[13] This statement has the vigorous ring of sober caution; it also must have been written by someone who has never tried to get such a patient into analysis. Unfortunately, no one has ever reported having reached such success by any psychotherapeutic technique. We must search for such techniques, but in the meanwhile it seems haughty to say that "only such treatment as will enable them to come to terms with the reality of their condition is open to the psychiatrist to offer or endorse." Since we have nothing to offer or endorse that can give these patients any relief, to make this a rule to put into practice when sitting in one's office with the patient who asks for your help means to do nothing. The problem for the psychiatrist then is only, Should he do this nothing gracefully or horsewhip the bloody beggar off the compound?

Benjamin, who has treated more patients requesting sex-transformation procedures than anyone else, has a method of evaluation and treatment on which he has reported favorably.[14] After weeding out those patients who obviously are psychologically unsuited, he suggests to his candidates that they actually pass as women for many months. He has found that for some, while the fantasies of being a woman are very rich, the rigors of living as a woman are either too frightening or the person is too masculine to be able to keep it up. During this time, Benjamin prescribes estrogens, believing that they not only give the patient an inner sense of femaleness and an observable change in body contours, but that the estrogens in themselves have a tranquilizing effect on males. If after this trial, the patient, in Benjamin's opinion is still highly motivated and sufficiently feminine, he then refers the patient for surgical procedures. When these have been performed, Benjamin continues to follow up these patients indefinitely. He has reported on 40 patients followed postoperatively, noting 34 "satisfactory" (on a three-point scale of satisfactory, doubtful, unsatisfactory).

At this point, it is worth mentioning a practical difficulty that arises should the psychiatrist choose to recommend a patient for such surgery. Almost no such procedures have been performed in the last few years in major American medical centers (with the exception of patients who had already gotten parts of the operation done somewhere else, or where the patient had already mutilated himself). There is much secrecy involved in finding a surgeon who will cooperate, and even then the patient must have thousands of dollars. These operations are not being done in medical centers with facilities for nonpaying patients except in the rarest of instances. Although there are clinics in foreign countries where sex-transformation surgery is performed, it is alleged that not all routinely adhere to the rigid standards of asepsis familiar in American operating rooms.

It is unsettling to realize that transsexualism was scarcely an issue for physicians until a few years ago. This knowledge may annoy physicians who are aware that had the techniques not been applied to transsexuals and then publicized, such people would have contained themselves, as hopeless people certainly can do.

Nonetheless, we have to come to terms with the problem. We cannot legislate it away, probably, and we do not know how to treat it psychiatrically.

I would suggest, because these procedures may be disastrous if used with the wrong patient, that they not be used except as research techniques. This would mean that they should not be done simply because the patient has the money to afford boot-legging. They should not be used unless the patient has been studied in depth and for at least six months by a team of psychiatrists, psychologists, endocrinologists, and urologists. I think that only those males who are the most feminine, have been expressing this femininity since earliest childhood, have not had periods of living accepted as masculine males, have not enjoyed their penises, and have not advertised themselves as males (e.g., female impersonators) should be operated upon. I fear that it is from the ranks of the less feminine males—and these make up the greatest number of people requesting such procedures—that the postoperative failures come: psychosis, depression, suicide, prostitution, malpractice suits, the patient's appalling feeling that it was all a mistake. (It is outrageous that there are surgeons in some parts of the world who will operate on any male who arrives in town asking for the surgery and with the required many thousands of dollars necessary.)

For those who do go to surgery, the follow-up should be intensively pursued for at least a year, and then at least several times a year for years, with the patient actually being talked to by members of the team. Participating physicians should be legally protected from suits. In the course of such a program, we would not only learn much about the treatment of transsexualism—hopefully, so much that one would not need to continue using these procedures—but, more important, we would learn much about the sources and manifestations of gender identity.

CHILDHOOD TRANSSEXUALS

This chapter can be closed with some comments, partly chilling and partly hopeful, about male children with gender perversions. Considering the very small number of these boys, any "conclusions" one reaches can at best be considered opinions to be verified or discarded when more such children have been seen. Thus, in any discussion of treatment, we must remember that this is written on the basis of very inadequate experience.

One boy has been treated successfully (he is now masculine and no longer thinks he is or should be a female); one is in early treatment (while more masculine, in times of stress he still falls back upon hopes of becoming a girl); the third has not started treatment. However, I hasten to discuss treatment because, if these hunches are right, one runs risks by delaying. If these boys are the adult transsexuals of future years, with their demands for sex-transformation procedures and the reportedly hopeless prognosis for psychiatric treatment, then the time to help them is in childhood, when their gender identity is still forming. At any rate, remembering that the reported findings must still be considered tentative, it is worth considering some of the issues in treatment.

The goal of treatment should be to make the child feel that he is a male and wants to be a masculine boy. It becomes apparent that successful treatment is possible only with proper diagnosis. If one thinks that these boys are passing through a normal phase, or are "simply" homosexuals, or are young transvestites who will become typical adult transvestites, then treatment may be badly skewed. Therefore, the first step in treatment is to establish that one is in fact dealing with a childhood transsexual. Next, since the fixing of character structure in children proceeds very rapidly and what has been established is not easily undone, one must start treatment *immediately*. If one waits until five or six or seven, the undoing is more difficult, and if one waits until pre-puberty or puberty, treatment will probably be only partially successful. I would guess that by adolescence or adulthood it is too late; one may then have to deal with the malignant end result of this process: the male who insists he is a female and wants to be transformed into a female. (There are no reports of an adult male transsexual having been cured of his pronounced femininity.)

What is hopeful is that we have a few clues that the process might be modified. There are a couple of reports of transsexual boys[15] who, with their mothers being simultaneously analyzed, gave up their cross-dressing and other feminine interests, this accompanied by changes in character structure beyond those naturally occurring with growing up.

The prognosis may be very good when the child is young. The essential task of treatment is to end the excessively gratifying symbiosis of the mother and her son. Since the boy's father has failed to do this, the therapist must. First, one must convince the family that the condition is pathological. In each case so far, this has been easy, for by the time such boys are four or five, their mothers can recognize the damage they have done when an authority clearly points it out to them. Then all the formerly unconscious guilt pours out, and treatment can begin.

Dealing with the fathers has been much more difficult. They have not been very cooperative in the evaluation stage of treatment, failing to come in for interviews themselves, though permitting their wives and sons to become involved. Apparently their own guilt over what they are doing is so great that they cannot stand the "accusation" implied in treatment. If the father can eventually be brought into treatment, this is by far the best solution, for then all three participants are involved in undoing the situation. If he cannot, however, then the boy's therapist must substitute for the missing masculinity in the boy's life. For this reason, it may be contraindicated to have a woman therapist if the boy is younger than five or six.

In summary, the treatment aims (1) to help complete the process of separation between mother and son; (2) to support the mother as she goes through this traumatic separation, and to change her character structure sufficiently so that she can not only survive the separation but also salvage her own sense of identity; (3) to have the therapist of the child serve as a model for masculine identification; (4) to support the child during the process of separation and to treat the ensuing anxiety states; (5) to involve the father in the family's life so that he will become a source of masculinity for his son.

However, there are as yet no adequate follow-ups. At this time, then, it seems that prevention by education of parents or treatment of the few who can be given such treatment are the best hopes in severe childhood cross-gender defects. Unfortunately, the former requires a revolution in the attitudes of many parents and of our society. The first successfully treated case of childhood transsexualism is that of Greenson; a report written after the treatment was ended gives a vivid and warm account of this boy's rescue.[16]

There are no reports I know of regarding treatment of little boys who are transvestites (intermittent, fetishistic cross-dressers).

CHAPTER 22

Moral Issues in
Sex-Transformation Procedures

While it is no longer immoral to give anesthetics to women in childbirth, and only a few of the more esoteric cults call upon the Bible to save sinning mankind from blood transfusions or smallpox inoculations, the gender defects of homosexuals, transvestites, and transsexuals can still stir the thunder of the righteous. Especially disturbing—and not to the religious alone—is the body mutilation and destruction of fertility that must accompany sex-transformation procedures. No other surgery is so radical simply to improve one's image of oneself. Since these moral problems arise to influence the treatment of both intersexed and transsexual patients, it may be worth discussing them now.

One concerned with the morality of sex-transformation procedures can find a clear expression of the issues in a recent article by Thomas J. O'Donnell, S.J.[1] The crux of the problem for Father O'Donnell is this:

The moral dimension allows for the development of the true hermaphrodite towards either masculinity or femininity and in accordance with the clinical judgment of the physician and the wishes of the patients or parents. The moral dimension though limits the development of the pseudohermaphrodite in the completion of the already established sex. Because of the human damage and grave moral danger involved in an only apparent change of sex, this becomes an area where values beyond the purely clinical must be considered.

The given in this situation is that tampering with procreative ability is sinful when there is no major physical illness.

This moral position leads us into dilemmas best revealed by examining clinical data. In arranging these data now, it will help to recall the different meanings we assigned to sex and gender, those two usually interrelated phenomena that are too often confused as being identical. The difference between them is not apparent in normals where, for example, the fact that one is a male (*sex*) is accompanied by a sense of masculinity (*gender identity*) and by one's living a role in society appropriate to a boy or man (*gender role*). But in intersexed and transsexual patients, sex and gender are often discordant.

Those cases in which elective destruction of gonads and genitalia may be entertained are these: "*true*" *hermaphrodites* (individuals having gonads of both sexes); *pseudohermaphrodites* (individuals having gonads of one sex only, who nonetheless have external and therefore observable anatomical defects of the genitalia in the direction of the opposite sex); and *transsexuals*.

In the case of the "true" hermaphrodite, no moral issue is raised because, with the patient having gonads of both sexes, one can remove the evidence of one sex and still feel comfortable that major biological criteria of the other sex remain. The pseudohermaphrodite, of course, poses many more questions, some to be discussed below. Undoubtedly, no moral uncertainty (in the Catholic sense) is present with transsexualism, for, there being no biological defect demonstrable, such a person by requesting sex transformation for psychological reasons only, is consciously, willfully, unerringly sinning. However, there is some value for us to extend Father O'Donnell's concern to cover even the transsexuals.

Although there are almost limitless variations in the anatomical defects found in pseudohermaphrodites, in this discussion we can restrict ourselves to just a few. Let us first consider two types wherein the Church raises no moral questions:

1. There is the pseudohermaphrodite whose condition is properly diagnosed at birth or shortly thereafter. If, when a little boy is born without a penis, the family is informed that they have had a boy, the child will grow up with no question that he is male. His problem in adolescence in trying to cope with the humiliation involved in being sexually inadequate are great, but none of these children ever seriously wishes to be a girl. In the case of the hermaphroditic female, if the diagnosis is made early in life, the physical corrections necessary are relatively easy to accomplish, and the little girl, always knowing herself to be a girl, has no problem with her gender identity. She can grow up to be a normally functioning woman.

2. Often, when the parents learn that there is a genital abnormality, a clear-cut assignment of sex is not made soon after birth. So they decide on their own or on the advice of a physician to keep the clear-cut identification of the child as a male or female in abeyance for a number of years. In such cases, this equivocal state of identity is maintained by the child without any great observed difficulty, and when a final decision is made (which at times can be as late as in adulthood), the patient moves to whichever sex he is directed without this being painful. (See Chapter 4.)

Now let us look at those hermaphrodites for whom the application of moral absolutes may be destructive. These are the people who, unequivocally considered to be of one sex at birth, are discovered years later to have been mistakenly assigned. For example, an infant is born with completely normal-appearing external genitalia of a little girl. There being no reason for question, the child is named and raised as a girl by the parents, without suspicion that they do not have a normal girl. Nonetheless, hidden from view are the following biological facts: The child has male chromosomes, cryptorchid testes, little or no vagina, no uterus or ovaries, some degree of male internal sexual apparatus, a bifid scrotum that looks identical with external lips, a penis which is identical in appearance to a clitoris, and a severe hypospadias so that the urethra opens in the same position as in a normal girl. When the proper sex is determined years after birth, should this child receive whatever medical treatment is necessary to render it a more biologically normal male, or should the child, since to herself she is a girl, have the testes removed, an artificial vagina produced, and estrogens given so that she will not develop facial and body hair but will develop breasts and other subcutaneous fat distribution typical of a woman? In addition to the poignant fact that a normal-appearing or functioning penis cannot be constructed and therefore the child is doomed to a humiliating and frustrating adulthood if changed to a boy (as compared to a normal sexual life if kept as a girl), there is the even more frightening likelihood that when this child is told that she is not a girl but really a boy, the experience will be so disturbing that psychosis may ensue.

This makes for quite a dilemma, since if one follows the clearly defined moral course of insisting that the hermaphroditic person, who had no idea that he was abnormal, nonetheless switch over to the opposite sex, one may be quite consciously forcing such a person into severe mental illness. But there is an even further peculiarity. A person who is brought up to have no question about his gender is likely to be heterosexual when an adult; that is, primarily attracted to people of the opposite sex and gender. What, then, do we do with the child who was brought up without any question as a girl and who is now told she is a boy? Such a child will have long since developed a heterosexual orientation in childhood that was appropriate for the gender developed over the years of childhood, namely, that she is a girl. Although she may not have begun having sexual relations, no one is any longer so naïve as to believe that children do not have romantic and sexual fantasies from earliest childhood; we also know that such fantasies in most cases already point to future heterosexual or homosexual interests that cannot be shifted by an act of will, or always even by psychiatric treatment.

In the above case, the child was a heterosexually oriented girl until she was told—let us say, at age twelve—that she is really a boy. If we now follow the demands of the "moral" positio.., we try to change her into a boy; we then find that she is unable to will away her formerly heterosexual orientation, which orientation now, by the surgeon's knife and by fiat, makes her into a homosexual. How moral is such morality? While Fat .r O'Donnell does not mention that abiding by the moral position may produce a homosexual, he is concerned about such perversion. He says, "A male, externally fashioned as a female, could not validly marry, nor even attempt marriage without sexual perversion." He seems here to be defining sexual perversion not by what the person feels he is doing (not even what he wills he is doing) but by the evidence of the patient's genitalia. This unique way of defining perversion has little logical or operational value.

On the other hand, if one removes the cryptorchid testes, creates a vagina, and gives estrogens, one has a little girl who can function normally in harmony with what she feels herself to be psychologically; she will have no doubt about her heterosexuality; she can have the capacity for mature love; she can have a sexually gratifying life, and if she adopts a child she can mother it appropriately. To maintain that this is morally wrong seems to put one in a position that is not as easy to defend as it may have been four hundred years ago.

Let us tackle a problem not mentioned by Father O'Donnell but which comes to mind in any discussion of so-called sex transformation: the increasing number of people demanding sex-transformation procedures when there is no biological abnormality by any known present-day tests. When this is considered from a moral viewpoint, at the heart of the issue is found the problem of free will. Do these people choose to change their sex? To what extent do they choose it and to what extent, if any, is the desire forced upon them? Certainly there is no evidence that such patients are suffering from an irresistible impulse or that the vast majority of them are psychotic in any usual use of the word "psychosis." Also, there is no question that after 1953, when there was great notoriety following on the publicity of such a case, more and more feminine men and, in lesser numbers, highly masculine women began seeking such transformations.

In the past, when surgical and endocrinological procedures were not available, these people managed to live out their lives without such transformations. The patients know right from wrong, and in their powerful need to pass as members of the opposite sex they show such skillful planning and shrewd awareness of the risks they run that it would be absurd to claim they have no control over their actions. Nonetheless, events from their past lives may play a part in their disorder in such a way that the problem of free will remains to haunt us. Recall our transsexual boys. Although biologically normal male infants, they came to believe by the time they were two or three years old that in reality they are females, and they have an overwhelming desire to grow up to be biologically normal females. They have a fierce need to dress in women's clothes, to wear women's shoes, to put on women's makeup, to fix their hair like women, to walk like women, and their fantasy lives are identical with those of little girls their own age. They are accepted in games by little girls as if they were little girls. In brief, they are very feminine. In studying these boys, we discovered that the process began even before the child could walk or talk: one has great trouble imagining that these children are willing this condition in any way that does not destroy the meaning of the phrase "to will."

When these boys get older, it would not .be surprising if, without treatment, they wanted a sex-transformation procedure so that their body could be converted from its "abnormal" state to the one that they feel will fit their gender identity—namely, a female body. They know perfectly well that their bodies are male; they are not delusional. Nonetheless, they are overwhelmed with a feeling that they are really females and should grow up to be women. When one watches this develop from infancy on and one sees that the child played no active part in creating his gender identity, but essentially had it "imprinted" upon him by his mother's attitudes and the failure of his father to stop her, one is at a loss to ascribe his "willful" insistence that he dress in girls' clothes to an act of complete free will; in order to be able to damn such a child for what he is doing, one has to suppress part of one's knowledge, and to call this a sin because he knows that he is doing it and also knows that society does not approve is to cry "sin" too quickly.

If a greater part of one's sense of gender is created by factors beyond one's control (e.g., what one's mother does to one) then, if one persists in expressing that gender, is one sinning? When a little boy develops a normal sense of maleness and masculinity because his mother and father treated him as though he were a masculine little boy, we give him full credit for not being sinful, telling ourselves that he has chosen his sense of gender, when in fact he received much of it passively from his biology and his culture (especially his parents). But when parents, placing their attitudes upon the child in the same way, so influence him that he develops a gender discrepant with his anatomy, we suddenly introduce the concept of sin.

As has been so often noted in recent generations, concepts of sin and morality have to be opened up to the new findings of infantile development, and if these facts complicate what had seemed to be solved problems, one may run greater risk to his soul by willfully refusing to acknowledge the demonstrable than by being made uneasy by the data.

CHAPTER 23

Conclusion

It may be useful now to ponder on implications of this study. So long as we remember that what follows is speculative, we can move freely beyond the observations, looking for leads to better research. Remaining consistent with the plan of this book, I shall not now discuss the sex and gender development with which we are familiar, especially from Freud's work. I have no question that conflicts between the growing child's instinctual drives and the opposing demands of the outside world are crucial to understanding masculinity and femininity. That I do not at length restate these findings, which are the glory of decades of psychoanalytic research, but rather report primarily my own data must not be read as some subtle statement that I believe that the early events I have described are the *"really* important ones." Rather, I merely intend to add a perspective to the main body of findings on masculinity and femininity.

As I have tried to indicate, I have been struck by the tremendous power that parents' attitudes and behavior have in shaping masculinity and femininity, and especially by the amount of gender development that occurs in a nonconflictual manner in the infant. It is hard to find a vocabulary in psychoanalysis suitable for describing these nontraumatic processes. So much of analytic thinking stresses conflict and defense; less has been written as yet about nonconflictual personality development. This is where our transsexual boys have been helpful for theorizing. Because of what their mothers have done, these bizarre boys give us an example—a magnified view of what occurs in the gender development of more normal people—of the powerful effects a mother can have upon her infant's development and on which the infant thrives without (in the beginning) pain and conflict. This suggests that other areas of personality development as important as masculinity and femininity originate in a similar manner; despite recent thinking on ego psychology, it does not seem that we have become receptive to this possibility.

Reviewing the data, I see three themes intertwined; the parental (especially mother)–infant relationship (symbiosis and separation), its effect upon the infant's growing capacity to make choices (the development of choice), and the difficulties to be met in trying to study these issues precisely (psychoanalysis as science). Let us now, finally, speculate—softly—on these.

1. SYMBIOSIS AND SEPARATION

I agree with Greenson[1] that there are special problems in a boy developing his masculinity that are not present in the development of femininity in little girls. In contrast to Freud's position that masculinity is the natural state and femininity at best a successful modification of it, Greenson and I (joining an increasing number of people, to judge from the literature) feel that the infant boy's relationship to his mother makes the development of feminine qualities more likely. To create her femininity, the little girl does not have to surmount her relationship with her mother. We can imagine that the more feminine her mother, the easier the girl's task of creating an appropriate gender identity. The boy, however, must manage to break free from the pull of his mother's femaleness and femininity, a task that is so frequently incomplete, to judge by the amount of effeminacy, passivity, or forced hypermasculinity one sees. (I refrain from philosophizing on the contribution that men's fear of being found feminine has made in the world's history of hatred and war, as well as of more positive contributions to civilization.)

Every infant in its weakness can dimly recognize the fact—it is not a fantasy, though a source of fantasies—that this immense mother-creature can easily give bliss, agony, or death, each of which can result from her capacity to engulf her infant (eat, smother, crush, poison). Every infant—of either sex—runs these risks. However, if the male infant is to succeed in becoming a separate masculine individual, he must not only escape from the effects of this fact and its associated fantasies but must also be free of profound identifications with his mother; for when these identifications are too strong and primitive, lurking inside like the monstrous woman so many men project into their view of the women in their real lives, a man can hardly love a woman or respect himself as a person who is different from women: he doubts his masculinity.

Even a good mother will appear monstrous at times to her utterly vulnerable infant, but as the months pass, a store of memories and an awareness of reality start to grow. With these comes the capacity to separate from mother and, in happy circumstances, success in mastering the world.

But part of the mastery will depend on the male becoming a boy and the female a girl. Thus, a task falls upon the boy in developing his gender identity that does not burden the girl. He must grow beyond the feminine identifications that resulted from his first encounters with his mother's female body and feminine qualities. Here is where the mothers of transsexuals show us so starkly how too much mother (made possible by too little father) does not allow the process of separation to proceed adequately. (I suppose that if a mother does not allow separation to occur in a different sector than gender a different, nongender pathology results.)

All this may shed light on the differences between men and women in perversions—the absence of fetishistic cross-dressing, voyeurism, and genital exhibitionism as sources of genital excitement in women; on differences in the ways male homosexuals look on their aberrations as compared with females and the ways society fears male and not female homosexuality; the fear of effeminacy in so many men and the relative lack of a corresponding fear of being masculine in most women; and the much lower rate of hallucinatory accusations of homosexuality in female than in male psychotics. . . . But these issues are too heavy to be safely carried by my small bits of data.

Some of men's fears of being unmanly may have been muffled throughout the ages. Since the males have had the greater physical strength, they have been able physically to dominate women, though the fear and expectation of being themselves dominated by women was showing through. One need only read the Church Fathers' statements on the abominations of women and of women's secret powers in destroying the equanimity of men to be able to see how men have been obsessed by their sense of weakness vis-à-vis women.

In addition, society has given a far greater outward show of rewards to those who achieve its standards of masculinity than it has given for being feminine. This must have had its practical reasons. Before machines, the physical power of males was essential for saving a society and permitting its children to grow. Therefore, strength and courage (which is at bottom defined by society as willingness to die for society) were crucial. Then, as protection could be produced by inanimate objects—that is, by civilization (science)—other, gentler qualities could be permitted (even a God of love, superimposed over phallic worship or stern-Father worship; and a sweet Mother who can scarcely procreate pushes back into unconsciousness the huge, devouring, blindly abundant, sex-loving Earth Mother, whose consuming biology was necessary for replenishing a world that was not yet inventing machines.)

However, the Industrial Revolution has diminished the importance of man's physical strength; machines work for both sexes. So we now see appearing above the surface man's sense of weakness and his fear of being attacked by his feminine tendencies. (Was Victorianism and its demand that women keep still in part invented by men as a response to, and defense against, a first dim awareness of man's vulnerability and women's approaching power?)

And the children of our most industrialized societies now say they no longer need to exaggerate the differences between the sexes much beyond what is anatomically obvious. So they dress alike.

To shift to being masculine, a boy must develop not only a capacity to let go of his mother but also to relinquish his sense of being like her, a process Greenson calls dis-identification,[2] and his mother must be able to relinquish her hold upon her son bit by bit, with love for him and respect for his independence; she should not operate at either end of the continuum between too much or too little holding. It is understandable that, having carried the infant within her for nine months, a mother will feel that it has been literally a part of herself; one aspect of this that has frequently been cited in psychoanalysis is her unconscious belief: The child is her penis. Turning that infant loose to become an independent creature can tax a woman. We all know that this process of letting go is complicated, with different timetables determining when certain aspects of the child are best let loose. The process goes on continuously throughout the day as the baby, with its increasing motor coordination and other developing ego functions, shows more and more capacity to move away from his mother. This causes a mother to be forever deciding (effortlessly, we would hope) whether and how much to permit her child to separate from her. Obviously, this process is especially dependent on the mother's personality, though the infant's developing personality will also be an important factor. There seems more leeway possible in the little girl's gender development than in the little boy's, for the mother who keeps her infant daughter close to her for too long may damage the independence of the child or produce other neurotic problems, but the damage to gender, certainly to core gender, may be much less.

If, however, other ego functions are distorted so that for instance, a girl is not relating well to her mother and father after infancy, her femininity will still come to be blighted. We see this ubiquitously in our practices, and I wonder if much of what Freud described as the origins of gender development are not actually the result of these later phases, from around the age of two or three on. I would also guess that in the adult it is only these later disturbances that are very modifiable by the analytic process.

In this discussion, the child's father has not been mentioned. We know that although he is essential, his effects are—in the earliest stages of his child's life at least—manifested primarily through the mother. However, gradually and as the infant becomes aware of this male and masculine (we hope) creature, his father's role becomes one of equal immediacy with his mother's. Then, as a boy disengages himself from his mother's body and psyche, he finds his father available as, for example, a man with whom to identify, and the girl finds him available as a heterosexual object, aspects of the oedipal situation described long ago by Freud.

Let us set up more projects in the future to study the different styles with which mothers hold and care for their infants and how mothers treat their infant sons differently from their infant daughters. Are they more casual about a little girl's body, since it is of their own variety? Does the little boy's body get a different and more special sort of handling; and if so, is there any subliminal message that accompanies it to express his mother's envy of her son's body or, more happily, pleasure to have shared in the production of a male body? Do healthy mothers hold their little girls longer than they do their little boys; do they hold their little boys more fiercely, though more episodically? Are more women comfortable with intimacy than are men? (I am not now talking about the capacity for sexual pleasure.) If they are, is this the result of their having been mothered by females? There are many questions of this sort that one can ask in an experimental way, so that precise measurements can be made without doing damage to the mother-infant pair who are being observed.

If these parental effects play their part from birth on, the psychoanalysis of adults probably cannot tell us what happened in the earliest months of the adult's infant life—neither what happened objectively nor what the infant made of it. We can see the outlines of these effects of the first months dimly yet monumentally visible as our analytic work proceeds with adult patients;

however, while these impressions are crucial for our work with patients, more precise understanding of forces creating personality in those first months is just not available—unless we turn to direct observation of infants and their immediate environment, especially their mothers. I know very well that this kind of observation from the outside is also flawed, since we still must infer what the infant feels and fantasies, but the incompleteness of the technique of observing the infant and talking with (ideally, analyzing) its mother should not inhibit us from making such observations. And, happily, it certainly has not, for more and more such studies are bringing to all of us the most exciting, incomparable data.

2. THE DEVELOPMENT OF CHOICE

When we were discussing moral issues in sex-transformation procedures (Chap. 22), we worried over the problem of moral responsibility—free will. I want to do so again, this time using some of Freud's thoughts about cause and motivation—biology and/or psychology, the pleasure principle and beyond, life and death instincts—as background. Freud's work has made it clear that most of the act of choosing—of will—is far less free than we feel it to be. He emphasized two factors that diminish free will: first, the power of repression and those mental contents that must be kept unconscious, and, second, inherited and other biological factors.

Some of the data outlined in this book make me suggest a third. I do not know a proper word to cover the area to be described,* but am referring to those changes imposed upon the infant's mind in a nontraumatic way by the environment, especially mother, changes which occur without conflict and are as impelling a source of behavior as are many prenatal constitutional factors.

It was, I believe, just these earliest created, fixed, driven styles of approaching objects, such as we see exemplified in core gender identity—grotesquely in transsexuals but no less insistent in normals—that made Freud invent the concept of a death instinct

*Learning theorists call it "learning," but I am sure that learning covers far more than what most academic psychologists are willing to concede.

as an ultimate source of behavior that he considered to be self-destructive and thus beyond the pleasure principle.[1] He saw people tenaciously persisting in doing things not apparently pleasurable or tension-reducing ("primary masochism"), and he was impressed with the limitations of psychoanalysis as a treatment,[2] feeling that the most compelling reason for this failure was the pull of the death instinct. He had to believe ("We shall find the courage to assume") that if one is inexorably compelled to repeat, one must be gripped by a repetition-compulsion, the outer manifestation of a hidden death instinct.

In view of what so many others have said in disagreeing with Freud about a death instinct, it may be no more than beating a dead horse to worry the issue any further. If so, the following can be taken simply as my own discomfort with exalting compulsively repetitive behavior, such as not getting better in treatment, to a biological principle.

It seems glamorous but unnecessary to conceive that such fixed behavior is due to a repetition compulsion (a Law of Nature), though we are all indeed captives of compulsions to repeat. Nor need we agree, when such blindly stubborn behavior destroys the organism, that this destructive persistence is evidence of a deeply unconscious, inherited drive to die and to become chemically inert, an instinct alleged to be found in every living cell on earth. Tenacity in damaging oneself may be in the service of pleasure; one will do anything to avoid the pain of shifting fundamentals of one's identity. Under the profound hedonistic logic of primary process, we are not about to give up positions only because it would be more realistic to do so.

Still, many of us believe with Freud that there are psychic processes that operate independently of a pleasure principle; among them, I think, are those areas to which the learning theorists and ethologists are trying to attract our attention. Evidence from animals shows that there are modes of behavior which, while not produced by genes, are induced in each neonate of a species by its environment (which often includes parents).

Humans share with lower animals capacities to modify behavior at a simple reflex level, at the level of reflex chains, at the much more organized level of drives ("instincts"), by conditioning of the nervous system, and by imprinting. While all are part of the genesis of human behavior, humans, in addition, have the capacity for fantasy and for the creation of internal objects. These last are minimally important at birth and in early infancy but increase in importance as the months pass, while physiological motivations no longer play as crucial a role in normal personality development. However, the capacity to learn by conditioning (proven to be so powerful a process in lower animals, and not likely suddenly to break off when evolution reaches man) persists throughout life—most often minimally, or at least silently—but under certain conditions (e.g., with traumatic neuroses, brainwashing, laboratory experiments, and monotonous repetition of identical conditions in life), may be a major source of a piece of behavior.

I believe that changes in behavior in animals that result from these special conditions, along with the central nervous system changes that result from imprinting or the organizing effects of hormones on the neonate's CNS, may be truly beyond the pleasure principle. The organism has little behavioral or biological defense against being modified by these processes (though the development of the capacity to fantasy, with its feeling of being able to make choices, may have evolved in part as a more successful technique for dealing with the environment). Certain other laboratory situations also point to events that are beyond the pleasure principle, because the organism has no choice (though whether these have their counterparts in real life is uncertain). I am thinking, for instance, of the production of conscious feelings of pleasure by electrical stimulation of pleasure centers in the hypothalamus, bypassing all psychological mechanisms. These experiments are beyond the pleasure principle in much the same way as is an epileptic seizure or being hit on the head with a hammer.

The feature differentiating all these effects (listed in the above paragraphs) from what we psychoanalysts habitually deal with—wishes, fantasies, memories, etc.—is the absence of choice. With conditioned learning and partly with imprinting in the CNS, the choice is more the outside world's than the organism's.

When such impingements as conditioning and imprinting by mothers on their newborns go awry, the individual is as unprepared for his environment as if his genes were defective.

While Freud shifted the scene of the struggle over choice from conscious to unconscious, secondary to primary process, or ego to id, his conceptual system still runs on the idea that one individual (cell or person) chooses—even if instinctively choosing to die. Yet the discoveries of such as the learning theorists, the ethologists, and the behavioral geneticists suggest that there are huge areas of learning that are stamped permanently into the psyche from the organism's earliest days on, without any agency of the personality (or even the cells or the "instincts") choosing to do so. But if an organism has from birth, or shortly thereafter, a mode of action already imposed upon it, then its choices henceforth are limited. It can no more escape from an imprinted pattern of behavior or a conditioned reflex (or can hardly even recognize the presence of such motivators) than it can from an inherited drive ("instinct"). This imprinted or conditioned part of personality must be coped with—made useful or defended against—by the organism, much as it must cope with its insistent, inescapable biological needs. It may then make choices, but now within a limited number of possibilities.

At a less ponderous level, these thoughts could lead toward further consideration of incorporation, introjection, and identification. While I do not wish to be involved in a discussion of these phenomena, I can note that the idea of taking in (psychologically) part and whole objects from the outside world, whether done in order to solve conflicts or in more tranquil circumstances, does not account for a great deal of the learning and growth of personality that occurs in the infant, especially in the first months of life. May not a better understanding of learning theory and ethology be necessary for all of us analysts who are concerned with earliest causes?

3. PSYCHOANALYSIS AS SCIENCE

It is generally conceded by psychoanalysts, including many of the greatest of the analysts of the past, that psychoanalysis is a science. That this is conceded by almost no one else is not, I believe, simply a function of the resistance of the scientific world to innovation, though this has played its role in rejecting parts of psychoanalysis. Everyone knows that an obstacle to the acceptance of psychoanalysis as a science has been the fact that no one ever sees the "experiment"—that is, the process by which the data are collected—the psychoanalytic treatment—except for the person reporting the findings. This failure to be able to demonstrate one's results continues in psychoanalysis, but not because analysts are trying to put one over on the scientific world. Since no one has yet discovered a method for reproducing the moments of discovery in a psychoanalysis without destroying it—what led up to the patient saying and feeling and thinking whatever he did, and the way in which the analyst perceived this—the analyst's report must suffice. Here is a terrible problem to be solved if analytic findings are to be taken seriously by the scientific world.

The claim that psychoanalytic findings are rejected because they touch on the neurotic problems of mankind is a partial but not sufficient explanation of why they are not accepted. Even the Church, with its resistances to the findings of such a man as Darwin, has gradually been able to accept these findings when they were adequately demonstrated. The underlying conflicts and defenses of the Church were not necessarily modified, but most nonpsychotic people who belong to great institutions are able, after a certain amount of embarrassment, and after the passage of enough generations, to admit into their consciousness incontrovertible findings.

All analysts know that not all the pronouncements of psychoanalysis are incontrovertible. In addition, psychoanalysis finds itself in a position analogous to that in which the more established sciences found themselves as they struggled to break free from philosopy. Philosophy, the art of introspective generalization, is colored by the fantasies that induce one to see the world from a particular perspective, propped erect by Logic and Rhetoric, and undeterred in its pronouncements by the discipline of the experimental method.* Its close relative, Intuition, is the essential first step of science, and at its best is original and imaginative. How-

* Please do not disturb my polemic by insisting on fairness or accuracy.

ever, the process working alone remains speculation, even if one prefers the more prestigious terms—Philosophy or Intuition—until the disciplined experimental method is applied—sometimes against all temptations to avoid it.

Even the implacable effort to be scrupulous, while essential to producing a science, is not a science in itself. If psychoanalysis is to leave the bloated and blissful pleasures of philosophizing and join the scientific community, it will have to consider speculation to be a beginning but not the end of scientific process.

In the last ten or fifteen years, attempts have been made to bring an interest in scientific methodology to psychoanalysis. Because these attempts so far have on the whole been primitive, they have been too easily dismissed by some psychoanalysts. However, it is to be expected that such attempts will in time become more sophisticated, and should that be the case, then the sorry state in which psychoanalysis remains as compared with the scientific community into which it is trying to enter will change. When the rules of the game in the psychoanalytic community stop encouraging speculation *in the absence of* experimentation, an essential step toward science will have been taken.

Appendix

Data on Transsexuals

Data on Transsexuals

In 1914, Freud said: "These [certain metapsychological] ideas are not the foundation of science, upon which everything rests: that foundation is observation alone. They are not the bottom but the top of the whole structure, and they can be replaced and discarded without damaging it (p. 77)."[1]

What really must be investigated with the greatest care, if the study of the psychodynamics of personality development is to become a science, are the minutest details of what mothers, and to a lesser extent fathers, do with their infants, moment by moment as the months pass. Researchers are beginning to record these events, and if one can couple these observations with the mothers' thoughts and fantasies, we might vastly increase our understanding of personality development.

People like Call, Mahler, and Spitz are actually showing that each mother's style of contacting her infant helps form its unique personality. When we know these details, we shall be closer to ending the stage of theorizing so vaguely about earliest personality development. For example, if we say that the mother-infant symbiosis was pathological, our audiences at that future time will not let us get away with such vagueness, but will want to know exactly what happened within that symbiosis. At the very least, we shall then know that the kind of symbiosis that may drive an infant mad is different from that which leaves him sane but thinking he is a girl.

The arguments and conclusions in the chapters on transsexuals are assertions that the reader should feel require confirmation. For example: Are these boys really so different from lots of little boys who play with girls' dolls and try on their mothers' hats or shoes, or have unconscious fantasies of having their own babies? Of what nature and how much was this body contact which is alleged to be far more than in the normal closeness between mothers and infants? How was the so-called bisexuality in these women different from that seen in so many women where it has no operational significance and does not harm their sons—and so on.

Unfortunately, data (in this case, the exact quotations of what the mothers have said) can be dull. Still, I see no way around it. I believe that much of the disbelief (or extravagant belief of the impossible) that exists regarding the psychological roots of normal or abnormal behavior is due to a worker not demonstrating his data. This is usually because data in our field are too difficult to present, but one suspects that at times it is because one does not have data.

However, it is not only the fault of writers that the exact findings are not presented and that imaginative speculation may be overvalued; the audience is almost as much at fault, because it does not expect the facts, does not miss them, and is more likely to counter theory with opposing theory and bias with opposing bias, rather than demanding to know just what was observed; some readers and listeners indulge themselves too much and in the long run depreciate psychoanalysis with their uncritical enthusiasm.

It is not the custom in psychiatric and psychoanalytic literature to attempt to present in detail the data from which one draws his conclusions (but Lord have mercy on the writer whose citation of authority is incomplete). As everyone knows, it is impossible to reproduce life with written words. Those who have been concerned enough to try to solve this problem in communicating findings for others' more objective review have found themselves entangled in huge masses of findings. Some have spent months unraveling but a few moments of a filmed interview and have been dismayed at the task of trying to objectify such a conglomerate of variables as those making up a psychoanalysis.

But even if one could develop a reliable method of studying another person, how could the information be summarized and presented to a wider audience?

I have no illusions that the following reports solve these problems. Even this attempt to be scrupulous places on the reader a burden that most of us are not anxious to bear when we pick up a book: undoctored, printed conversation and much repetitious (for the reader), ungainly material. But I feel it should be put down, for only then can the reader judge whether what is reported to have been said in one case is in fact repeated in each case. Only in this way can readers see the features (listed below) that distinguish each of these cases being discussed.

1. The boys' desire to be anatomically female.
2. The mothers' need to keep their infants close to their bodies too long.
3. The mothers' excessive permissiveness of whatever their sons want.
4. The mothers' bisexuality, marked especially by their acting like masculine boys in childhood.
5. The mothers' sense of emptiness that helps keep them from remembering an earlier close relationship with their fathers and the disappointment and loss that ended this closeness.
6. The empty, angry mothers of these mothers.
7. The passive, distant fathers who are almost never seen by their sons, and who do not stop the feminizing process.

Glover, in a provocative paper that questions the vagueness of such terms as "identity," says that ". . . in the conflict of modern theories the role of clinical observation has been vastly neglected (p. 183)."[2] The purpose of this appendix is to present clinical observations. The following written direct quotations are not as rich in information as are the voices heard on the tapes from which these have been transcribed, and are also inferior to being part of the interviews. But for all their absence of the drama and excitement, I feel that the transcripts of what these people say is more dependable for the reader than even the finest and most poetically written descriptions of great writers.

THE MOTHERS

Subject A is a woman in her early thirties, married about ten years. A′ is her 4½-year-old son (at the time of the evaluation), so active in the interviews that he could not stop jumping, wriggling, sliding, and crawling unless sitting in her lap. He constantly returned from a few moments' precipitous activity to touch her limbs, trunk, face, and hair, or to sit or lie on her. Both were referred to other members of the Clinic for treatment but quit after a few visits. Father refused to cooperate. All the evaluation interviews were taped.

Subject B is a woman in her early forties, married fifteen years. B′ is her 4½-year-old son (at the time of the evaluation); he literally never released himself from physical contact with her for one moment in any of the hours of consultation. His father refused to come in for evaluation. Mother and son are now in psychotherapy, each being seen two times a week. Father refuses treatment. All the evaluation interviews were taped.

Subject C is a woman in her middle forties, married twenty years. C′ ("Lance") is her five-year-old son (at the time of the evaluation); he had been able to separate himself physically from her during the interviews, but was terribly active in a curious and intelligent way. Her husband was fully cooperative consciously, but kept arrangements confused because of his being late and forgetting after promising to help out with baby sitting and transportation. Both mother and son are being seen four times a week in analyses, the mother so far for three years, the son so far for two. After being pressed for three years, the father has now consented to be seen by an analyst (not for analysis) once a week. None of the interviews is taped, but notes are taken during hours with the mother to get certain quotes (e.g., dreams) worded exactly. All hours with the mother are described in detail on tape immediately after the hour. If the patient's words are given here in quotes, it means that I took her words down verbatim as she spoke.

Subject D is a woman in her late fifties, widowed for twenty years. D' is her 28-year-old "daughter," an adult transsexual male who has been "transformed" to appear externally like a normal adult female. D' has been seen intermittently (but not for formal therapy) for nine years. All the interviews are taped.

QUOTATIONS FROM INTERVIEWS WITH THE MOTHERS

Note: These quotations have been edited in the following ways only: (1) clearly identifying data—who these people are—have been removed or made vague; (2) large chunks of talk have been removed en bloc to focus the data onto the described category; (3) quotes that are actually separated in time are at times run together as if spoken in continuity, if they are on the same subject; (4) an occasional word is modified if its grammatical use is so conversational as to be confusing.

The reader will realize that many of the quotes exemplify more than the category they are chosen to represent; e.g., when Mrs. B talks of her son's pleasure in feeling fabrics, she demonstrates how she is so permissive in gratifying him; she knows how while being in close body contact with her, he would handle her beads, developing his beginning sense of esthetic pleasure in jewelry; and she tells of his need for cloth as a transitional object bridging the gap between what is "mother" and "not-mother."

It may only be a coincidence, but all three little boys have unusual (though not bizarre) names of a single syllable, and having a definitely masculine ring; to pronounce each of these names requires a forceful shot of breath. Considering how feminine the boys became, the lean masculinity of their names seems odd.

To introduce the reader quickly to the data, we can begin with an excerpt from the interview of one of the mothers at a conference of members of the Gender Identity Research Clinic.

MRS. B

DR. STOLLER:　Why are you here?

MRS. B:　Because we feel B' has a problem. We feel he doesn't identify in a male way, and my greatest fear is that he may grow up to be a full-blown homosexual because at this point of his development he is very much interested and attracted to all things female, to the point of wearing my shoes when he can, dressing in his sister's clothes. A certain amount of this I'm sure is normal; at least, I always felt this because I know other children, boys particularly, with sisters in the family who go through a period of this. With B' it just seems more intense, and since I started censuring his wearing of his sister's clothes—I didn't want him to wear his sister's clothes—and I told him that that's not suitable and these are her clothes and these are her private things and she doesn't wear your things and you don't wear hers. That isn't a good way to behave. He began taking the clothes and actually hiding them in his room, and that's when I was certain that we had a real large problem, because then he was doing it and being guilty about it because our children don't normally do things that we don't approve of. They're not too secretive; they have their own privacy, but by the same token if I say that we're not going to do it, I never have to go back and check because they just don't find it necessary to sneak something, because there's a lot of latitude in the family, a great deal of permissiveness and they don't seem to need this. But B' really seems to need this now. I found two of his sister's dresses under his pillow. I was straightening out his own wardrobe closet and I found a couple of dresses there, some party shoes of hers. B' was always playing with the girls at nursery school, which isn't easy to do because there are something like sixteen children in this age group and there were three girls at the time and the rest were boys and he always managed to find the girls and vice versa.

He was always in the doll corner and when they played dress-up, he always wore the girls' dresses in school, which a lot of boys do, but he wore it with more intensity always and even when he played with another boy, he always immediately said, "I'm the mother and you're the father," and when he played with the girls when he was playing house at school, even at home he would tell the girls, "You have to be the father. I'm the mother." And this is why we started to come for help.

DR. S: When did it start?

MRS. B: About two and a half, I think, he began showing a great interest in his sister's toys, which were primarily dolls, Barbie dolls, it was a big craze then. Up until then he didn't seem to be particularly concerned with anything. He used to like to watch me put on lipstick and get dressed to go out of an evening, he was always interested, but he started wearing my shoes, you know, getting out my high heels and showing off and prancing around from about that age, maybe a little earlier, I really don't remember. He didn't start walking until eighteen months. So I don't know whether he was adept with the high heels at two or two and a half. He began doing this for fun, nothing else, just the shoes and sometimes trying to get into the jewelry—you know, looking at the beads, trying them on and handling them, and then by the time he got into nursery school, which was at 2 years, 9 months, he found they have lots of wonderful toys there. They have pots and pans and dishes. They have a whole doll-house corner all scaled down for children. He enjoyed that more than the trucks, which surprised me because at home he was a big car collector; he has about sixty model cars, friction cars and various varieties, and he's just crazy about them. And so he just got to about that age, and more and more he began getting interested in the girls' things and even his block play was never building ramps or forts and things that most of the boys—it's a co-op nursery so I can get to see other children play, so I have a good yardstick or a pretty good yardstick. Even when friends come to the house, they play with his boys' toys, and he either plays with them in a different way or else he goes and takes his sister's dolls, or he has some of his own dolls since we bought him some dolls too and he had a choice of a birthday present and that's what he wanted most of all. I just felt that it was better to go along with it than to say absolutely No, because I knew he'd find a way of getting dolls if he really felt he needed them that sincerely.

At the nursery school I watched and the only thing he builds with the blocks are houses for the animals or for flexible people; they have the creative-type playthings, and he acts out lots of situations. He is very drama-oriented. He has marionettes and puppets and even at the beach, if he's walking on the beach with us and he picks up three stones, he immediately starts assigning them roles—"This is the mother stone and this is the father stone and this is the sister stone"—and he goes on with a whole big play. He talks for each one and then they interrelate and that's why we decided this is as good a time as any, if not too late, to do something about it. Because my husband is very distressed by this.

DR. S: How does he express his distress?

MRS. B: He feels I've been too permissive. He feels that if I had stopped it earlier B' wouldn't be this way now; he feels that— last night he said he would not come to talk with you. He decided he would not waste his time and he doesn't believe in it, but that he certainly feels that we do have a problem and he wants me to go for a limited time, he said last night, and he feels that I have just been too permissive and that the fault is mine and the results that we now face are my fault and that I should do something about it.

DR. S: Has he changed his way of relating to the boy?

MRS. B: In the last few weeks [since the evaluation started], yes. He's taken more time to be with B'. Before, he never saw him. Yes, he's seen him at night, sometimes, but my husband gets home very late. He sometimes doesn't get home until pretty near ten thirty. So that means B' never sees him. He would see him in the morning sometimes, but then when B' goes to school, he has to have breakfast by eight-thirty. My husband leaves the house by eight-twenty, so there are many days when he doesn't see him.

DR. GREENSON: What about Sunday? He doesn't work Sunday, does he?

Mrs. B: He doesn't work at the office but he is very creative, so for a year he was working at his hobby every Sunday. He would leave early in the morning, like nine o'clock, and come back for dinner, sometimes six or six-thirty. He would be gone for the entire day. He works at it all day Sunday. And he was doing this for two years before.

I carried B′ a lot. My husband could never lift B′ [because of a physical problem], and it has just been of late that he has been able to carry him on his shoulders if we go anywhere, but normally I've been carrying him. So my husband hasn't been having much of this touching contact which I have had a great deal of. The children don't see an awful lot of him. He's more aware of it now, and he is making a deliberate effort to take time out and spend time with B′. We used to go out every Wednesday night for dinner. We'd eat dinner and then he'd go back to the place where he worked at his hobby and we'd go back home.

Dr. G: Is he against your coming for help with the boy?

Mrs. B: No, he's not against it—he won't come. He doesn't believe it's going to help. You see, we had my daughter for six months for therapy here at UCLA.

Dr. G: Why did she go to therapy?

Mrs. B: She was having temper tantrums. She went back to bed-wetting. She was a terribly unhappy, depressed child and I could find no solution out of the problem.

Dr. G: How long ago was this?

Mrs. B: Two and a half years ago. Dr. X has the records and I used to go once a month and my husband used to go once every month or six weeks, whenever Dr. X felt he had to see him, and this was when B′ was a baby. His sister didn't welcome B′. She was very happy as an only child, and then B′ took a lot more of my time up than she had anticipated, far more than she did because he wasn't a healthy youngster. He had problems, not that he was unhealthy. He came home from the hospital with a staph infection and when I got home—then my daughter had a virus X which is not good for a newborn baby because it can be extremely dangerous, so I had two sick children and the baby nurse was not too capable and she only lasted a week because I was late and the next woman was early or some such thing, so he was sick with a staph which caused extreme gaseousness and great stomach distress, large cramping, and he screamed constantly day and night. He wasn't a good sleeper; he had colic; he had difficulty adjusting to the formula; he was rashy; it was quite a frantic household and at two weeks of age he was cast because he had a tibial torsion so he had a cast from his toes to his hips, and I was busy with him, walking night and day. I think I had less sleep than any time in my life. I was walking him nightly. . . .

I. ARE THESE BOYS LIKE OTHER BOYS WHO CROSS-DRESS?

Because it has been so often observed that many children will occasionally try on garments of the opposite sex, statements that these boys' needs to do so are fierce and express a far more powerful process of cross-gender identification have sometimes been received skeptically. It is therefore best that the reader himself judge the data rather than his joining the argument on whichever side his biases propel him.

MRS. A

MRS. A: . . . and he asked me if he could be a girl when he married. He even asked if he could cut off his penis. And I say, "No, you couldn't do that. You would die." And he asked me if I was sure he would die and I said, "Yes, I am sure you would," and he really seriously was considering it, I guess, in his little mind. He just didn't want to have any part of it [his penis]. And that kind of worried me because I didn't know if he really might go ahead and do something, you know. He definitely wants to be a little girl, because at times I'll say to him, when he is playing with a doll or wanting to wear a dress, "Well, you're not a little girl," and he will say, "Yes, I am."

When he was wearing this dress he did not want to have Levi's on; he just wanted to wear the dress and he would make quite a complaint if I made him wear his Levi's underneath it. He hadn't dressed up in anything for quite a while; in fact, he was to a point where he would put a dish towel around him, tuck in his pants and make a skirt out of it. He had quit doing that for quite a while when last week he took a dress off a doll that he had and started wearing that—it was quite a big doll—and that night I put it away in a drawer underneath some stuff to throw it out and he didn't miss it, but when it is there you know he would wear it. For the last three days he has been carrying a doll around and combing her hair and went off to play this morning before he went to school and when the woman came to pick him up for school, he shot in the house without his doll; he had to take it with him. So I was kind of hoping that we had gotten past that. As I say, he had thrown two of his dolls away— I don't know why—he just threw them away, and I asked if he didn't want them, and he said, "No." So I was pleased and elated— and then he is right back at it again.

He likes to wear jewelry if he can. This started when he was about one and a half or two years old. I think I was most aware of it, I think, when a little girl in our neighborhood—they had played dress-ups in the neighborhood where we used to live—and one of the little girls there—they dressed him up like a little girl. They thought this was fun. It must have been between a year and one half and two. And he liked the dress so much that the little girl let him have it. This was when it seemed to start, when he wanted to wear this dress all the time. He doesn't seem to be interested in regular little dolls that have the rubber head and no hair, the little baby dolls; he is not too interested in that. He is interested in dolls with hair. He got a doll for Christmas from my mother, and it has hair and he carried around a little hairbrush all the time—every place he went out to play; he took it to bed with him and everything. And then about two weeks ago he threw it away. Just threw it in the trash can and that was it. He would like to have another one. He keeps asking for a doll and I told him "No," that we weren't going to buy him any more dolls.

He was taken out of class where they have the dress-up and put into one where they don't have it. They have a big box of clothing, and the children can pick out what they want to wear and then they assume this role for the time they are in class. He didn't like to go to school anymore, because he is not in the class where they can put on dresses.

Combing my hair was an everyday thing. He had to get the brush and comb my hair. He does like to—and every time I put makeup on he wants to put it on me. Now since coming to the NPI I won't allow him because he makes a terrible mess [*chuckle*]. Boy, what a mess. He would like to do that!

His older brother plays very boyish games, cars and cowboys and this kind of thing, but A' played mostly with little girls in the neighborhood because they had dolls and dress-ups and things like that. He seems to like the little Barbie dolls, and so on—the smaller ones with the hair, because he likes to comb and fix their hairdos. He carries a brush and comb around with him constantly if he has a doll. He is very interested in fixing women's hair. My sisters come over or my mother and right away he wants to fix their hair. They say he is very imaginative at school. They say that his pattern of play is much advanced to the other four-and-a-half-year-olds, that their pattern is rather helter-skelter when they play house or when they play any kind of games. They say he plans everything out and does it with a pattern. They say that he is very dramatic and that he lives . . . actually he gets into a role and plays it . . . he gets a little upset with the other children that they can't be as fixed along the lines as he is.

He is extremely observant about changes. If I have a different arrangement of flowers in the house, he notices immediately upon coming in. This has gone on for quite a while. He has always been very observant. Or if I have a different dress on or set the table differently, he notices every little change and then he makes comments about it. I don't think he is as observant with his father. He is pretty observant about what people wear. He can tell me after they leave sometimes what people have had on and makes comments about it.

For a while he walked around all day with an apron on and he wouldn't wear Levi's, just the apron. He would go outside and play like this, and he would come all apart if he couldn't wear the apron. But we put it away and my mother had taken it down to her house—and he had forgotten all about it, and she had it on when we went to her house for dinner and right away he said, "Hey! that's mine; how come you've got it down here?" Mother said she needed to have it and he didn't make any issue out of it, which I was very surprised about. . . .

At another time, Mrs. A describes the situation as follows: Where we used to live, these little children were playing dress-up. They dressed him [age 2 to 2½] in a little green plaid dress which hit him way down around the sidewalk. He just fell in love with this dress. So the little girl—when they went to take it off him, he put up such a stink that the little girl asked her mother, and she said Yes. So he brought it home and wanted to wear it all the time. We didn't let him wear it all the time, needless to say, but occasionally we would let him wear it around to play in. Then I took the dress away. He asked about it quite often and I told him I didn't know where it was. Then he got into my apron drawer and got out one of my aprons as a dress. This went on for quite a while. Then I refused to let him have the apron. Then he would get a blanket or anything he could get to wrap around to make a dress out of it. When he did this, he didn't want to wear his Levi's or his little slacks. He wanted to have his underwear and then the little dress. . . . In the last three months, he has gotten this towel thing with a hood in one corner. He puts it over his head and that's his hair, this long flowing thing behind him. He is very interested in hair. He likes to comb my hair. He likes to comb my mother's hair and any women that will stand for it—comb their hair. He is very observant. Yesterday I went to the beauty shop and got my hair fixed in a different style and right away he said that it looked very pretty and could he comb it. I said no, he couldn't. He notices things in other people's houses that are new: if I go into my mother's house and she has a new flower arrangement, he will notice this right away, much before I do.

He isn't as interested in men as he is in making friends with women. If there were a choice in a room whether to go sit with a man or a woman, he would pick the woman to sit with, talk to.

He likes to touch their hair. He has combed mine for as long as one half hour and then stops spontaneously. The interest in hair started around the time the dress fixation started. He combs dolls' hair until they are bald. He will keep *that* up all day. He will spend most of his day playing with this doll and fixing her hair, combing it, washing it, putting bobby pins in it.

When he first started preschool they had dress-ups. The children were allowed to go into this big box and pick anything they wanted to and wear it the entire morning at school. A' had a little fuchsia outfit he had picked out—a little skirt and bolero. Immediately when he came into school in the morning this is what he would put on. He was quite contented playing this role. Then they put him in a class where they no longer allowed him to dress up, though they had shoes, men's shoes and high heels. The teachers called me in to talk to me because they noticed this tendency toward wanting to dress up as a girl. When they moved him into this new class, he was full of anxiety. They wondered if that was because he wasn't allowed to dress up anymore in this little outfit he had worn for so long. He did then start to wear women's high heels in this other class. One of the little girls was the mother of the house; they have a stove, a refrigerator and a little house in this one room at school. A' came clomping in in these high heels, and the little girl said he was a boy and he wasn't supposed to wear the high heels and if he didn't take them off, he couldn't come into her house. So he went out, didn't argue, and got the high heels off and put a pair of men's shoes on. They said it lasted for around fifteen minutes and he went and took the men's shoes off and put the high heels on and stayed out of the house. [Note that there *are* little girls who do not like little boys to be dressed up as little girls.—R.J.S.]

They said they noticed the difference in his painting, and his ability to get along with the other children was very strained after this change from the one class into the other. They felt it was due to the fact that he could no longer play the role of the little girl.

At the beginning it was funny. It didn't bother me. I didn't think it was a problem. It began to bother me in the first year that he was doing it. I could not understand why a little boy would be interested in dressing up like a little girl and wanting to be a little girl. He actually talked about, wanted to be a little girl. If he doesn't get his way the first time he asks, he will hound you for an hour. [Because she doesn't say No unequivocally.—R.J.S.] It's very hard to stick to your guns.

MRS. B

DR. S: How did it begin?

MRS. B: I didn't really notice it until he was almost three. Until that time he was a dependent child but his sister was also. So I didn't feel this was unusual. . . . He began playing quite seriously with Barbie—with all the girls' dolls, and he became quite enamored of this whole business. Then I discovered he wasn't playing much with boys in nursery school. There were sixteen children, three girls and the rest were boys and he played more with the three—and it's very hard to find, to get in with three girls [he was 3½ at this time]. He was always in the doll corner. He liked to be the mommy in the situation. He likes to imitate me a great deal. At home he was putting on my high heels and running around the house—not my clothes, just my high heels. A lot of boys enjoy playing with Mommy's high heels. At nursery school we did not discourage the boys in the doll corner playing with the dolls, because they also have to express some feeling of mothers, I guess. They are just tender kids and they like playing with the babies.

B' started this around 2 years, 9 months or three. He was shyer than most boys are. He was less physically coordinated than most boys; that is, he didn't gravitate to the swings or the rough play of the sandbox or the slides. He tended to be more interested in the park, in the rhythms, and the music. Not that he participated in this. Other kids would get up and dance or go in a circle and do ring-around-the-rosy. He sat on my lap and wouldn't leave me, but was very aware and very excited by it and wanted to go but he didn't want to participate. He didn't like to be forced into participation—and he is extremely athletic and very creative and has a more lively imagination than—a more creative world than most boys seem to have, just watching him play with his friends, who are certainly equally as bright.

Dr. S: Before two and a half or three years old did he have any interest in your clothes or your makeup or your hair?

Mrs. B: Yes. Very much. He always wanted lipstick from two, two and a half, every time I put on lipstick. He would cry whenever I wouldn't let him use it.

Dr. S: Has he ever wanted to put on your clothes?

Mrs. B: Yes, he has wanted very much to wear my clothes. Stockings, shoes, jewelry—my clothes are too large for him, naturally, but——.

Dr. S: Would that be his preference or would his sister's be his preference or doesn't it make that much difference?

Mrs. B: I think he prefers to put on hers because they fit him better. In mine, he falls flat on his face.

Dr. S: He doesn't look real enough, is that what it is?

Mrs. B: It isn't comfortable. Also, he can't reach them as easily, my hangers are up high and hers are on the same level as his own in his wardrobe so he can reach in and take anything out. He knows her wardrobe very well, so he can just walk in and take out her clothes and he plays a lot in her room with her. I have come home and found that he was completely dressed in her clothes, with makeup, a headband, her party shoes and socks, her purse, and having a marvelous time. And she got a big kick out of it too. She thought it was kind of funny and cute because she really wanted a sister to be in with her. She's very happy to play because he plays very well, and she can be Barbie and he can be Midge and he'll talk for the one girl and she'll talk for the other and they'll go through a whole life situation. They won't really spend so much time in the dressing and undressing; it's mostly getting set up for a production, a play, and then they act out a whole situation. I should tape some of this for you. It's unbelievable.

Dr. S: At five years?

Mrs. B: He'll be a dandy script writer some day. He has a lively imagination. He likes long hair. He wants a wig for Halloween. He wants to be Alice in Wonderland. "Wouldn't that be funny?" he says. He just lives for Holloween; it's a big deal. And he would like to be a girl for Halloween. "Wouldn't that be fun, with makeup?" and the whole bit. And he says, "Boys wear lipstick on TV." He shows me commercials and he says, "He's wearing some lipstick." "That's not lipstick, that's vaseline, that's something they use for the camera. The camera has to reflect better"—because I can't honestly tell him it's nothing because he's smart enough to see when there's something applied. And he likes the theater much better than the movies because he likes to see the actors and get the autographs, and he loves the girls but I wouldn't even say this is unusual because so many of the characters of children's fiction are females, the heroines; even Peter Pan—he was so surprised—was a female when he saw it acted twice, saw the play. He loves Alice in Wonderland and Snow White and Sleeping Beauty and Cinderella. He does have a "Cinderfella" album, which is Jerry Lewis playing the male Cinderella, a young man who marries a princess.

DR. S: He would—when you were away—dress up?

MRS. B: Yes, if he knew that I was not going to be home, he would dress up or he would go into his sister's room, take out the Barbie dolls and a whole box of clothes and probably enjoy playing with that more than anything else. He would either dress up or dress the dolls. I don't know, in the past few weeks I have been stressing, that's not to do for a boy, there are so many other things that are fun for a boy, you're going to outgrow this soon. Like he has a long list he wants for his birthday. Most of all on our whole trip on our summer vacation he wanted an Alice in Wonderland doll. Of all the goodies you can buy in X, which is a veritable treasure trove of toys from around the world, very inexpensively, it's a duty-free port, he ended up with a clock which has dancing figures on it, but he didn't pick the dancing ballerinas; they were dancing adults, male and female, but that's what he wanted. And he likes flexible figures, but the one that he chose, he's mad for mermaids, a flexible mermaid with the exposed bosoms, and I didn't see any reason for not getting these for him because he wanted them so desperately and I figured that maybe

this too shall come to pass [*sic*]. I didn't know how to handle it—
I offered him many other things; they have wonderful soldiers, you
know the English toys, but he likes what his sister likes. He had
one choice of something to buy at Y as a souvenir; he picked a
Dutch doll; his sister has a Spanish doll.

DR. S: How efficient is he in high heels?

MRS. B: He maneuvers just fine. He walks very well.

DR. S: You know you put a teen-age girl in high heels for
the first time and she's very awkward.

MRS. B: No, he's quite adept. He would be a very good stilt-
walker. He started playing with my high heels when he was about
two and a half, I think, when he discovered there was such a thing.
He noticed that I had different shoes and he liked pointy shoes.
When he buys shoes, I have much trouble selecting shoes for him
that are orthopedically correct, because he really prefers the points
and his whole objection now is, "Why can't I have them? They're
for boys. Look at the Beatles." And sure enough, they are wearing
the Spanish toe and he likes the pointed look.

DR. S: Does he want to be a girl?

MRS. B: Yes, he says so. Yes, he said—probably at the birthday party when his sister got all these wonderful girls' things—
that he didn't get and I said he couldn't have, that I wouldn't
duplicate for his birthday—he said, "I'd like to die and I'd like to
be born back a girl. I don't want to live this way; I want to be a
girl. It's not fair."

MRS. C

*The following quotations are taken from notes dictated
immediately after each hour of this patient's analysis. The
first quotation, which follows immediately, was dictated after the
conference of the research team at which this family was seen
by us for the first time:*

". . . We [the research team] also saw the child for some
time. He is a very alert and intelligent boy, smiling all the time,
apparently completely at ease with all of us, talking away at a

great rate, answering any questions and taking anybody on who spoke to him. His hair was long; he is almost a beautiful child, a little round-faced, and to me he did not seem rugged or very masculine. On the other hand, he did not seem effeminate either. I could not have guessed he was a transvestite.* However he is. Both parents say they don't know why he is, but that since he could walk he would walk up and down the steps on high heels, and what should have been a very precarious maneuver the child did without any trouble at all. He has always been encouraged in dressing like a girl, using his sister's or his mother's clothes, and the whole family thought it was 'cute.' It was only recently when a woman [a stranger] in a market expressed dismay openly, that Mrs. C felt there was anything unusual. And following this she looked for help."

"She [Mrs. C] then went on, in response to a question of mine as to when his awareness of her clothes began, to describe how as an infant, by which she means a toddler (I couldn't get from her a specific age and whether she means when he was just able to sit up or when he was able to struggle around weakly on his feet I could not determine; it was somewhere between 8 months and a year), he and she would sit on the floor leafing through magazines, and whenever there would be an illustration of something relating to cooking that was pleasant, such as cookies, he would stop her from turning over the page and make happy, cooing exclamations. He would do exactly the same when there was a picture of a well-dressed, beautiful woman. I asked if there was a time when he was not interested in women's clothes, and she said there never was a time, scarcely."

"She wondered how she could have felt that there was nothing wrong. She said that even now, except intellectually, she doesn't feel that this is a problem. And she said, 'I wonder what he would look like as a grown-up man [dressed as a woman].' But this was said without any strong feeling, and I asked her to try to imagine what he would look like as a grown-up man. She was

*At this time, like most psychiatrists, I called everyone who insistently cross-dressed a "transvestite."

somewhat evasive, and I said, 'No, I mean that you literally picture his appearance.' She said, at first, it would be strange to see a man dressed as a woman and then she said, 'No, it wouldn't be for C'. He would be beautiful.' She then went on to describe how her feeling about him is that he looks like a girl and always had, though she feels he looks less so now than he used to. She said, 'He looks more like a girl than anything else in the face, and with his long hair he looks more like a girl than many little girls that I know. He was such a pretty boy. When I would take him shopping the women would call him a beautiful boy, and I would feel so embarrassed because my daughter was with me, and people were saying that he was more beautiful than she was. So many women commented on this that I finally stopped taking him to the store.' This was interrupted by a pause, and then she said, 'Oh, what am I talking about! Let's change the subject.'

"Then she went on and said that the acceptance of C's transvestism was 'a conspiracy.' This is very interesting to me because I have recently, in writing up this material, been using the word 'conspiracy,' but I have not ever used it in talking with her. What she means by conspiracy is not simply her own and her husband's silence but the conspiracy of a lot of other people—and she has proved her point to me. She told me how when he was in nursery school the school accepted this behavior and did nothing to stop it. Later, when he went to grammar school, they knew about it and said nothing to her about stopping it.

"She says this whole business is like the Emperor's new clothes; all the adults kept seeing the transvestism as being nothing remarkable, but it was the children, she says, who asked questions of her and of him—the children who thought that this was so unusual. She was affected by hearing one child ask him, 'Are you a boy or a girl?' but despite these hints, she did nothing until she was hit by the woman in the market place who questioned her dressing him up. She also kept from taking it too seriously because she had noticed that there are lots of little boys who are effeminate or who have some slight tendency at least to dressing up, but she realizes that although C' is similar in this respect, the degree to which he has gone is much more pronounced. She realizes the difference between him and these other boys is that they usually are furtive and embarrassed about it and he has never been the least bit ashamed of this dressing up."

MRS. D

DR. S: Was she at all feminine?

MRS. D: Always. Ever since she was a baby. In fact, we didn't cut her long curls off until she was two years old; we kept her in feminine coveralls. It was so becoming to her when she was small. During Halloween and every chance she would get, she would dress as a girl. Everyone said how beautiful she was as a girl. We never said anything about it. . . .

When I saw her as a girl at age sixteen for the first time, I took her in my arms. She said she would rather die than be anything but a girl. She told me of her years of suffering and at one time my son tried to tear off her T shirt and show me what was happening. I was very disgusted with him and told him I never wanted to see anything like that happen again. . . .

Children noticed that D' had breasts, and his mother did too, but—"I didn't think anything about it—she will outgrow that."

DR. S: How did you feel when you saw her changed?

MRS. D: How does a mother feel when her child says, "I would rather die than change back to a boy"? I wanted her to be happy, to be what she wants to be. I have never fought it. . . .

D' had long, curly hair until she was two. We dressed her in little clothes that might—they were blue denims but they were piped in white and looked little-girlish. She resented people telling her she looked like a girl. Everybody took her for a girl; the barber said, "Little girl, how do you want your hair cut?" She said, "I am a boy. I want a barber man haircut." She always acted feminine even at two. She liked to work around the kitchen, to learn how to sew. She liked to do things a girl did, right straight through. In kindergarten, D' told the teacher she wanted nothing but that she wanted to be a girl. She told a lot of people more than anything else she wanted to be a girl. At two she was very dainty, dressed up a lot in girls' clothes. My son [not D'] knew of this a long time before I knew about it [years]. . . .

When D′ was born, I thought the baby a beautiful, beautiful child. Everyone thought she was a girl. She had long blonde hair and blue eyes. . . .

II. BISEXUALITY

It is not easy to describe in a few words what I mean when calling these women "bisexual," but what they say will help clarify this. In addition, one can try to picture these women while reading their words. Each is dressed naturally and unobtrusively, not in a flowery or unusual manner or with splashy colors. Mrs. A wears simple dresses each visit; Mrs. B, slacks or skirt and a shirt-blouse each visit; Mrs. C, suits or a shirt-blouse and skirt each visit (four times a week for three years); Mrs. D, simple, tasteful dresses each visit. All wear stockings and unobtrusively styled, one-color high-heeled shoes. Each has her hair cut short but not severely, except Mrs. B, whose hair is pulled back on her head so tightly in a bun that it looks like a man's haircut unless one sees it from the side or back. None wears makeup except for a little lipstick. None moves or otherwise behaves seductively or as if she feels herself to be sexually interesting or beautiful.

(These descriptions might indicate less about gender identity if these were teen-agers or women following the latest styles that stress boyishness in women. However, none of these subjects looks like a teen-ager or woman of haute couture. In other words, while these women have a feminine quality, inextricably woven in is this other, difficult to describe but easy to observe use of certain boyish or "neuter" external features.)

In each case, following a period of femininity in childhood, the woman has been sorely disappointed so that her formerly loving relationship with her father is broken off in childhood and replaced by a degree of masculinity beyond what would usually be called tomboyishness: These girls dressed in boys' clothes (not just boyish clothes) in childhood and would have preferred not to do otherwise. Their friends were boys, with whom they played boys' games exclusively and as equals. Their fantasies were of being boys, but while they wished they could grow up to be men, they did not believe they would. In a manner different from transsexual girls, when the changes of puberty manifested themselves, these women gave up their masculine interests, looked and acted like girls, simulated a heterosexual life, married, and had children. Nonetheless, they have carried throughout life a profound sense of emptiness that covers over their forgotten, earliest, rather feminine years.

MRS. A

Mrs. A: I had something particular that I wanted to discuss today—the fact that I wonder how this parallels in girls as it does with boys, my little fellow having a tendency to wanting to be a girl. When I was a youngster, I wanted to be a boy my whole life. Now this was every morning that I woke up hoping that I had changed to a boy. And I dressed in boys' clothes. My mother and dad bought me plaid shirts and Levi's and the whole bit and guns and balls and everything. And I guess——I don't know whether my folks worried about it or not. I have talked to my mother about it, and she says she just didn't have good sense enough to think about it, you know. She said it did bother her because she bought frilly little dresses and I wouldn't wear them, and so on. Then when I got to be about twelve or thirteen, that was it. The whole thing just disappeared and I made a complete changeover. There was no outside thing that I can think of that made me change, other than I was becoming interested in boys at this age. But up until that time I played with boys, and very rarely played with girls, and I just wonder if this works the same way with boys having this tendency, or whether it's a different thing altogether or what.

I wanted to be a little boy. My mother and father were, I guess concerned about it, but they didn't do anything about it. My mother said she didn't think I would grow up and wear a dress. I actually wore boys' clothing. We went to the boys' department and I wore pants with fly, plaid shirt, the whole bit. To school, of course, I wore dresses. In winter, because it was very cold, I would wear corduroy boys' pants. At play time after school I was always in boys' pants, plaid shirts. I outgrew it around twelve or thirteen. This was the end of it. I wasn't interested after that. I liked boys' clothing. I liked to play rough and be rough. My mother bought me frilly hats and purses. The only time I wore them was when I went to Sunday school.

One of the girls I chummed with in high school is a homosexual. She says she had those feelings as a child. She dressed up in boys' clothes. I dressed up in boys' clothes as a child.

I was interested in boys' clothes. As a child back East in the winter the girls were allowed to wear slacks. In the third grade I took an interest in wearing boys' clothes. In the fourth grade my mother took me to shop. I wanted clothes out of the boys' department, corduroy pants. My mother has always bought them for me. I always liked boys' things. So all my play time I spent in boys' attire. I used to think they would never see me in dresses. But I did. I am not interested in boys' things any more. It stopped in high school—a slow thing.

DR. S: Was this related to developing your breasts and female figure?

MRS. A: I don't know. I was happy with the change and excited with my first bra. I was the last girl in my age group to get my period. Now I think I could have waited a few years—but then it was a big status thing.

I never played with girls. I was quite a fighter. Not many people would hit me, not even boys. I ran everything—had my own football team and baseball team. This was a team of boys, not girls. And if they didn't like it, they didn't get to play. I remember playing tackle football until I was around twelve. Baseball and softball I played right up to high school, but I guess I changed then to playing with girls on girls' softball teams. I swam in competition. I did a lot of diving.

The area I was raised in was real great for kids—wide-open spaces. The whole town was surrounded by wooded areas with creeks, and so I spent a lot of time hiking through the woods and fishing and baseball. I played baseball primarily with boys until I was twelve or thirteen and then I went into playing with school groups that were all girls. As a child most of my friends were boys. I rarely played with girls. I didn't enjoy playing girls' games.

If the girls had gotten out and played boys' games they would have been all right. I couldn't see sitting in the house and taking a dress off a doll and putting a dress on her and taking that one off and putting that on—I didn't want to be indoors. I think girls have a tendency to be more selfish than boys. They don't seem to be able to play with more than one person at a time. When a third individual comes in, there is always dissension. Whereas boys can stay as large groups. They don't stay angry. They don't hold grudges like girls do. As I got into junior high and high school I formed relationships with girls. I could get along equally well with a group of boys as girls. I felt I could do anything a boy could as well as if not better. I would attempt anything boys would do. It was a bigger challenge. I felt as if I could do things as well as any boy could. When I was playing I assumed the role of a boy. I always was playing as if I were a boy.

In regard to boys' penises, I was very put out God didn't give me one of those. This started when I was four or five. I kidded myself and probably thought that maybe I would have one eventually. I can remember at night when I would say my prayers that I would wake up a boy the next morning, that was until I was nine or ten. But then when I got older I enjoyed kissing, and so on. My attitude towards boys at that time was the attitude of the other girls. I enjoyed dating and necking with the boys. . . .

MRS. B

The following are quotations from notes dictated by Mrs. B's therapist; none of this material came out in the evaluation interviews, for I did not know enough about such data to ask for it specifically when it did not come up spontaneously:

"Mrs. B on a number of occasions has described in some detail the tomboy activities she engaged in as a child. She reports for example that she was always a tomboy; she was always aggressive, not only as a child but as an adolescent and as an adult, frequently finding herself in the male role in school and work. She stresses she did not just take masculine jobs; she took men's jobs.

"She played baseball, stickball, hockey, handball, and was always an enthusiastic competitor in all sports. She was the pitcher on the girl's high-school softball team. She always wanted to be a winner, had to be. As a child at the age of eight, she remembers playing Tarzan and Jane, and she was always Tarzan and some other girl was Jane. When thirteen, she played with her father at the 'father and son' baseball game, largely at her father's request. Her father taught her many masculine sports. He taught her to roller skate, jump rope, and play ball. Even now she feels herself competing in a masculine way. Only recently has she given up wearing man-tailored shirts and man-tailored slacks, and this is primarily for B''s sake. Looking at the chronology, it seems to me that the upsurge in masculine behavior occurred following the birth of her sister when Mrs. B was seven years old. She feels she has never outgrown being a tomboy.

"She described a photograph of herself with a Buster Brown haircut, her father's tie and hat, and a pair of shorts. Her father was putting her in a wagon—age 6 or 7. She says, 'I looked like a boy.' "

MRS. C

NOTES: "I asked her [Mrs. C], 'Have you ever wanted to be a boy?' She said, 'Well, I was a tomboy. I was very good at sports and I was highly competitive. I was as good as some of the boys—let's face it.' She said, 'At that age [10 to 12] there isn't much difference between you [meaning herself] and a boy. I competed scholastically against the boys, even though in our school the boys were in a separate building from the girls, but I couldn't compete with my brother. He was much better than I was.' "

"She has a fear of her daughter touching her at times. When her daughter comes over and puts her arms around the patient, the patient has to consciously control herself. She says she has no idea why this is, but at this point she's feeling rather uneasy."

"She used to dress up often in those days to take parts in the

various plays, and she would be equally dressed as a male or female. 'I tell myself that these things aren't either masculine or
feminine, but I don't know why I have to tell myself that.' The
implication is that she's trying to convince another part of herself that there is nothing unusual about playing both masculine
and feminine roles in plays. In regard to this dressing up and
changing of clothes, she says, 'When you took off your clothes
and put on other clothes, then you can be anything and anyone.' "

"The patient was again talking on sexual matters. She said
that all penises disgust her, including her husband's, except for C′,
and she considers his penis beautiful. When I asked her how come,
she said because she was not afraid of it, and because it was in a
way hers. She elaborated the latter by indicating he was her son
and therefore from her own body and her own flesh, so that in
effect (though she did not say this) it was a penis that she had
produced from her own body. But this is the only exception. All
the rest of the penises are disgusting. This led to her talking about
her lack of sexual intercourse with her husband."

"A dream reported by the patient, which took place the night
before she had an appointment to see C′'s teacher to see how he
had been progressing: In this dream, she was being chased by a
very evil man who is going to do something to her—possibly kill
her, but he will do it only by talking. She was not sure that the
man might not also be herself. Then off in the distance she saw
three Boy Scouts, youths of about seventeen whom she called
to help her. But the evil man, in order to demonstrate his power,
converted them into something evil also. All this took place on a
gentle slope. As she said it, it hit her for the first time that the
man who could kill by talk might be myself. I then pointed out
to her that the gentle slope was probably the slope of my couch.
She said that when she awakened from this dream the thought
hit her for the first time that she really doesn't know who she is,
and that she is not certain whether she is a man or a woman. She
said she had never thought of such a thing before, and since this
dream occurred, over a week ago, she has not been able to make

anything of this thought, but felt that it was very important. She said, 'I feel it in my body; I just know that it's right but I don't know why.' The patient tied up the idea of C''s transvestism with her own problem of not knowing whether she is a male or female, and then she expressed puzzlement that while C' has this problem in gender identity, her daughter apparently has none whatsoever.

"This talking about C''s transvestism brought us to talk about her feelings about it prior to the time she came in for help. I have never understood what her feeling was about his transvestism, that she could ignore its significance. And she now told me more about these feelings. She says that she had never thought there was anything unusual about it, but had presumed that all children were this way, that they liked to dress up. Later in the hour I learned further what 'dressing up' means: It doesn't only mean dressing up in clothes of the opposite sex, but various kinds of play-acting with children. So when C' was expressing his interest in 'dressing,' neither she nor her husband felt there was anything unusual in it, but it was simply an indication of many qualities that the child had. He is very sensitive and perceptive, loves music and loves drama, and so the patient thought this was just evidence of his creativity; and he also liked to dress like a girl. She says, 'I thought everyone was that way, I was that way, my brother was that way.'

"Following another pause, she said that she has never been like so many women, and like many of her friends, who feel uneasy because their breasts are not large enough. She says she has never, despite her small breasts, had any desire to wear falsies, and for that matter is rather pleased that her breasts are small. This led to her recalling that last night she had been looking through an old photo album and saw a photo of herself when she was twelve and that she was 'straight as a stick,' so different from her daughter at the same age. She remembers with some pleasure a remark by a woman who had looked at this photograph and said, 'I wouldn't have known that it was not your brother' (this being because the patient's hair had been drawn straight back so that she didn't even seem to have a woman's hair).

"She now recalls, and says with some mild surprise, how interesting it is that you forget things and yet you've never forgotten them, that she really did take great pleasure in being like a boy as a child. She also now recalls for the first time that she had been wrong in answer to a question that I had asked some months ago about whether she ever liked to dress up as a boy. She now recalls that she did very much like to and would invariably—when there was any masquerade, like Halloween or Thanksgiving—dress as a boy and was always complimented and took pride in the compliment that she could have passed for a boy.

"This led immediately at the end of the hour to her remembering a dream from last night. The dream in its entirety is: 'I was radioactive.' She says she was dreaming this when C′ came in as he always does and woke her. As she was awakened, still under the influence of the dream, she felt he shouldn't touch her to waken her because he might be affected by her.

"She had a dream which she reported. This was the first dream she has ever had in which C′ appeared so far as she can remember. He had taken off his shoes in the dream, as he likes to do in reality, and had stepped on something and was crying, so she said to him, 'Let me take it out,' and he said, 'No, you'll hurt it,' and she said, 'O.K.,' and went away and returned a little bit later. At that point he was kneeling so that the backs, the soles, of his feet were showing and she could see a huge black hole in his foot. She went over to it and squeezed it and a great big thing came out and left a hole behind it. This thing had the head of a snake which reminds her of the snake in a caduceus. She thought that it could have poisoned him and that she would have to tell the doctor. He wasn't even aware that she had gotten it out. When she awoke, she thought, I mustn't forget this. I have to tell the doctor—meaning myself, but in the dream the doctor was not overtly me. I asked her about the black hole, and it led her to talking about his dressing up and his fear that he might get some illness from her. I reminded her of a dream she had a long time ago of contaminating him in some magical way. She equated then the big black hole with some kind of illness that he might get with femininity, so I said to her, 'Well, what's the big black hole?' and she knew then

that this was the female genital, and she said, 'Is that what I want
to have happen to him?' "

"She is not concerned with the kind of stockings that she buys
and she has no idea whether her legs are similar to or different from
other women's."

MRS. D

MRS. D: I feel that a human being should do what they want
to do, be what they want to be. I had the same desire when I was
a child. I wanted to be a boy. That may seem very unusual to
you, but I did. I did everything a boy would do—played football,
was the best football player, could clean up any boy in the neighborhood, could climb the highest tree, jump off the bridge into
the river. I might have ruined myself doing these things, but I
felt—I was the only girl in the neighborhood that would wear a
pair of pants. My mother was furious with me all the time. She
had a bad time with me. I gave her a very bad time because I was
a healthy, husky girl, and I loved sports so much. I was always
at the ballfield with the boys, and even made my girl friend cry a
lot because I would not give her much attention because I was
always playing with the boys. I could always hold my own with
the boys until I got to be about fifteen. Then I started working
and changed right along—growing up. My periods didn't start until I was sixteen. Same with my mother and sister. When I started
to develop, by the time I was eighteen, I was a very well-developed
girl. It was a little disappointing to me, because—you know—I
rode bicycles and everything, but the feeling I had came mostly
from the boys, because I no longer wanted to play ball or anything. I can still remember when I was about sixteen, a boy
wrapped a rope all the way around me, getting it around my
breasts. It was real tight, and he said, "Now I am going to squeeze
the milk out of you," and that embarrassed me so much I never
played with the boys after that—never—until I started going with
them to dances. When he said that, I had had it. Seemed I was
growing up then.

Every boy I knew, I could lick him. I was the leader of my gang. I don't give a hoot for sports today. I got them all out of my system when I was young. It practically ruined my life because I didn't want a boy near me. I couldn't adjust right away to boys, because I had felt I was one and wished I had been one for so many years. I had a hard time adjusting myself to my husband.

We dressed in boys' clothes and girls dressed in boys' clothes and boys dressed in girls' clothes. It's not an uncommon thing. All children go through that. When I was little, we would put on shows for pins, needles, and buttons, around five or six. I wanted to be a boy more than anything when I was small, and I think that when D' wanted to be a girl, I just thought it would be something she would outgrow, just like I did. Of course, I could never have been a boy. I thought: If I could be a man someday and help my mother because she struggled so to support us. Being a girl, I couldn't give her the help she needed. . . .

III. BODY CONTACT AND EXCESSIVE MOTHER-IN-FANT SYMBIOSIS

This factor is being separated in this discussion from the next one—the mothers' excessive permissiveness—for, while it is a prime example of that permissiveness, this skin-to-skin contact and envelopment of the little boy by his mother from birth on for many hours a day has, I feel, its own highly specific effects: The child is kept in a physically extremely gratifying environment—his mother's loving body (not all mothers' bodies love)—which quells whatever urge he would otherwise have gradually to separate himself successfully from her. As a result, he does not develop an early enough or adequate sense of being a separate and different creature from her, and so at the earliest stage in the development of gender identity—the development of the core gender identity—the categorizing of oneself as male or female—is terribly flawed. He thinks of himself as part of his mother, a female.

All these mothers hold their infants against their bodies for many hours a day, frequently skin to skin. Not only is this excessive in amount every day, but probably, of more pathological importance, the gradual separation that begins in most mother-infant symbioses before the end of the first year does not occur, and so this mother-infant body contact persists for years. These mothers are nude with their sons, permit them as equals with themselves into what is privacy from which the mothers would exclude anyone else; for instance, when they are in the toilet, bathing, or dressing.

At first the mothers create contact; then, as the child becomes more mobile and coordinated, they encourage it; when the child's size and ego strength make this wearing, they patiently permit and finally endure it, never bringing it to an end themselves.

It should be understood that from the beginning, while this body contact helped shape the identity of these boys in a way that the world must judge is pathological, there is no evidence that the process is felt as a trauma by the child, but is instead a most happy and excessively gratifying experience. (The later traumatic intrafamilial processes are not the focus of this research, and so the evidence of them need not be stressed.)

MRS. A

MRS. A: If he is in the house, he is always on me. If I am sitting down, I've had it.

DR. S: How old was he the first time he saw any female body, including your own?

MRS. A.: Well, he's . . . I'm not very modest in front of the kids. I don't know whether this is good or not but I don't cover up when they come in, and so this has been part of his life. He has always been wandering in and out when I am taking a shower or getting dressed or something, so this has been since—whenever he first noticed it, whatever age that would be.

MRS. B

DR. S: I want to talk to you. Is it possible for B' to wait outside, or is he too active and peppy?

MRS. B: Not too active and peppy—*attached*. [to B'] Would you wait outside?

B': No.

Mrs. B: With the secretary?

B': No.

Mrs. B: You might draw with crayons.

B': No.

Mrs. B: You think you might try? You will be right outside the door.

B': No.

Mrs. B: They have magazines and comics.

B': No.

Mrs. B: You can't get lost. I would be very pleased—

B': No. No.

Dr. S: How come?

Mrs. B: B' is very concerned that I am not going to be there all the time, and even at home where I am involved a good deal of the time and he is happily playing, he will check several times in the course sometimes of an hour, call my name to make certain I haven't gone, which is quite unusual because I never go anywhere without telling either of the children. Even if I am going up front to the mailbox I will say, "I am going to the mailbox now," because the few times I forgot to say it there has been a small panic session. B' usually likes to hold my hand when we walk, or if not my hand another part of me, because he likes to be with me.

Dr. S: To be with you even to the extent of being able to be in contact with you?

Mrs. B: Physical contact is quite important. The first year and one half of his young life he had to be in the same room with me, even the john—which we finally broke from but it took a very long time . . . it seems to be something I have been doing. I do spend more time with the children than most mothers do, I will admit.

The nursery school to which B' now goes is about a block from their home. From infancy he has gone there every day when his mother walked his sister to school, and so he did not look upon it as much more than an extension of his home, and therefore a safe place. In addition, his mother worked there on a regular basis, so he thinks of it as "our school." "He knew it was our school. He knew we were part of the school." Some of his need to touch his mother constantly is also present at school. Once he gets adjusted to the teacher, he still has to keep in physical contact with her.

MRS. B: He is anxious about the entrance to kindergarten [to which he will transfer in a few months], whether he can hold his teacher's hand. At the beginning when he entered nursery school, one of the teachers said he insisted on holding and clinging, like now. [*At the moment, while she is talking, he has let go of her for a moment and suddenly realizes it. Throughout the interview he is either holding his mother's hand or touching some part of her body and for scarcely one moment does he let go. He just suddenly realized he has let go.*] (*To B'*) You cannot get lost, kiddo, as long as you can see me. (*To Dr. S*) I tell B' that as long as he can *see* me it's the same as holding hands. He can't get lost as long as he can see me.

DR. S: Does he agree with that?

MRS. B: He seems to agree verbally, but he quickly reaches for the hands and if I say my hands are busy—in fact, I just adopted a shoulder-strap handbag because I find that I do smoke, and if I carry a handbag in one hand and a cigarette in the other, I am running out of hands. So now I carry a shoulder-strap bag so that at least there is one hand available when the need arises.

He doesn't play at other children's houses unless I am there . . . he *will* go to friends' houses, provided I will stay. As a little one we did have a young Swedish student living with us. She would take him out for a walk in the morning and you could hear the walk commencing by the sound of the screaming until she got to a half or three quarters of a block away and then it would calm down. A perfectly lovely girl, friendly and warm, but he just didn't want the separation. Of course as a baby, we were together a good deal. He had many physical problems. He came home from the hospital with a staph infection so that he needed medication. Erythromycin was used, which caused extreme cramping; he had colic. At two weeks of age he was cast practically from the scrotal sac to the toes because he was born with bad tibial torsion. So he was cast. He needed a great deal more attention than a newborn would, which meant he was up day and night—very little sleeping because he was hungry a good deal of the time. With each feeding, he required medication, which caused extreme intestinal discomfort. So I used to walk him day and night.

DR. S: You had him in your arms?

MRS. B: Constantly. Absolutely. It got so—he was a large baby, very large, and by the time—he must have weighed thirty-five pounds at eighteen months and still was not a walker. . . . We were very much closer than—the normal baby would sleep a full night through and nap a good deal during the day. His disposition was happy. . . . He was also extremely rashy, which meant a lot of times no diapers, not even—he was handled a great deal more than the base . . . I would say that he had a great deal more mothering than the normal child would need, a great deal more contact. I was in terrible shape at the beginning, because I was physically worn out, and then to add to the joys the grandpa and grandpa [sic] moved in with us when he was about two months old. And then there was the additional stress and strain, meaning more attention. I think he was concerned even at that age, who was really going to take care of him . . . and that made for more tension and exactly at that point my oldest child began visiting the NPI because she reacted very severely to the sibling rivalry. She had looked forward to his arrival, but she didn't really expect that she would lose a mother and gain a brother. Who needed that? I was terribly involved at that point. . . .

DR. S: Was he interested in your jewelry before he wanted to wear it?

MRS. B: He used to like looking at it, yes. He enjoyed looking at it. He was esthetically pleased by my beads. I always wear beads; he would always feel the beads.

DR. S: How early did that happen?

MRS. B: Since I've always worn beads, I think he's always been handling my beads.

DR. S: When he was an infant on your bosom?

MRS. B: Yes, he would hold the beads and I would say, "Don't," because they break, and sometimes I would take them off but mostly he was careful; so I always wear beads—I don't wear much in the way of jewelry but I always wear beads.

DR. S: About your clothes, so far as his wanting to touch them or be in contact with them, has he shown any interest?

MRS. B: More of late; he's very interested in textures. I have some wool and linen shorts and they're very scratchy. When I wear them, I notice—in fact, I've stopped wearing them—he always reaches and scratches. He likes to feel them.

DR. S: He actually plays with and touches——

MRS. B: He plays with . . . the tactile sensation is very sensitive. Even when we go shopping for clothes for him or if he's with me when I'm shopping—for he's with me most of the time—he'll say, "Buy this, it's so soft." You know, artificial fur, dynel fabrics, and he just mentioned it yesterday when we left here; we bought a vest for his father and he said, "Why don't you buy this one? This is that nice scratchy texture." It was a rough woven hopsacking. He's very sensitive to textures and even his blankets—he has two blankets, both of which he has had since he was born; one of them he uses as a pillow. How come a blanket is a different texture from the other, I don't know; it's the same manufacturer, but one is more pilly than the other, and the pilly one he always feels for. I couldn't feel the difference. I've now learned to; I can identify them now in the dark. When you look at them by daylight you can see the difference, but even in the dark he can say, "Oh, my blanket," and when I hand him the two blankets, he can immediately feel, and he gets the pilly one and that's the one he likes as a pillow. He doesn't suck it; he doesn't twiddle it; he just puts himself on it, and the other one he likes under his body.

MRS. C

NOTES: "She [Mrs. C] then went on to talk about how close to each other they [she and her son] have always been. When he was an infant, she felt as if he could literally absorb things through his skin. She said that he had a very fine, white skin and huge black eyes that he would just keep fixed on her all the time. She was with him practically continuously day and night throughout his infancy and small childhood. During the night he never slept more than an hour and a half in the first year and he would wake up screaming. She says that she has never been able to stand to hear a baby cry. So she was exhausted every night because she would sleep maybe an hour or an hour and a half, and then she'd have to get up and be patting him or feeding him or singing to him or cooing to him, so that all night long he and she were together whether he was awake or asleep. In the daytime it was the same. If she put him into his bed, either to play by himself in the room or in the bed for a nap, he would very shortly be screaming. So she gave up trying to do this and instead would just keep him in the same room that she was in if she was working or cooking or whatever. As long as she was there, he was completely happy. This means that he felt her presence twenty-four hours a day. She never went away—as a matter of fact, this coming weekend will be the first time that she has ever left him. [He was over 6 when this was dictated].

"Because of this closeness, she had the feeling that as an infant he always knew exactly what was going on in her. He would keep his big black eyes focused on her and seemed to be just soaking her into himself. I asked her how come she never let him cry to see if he would get over it, and she said it was because she just couldn't stand the crying. The pediatrician had told her that she should let him cry and he would then be able to get through the night, but she was incapable of doing this. In addition to her presence, the other main thing that comforted him was his quilt and then her bedjacket, objects that he latched onto when he was only a few months old and which he carried with him continuously for five years."

" 'When he was an infant, if he was restless or had the hiccups, I'd roll up my pajama top, roll down his diapers and lay him on my abdomen. It always quieted him.' "

" 'This morning I was in the bathroom undressed. He came in while I was facing backward and didn't know he was there and slapped me on the fanny and said with a laugh, "What a lovely butt." I laughed and told him how cute he was.' "

"She describes C' as a very happy baby and a very funny baby. By this she means that even before he could talk, but especially after he began to talk, he conveyed ideas which were humorous and which he knew were humorous and which extracted from people in the environment a sense of sharing in laughter with him. She says, 'I enjoyed him so much. I didn't want to pamper him and make a mother's boy of him. I can remember thinking this at the time.' "

"The patient had been thinking how outspoken, adult, and comfortable C' felt with her. What happened was that he commented appreciatively today, 'I see your bosoms,' and she was impressed with the 'mature' quality with which he remarked on this and his lack of embarrassment. To my question about her feelings about her children seeing her nude, she said that she doesn't run around the house nude, but if they come upon her if she is either completely or partly undressed, she doesn't make a big fuss about it because she feels then she doesn't emphasize the whole issue. They have a tendency to just walk into her room or into the bathroom. She is her usual permissive self, and so her children are walking in on her all the time; she'll be in the bathtub, for instance, and C' will come in and sit down and talk to her while she is taking a bath. Once he has found her, she makes no effort to put on clothes but continues nonchalantly about her business, conversing with him. She has noticed that in recent months (since he has been in treatment) he seems to have gotten rather keenly interested in her body. She tells how the other day he came in while her back was to him, and he said in a cute manner, 'Well, I say, and gave her a slap on the fanny.' Following this, she became a little sad and said how she feels her relationship with C' is changing (since treatment has started). She says, 'I can't touch him,' by which she doesn't mean anything physical, but their symbiosis seems to be falling apart, which makes her sad."

MRS. D

MRS. D: I don't think I was overly affectionate. I wasn't overbearing. I guess I was affectionate. We did everything together [in D"s first few years of life]. I had to take her everywhere I went. . . .

I can't remember anything except D' wetting the bed until she was eight years old. . . . She slept with me for about three years [sic]. She slept in her own bed till she was two—then with me till she was eight. . . .

D' was the most precious thing I had had, even if she was my fourth child. There was something very close between us. . . .

From infancy on, nudity between D' and her mother was all right. Her mother never locked her out of the bathroom.
D' says: "I remember—she would be the mother hen and I would be baby chick, and she would lay on her side like this [*she makes a circle of her arms, trunk, and thighs*] and I would lay up next to her, and then she would put her arm over me and that's the position we always went to sleep. Anyone who would wet all over anyone every night of the week, they would have to be doing it for pretty good reason. She would get so mad [*but never stopped it*]." (*The sleeping arrangements were that D' and her mother slept in one bed, the father and brother slept in another bed, and her two sisters slept in a third bed.*)

The following quote comes immediately at the beginning of the hour after Mrs. D's first interview with me and is not in response to any question by me:
MRS. D: I had a lovely dream last night. I dreamed that D' was six months old. I forgot to feed her breakfast. I had taken her someplace and she became a little fussy and I happened to think it was lunchtime and I hadn't given her her lunch. So I quick took all her clothes off and gave her a bath and started

to give her some lunch and that was the end of the dream. I was spoon-feeding her.

IV. EXCESSIVE PERMISSIVENESS

Note that, where we have data, the mothers did not want to oppose their sons' demands. Thus, in addition to permitting the boys unlimited freedom on their bodies, these mothers did not wean or toilet-train the boys, did not significantly restrict the use of women's clothes, jewelry, makeup, or girls' games, or gradually restrict the use of transitional objects. If the boys would not obey their mothers' request to restrict some activity, the mothers gave way to their demands.

MRS. A

If the reader will refer back to the material already quoted (in Section I), regarding the child's intense need to cross-dress, he will find running through the quotes (from Mrs. A) this mother's attitude of allowing the boy almost unlimited freedom, and her unending patience as she lets him dress in women's clothes, comb her hair, touch her, and interfere with her housekeeping routine. While she could say No on occasion, one doesn't get the feeling in her interviews that she ever persisted in denying him what he demanded.

Unfortunately, I did not ask her about when (or if) weaning and toilet-training were imposed on him.

MRS. B

Note earlier quotes (in Section I) which demonstrate Mrs. B's unwillingness to restrict her son and her attempts to submerge her own needs to his demands, not only in infancy, when this is an essential part of good mothering, but also years later when the same behavior that is supportive for the infant becomes destructively gratifying for the three- and four-year-old.

MRS. B: He gave up the bottle whenever he wanted to, I

don't remember exactly when, probably at sixteen or seventeen months. He did it, I didn't. . . .

He didn't have his hair cut until he was almost two. I liked it shaggy; he didn't have a lot of hair and I don't like little boys with that bald look. I just don't like it particularly, and he was a chubby baby, chubby boy, and I thought a full head of hair would be all right. . . .

And he threw himself down, not angry, all smiling and happy; he evidently had a nice day at school, and he began rubbing. I didn't say anything about it because I just decided it was a good release from tension but he even emulates that technique of masturbation [the way his sister does], rather than the handling of the genitals that other friends tell me their boys do. . . .

DR. G: Was toilet-training a problem?

MRS. B: No, I didn't make an effort. He learned by himself. With his sister neither. But you know what was the problem? He didn't know how to urinate standing up; he only sat down on the potty, and I tried to explain to him that this is much more convenient for boys and he wouldn't; he just sat there and pressed his penis down to aim it properly, and liked the gurgling sound because he had never seen a male urinate. My husband likes privacy and B' never sees his father. . . .

DR. S: How about you?

MRS. B: Not anymore.

DR. S: Until when did he?

MRS. B: Occasionally, maybe until he was two and a half, and after that I made a point to . . . you know, because I personally like privacy, and I don't want to be prudish with him but I felt that this was getting to be too much of a game.

DR. S: He would be in a lot—is that what you mean?

MRS. B: No, not a lot, but he would try to come in when I was getting dressed in the morning, because I would dress him and then I would get dressed. Maybe even earlier, because I'm much too puritanical. I didn't make a big deal about it . . . if he walked in and I wasn't fully dressed, fine; but I didn't permit him to come in while I was still in the bath or something like that.

I've never bathed with him, which some mothers do with their youngsters.

DR. G: You say you're puritanical. Is this boy showing interest in his penis?

MRS. B: Yes.

DR. G: What's your attitude toward that?

MRS. B: This is perfectly fine.

DR. G: You permit this?

MRS. B: Permit this? He masturbates; his sister masturbated. He does it in the same manner that she masturbated. She used to lie down flat on the ground and rub and rub and rub and get great satisfaction. And would sometimes do this maybe for a half-hour. B' doesn't handle his genitals, which I thought was a more normal way of masturbation for boys. . . .

I bought him men's underwear—you know the type. I finally found a store that sold those, but those he wouldn't wear; those he thought were icky-looking, so I ended up letting him wear tights. He still likes to dress up in tights. . . .

I disapproved but I permitted; I didn't approve to the point of . . . I would distract him if I saw him playing actively with the dolls, and I got tired of this after a half-hour and I would distract him and we would do something else. But this was an alternative; this wasn't actually saying "I don't want you to do this." I'd say, "Come on, let's go out and we'll go find the cat or we'll read a book." He didn't know I was unhappy about it or maybe he did know but it didn't affect him.

MRS. C

NOTES: "Formerly he [C'] used to put on his sister's dresses all the time, but this now forbidden: [Mrs. C] 'We forbade him his sister's dresses so he went to her slips.' She says this without any conscious awareness that it was also within her and her husband's power to forbid him the slips. At any rate, she has never forbidden this, though she disapproves of the slip: 'I'd say to him, "Oh, let's get it off!" and he says, "Oh, just a few minutes," and at times becomes hysterical, so I say, "O.K."'"

"He has been so attached to a quilt and then a bedjacket that it is practically impossible to disentangle him from them. Then she [Mrs. C] remarked that she was unable to wean him from a night bottle until six months ago (age 6). 'It was life and death to him. I told him that when he was five years old he should be thinking seriously of getting rid of it; we talked it over many times, and he tried many nights to give it up, but he would just get hysterical without it.' She said she would rather have him walking around sucking on a bottle than sucking his thumb. In this discussion, it is obvious that there is an element in their relationship that has persisted at all times and that I have heard expressed in many other hours, which is the way she treats him as an equal, as a colleague, pretty much as an adult. This is apparently in part due to his very winning, precocious, and intelligent personality, but, in addition, it seems to be something she needs to do. I suspect that she so identifies with children rather than with adults that she easily treats them as equals.

"He finally gave the bottle up, and when he did so she and he sat down and had a formally planned big celebration, in which she gave him a pound box of chocolates and spoke to him in a very mature way about his wonderful accomplishment. This whole description above is in keeping with her permissiveness in regard to his transvestism as well.

"She then remarked to me that she never toilet-trained her children. When they were ready to have their B.M.'s by themselves and much later, when they were ready for urinary continence, that is when they were found to be trained. But she never spoke to them or disciplined them regarding toilet-training. She did, however, talk to them (again, this colleagues-talking-together), explaining to them the advantage of toilet-training. She denies any difficulties with C', though he continued to have bed-wetting accidents up until last year."

MRS. D

MRS. D: She is just such a marvelous person. She is still the same good D' she was when she was a boy. She is a full-fledged

girl. There is no reason in the world why anyone couldn't accept
this. In fact, she is more girl, more fun, than my daughters are.
To me, she fits into society beautifully. I don't see any problem.
I am very proud of her. I have almost forgotten she was a boy.
I can truthfully say I have my daughter today. . . .

(*According to D', her mother saw her dressed as a girl around
age three and after that, and never said anything against it. She
would say, "Oh, isn't that cute! You are more like a girl than a
boy. You would make such a cute girl."*)

D': After I came back [following the change at age 17],
she [her mother] found the estrogen pills in a shirt I had hanging
in the closet. She said, "What are you doing with those?" I told
her I was taking them.

DR. S: And she said?

D': My mother does anything for me. She will conspire
with me to have or do anything I want.

V. THE MOTHERS' EMPTINESS AND ITS ROOTS IN THEIR CHILDHOOD OEDIPAL SITUATION

It seems likely that each of these mothers has tried to cure
her pervasive sense of emptiness by holding her son close to her
for too long. In this way, she prolongs her own blissful experience
of possessing this marvelous flesh of her flesh. In addition, since
part of her knows that he is a separate being, she hopes to undo
her own awful experience with her distant, unloving mother, by
being all too alert not to let her own child suffer from similar neglect.

As noted before, this emptiness results from a bleak relationship with her own distant, angry, empty mother, plus the
disappointment which resulted when her father, who was to be
both mother and father, abandoned her without being close and
loving, by death or at the advent of a sibling.

I believe that these mothers' bisexuality is induced by their
search for a good mother and by their angry, disappointed rejection of their fathers. It can't be conjectured that as a result of the
deprivations of childhood, their sons become the intended vehicle
of salvation and revenge.

For all their expressed anger toward their mothers, each of these mothers has arranged it so that their mothers live very close to them and are in almost daily contact.

MRS. A

This patient was referred to me by the psychiatrist who had treated her for an acute depression and a chronic sense of emptiness and worthlessness. Although we did not dwell on these feelings during the evaluation, she expressed them frequently; for example, in the tired and patient way she talked of how she has willingly persisted for so many years in her hopeless marriage, or in her opinion that she has achieved little and leads a meaningless life every day of every year:

"My father was very attentive. When I was three he taught me to play ball. My mother did not spend much time with me. I cannot remember her ever sitting down with me—she was working around the house all the time—but my father did. There was a terrible void in my life when my father passed away [age 12]. My mother was extremely strict. Don't spare the rod. She spanked me often and hard. My teens were unhappy. I paid no attention to my mother. If she would slap me, I would just stand up to her and defy her. My mother and I clash an awful lot. She leans on people to get them to do things for her. She lives a half a mile away. I see her or call her often.

"My mother's father was an alcoholic, and so my grandparents split up. My mother was a very hard-working and humorless woman. She lives very well for a person with no income. I don't know if she has any feeling for me. She isn't very demonstrative. I am sure she does [rising, questioning inflection]. She won't listen to what you have to say. She was extremely strict—very short-tempered. She spanked us kids an awful lot and very hard. I was scared to death of her. I am like my mother. I have a bad temper. So I am more lenient with my children than she was. I try to keep it in check with my children. I have a violent temper. I throw things."

MRS. B

The following are quotations from notes dictated by Mrs. B's therapist:

"Her father never actually said to anyone in the family that he loved them, and yet she felt him to be warm. She always loved him more than her mother. He was attentive; for example, he always tucked her in at night since infancy, not her mother. He spoiled her, while mother was the disciplinarian. He taught her to roller-skate, jump rope, and play ball. He was ineffectual in a crisis, however.

"Her sister (only other sibling) was born when she was seven, after which her father's attention was deflected from her. Her mother withdrew all interest and affection from Mrs. B at this time because Mrs. B showed some independence."

"Her mother always said, 'Men are nothing. Don't trust them.'"

"Mrs. B's mother and father live about a mile away. She is in touch with her mother almost every day."

Regarding her sense of emptiness, she is described by her therapist as "self-sacrificing—planning all the time how to take care of all the details of everyone's life—her son, daughter, husband—except herself."

MRS. C

The patient has often described herself as a "nothing," "a cipher," "a mirage." Notes follow:

Her mother didn't care at all about her. It was her father who took care of her, did the shopping, paid attention to her, got the doctor, and so forth. She once had a dream in childhood which typifies what her mother was like. The dream was that the patient had died, but her mother kept sending her to the store on errands because her mother didn't even know that she was dead."

"*Dream:* 'I was in a room trying to reach some wooden milk bottles—like children's toys—on a shelf. I couldn't reach them.' "

"She talked about how much her father loved her when she was little and how she would sit by the hour watching him at his work or sitting on his knee. She says that for some strange reason when he would go to track meets or baseball games when she was very young, he would never take his sons but only took her. Also, it was his pleasure to buy her clothes, and so her mother almost never bought her clothes; her father did. He bought her very frilly and feminine clothes, which is completely the opposite of the way she dresses now, which is more sporty and boyish."

"She talked about her angry relationships with her father, though in very general terms, and then apparently interrupted this train of thought to tell me the end fragment of a dream she had last night: 'C' had gotten into my drawer and took something valuable. He was with some man I didn't know, a doctor or something. I was enraged in the dream. I woke up enraged with my jaws clenched.' Her associations to this were that she had always been very concerned about people getting into her drawer without getting permission to do so. Her daughter does it all the time. C' does not. On the other hand, her husband doesn't ever care and is not a particularly neat person. When the patient was sixteen, her sister took from her drawer a sweater which the patient had just bought and of which she was very proud, and had worked hard to get the money for it. She became enraged at her sister, who was ten years old; her father came into the room, picked up a chair and hit her with it. She said she wasn't going to stand for this anymore, and he was never going to touch her again, and she was going to leave home. And at that point, when she was sixteen years old, she did in fact leave home, because someone stole something precious from her drawer.
    "The poignancy of this episode with her father was brought out by the patient's next association, when she talked about how

her then-ten-year-old sister was his favorite, but how in former years she, the patient, had been his favorite, but that he was so unpredictable and, especially as time went on and he was drinking more, he became more easily enraged, and the patient fought him inch by inch in this rage by refusing to do what would be most cooperative and which would take the heat off her. Her brother would often tell her to stop acting that way, that she was just aggravating her father more, but she couldn't stop doing this. While she was talking about all of this, she was crying because of the loss of tenderness and happiness she had had with him. She described him as a very creative, talented, humorous, warm man, but one who was completely unpredictable because at any time without warning he could become enraged. During the time that their relationship was very warm, in her younger years, she expressed with some feeling the fact that he loved her so much that he would buy her clothes, and that he always bought her clothes that were better than the few her mother bought.

"She started to talk about the drawer of tools her father had for his carpentry work. She described how beautiful his tools were in the drawers, and she expressed anger, saying she didn't know why she was angry but that in one special, beautiful chest, a drawer-chest, he would keep the drawers locked so no one could get into his beautiful tools."

"The patient says that when she was her daughter's age, she never thought about getting married, or even that she was a girl or what femininity consisted of. As she discusses this, the impression is one of a kind of emptiness. In other words, it is not as if the patient is protesting too much, or in some other subtle way showing a strongly defensive reaction against conscious or unconscious knowledge. Rather, there is a kind of bland, peculiar quality as she tries to sense the difference between her daughter's active and vigorous search for femininity and her own lack of any such feelings consciously in her own puberty and adolescence. There must be fantasies and there must be a much more clear-cut structure of feminine gender identity than the patient is now able to report. At any rate, she has no memory of thinking that she would get married, or wondering whom she would marry or what the responsibilities of getting married would consist of. She says that she never as a child played the games that her daughter does: of house, of being a mother, of being a wife, of dressing up dolls, of pretending to have a baby, etc. She also contrasts her own lack of awareness of her changing body in adolescence with the great interest that her daughter has. She says with surprise that her daughter is always saying such things as, 'When I get married. . . .' The patient acts as if she were a young girl herself, learning these attitudes for the first time.

"Her sister-in-law, who is usually the sitter, is going to have to be in the hospital. This then made her remark further on her sister-in-law's operation (panhysterectomy) and the sense of empti-ness and neuterness that this would produce. She said that this is such a terrible thing to contemplate, which is a great change from the way she used to talk about her body before, as being neuter, as much boy as girl, empty inside, and so forth. Now, following my reminding her that she had been so proud of being neuter as a child, she said that it really hadn't been that way as I had heard it in the past, but that when you dress up as a child there is the fun of being what you are not; in other words, not becoming what you are inside—namely, neuter—but of pretending to be something that you really know you are not.

"Mrs. C's mother lived with her for years before and for years after Mrs. C married, but in the last few years her mother has lived a few miles away, seeing Mrs. C several times a week."

MRS. D

In regard to this mother's sense of emptiness: "I led a life alone [because her mother was working] from early childhood. My mother was not lovable or a loving woman." D''s mother was never hugged by her own mother and says that she tried to make up to her own children for what she didn't get from her mother.

"My mother and father idolized my little brother so much that there was never any time for me."

Mrs. D was picked to be the family worker in the way Mrs.

C was. She was the cook, the housekeeper, the gardener, and the cleanup man.

VI.   FATHERS' ABSENCE

In each case, there was evidence that the boys were severely deprived of their fathers' presence, and in a very special way. These fathers had not died or left the families; they were crucially built into the atmosphere of the family; they were responsible, in that they financially supported their families; they were clearly labeled as the father and husband; and for all of these reasons they aroused hope that they would participate in the family—and then they were physically almost never there. This produced a completely different message for the child than if his father were dead or had left through divorce or separation. In addition to this poignant abandonment of much of their fatherliness, these men, by not being home, were not there to stop the excessive mother-infant symbiosis and the resultant feminization of their sons. On the infrequent occasions when they saw what was happening, they either encouraged the process, ignored it, or made noises of disapproval without acting.

Like their wives, they did not try to improve or end their empty and futile marriages.

In the three cases, where something is known of the fathers' childhood (A, B, C), there are statements that he was mildly effeminate and/or passive, and residues in the form of marked passivity persist to the present, though all are very clearly not effeminate-appearing men (just as their wives are not masculine-appearing women). Of the three who are alive (A, B, C), all refused to take on the responsibility of getting treatment for themselves, though willing to let their wives do so.

MRS. A

Mrs. A: Daddy spends no time with the children at all or with me. He has gotten this hobby, and he is with that almost every night out in the garage. He has had it all fixed up and on Sundays he spends most of his time doing this. So we don't have many outings together or times with the children. So I wind up spending the time Daddy should spend flying kites, playing ball, this kind of thing which I do not feel is my role, but I feel somebody must spend the time with them. This responsibility should be taken by the father. It should not be my task at all. . . .

(*She adds, regarding his attitude toward A', that he says that since he works six day a week, he feels that Sunday is his day; so he spends it alone in the garage with his hobby.*)

My husband didn't like it [cross-dressing] at all, even the first few times. He didn't *do* anything about it. He would blame me for it. . . .

He reacts to A''s dressing by having fits. He yells at everybody in the house, "Don't let him wear them. You've caused this thing." Telling me that it's all my fault because I allowed him to have dolls and I allowed him to dress this way. And I contend that our other boy had dolls; he had one when he was two and he kept it for about a year, and then he discarded it and that was it. When my husband saw him playing and dressing up like a girl he made fun of him and told him that little boys didn't dress this way.

DR. S: Did he get him out of the clothes?

MRS. A: No. . . . Because of his drinking, he was getting home like seven, eight, nine, and it just progressively got later to a point where he was going right from work to a bar and drinking, until most of the time when the bar would close, and then last year—I would say the last year and a half of his drinking—he was very rarely home. He was out . . . and of course this was when my little one was fairly small, and I don't think he even knew he had a father because he never saw him, maybe on Sundays, but my husband was getting home at two, three, four, five, sometimes even seven-thirty A.M., and he would shower and leave for work, and this was an every-night thing. If I had any sense at all I would have thought that he was not going to be home for dinner—"I won't fix dinner for him," and go ahead and eat, but I always waited. Every night we would wait and wait and wait, until seven, seven-thirty, and we would be eating so late. So . . . because he never came home for dinner. Some night he might get home at eight-thirty; I don't know why, I guess he must have fallen out of the bar by mistake, but he sometimes would get home at maybe eight-thirty or nine, but this was very rare; most of the time it was two or two-thirty, and he would usually stay home on Sunday, but of course he would drink all day. Now he has given up drinking and has taken up his hobby, and we have no companionship. I mean—there is no companionship at all. He comes home and he eats and he goes out to the garage. He has the garage all built; he has cabinets built out there and the whole bit. So almost every night he is out there and on Sunday. . . .

I think my mother-in-law would have been tickled to death to have her son be a little boy like A'. She wanted a girl so badly and my poor husband—you should have seen his bedroom. She had told him many times that she wanted a little girl and she always fixed his room up with frills, skirts around the bed and frilly drapery and everything. He said he was embarrassed to have his friends in to see his room. I know that she was overly protective with him. He said he was fourteen or fifteen before he was allowed to go on a bus by himself or go anywhere by himself. She had to go with him, and he said he was treated like a girl from the standpoint that when the other fellows were allowed to go out when they were in high school, and they were allowed to go to movies and dances, and they were allowed to stay out until twelve or one, he had to be home at ten-thirty or eleven. He resented this very much, because he felt his mother was treating him like a girl, putting hours on him like the girls had. I know she was very disappointed when I had the boys. She had hoped that maybe she would have a granddaughter, and she made comments about this many times that she was very disappointed at not having a girl. His mother tells the story about how his father was so proud of him, and he said his dad brought someone home from work one night to show off his boy and my mother-in-law had him dressed in a dress with a bow in his hair. He was only about nine months old, I guess. If she did it once, probably the chances are that she may have done it more often.

MRS. B

DR. S (to B'):   What does your daddy do [for a living]?
B':   Go out.

MRS. B: . . . and my husband isn't home an awful lot. He isn't home for dinner, for instance, most evenings and on Sundays. He is home very late on Saturdays. Saturdays his office theoretically closes at one, but he very seldom gets home until three-thirty or four, and at that point he doesn't play with the children because he has had a long, tiring day. And he has a hobby. So he usually works at it on Saturday when he gets home. Sunday he spends— well, last year he spent most of it at his hobby, which meant he would leave the house nine o'clock Sunday morning, come home for dinner sometimes. So B' didn't have much of a male influence, didn't have someone with whom he could really identify. He is very fond of Daddy but if he falls down and hurts himself, he will very seldom go to Daddy. I have to make a big deal about it: "Daddy can fix it for you." Even when he was young, with the car business [he was fascinated with various makes of cars], he liked a lot of cars that were not ready-made— ninety-eight-cent friction models—and so I bought the plastic models, you know, the kind of things little boys play with or teen-agers assemble, and very often I wouldn't assemble them with him during the day. In fact, more and more I would say, "Daddy will do this. This is more Daddy's job." And I would do it at night, because his father was home too late and didn't have the time or the patience. And I would say, "Daddy did this for you." The next morning he would thank Daddy for it. I think I have overcompensated with both children for the fact that I think their father hasn't been home more with the kids.
DR. S: Does your husband see anything wrong with B'?
MRS. B: Yes, he said to me—which is why we started immedi-

ately to come to you, that's why I called you; I was very distressed one day, because he had a free day and I just feel if he
had someone else with whom to identify he wouldn't always be
quite as female-interested. I asked him please to spend some time
with him [B'] that day, and he didn't get around to it; he was
busy with his hobby and at about ten o'clock that night he
finally came in—the children had gone to bed—he had seen them,
he had stopped for dinner, and I said that I really felt that so
much of what was wrong with B' was the fact that he had really
a lack of father. My husband played it back, which he seldom
does because he's very controlled and extremely patient and very
mild-spoken: "It's a thing of genes and there's not a thing you're
going to do about it." . . .

He thinks it's just necessary to support the family financially
and to be there in moments of stress, because he never knew
his own father until my husband was out of the Army. . . .

He has made it a point, they have man-to-man dates. In
fact, as I was going out today, he said, "When will Daddy be
home? I want to have a date with him."

DR. G: Did you want to have a boy?

MRS. B: I was afraid to have a boy because I was afraid
after my daughter that it would be very hard for me. How was I
going to play baseball with a boy? How would I ever get a
boy to identify with a father?

DR. S: Because of your husband's absence?

MRS. B: Because he wasn't always there—that's right.

MRS. C

Throughout their marriage, but most of all since the children
were born and prior to treatment, Mr. C has worked almost
every evening, usually not coming home till the children were
in bed and leaving before they awoke. In the evenings, when he
was not away working at his business, he isolated himself at
home to do paper work, or was out of the house busy at his hobby.
The latter activity, which by its nature is done alone, also removed
him from the family on weekends. Notes follow:

"She had been so angry at her husband that she threw a tray of dishes against the wall, because of some obtuseness (not yet clear to me) in regard to his lack of feelings for his daughter's struggle with puberty. The patient, trying to make him feel this, and frustrated with his lack of interest and his just wandering out of the room in the middle of a conversation (not in anger but just because he wasn't listening), became enraged and threw the tray at him. I asked her what his response was and she said that he was somewhat surprised, but he didn't say anything, he just very casually asked her why she did that. She said she did it because she didn't want to kill him (and so threw them, not at him but at the wall). He didn't even ask her then why she was enraged. She spent the rest of the hour describing his complete absence of feeling in regard to her, and by this she doesn't mean anger or reaction formation or anything else; she just means he doesn't seem to feel anything at all. She can be enraged and flaming mad at him and he can fall asleep that evening as if nothing had happened. She says that he can practically fall asleep while it is going on. If her description is correct, then he is supremely empty himself."

"She says that although she has finally learned by experience never to talk with him about anything significant, she was driven to do so about two months ago, shortly after the conference which they both attended here regarding C'. It was after this conference that she got into an argument with her husband, which is unusual, although it used to be fairly frequent in the past; but it's unusual now because, she says, she has just given up talking to him, because he just doesn't listen or doesn't respond, but she felt it was important to indicate to him that there was reason for both of them to be concerned because the child might grow up to be an effeminate man."

"The patient came in today almost white with rage and yet not in any other way showing this affect. She had arranged with her husband to take care of C' this afternoon, and Mr. C had said that he would and then had never showed up. She said that this is typical, 'It always goes this way.' So at the last moment she had to drop C' off at her sister-in-law's in order to get here. She had not told him what she was going to do. He had said in a casual way, 'Where are you going?' and she had said, 'Oh, I'm going someplace,' and he had asked no further. She is so disgusted with this that she no longer has any feelings about it. (This means his attitude, that he isn't even sufficiently interested to care when he doesn't get an answer to his questions.)"

"She described the number of things around the house that needed to be fixed, but Mr. C never fixes these and he never suggests to C' that he get out a screwdriver and fix them, although C' is an extremely active child and wants to always do things and would be happy to do anything. She then went on to say that Mr. C has no distinct idea of the differences between the two genders and she is now becoming aware that in addition to her own contribution to neuterness, that he has never treated her as if she were distinctly a woman, and so never encouraged any femininity in her. She says that there is only one part of her that he treats like a female, by which she means her vagina."

MRS. D

"The narcolepsy [Mr. D's] was discovered when D' was six months old. He [the father] would fall asleep over his food. He wouldn't take his pills at the proper time. He would take them so he could stay up all night and work. He worked nights [and slept all day]. . . . He was out of the house on the WPA during the Depression. He had a machine shop and would lock the door." [This means that when he was home he would work in the machine shop as a hobby and was not with the family.]

The father was a different man when his first son was an infant. Mrs. D describes him as being more of a father and as having wanted the boy very much. This was before he had narcolepsy. At that time he was an angry, violent man who beat his wife, but nonetheless he was present as a part of the family. He was happy then to have a boy and was so until the child was 2 to 2½, but this was never so with D': "I doubt if he wanted more children. He never even came to see the baby [D'] on the day she was born or to visit at the hospital." When his wife came home from the hospital, "he was out all the time. . . . He didn't play with her like he did with the first and second child and then with the first son."

VII. STATUS QUO

One of the main techniques these women use, all too often, in order to survive emotionally is to deny that a situation is grim or dangerous; or, if forced to admit to the danger, they tell themselves that at least one can survive in the present situation, whereas, on the other hand, any change will only bring disaster. Thus, they tell themselves that their sons are not threatened and that their marriages are tolerable or even happy; that their husbands won't change and so why even try to make them change.

One attribute that assists them in being able to bear life in this limbo is their sense of emptiness, acquired as a defense to anesthetize the terrible disappointment when their fathers turned from them in childhood.

The reader can see this capacity to not "make waves" interwoven in much of the already quoted material, where, for example, these women reveal indirectly how, while they patiently complain about their marriages, they persist without either trying to force a change in their husbands or making use of separation or divorce as an escape.

MRS. A

"Last Sunday he played golf in the morning and in the afternoon he had a schedule set up for his hobby. And so all Sunday we [she and the children] were alone, and I was pretty upset about it. In fact, we had an argument about it before breakfast, about him going out. I insist that Sunday is the day for him to spend with the family. It's the only day that he has off, and I feel that the boys need this and I do too. This is something that has to be worked out, I know. It won't change overnight to being good. Sometimes I get a little anxious because I would like it to have happened yesterday instead of tomorrow, you know, but I am aware that it's not suddenly going to come to a halt and be completely different. I know it's going to take time."

MRS. B

"We get along very well. No problems, a happy marriage. I wish he had more time to be at home, but no major problems. We're very compatible; we like one another; we were not little kids when we were married; I was almost 24, had dated a good deal before then; he had been in the service; he had dated before then too. This wasn't any two little kids in high school finding a sexual attraction at nine. We were very deliberate about it. I think we have a perfectly marvelous marriage, except the children are not having as easy an adjustment as I would like."

MRS. C

". . . It is apparent that she [Mrs. C] did not rush into treatment on her own, but has been carried along rather willingly at each stage. For instance, she did not think something was wrong until a strange woman in a market told her that was the case. I'm not certain yet how she sought out treatment; there's a certain lack of pressure from *her*, it seems, in this beginning of the treatment situation with the son. . . ."

". . . she [the mother] says that although she has finally learned by experience never to talk with him [her husband] about anything significant, she was driven to do so about two months ago, shortly after the conference which they both attended regarding C'. It was after this conference that she got into an argument with Mr. C, which is unusual though it used to be fairly frequent in the past. It's unusual now, she says, because she has given up talking to him since he doesn't listen or doesn't respond. But she said she thought it was important to indicate to him that there was reason for them both to be concerned because the child might grow up to be an effeminate man. It was as if this were the first time that Mr. C had ever considered this, because he was taken aback by it, and since that time he has been more cooperative, and has on a number of occasions, for various reasons, told her that he was sorry for one thing or another that he has done—a remark that he had never before made in their relationship."

She was in treatment nine months, in psychoanalysis six months, before telling her husband that she was receiving psychiatric treatment. After three years of analysis, she still has not told him my name—and he hasn't asked.

"I asked her, 'How did you happen to have C'?' She acted as though she didn't understand what I meant, so I tried to make it clearer for her: I wanted to know how come. She said, 'It wasn't a mistake. We planned to have C' even though my husband and I were fighting all the time.' She talked a bit about the fighting and how sometimes she became so enraged she'd throw things at him and would break the windows. She said she didn't care how much she hated him at this time. She just had to have another baby. She had wanted to have lots of babies."

"I asked her what she thought about C' being a transvestite and she said it was too bad, because when he grows up it's going to be very dangerous. But otherwise, she says, she doesn't care. He's a free agent and should be able to do whatever he wants. There's a very peculiar quality when she talks about this. It's really empty. She really doesn't seem to have any judgment—morally, or in any other way—that there may be any difficulty in being a transvestite, or that it reflects some problem in personality. She doesn't even question his masculinity, although she does use the word. . . .

"I remarked to her that even now in a curious way she might be considered to have never gotten married. She agreed with this. She said that she really didn't know Mr. C; although she had been attracted to him, they really had not much in common. Because of the war, he was not with her during much of their 'courtship,' which occurred by letter, and she says that she undoubtedly never would have picked a man who himself could feel truly married. The course of their marriage has borne all of this out. They live under the same roof with not a great deal of communication except for the occasional times when they get angry. They hardly talk to each other. They have given up their sexual relations completely. He goes to work and on his return at the end of the day, he sits reading or continuing his work in the evening without talking to her, while she goes to classes or plays or whatever. So although they are legally married, there is very little else to the marriage at this time.

"Her final remark in describing herself in this hour was: 'I'm a cipher.' "

MRS. D

Rather than her remarks, which are rather diffuse and dispersed bit by bit throughout her interviews, I can quickly epitomize Mrs. D's capacity for silent and passive suffering by pointing out that, as with the other three mothers, she remained with her husband for twenty years, until his death, while quite dissatisfied and unhappy, yet not held by moral or religious scruples.

VIII. TRANSITIONAL OBJECT

It is of great theoretical interest whether and to what extent these boys' interest in women's clothes was influenced by their clinging to a beloved piece of cloth as a bridge between the bliss of mother's body and the more indifferent world of outer reality: mother—mother's skin—mother's garments—nonmother object equated with mother (transitional object)—outside world. It would seem that in these children in whom the process of separating from mother is so slowed down, to cling to a cloth that substitutes for her would be even more crucial than it is in the many children without gender problems who also use this technique. Also, our boys' continuing sensuous relationship to cloth and clothing (implying here textures and colors rather than that the cloth is made up as woman's clothes) may spring especially from an intense experience with a cloth transitional object. However, the data are too imprecise; one cannot tell if these boys used transitional objects qualitatively or quantitatively differently from other children.

MRS. A

"He started out when he was very small—I used to put a diaper, stretch it across the top of the mattress where his head lay because it was softer than the sheet and this may be the reason why he latched on to it. But now it can be any piece of rag—in fact, I have one. He brought one with him. He brought it with him this morning in the car and I didn't realize it. It was in the back seat of the car on the way over here, and then he noticed it when he got out of the car and he brought it out with him."

MRS. B

MRS. B: . . . He was esthetically pleased by my beads. I always wear beads; he would always feel the beads.

DR. S: How early did that happen?

MRS. B: Since I've always worn beads, I think he's always been handling my beads.

DR. S: When he was an infant on your bosom?

MRS. B: Yes, he would hold the beads and I would say, "Don't," because they break, and sometimes I would take them off but mostly he was careful; so I always wear beads—I don't wear much in the way of jewelry but I always wear beads.

DR. S: About your clothes, so far as his wanting to touch them or be in contact with them, has he shown any interest?

MRS. B: More of late; he's very interested in textures. I have some wool and linen shorts and they're very scratchy. When I wear them, I notice—in fact, I've stopped wearing them—he always reaches and scratches. He likes to feel them. . . .

[The rest of this quote can be found on pages 311–312, where it was then used to illustrate the excessive symbiosis.]

MRS. C

"He started as an infant playing with a satiny blanket as a transitional object and went from that to a bedjacket that the patient [Mrs. C] had. He apparently took over this bedjacket immediately and with her permission—and, again, a peculiar permission without her awareness that she is being permissive. After saying he still has it—he's now six—and that he had had it since he was three and a half, I asked her whether she gave it to him, and she said, 'Oh, no, he took it and after dragging it around on the floor for a few weeks, it was such a mess I had to let him have it.' She isn't aware that she let him take it and let him drag it for several weeks before permitting him to keep it as his own. So he now takes it to bed with him still and plays with it each night. She has noticed that even while he's asleep his fingers still are running over the satin. She remarked that his sister never did that at all, and actually had an antipathy to feeling fur in any toys. C' inherited many of his sister's toys unused because she couldn't stand the feeling of furriness."

MRS. D

"She [D'] had a favorite teddy bear—just a couple of years."

IX. CREATIVITY AND SENSITIVITY

Without being asked about it, the mothers of the three little boys stressed that they had noticed, and teachers had noticed, that these boys were outstanding as compared with other children in their appreciation of artistic creations like paintings and music, and especially in their pleasure and skill in expressing their own artistic creativity. It also seems that these boys are unusually sensitive with their physical senses—seeing, hearing, smelling, and proprioception.

There are hints in the mothers' remarks suggesting that this sensitivity goes back to infancy and is enhanced by the physical intimacy between mother and infant.

MRS. A

"At school, they said that in his drawings he is drawing about as a six-year-old would, that his drawings have a great deal of detail. In most of his paintings, he uses quite a lot of color. He draws pictures of girls mostly. He will put earrings and necklace and bracelet and high heels on the girls, which I don't know too much about. The teacher said that the other four-and-a-half-year-olds don't go into this much detail.

"The teachers brought up a curious thing which I don't know and they don't really, either. They had to put him in another group of children because with the other children he starts out with—and every day he came in and took his shoes off and put this skirt and bolero and high heels on, and while he had this on he generally was doing drawing. Now they put him in a class where there were children more his own age and he doesn't do it in class because they don't do that, only at playtime, and he won't draw. So they wondered if he was playing this role and in this role he could express himself in drawing." [Only when he gets dressed up in girls' clothes does he then draw.]

MRS. B

"Good sleeper with minuscule number of nightmares considering the active imagination—highly creative play, very fond of theater, goes to all the UCLA things, long, good attention span, large fantasy world."

MRS. B: He likes the touch of it; he's very sensitive to things and how they feel. He has a very sensitive skin also. He tends to be rashy; he tends to be itchy, has to have medication for his back; it will break out, dermatologically, for no reason that we can find except he's probably allergic to wool. When he buys sweaters, he won't wear some clothes, very sensitive skin, even jeans—you know, boys' jeans; the winter-weight pants are very heavy, and they're very coarsely woven. I've had to put him in tights, which boys don't normally wear but he can't wear winter-weight pants because the seams, the welted seams, bother him and he actually gets reddened from them. So it isn't all imaginary. He has a physical response to it. I bought him a number of guns, but he didn't like the noise of them and holds his ears. Very large on play-acting; that's why he has lots of marionettes and puppets and even if you give . . . typical of B', he'll find three stones at the beach and you know other children may look at the color, the texture, or just look at them or throw them . . . he will immediately set up a family situation and he'll play: This is the mother, this is the father, and this is the sister, and he works them around and he acts out a whole big fantasy by himself, not for anyone's benefit, but just sitting there talking to himself and playing—usually the sister. In television, all of his idols are the females. He's a marvelous mimic. He actually mimics someone who has a very swinging, hip kind of thing. Yes, I think he's quite graceful. If you've ever seen him in his leotards dancing around—he'd make a dandy ballerina or ballet dancer, a male ballet dancer—loves to dance.

He doesn't like to play with ropes like the boys do at school, doesn't build too much except cages, houses for the animals, but doesn't actually structure blocks the way kids do, for . . . I watch the kids and they build airports or they build all sorts of things with blocks, but B' always builds the same things: a house for himself or a house for the rabbits or guinea pigs, the rats, whatever he can get. Very house-oriented: likes to play in the house when we go driving just to take a drive, wants to stop at new houses when we go for a drive, newly built houses; this is the kitchen, there is the bathroom, is quite interested in houses and what goes on in them and the people who live there. Likes to go visiting with me even when there are no children in the house if I have to stop somewhere, like I collect money for various assorted charities and he enjoys going with me. . . .

She [the sister] is very happy to play because he plays very well, and she can be Barbie and he can be Midge, and he'll talk for the one girl and she'll talk for the other, and they'll go through a whole life situation. They won't really spend so much time in the dressing and undressing; it's mostly getting set up for a production, a play, and then they act out a whole situation. I should tape some of this for you. It's unbelievable.

DR. S: At five years?

MRS. B: He'll be a dandy script writer some day. He has a lively imagination. At this age he admires one of his girl friend's mother's clothes. She has very elegant things, very dressy, very unlike the things I wear. When we go shopping, he always asks me to buy red shoes, why don't I like prettier colors, because I tend to dress rather monotone. "Why don't you get some prettier things?" And even on television he'll pick out people to like and not like on the basis of, this one's much prettier because she has much prettier eyes or this one has a prettier flip hairdo or bouffant, or things, you know, that I don't——

DR. G: Does he know these terms?

MRS. B: He uses them, and this is not in my conversation. But this is TV exposure, and his sister and her friends, and she has a lot of girl friends eight and a half or nine who play at the house, and he likes to interject himself in that play and they permit him to a great extent, and if you have occasion to turn on the television, it is constant. He makes commercials, that's another thing. He sits there at breakfast and says, "Do you mind if I do a commercial?" I'll say, "Fine," and then he says, "Well, now you take cereal, and it's *crunch*," and he gives me a lot of the conversation that I'm sure he hears on TV.

DR. G: But not only does he like to be touched—does he like to touch?

MRS. B: Yes, he likes to hold on to me—he loves to touch; he likes to stroke my dress; today he was touching it; he likes to cling to me, to his sister—he's always fooling around with her buttocks; she says—I'm surprised she didn't say it, because when we were driving over, she said, "I'm going to tell them my real true feelings, that B' is a pain in the ass and I hate him and he's always fooling around with my butt," and of course here she was all sweetness and light and got over those bad feelings since she said them out in the car.

DR. G: Then he likes to touch your dress?

MRS. B: Yes.

DR. G: Is he aware of cloth and materials?

MRS. B: Yes, he has a greatly developed tactile sense. He— we were shopping right after we saw Dr. S on Wednesday, looking for a vest for my husband—I buy a lot of my husband's clothing; he doesn't have time to shop and the kids help me to pick it out—

this was his birthday present—and he wanted a vest unlike B′'s taste in colors; it wasn't a color he is ever attracted to, and I looked at it and I wondered why he wanted to pick this one, because it was a very rough-textured raw-silk kind of thing, and he likes to feel it. I have a pair of shorts, summer shorts, that are a slubbed material and he always—whenever I wear them, he is scratching like a cat. He has two blankets he picked up that he learned to adore and become attached to at just about two and a half. I finally was thinking back. They're both the same age; they're both the same synthetic Acrylon; one of them is more pilly than the other. That's the one he always wants when he goes to sleep, to put under his head or to have, to hold. He doesn't suck it; he doesn't tangle it or twist it or manipulate it; he just likes to touch it and if you walk in before he's asleep, you can see he's stroking it, very, very sensitive to it. He's always touching fabrics; even when we buy clothes for him, he's very concerned about looking at the fabric and touching it, the feel of it; he likes to absolutely get his hand on it and decide if he likes it or not.

He's the most aware boy of hair styles, hair products, shoes, clothes. He's very—you know, laughingly we said last year, you know this is going to be a dandy dress designer, and even now, at this point, if you go shopping—he shops with me for all of his clothes—he's terribly fussy and he knows what he wants. He'll say to the lady—and the saleswomen look at me as though I have some kind of a monster—"That's not my taste." And you should see her; he doesn't like the color and he doesn't like the texture of the fabric. . . .

He has a very acute sense of smell. He's the only youngster who, when we get into a car, will say, "The gasoline is leaking." He will walk into a restaurant [and say], "I don't like the way this place smells. Too greasy." He has a highly developed sense of smell and also he's acutely aware of noise. Other kids can listen to noisy things on TV but he'll cover his ears and run out of the room crying. We took him to a Beatle movie. He was so anxious to go. We sat through one-fourth of that film; even though he wanted to see it, he couldn't stand the girls screaming, and yet when the Beatles are on TV at home, when he's watching it, he screams just like the girls. And I say, "Why does your noise not bother you and why does it bother you to hear them?" He says, "It's too noisy."

DR. G: He's discriminating about sound?

MRS. B: Yes, very discriminating.

DR. G: He likes music?

MRS. B: Yes, and some records he insists I play on my phonograph, on our phonograph, the adult one, because he says it sounds better; he says it sounds tinny on his, because a lot of the records are children's records and he discriminates; he knows the difference between a little Columbia portable twenty-dollar one and a big Fisher.

He's sensitive to colors. He notices people's eyes. I'm sure if we talk about it today [conference], he's going to tell me who has pretty eyes in this room. He just told me the other day he likes someone's father better than his own, which surprised me, because he doesn't see the man much; the man runs a restaurant. He said, "I like Z's daddy better than mine." And I said, "How come?" "He has much prettier eyes." He's always commenting; he's always looking at people. If he wanted to be verbal, I venture to say he could describe each one of you, although he doesn't seem to be looking at you, by the time we'd get out—tell me the colors you were wearing and what you look like, describe who has pretty eyes, who has blue eyes, who has a sad face. He is very concerned about the tone of my voice. If I'm reading a story and I kind of act it as I read it, he says, "Don't read it with a sad face or a sad voice even if it is a sad story; keep smiling and be happy." His sister was taking a dance class, and he used to go and watch that. I'm sure he would like to have a dance class himself. He sees a good deal of theater, I mentioned. My husband feels this may be a mistake and be overstimulating for him, but this is the esthetic standard he has and I don't see anything particularly wrong in a boy enjoying theater. We go to museums, and he goes with us; now he's getting to the bored stage and, fine, we don't do this anymore with him; but he used to enjoy it to a large extent, looking at the paintings and the textures and the prettiness of the picture and the ugliness he saw.

MRS. C

"He's always loved color; he's always loved textures of things. He's always had—in fact, he still has—a satin thing he feels. He's always responded to music. He's responded to music since the time he's been a little—just a baby—and still does, still does—a tremendous response to music. When he was two years old, he was talking about how much he enjoyed listening to the Gregorian chants on my records. The other day he was singing the male and female parts word for word [in Latin] of 'Carmina Burana.' He loves to dance when he listens to music, and is so graceful that at school last year they made a movie of him dancing. He loves materials—that is, cloth. He gets great pleasure from looking at paintings and also from doing his own painting. He just thrills to colors and likes to talk about them with me.

"He's got a tremendous sense of smell and a tremendous sense of hearing. He can hear fantastically well—and his sense of smell ——Now this sounds ridiculous—it took me months to realize what was happening! When he was an infant, he use to start—the food would start cooking and the smell would pervade the atmosphere —and he would start screaming and screaming and it took me— slow as I am—to realize he was hungry—and I started to feed him at the same time as I—the food was cooking and then everything was fine. And he loves the smell of perfume, flowers—he'll always comment on this.

"And hearing. One night not too long ago he was sound asleep, and I went to let the window down and it made a *rrrr* sound, and in his deep sleep he raised his hands to his ears; and I thought, If that hurts him so much in his sleep—good grief—some of the sounds that he hears during the day must really bother him. He can hear the front gate closing and my hearing is quite good and I can't hear it.

"I say, 'Why don't you paint in school?' 'Don't want to.' But if we just pile it on and leave him alone, he paints like mad—good separation of color, without muddiness, very carefully defined things. Use of space, the whole thing.

"He was always a very curious child. He would pick everything up and examine it, set it at a different angle and then I would look at it from the new angle and be surprised myself at how he changed the significance of any object by the way he would look at it."

MRS. D

I failed to ask this mother for any evidence of creativity in her little son. On the basis of the experience with the other mothers, all of whom spontaneously brought up such information, I doubt if D' was especially artistic. She is not so as an adult.

X. PHYSICAL ACTIVITY, CURIOSITY, AND INDEPENDENCE

Unexpectedly, despite the evidence of blurring of boundaries between mother and child, there is one attribute in these boys that clearly shows an independence from their mothers' bodies. This is their great curiosity, which is coupled with great physical activity and with a certain independence all the more odd in the face of their need to keep touching their mothers. In the oldest of the boys, C', the touching had died down before treatment started, though not the identification with her, which, one can speculate, makes it less necessary to keep touching her physically, since he now had practically completed the task of building her inside himself. In C', the need for body contact alternated with periods when, even as a toddler, he completely left his mother.

B' is less active than the other two. This may mean that this whole category is not significant, but one cannot yet be sure, for we know that B' was immobilized by his cast for 18 months, and the effects of such a traumatic restriction on activity may mask a tendency to great searching activity.

If this trait is related to the production of femininity in these boys I cannot guess to what extent it might be biologically determined or is a psychological effect of the closeness to and identification with the mother. It would be fun to speculate on the theme of orality: voracious infantile feeding, voracious curiosity, and voracious incorporation—introjection—identification with the mother's body, but the illumination provided proves nothing and may only give false security.

MRS. A

There are no specific quotes that when extracted from the tapes would make much sense to the reader. However, throughout the interviews, Mrs. A is trying, mostly without words or with only exclamations, to control A', whose activity is more intense than with any child I have ever seen. He is on and off her lap, under the furniture, banging at the walls and furniture, sliding on the couch, pausing for a few moments but only when sitting in her lap. This is not random movement, but searching, curious, and motivated. Because of it, his mother did not dare let him leave the office, for instance, to draw or read as can other small children. Psychological testing, attempted on six different days, failed, even when we had his mother sit in the room, because the boy would attend only for a few moments and then start searching the environment.

MRS. B

Because of the cast, B' was very restricted in his movements for eighteen months. The only clue to independence we heard in the evaluation that sounded like any of the other boys was this:

"He had a pacifier until he was about seven months of age, and then he threw it away. He was able to drink from a cup right off the bottle and he nixed the nipples. I think he said he didn't like it, or he didn't even say it—he just showed it."

MRS. C

'I didn't want to pamper him and make a mother's boy of him. I can remember thinking this at the time. He always did things first and then would learn the proper way to do them. For example, when he was just a toddler, he got up on a high place and tried to fly. Of course he fell on his head. Also, when he could scarcely walk and didn't know how to swim, he was fearlessly diving into the swimming pool, and we would have to fish him out. Right from the start and up to the present, he has been daring and completely unafraid. He has always wanted to do things for himself. He is just covered with cuts and bruises and scars all over his head. I remember when he could hardly walk that he would climb over the fence and go out into the street. He was also very independent about his eating, as soon as he could coordinate at all. He wouldn't let let me feed him right from the start when he went on solids. And so I encouraged him to feed himself, which he did very easily.

"He was always pushing me away when he first was trying to walk. A long time before he was able to walk, he was still getting up and trying. I tried to nurse him right after he was born, but I had no milk; but I tried for three weeks. He was a very erratic sleeper right from birth. I didn't get more than three hours of uninterrupted sleep until he was over three years old. He never could get enough to eat. He was a prodigious eater and still is. He still would like to eat meat and cheese for breakfast, lunch, and dinner if I would let him. As an infant, he cried louder, laughed harder, ate more, had screaming anger, and had less sleep than any child I have ever heard of. He just overdid everything. He was so different from his sister. . . .

"He was such a beautiful baby. Everyone talked about it. And even as a baby he loved all people. I had to stop taking him shopping because as soon as he could toddle around, he would wander off and would get into conversations with people, so that it took me hours to finish my shopping. He was always a very curious child. He would pick everything up, examine it, set it at a different angle and then I would look at it from the new angle and be surprised myself at how he changed the significance of any object by the way he just looked at it. In the mornings he gets up like a rocket and at seven o'clock I will find him all up and dressed and out digging in the garden or looking at birds.

"He's also very funny. The other day I was driving him and I turned around and saw that he was picking his nose; I said to him, 'When Dr. Y returns in a couple of years, you won't be picking your nose any longer.' To which he replied, 'You hope.' "

MRS. D

Mrs. D made no mention that D' was unusually active, curious, or independent as a child; D' never commented on this; I never questioned either about this.

Chapter References

Chapter References

(Identification of titles listed below is by first-named author, date, and shortened title. Complete title and publication data will be found in the Bibliography, listed alphabetically by first-named author's name.)

Preface

1. S. FREUD (1920; 1955). The Psychogenesis of . . . Homosexuality in a Woman.
2. N. LEITES (1967). Talking about Identity.

Chapter 1—Biological Substrates of Sexual Behavior

1. S. FREUD (1905; 1953). Three Essays on . . . Sexuality.
2. H. LICHTENSTEIN (1961). Identity and Sexuality.
3. R. K. BURNS (1961). Role of Hormones . . . .
4. C. A. BARRACLOUGH AND R. A. GORSKI (1962). Studies on Ma Behavior in the Androgen-Sterilized Female Rat . . . .
   H. H. FEDER AND R. E. WHALEN (1965). Feminine Behavior in . . . Male Rats.
   R. W. GOY, C. H. PHOENIX, AND W. C. YOUNG (1962). A Critical Period for the Suppression of Behavioral Receptivity . . . .
   K. L. GRADY AND C. H. PHOENIX (1963). Hormonal Determinants of Mating Behavior . . . .
   R. E. WHALEN AND R. D. NADLER (1963). Suppression of the Development of Female Mating Behavior . . . .
   W. C. YOUNG, R. W. GOY, C. H. PHOENIX (1964). Hormones and Sexual Behavior.

5. R. W. GOY, C. H. PHOENIX, AND W. C. YOUNG (1962). A Critical Period for the Suppression of Behavorial Receptivity . . . .
W. C. YOUNG, R. W. GOY, AND C. H. PHOENIX (1964). Hormones and Sexual Behavior.
R. P. MICHAEL (1964). Biological Factors in . . . Sexual Behavior.
6. R. P. MICHAEL (1964). Biological Factors in . . . Sexual Behavior.
R. P. MICHAEL AND J. HERBERT (1963). Menstrual Cycle Influences . . . in Rhesus Monkey.
7. W. C. YOUNG, R. W. GOY, AND C. H. PHOENIX (1964). Hormones and Sexual Behavior.
8. S. RADO (1940). A Critical Examination of . . . Bisexuality.
9. S. FREUD (1905; 1953). Three Essays on . . . Sexuality.
10. C. S. FORD AND F. A. BEACH (1951). Patterns of Sexual Behavior.
11. M. J. SHERFEY (1966). The Evolution and Nature of Female Sexuality . . . .
12. K. LORENZ (1952). King Solomon's Ring.
13. S. EIDUSON. Personal communication.
14. J. BOWLBY (1960). Ethology and . . . Object Relations.
P. H. GRAY (1958). Theory and Evidence of Imprinting . . . .
15. J. MONEY, J. G. HAMPSON, AND J. L. HAMPSON (1955). An examination of . . . Human Hermaphroditism.
16. W. H. MASTERS AND V. E. JOHNSON (1966). Human Sexual Response.
17. M. J. SHERFEY (1966). The Evolution and Nature of Female Sexuality . . . .
18. M. L. BARR AND E. G. BERTRAM (1949). A Morphological Distinction . . . during Accelerated Nucleoprotein Synthesis.
19. M. L. BARR (1959). Sex Chromatin . . . in Man.
20. F. N. KALLMAN (1963). Genetic Aspects of Sex Determination . . . in Man.
21. S. E. WAXENBERG (1963). Some Biological Correlates of Sexual Behavior.
22. W. FULLER AND N. DREZNER (1944). The Results of Surgical Castration . . . .
A. C. KINSEY, W. B. POMEROY, C. E. MARTIN, AND P. H. GEBHARD (1953). Sexual Behavior in the Human Female.
23. W. FULLER AND N. DREZNER (1944). The Results of Surgical Castration . . . .
24. A. S. PARKES AND H. M. BRUCE (1961). Olfactory Stimuli . . . .
25. R. SPITZ (1962). Autoerotism Re-examined: . . . Personality Formation.
26. J. CALL. Personal communication.
27. J. CALL. Personal communication.
28. E. S. SCHAEFFER AND N. BAYLEY (1963). Maternal Behavior, Child Behavior . . . Through Adolescence.

29. J. MONEY, J. G. HAMPSON, AND J. L. HAMPSON (1955). An Examination . . . of Human Hermaphroditism.
30. R. J. STOLLER (1964). A Contribution to . . . Gender Identity.
31. J. OLDS (1958). Self-Stimulation Experiments . . . .
32. R. G. HEATH (1963). Electrical Self-Stimulation . . . in Man.
33. C. FISHER, J. GROSS, AND J. ZUCH (1965). Cycle of Penile Erection . . . (REM) Sleep.
34. A. H. PARMELEE, JR., W. H. WENNER, Y. AKIYAMA, M. SCHULTZ, AND E. STERN (1967). Sleep States in . . . Infants.
35. P. H. WOLFF (1966). The Causes, Controls . . . of Behavior in the Neonate.
36. P. D. MACCLEAN (1963). Phylogenesis.

Chapter 2—The Intersexed Patient with Normal Gender Identity

1. H. LICHTENSTEIN (1961). Identity and Sexuality.

Chapter 4—The Hermaphroditic Identity of Hermaphrodites

1. J. G. HAMPSON (1955). Hermaphroditic genital appearance . . . .
   J. L. HAMPSON, J. G. HAMPSON, AND J. MONEY (1955). The Syndrome of Gonadal Agenesis . . . .
   J. MONEY (1955). Hermaphroditism, Gender and Precocity . . . .
   J. MONEY, J. G. HAMPSON, AND J. L. HAMPSON (1955). Hermaphroditism: Recommendations . . . .
   J. MONEY, J. G. HAMPSON, AND J. L. HAMPSON (1957). Imprinting and . . . Gender Role.
2. J. MONEY, J. G. HAMPSON, AND J. L. HAMPSON (1957). Imprinting and . . . Gender Role.
3. J. MONEY (1952). Hermaphroditism: . . . a Human Paradox.
4. A. S. NORRIS AND W. C. KEETTEL (1962). Change of Sex Role During Adolescence.
5. J. MONEY, J. G. HAMPSON, AND J. L. HAMPSON (1956). Sexual Incongruities . . . .
   J. MONEY, J. G. HAMPSON, AND J. L. HAMPSON (1957). Imprinting and . . . Gender Role.
6. PLATO. Symposium.
7. J. MONEY (1963). Factors in . . . Homosexuality.

Chapter 5—The Sense of Maleness

1. P. GREENACRE (1958). Early Physical Determinants . . . Sense of Identity.
2. A. I. BELL (1961). Some Observations on . . . Testicles.
   A. I. BELL (1965). The Significance of Scrotal Sac . . . .

3. J. MONEY, J. G. HAMPSON, AND J. L. HAMPSON (1955). An Examination . . . of Human Hermaphroditism.
J. MONEY, J. G. HAMPSON, AND J. L. HAMPSON (1957). Imprinting and . . . Gender Role.

Chapter 6—The Sense of Femaleness

1. W. H. MASTERS AND V. E. JOHNSON (1961). The Artificial Vagina. . . .
2. S. FREUD (1931; 1961). Female Sexuality.
3. K. HORNEY (1924). On the Genesis of the Castration Complex . . . .
K. HORNEY (1926). The Flight from Womanhood.
4. E. JONES (1927). The Early Development of Female Sexuality.
E. JONES (1933). The Phallic Phase.
5. G. ZILBOORG (1944). Masculine and Feminine.
6. B. BETTELHEIM (rev. 1962). Symbolic Wounds.
7. J. MONEY, J. G. HAMPSON, AND J. L. HAMPSON (1957). Imprinting and . . . Gender Role.
8. S. FREUD (1931; 1961). Female Sexuality.
9. S. FREUD (1931; 1961). Female Sexuality.
10. S. FREUD (1925; 1961). Some Psychical Consequences of the Anatomical Distinction . . . .
11. A. J. LERNER (1956). My Fair Lady.
12. S. FREUD (1931; 1961). Female Sexuality.
13. S. FREUD (1931; 1961). Female Sexuality.

Chapter 7—A Biological Force in Gender Identity?

1. S. FREUD (1905; 1953). Three Essays . . . on Sexuality.
S. FREUD (1937; 1964). Analysis Terminable and Interminable.
2. L. M. BAYER AND N. BAYLEY (1959). Growth Diagnosis.
3. A. JOST (1958). Embryonic Sexual Differentiation.
4. H. J. BAKER AND R. J. STOLLER (1967). Can a Biological Force Contribute . . . ?
5. D. BARTON AND P. D. WARE (1966). Incongruities in the . . . Sexual System.
6. P. W. DAVIDSON (1966). Transsexualism in Klinefelter's Syndrome.
7. D. H. CARR, M. L. BARR, E. R. PLUNKETT, M. M. GRUMBACK, A. MARISHIMA, AND E. H. CHU (1961). An XXXY Sex Chromosome Complex . . . .
W. M. COURT-BROWN (1962). Sex Chromosomes and the Law.
T. J. CROWLEY (1965). Klinefelter's Syndrome and Abnormal Behavior . . . .
C. J. DEWHURST AND R. R. GORDON (1963). Change of Sex.

A. M. DON (1963). Transvestism and Transsexualism.

M. A. FERGUSON-SMITH (1966). Sex Chromatin . . . and Mental Deficiency.

F. J. KALLMAN (1952). Twin and Sibship Study of . . . Homosexuality.

J. KNOL AND P. L. LOS (1966). A Mentally Disturbed Patient . . . .

H. G. MANTHEY (1958). Psychological Studies in . . . Gonadal Insufficiency.

J. MONEY, J. A. HAMPSON, AND J. L. HAMPSON (1957). Imprinting and . . . Gender Role.

J. MONEY AND C. WANG (1966). Human Figure Drawing I: Sex of First Choice . . . .

H. D. MOSIER, L. W. SCOTT, AND H. F. DINGMAN (1960). Sexuality Deviant Behavior . . . .

R. Q. PASQUALINI, G. VIDAL, AND G. E. BUR (1957). Psychopathology of Klinefelter's Syndrome.

J. RABOCH AND K. NEDOMA (1958). Sex Chromatin and Sexual Behavior.

R. A. ROHDE (1963). Chromatin-Positive Klinefelter Syndrome: . . . .

H. ROSKAMP (1959). A Contribution to the Psychopathology . . . .

S. F. SCHNEIDER, S. I. HARRISON, AND B. I. SIEGEL (1965). Self-Castration . . . in Sexuality.

R. J. STOLLER (1964). Gender Role Change . . . .

8. I. K. BOND AND A. I. MARGULIES (1964). Paranoid Schizophrenia . . . Klinefelter's Syndrome.

L. H. DOWLING AND S. J. KNOX (1963). Tranvestism and Fertility. . . .

H. J. KARL AND J. E. MEYER (1964). Sex Characteristics . . . .

A. MILLER AND J. CAPLAN (1965). Sex Role Reversal . . . .

J. MONEY AND E. POLLIT (1964). Cytogenetic . . . Ambiguity.

C. OVERZIER (1958). Transvestism and Klinefelter's Syndrome.

C. N. ARMSTRONG (1958). Transvestism.

K. WALTER AND W. BRAUTIGAM (1958). Transvestism in Klinefelter's Syndrome.

9. J. MONEY AND E. POLLIT (1964). Cytogenetic . . . Ambiguity.

10. J. N. KVALE AND J. R. FISHMAN (1965). The Psychological Aspects . . . Klinefelter's Syndrome.

11. H. BENJAMIN (1964). Nature and Management of Transsexualism . . . .

12. H. I. LIEF, J. F. DINGMAN, AND M. P. BISHOP (1962). Psychoendocrinologic Studies in a Male . . . .

13. P. C. S. HOAKEN, M. CLARKE, AND M. BRESLIN (1964). Psychopathology in Klinefelter's Syndrome.

14. R. J. STOLLER (1964). A Contribution to . . . Gender Identity.

15. R. J. STOLLER (1964). A Contribution to . . . Gender Identity.
16. H. BENJAMIN (1964). The Transsexual Phenomenon.

Chapter 8—Male Childhood Transsexualism

1. R. GREEN AND J. MONEY (1960). Incongruous Gender Role . . . in Prepubertal Boys.
   R. GREEN AND J. MONEY (1961). Effeminacy in Prepubertal Boys.
2. H. BAKWIN (1960). Transvestism in Children.
3. M. SPERLING (1959). A Study of Deviate Sexual Behavior in Children . . . .
   M. SPERLING (1963). Fetishism in Children.
   M. SPERLING (1964). The Analysis of a Boy . . . .
4. J. J. FRANCIS (1965). Passivity and Homosexual Predisposition . . . .
5. L. BENDER (1954). A Dynamic Psychopathology of Childhood.
6. F. B. CHARATAN AND H. GALEF (1965). A Case of Transvestism . . . .
7. I. PAULY (1965). Male Psychosexual Inversion: Transsexualism.
8. R. R. GREENSON (1966). A Tranvestite Boy . . . Hypothesis.
9. H. HARLOW AND M. HARLOW (1966). Learning to Love.
10. E. KRIS (1947). The Nature of Psychoanalytic Propositions . . . .
11. H. W. LOEWALD (1966). Book review: Psychoanalytic Concepts . . . (Arlow and Brenner).
12. W. MUENSTERBERGER (1967). Psyche and Culture.

Chapter 9—The Mother's Contribution to Boyhood Transsexualism

1. O. FENICHEL (1930; 1953). The Psychology of Transvestism.
   E. J. HARNICK (1932). Pleasure in Disguise: . . . Sense of Beauty.
   M. D. LEWIS (1963). A Case of Transvestism . . . Identification.
2. M. SPERLING (1964). The Analysis of a Boy . . . .
3. H. BAKWIN (1960). Tranvestism in Children.
   R. GREEN AND J. MONEY (1960). Incongruous Gender Role: . . . in Prepubertal Boys.
   R. GREEN AND J. MONEY (1961). Effeminacy in Prepubertal Boys.
4. R. C. BAK (1953). Fetishism.
   P. GREENACRE (1953). Certain Relationships . . . Body Image.
   P. GREENACRE (1955). Further Considerations . . . Fetishism.
   P. GREENACRE (1959). On Focal Symbiosis.
   P. GREENACRE (1960). Further Notes on Fetishism.
   M. M. R. KHAN (1963). The Concept of Cumulative Trauma.
   M. M. R. KHAN (1964). The Role of Infantile Sexuality . . . Female Homosexuality.
   A. PARKIN (1963). On Fetishism.

5. M. SPERLING (1959). A Study of Deviate Sexual Behavior in Children . . . .
   M. SPERLING (1959). The Analysis of a Boy . . . .
6. M. SPERLING (1959). A Study of Deviate Sexual Behavior in Children . . . .
   M. SPERLING (1963). Fetishism in Children.
   M. SPERLING (1964). The Analysis of a Boy . . . .
7. R. C. BAK (1953). Fetishism.
   W. H. GILLESPIE (1952). Notes on . . . Sexual Perversions.
   H. LICHTENSTEIN (1961). Identity and Sexuality.
8. R. C. BAK (1953). Fetishism.
9. P. GREENACRE (1955). Further Considerations Regarding Fetishism.
10. D. W. WINNICOTT (1953; 1958). Transitional Objects and . . . Phenomena.
11. O. FENICHEL (1930; 1953). The Psychology of Transvestism.
    S. FREUD (1927; 1961). Fetishism.
    S. FREUD (1938; 1964). Splitting of the Ego in . . . Defence.
12. P. GREENACRE (1953). Certain Relationships . . . of the Body Image.
13. H. LICHTENSTEIN (1961). Identity and Sexuality.
14. D. W. WINNICOTT (1956; 1958). Primary Maternal Preoccupation.
15. P. GREENACRE (1959). On Focal Symbiosis.
16. M. M. R. KHAN (1963). The Concept of Cumulative Trauma.
17. M. M. R. KHAN (1965, unpublished manuscript). On Symbiotic Omnipotence.
18. E. KRIS (1956). The Recoveries of Childhood Memories . . . .
19. R. H. SHIELDS (1964). The Too-Good Mother.
20. S. FREUD (1920; 1955). Beyond the Pleasure Principle.
21. D. W. WINNICOTT (1950; 1958). Aggression . . . Emotional Development.
    D. W. WINNICOTT (1950; 1958). The Theory of the Parent-Infant Relationship.
22. M. M. R. KHAN (1964). The Role of Infantile Sexuality . . . in Female Homosexuality.
23. M. M. R. KHAN (1965, unpublished). On Symbiotic Omnipotence.
24. R. C. BAK (1953). Fetishism.

Chapter 11—Etiological Factors in Adult Male Transsexualism

1. D. O. CAULDWELL (1949). Psychopathia Transsexualis.
2. H. BENJAMIN (1953). Transvestism and Transsexualism.
   C. HAMBURGER, G. STÜRUP, AND E. DAHL-IVERSON (1953). Transvestism.

3. I. PAULY (1965). Male Psychosexual Inversion: Transsexualism.
4. R. GREEN AND J. MONEY (1960). Incongruous Gender Role: . . . in Prepubertal Boys.
   R. GREEN AND J. MONEY (1961). Effeminacy in Prepubertal Boys.
5. A. D. SCHWABE, D. SOLOMON, R. J. STOLLER, AND J. BURNHAM (1962). Pubertal Feminization in a Genetic Male.
6. R. J. STOLLER (1964). A Contribution to . . . Gender Identity.
7. R. R. GREENSON (1966). A Transvestite Boy and a Hypothesis.

Chapter 12—The Transsexual's Denial of Homosexuality

1. S. FREUD (1905; 1953). Three Essays on . . . Sexuality.
2. S. FREUD. Quoted in E. Jones (1955). The Life and Work of Sigmund Freud.
3. G. BYCHOWSKI (1956). Homosexuality and Psychosis.
4. P. WEISSMAN (1962). Structural Considerations in . . . Bisexuality.
5. J. MARMOR (1965). Sexual Inversion.
6. R. R. GREENSON (1966). A Transvestite Boy . . . .
7. J. MARMOR (1965). Sexual Inversion.
8. S. FREUD (1910; 1957). Leonardo da Vinci . . . His Childhood.
9. R. R. GREENSON (1964). On Homosexuality and Gender Identity.
10. R. R. GREENSON (1964). On Homosexuality and Gender Identity.
11. I. MACALPINE AND R. A. HUNTER (1953). The Schreber Case.
12. M. KLEIN (1936). The Psychoanalysis of Children.
    M. KLEIN (1946). Notes on Some Schizoid Mechanisms.
13. H. ROSENFELD (1949). Remarks on the Relation of Male Homosexuality to . . . Narcissism.

Chapter 13—Identity, Homosexuality, and Paranoidness

1. N. A. LEITES (1967, unpublished). Talking about Identity.
2. E. HOOKER (1959). What Is a Criterion?
3. R. R. GREENSON (1964). On Homosexuality and Gender Identity.
4. R. R. GREENSON (1966). A Transvestite Boy . . . .

Chapter 16—Differential Diagnosis: Transvestism and Transsexualism

1. B. M. DAVIES AND F. S. MORGENSTERN (1960). A Case of Cysticercosis . . . and Transvestism.
2. O. FENICHEL (1930; 1953). The Psychology of Transvestism.
3. O. FENICHEL (1930; 1953). The Psychology of Transvestism.
4. R. R. GREENSON (1964). On Homosexuality and Gender Identity.
5. H. BENJAMIN (1966). The Transsexual Phenomenon.
6. J. WÅLINDER (1967). Transsexualism.

Chapter 17—Female (versus Male) Transvestism

1. H. S. BARAHAL (1953). Female Transvestism and Homosexuality.
   H. BENJAMIN (1953). Transvestism and Transsexualism.
   O. FENICHEL (1930; 1953). The Psychology of Transvestism.
   N. LUKIANOWICZ (1959). Survey of . . . Transvestism . . . .
   R. S. REDMOUNT (1953). A Case of Female Transvestism . . . .
   L. H. RUBINSTEIN (1964). The Role of Identification in Homo-
   sexuality . . . .
2. I. PAULY (1965). Male Psychosexual Inversion: Transsexualism.
3. H. BENJAMIN (1966). The Transsexual Phenomenon.

Chapter 18—Transvestites' Women

1. O. FENICHEL (1930; 1953). The Psychology of Transvestism.

Chapter 19—Bondage and Cross-Dressing

1. C. ALLEN (1962). A Textbook of Psychosexual Disorders.
   J. BLOCH (1908). The Sexual Life of Our Time.
   M. BOSS (1949). Meaning and Content . . . Perversions.
   H. ELLIS (1921). Studies in the Psychology of Sex.
   E. A. GUTHEIL (1947). A Rare Case of Sadomasochism.
   M. LEIGH (1963). The Velvet Underground.
   E. PODOLSKY and C. WADE (1961). Sexual Sadism: . . . Love and Pain.
   W. STEKEL (1929). Sadism and Masochism.
   A. STORR (1964). Sexual Deviation.
2. H. BAKWIN and R. M. BAKWIN (3rd ed., 1966). Clinical Management
   of Behavior Disorders . . . .

*Chapter 20—Treatment of Patients with Biological Abnormalities of
Sex*

1. H. W. JONES, JR., and W. W. SCOTT (1958). Hermaphroditism . .
   Endocrine Disorders.
2. R. VON KRAFFT-EBING (12th ed. rev., 1932). Psychopathia Sexualis.
3. V. M. PENNINGTON (1960). Treatment in Transvestism.
   V. M. PENNINGTON (1960). Phrenotropic Medication . . . .
4. H. YOUNG. Quoted in H. W. Jones, Jr. and W. W. Scott (1958).
   Hermaphroditism . . . Endocrine Disorders.
5. D. CAPPON, C. EZRIN, and P. LYNES (1959). Psychosexual Identification . . . .
6. J. G. HAMPSON, J. MONEY, and J. L. HAMPSON (1956). Hermaphroditism . . . Case Management.

J. MONEY, J. G. HAMPSON, and J. L. HAMPSON (1955). An Examination . . . Human Hermaphroditism.

Chapter 21—The Treatment of Transvestism and Transsexualism

1. R. E. MCKENZIE and I. M. SCHULTZ (1961). Study of a Transvestite.
2. O. FENICHEL (1930; 1953). The Psychology of Transvestism.
   S. FREUD (1927; 1961). Fetishism.
   S. FREUD (1938; 1950). Splitting of the Ego . . . .
   E. A. GUTHEIL (1954). The Psychologic Background of Transsexualism . . . .
   E. J. HARNIK (1932). Pleasure in Disguise . . . Sense of Beauty.
   M. D. LEWIS (1963). A Case of Transvestism . . . .
   M. M. SEGAL (1965). Transvestism as an Impulse . . . .
3. E. A. GUTHEIL (1954). The Psychologic Background of Transsexualism . . . .
   E. J. HARNIK (1932). Pleasure in Disguise . . . Sense of Beauty.
   D. DEUTSCH (1954). A Case of Transvestism.
   E. L. EDELSTEIN (1960). Psychodynamics of a Transvestite.
   V. W. GRANT (1960). The Cross-Dresser.
   N. LUKIANOWICZ (1960). Two Cases of Transvestism.
   N. LUKIANOWICZ (1962). A Rudimentary Form of Transvestism.
   G. S. PHILIPPOPOULOS (1964). A Case of Transvestism . . . .
4. C. E. ALLEN (1964). Electrical Aversion Therapy.
   J. C. BARKER, J. G. THORPE, C. B. BLAKEMORE, N. I. LAVIN, and C. G. CONWAY (1961). Behaviour Therapy in a Case of Transvestism.
   J. C. BARKER (1963). Aversion Therapy . . . Perversions.
   J. C. BARKER (1964). Electrical Aversion Therapy.
   J. C. BARKER (1965). Behavior Therapy for Transvestism.
   C. B. BLAKEMORE, J. G. THORPE, J. C. BARKER, C. G. CONWAY, and N. I. LAVIN (1963). The Application of Faradic Aversion Conditioning . . . .
   C. B. BLAKEMORE, J. G. THORPE, J. C. BARKER, C. G. CONWAY, and N. I. LAVIN (1963). Follow-up Note to: The Application of Faradic Aversion Conditioning . . .
   D. F. CLARK (1963). Fetishism Treated by . . . Conditioning.
   A. J. COOPER (1963). A Case of Fetishism and Impotence . . . .
   J. D. GLYNN and P. HARPER (1961). Behaviour Therapy in a Case of Transvestism.
   N. I. LAVIN, J. G. THORPE, J. C. BARKER, C. B. BLAKEMORE, and C. G. CONWAY (1961). Behaviour Therapy in . . . Transvestism.
   R. J. MCGUIRE and M. VALLANCE (1964). Aversion Therapy by Electric Shock . . . .

M. J. RAYMOND (1956). A Case of Fetishism . . . Aversion Therapy.
M. J. RAYMOND (1964). Behaviour Therapy (Correspondence).
5. W. H. ALLCHIN (1964). Behavior Therapy (Correspondence).
S. COATES (1964). Clinical Psychology in Sexual Deviation.
I. J. MACDONALD (1961). Behaviour Therapy in a Case of Transvestism.
P. C. MATTHEWS (1964). Behavior Therapy (Correspondence).
F. A. WHITLOCK (1964). (Correspondence).
6. F. A. WHITLOCK (1964). (Correspondence).
7. S. COATES (1964). Clinical Psychology in Sexual Deviation.
8. V. M. PENNINGTON (1960). Phrenotropic Medication in Transvestism.
V. M. PENNINGTON (1960). Treatment in Transvestism.
9. A. E. EYRES (1960). Transvestism: Employment of Somatic Therapy . . . .
10. C. HAMBURGER, G. STÜRUP, and E. DAHL-IVERSON (1953). Transvestism.
C. HAMBURGER (1953). Desire for Change of Sex . . . Men and Women.
11. I. PAULY (1965). Male Psychosexual Inversion: Transsexualism.
12. D. STAFFORD-CLARK (1964). Essentials of the Clinical Approach.
13. M. OSTOW (1953). Transvestism (Correspondence).
14. H. BENJAMIN (1964). Nature and Management of Transsexualism . . . .
H. BENJAMIN (1964). Clinical Aspects of Transsexualism . . . .
15. M. SPERLING (1964). The Analysis of a Boy . . . .
R. R. GREENSON (1966). A Transvestite Boy . . . .
16. R. R. GREENSON (1966). A Transvestite Boy . . . .

Chapter 22 Moral Issues in Sex-Transformation Procedures

1. T. J. O'DONNELL (1966). Current Medical-Moral Comment.

Chapter 23—Conclusion

1. R. R. GREENSON (1967). Dis-Identifying from Mother: . . . .
2. R. R. GREENSON (1967). Dis-Identifying from Mother: . . . .
3. S. FREUD (1920; 1955). Beyond the Pleasure Principle.
4. S. FREUD (1937; 1964). Analysis Terminable and Interminable.

Appendix: Data on Transsexuals

1. S. FREUD, (1914; 1957). On Narcissism.
2. E. GLOVER, Metapsychology or Metaphysics.

Bibliography

Bibliography

ALLCHIN, W. H. "Behaviour Therapy (Correspondence)," *Brit. J. Psychiat.*, 110:108, 1964.

ALLEN, C. *A Textbook of Psychosexual Disorders*, p. 144. London and New York: Oxford University Press, 1962.

ALLEN, C. E. "Electrical Aversion Therapy," *Brit. Med. J.*, i:437, 1964.

ARMSTRONG, C. N. "Transvestism," in *Symposium on Nuclear Sex*, eds. D. R. Smith and W. M. Davidson, pp. 84–92. London: William Heinemann Ltd., 1958.

BAK, R. C. "Fetishism," *J. Amer. Psychoanal. Assoc.*, 1:285–298, 1953.

BAKER, H. J., and STOLLER, R. J. "Can a Biological Force Contribute to Gender Identity?" Read at the American Psychiatric Association Annual Meeting, Detroit, Mich., May, 1967.

BAKWIN, H. "Transvestism in Children," *J. Ped.*, 56:294–298, 1960.

———, and BAKWIN, R. M. *Clinical Management of Behavior Disorders in Children*, pp. 555–556. Philadelphia and London: W. B. Saunders Co., 3rd ed. 1966.

BARAHAL, H. S. "Female Transvestism and Homosexuality," *Psychiat. Quart.*, 27:390–438, 1953.

BARKER, J. C. "Aversion Therapy of Sexual Perversions (Correspondence)," *Brit. J. Psychiat.*, 109:696, 1963.

———. "Behaviour Therapy for Transvestism," *Brit. J. Psychiat.*, 111:268–276, 1965.

———. "Electrical Aversion Therapy," *Brit. Med. J.*, i:436, 1964.

———, THORPE, J. G., BLAKEMORE, C. B., LAVIN, N. I., and CONWAY, C. G. "Behaviour Therapy in a Case of Transvestism," *Lancet*, i:510, 1961.

BARR, M. L. "Sex Chromatin and Phenotype in Man," *Science*, 130:679–685, 1959.

———, and BERTRAM, E. G. "A Morphological Distinction Between Neurones of the Male and Female, and the Behavior of the Nucleolar Satellite During Accelerated Nucleoprotein Synthesis," *Nature*, 163:676–677, 1949.

BARRACLOUGH, C. A., and GORSKI, R. A. "Studies on Mating Behavior in the Androgen-Sterilized Female Rat in Relation to Hypothalamic Regulation of Sexual Behavior," *J. Endocrinol.*, 25:175–182, 1962.

BARTON, D., and WARE, P. D. "Incongruities in the Development of the Sexual System," *Arch. Gen. Psychiat.*, 14:614–623,1966.

BAYER, L. M., and BAYLEY, N. *Growth Diagnosis*. Chicago: University of Chicago Press, 1957.

BELL, A. I. "Some Observations on the Role of the Scrotal Sac and Testicles," *J. Amer. Psychanal. Assoc.*, 9:261–286, 1961.

———. "The Significance of Scrotal Sac and Testicles for the Prepuberty Male," *Psychoanal. Quart.*, 34:182–206, 1965.

BENDER, L. *A Dynamic Psychopathology of Childhood*, pp. 152–171. Springfield, Ill.: Charles C Thomas, 1954.

BENJAMIN, H. "Clinical Aspects of Transsexualism in the Male and Female," *Amer. J. Psychother.*, 18:458–469, 1964.

———. "Nature and Management of Transsexualism, with a Report on Thirty-One Operated Cases," *West. J. Surg., Obst. & Gynec.*, 72:105–111, 1964.

———. *The Transsexual Phenomenon*. New York: Julian Press, 1966.

———. "Transvestism and Transsexualism," *Int. J. Sexol.*, 7:12–14, 1953.

BETTELHEIM, B. *Symbolic Wounds*. New York: Macmillan Co. (a Collier book), rev. ed., 1962.

BLAKEMORE, C. B., THORPE, J. G., BARKER, J. C., CONWAY, C. G., and LAVIN, N. I. "The Application of Faradic Aversion Conditioning in a Case of Transvestism," *Behav. Res. Ther.*, 1:29–34, 1963.

———,THORPE, J. G., BARKER, J. C., CONWAY, C. G., and LAVIN, N. I. "Follow-up Note to: The Application of Faradic Aversion Conditioning in a Case of Transvestism," *Behav. Res. Ther.*, 1:191, 1963.

BLOCH, J. *The Sexual Life of Our Time*, p. 571. London: Rebman Ltd., 1908.

BOND, I. K., and MARGULIES, A. I. "Paranoid Schizophrenia in a Patient with Klinefelter's Syndrome," *Canad. Psychiat. Assn. J.*, 9:439–443, 1964.

BOSS, M. *Meaning and Content of Sexual Perversions*, pp. 79–114. New York: Grune & Stratton, 1949.

BOWLBY, J. "Ethology and the Development of Object Relations," *Int. J. Psycho-Anal.*, 41:313–317, 1960.

BURNS, R. K. "Role of Hormones in the Differentiation of Sex," in *Sex and Internal Secretions*, ed. W. C. Young, pp. 76–158. Baltimore, Md.: Williams & Wilkins Co., 1961.

BYCHOWSKI, G. "Homosexuality and Psychosis," in *Perversions, Psycho-*

dynamics and Therapy, ed. S. Lorand and M. Balint, pp. 97–130. New York: Random House, 1956.

CALL, J. Personal communication.

CAPPON, D., EZRIN, C., and LYNES, P. "Psychosexual Identification (Psychogender) in the Intersexed," *Canad. Psychiat. Assn. J.*, 4:90–106, 1959.

CARR, D. H., BARR, M. L., PLUNKETT, E. R., GRUMBACK, M. M., MARISHIMA, A., and CHU, E. H. "An XXXY Sex Chromosome Complex in Klinefelter's Subjects with Duplicated Sex Chromatin," *J. Clin. Endocr.*, 21:491–505, 1961.

CAULDWELL, D. C. "Psychopathia Transsexualis," *Sexology*, 16:274–280, 1949.

CHARATAN, F. B., and GALEF, H. "A Case of Transvestism in a Six-Year-Old Boy," *J. Hillside Hosp.*, 14:160–177, 1965.

CLARK, D. F. "Fetishism Treated by Negative Conditioning," *Brit. J. Psychiat.*, 109:404–407 1963.

COATES, S. "Clinical Psychology in Sexual Deviation," in *The Pathology and Treatment of Sexual Deviation*, ed. I. Rosen. London and New York: Oxford University Press, 1964.

COOPER, A. J. "A Case of Fetishism and Impotence Treated by Behaviour Therapy," *Brit. J. Psychiat.*, 109:649–652, 1963.

COURT–BROWN, W. M., "Sex Chromosomes and the Law," *Lancet*, ii:508–509, 1962.

CROWLEY, T. J. "Klinefelter's Syndrome and Abnormal Behavior: A Case Report," *Int. J. Neuropsychiat.*, 1:359–363, 1965.

DAVIDSON, P. W., III. "Transsexualism in Klinefelter's Syndrome," *Psychosomatics*, 7:94–98, 1966.

DAVIES, B. M., and MORGENSTERN, F. S. "A Case of Cysticercosis, Temporal Lobe Epilepsy, and Transvestism," *J. Neurol. Neurosurg. Psychiat.*, 23:247–249, 1960.

DEUTSCH, D. "A Case of Transvestism," *Amer. J. Psychother.*, 8:239–242, 1954.

DEWHURST, C. J., and GORDON, R. R. "Change of Sex," *Lancet*, ii:1213–1216, 1963.

DON, A. M. "Transvestism and Transsexualism," *S. African Med. J.*, 37:479–485, 1963.

DOWLING, L. H., and KNOX, S. J. "Transvestism and Fertility in a Chromosomal Mosaic," *Postgrad. Med. J.*, 39:665–669, 1963.

EDELSTEIN, E. L. "Psychodynamics of a Transvestite," *Amer. J. Psychother.*, 14:121–131, 1960.

EIDUSON, S. Personal communication.

ELLIS, H. *Studies in the Psychology of Sex, III*, 153–156. Philadelphia: F. A. Davis Co., 1921.

EYRES, A. E. "Transvestism: Employment of Somatic Therapy with Subsequent Improvement," *Dis. Nerv. Syst.*, 21:52–53, 1960.

FEDER, H. H., and WHALEN, R. E. "Feminine Behavior in Neonatally Castrated and Estrogen-Treated Male Rats," *Science*, 147:306–307, 1965.

FENICHEL, O. (1930). "The Psychology of Transvestism," in *Collected Papers*, I, 167–180. New York: W. W. Norton, 1953.

FERGUSON-SMITH, M. A. "Sex Chromatin, Klinefelter's Syndrome and Mental Deficiency," in *The Sex Chromatin*, ed. K. L. Moore. Philadelphia: W. B. Saunders Co., 1966.

FISHER, C., GROSS, J., and ZUCH, J. "Cycle of Penile Erection Synchronous with Dreaming (REM) Sleep," *Arch. Gen. Psychiat.*, 12:29–45, 1965.

FORD, C. S., and BEACH, F. A. *Patterns of Sexual Behavior*. New York: Harper & Row, 1951.

FRANCIS, J. J. "Passivity and Homosexual Predisposition in Latency Boys," *Bull. Phila. Assn. Psa.*, 15:160–174, 1965.

FREUD, S. (1937). "Analysis Terminable and Interminable," *Standard Edition* (London: Hogarth Press), 23:216–253, 1964. (*Standard Edition* hereafter noted as *SE*.)

—— (1920). "Beyond the Pleasure Principle," *SE*, 18:7–64, 1955.

—— (1931). "Female Sexuality," *SE*, 21:225–243, 1961.

—— (1927). "Fetishism," *SE*, 21:152–157, 1961.

—— (1910). "Leonardo da Vinci and a Memory of His Childhood," *SE*, 11:63–137, 1957.

—— (1914). "On Narcissism," *SE*, 14:73–102, 1957.

—— (1925). "Some Psychical Consequences of the Anatomical Distinction Between the Sexes," *SE*, 19:248–258, 1961.

—— (1938). "Splitting of the Ego in the Process of Defence," *SE*, 23:275–278, 1964.

—— (1920). "The Psychogenesis of a Case of Homosexuality in a Woman," *SE*, 18:147–172, 1955.

—— (1905). "Three Essays on the Theory of Sexuality," *SE*, 7:130–243, 1953.

——. Quoted in E. Jones, *The Life and Work of Sigmund Freud*, II, 329. New York: Basic Books, 1955.

FULLER, W., and DREZNER, N. "The Results of Surgical Castration in Women Under Forty," *Am. J. Obstet. Gynec.*, 47:122–124, 1944.

GILLESPIE, W. H. "Notes on the Analysis of Sexual Perversions," *Int. J. Psycho-Anal.*, 33:397–402, 1952.

GLOVER, E. "Metapsychology or Metaphysics," *Psychoanal. Quart.*, 35:173–190, 1966.

GLYNN, J. D., and HARPER, P. "Behaviour Therapy in a Case of Transvestism," *Lancet*, i:619–620, 1961.

GOY, R. W., PHOENIX, C. H., and YOUNG, W. C. "A Critical Period for the Suppression of Behavioral Receptivity in Adult Female Rats by Early Treatment with Androgen," *Anat. Record*, 142:307, 1962.

GRADY, K. L., and PHOENIX, C. H. "Hormonal Determinants of Mating Behavior; the Display of Feminine Behavior by Adult Male Rats Castrated Neonatally," *Am. Zoologist*, 3:482–483, 1963.

GRANT, V. W. "The Cross-Dresser: A Case Study," *J. Nerv. Ment. Dis.*, 131:149–159, 1960.

GRAY, P. H. "Theory and Evidence of Imprinting in Human Infants," *J. Psychol.*, 46:155–166, 1958.

GREEN, R., and MONEY, J. "Effeminacy in Prepubertal Boys," *Ped.*, 27:286–291, 1961.

——. "Incongruous Gender Role: Nongenital Manifestations in Prepubertal Boys," *J. Nerv. Ment. Dis.*, 131:160–168, 1960.

GREENACRE, P. "Certain Relationships Between Fetishism and the Faulty Development of the Body Image," *Psychoanal. Study Child*, 8:79–98, 1953. New York: International Universities Press.

——. "Early Physical Determinants in the Development of the Sense of Identity," *J. Amer. Psychoanal. Assoc.*, 6:612–627, 1958.

——. "Further Considerations Regarding Fetishism," *Psychoanal. Study Child*, 10:187–194, 1955. New York: International Universities Press.

——. "Further Notes on Fetishism," *Psychoanal. Study Child*, 15:191–207, 1960. New York: International Universities Press.

——. "On Focal Symbiosis," in *Dynamic Psychopathology in Childhood*, ed. L. Jessner and E. Pavenstedt, pp. 243–256. New York: Grune & Stratton, 1959.

GREENSON, R. R. "A Transvestite Boy and a Hypothesis," *Int. J. Psycho-Anal.* 47:396–403, 1966.

——. "Dis-identifying from Mother: Its Special Importance for the Boy." Read at the 25th International Psycho-Analytical Congress, Copenhagen, July, 1967.

——. "On Homosexuality and Gender Identity," *Int. J. Psycho-Anal.*, 45:217–219, 1964.

GUTHEIL, E. A. "A Rare Case of Sadomasochism," *Am. J. Psychol.*, 1:87–92, 1947.

——. "The Psychologic Background of Transsexualism and Transvestism," *Am. J. Psychother.*, 8:231–242, 1954.

HAMBURGER, C. "Desire for Change of Sex as Shown by Personal Letters from 465 Men and Women," *Acta Endocr.*, 14:361–375, 1953.

———, STÜRUP, G., and DAHL-IVERSON, E. "Transvestism," *J.A.M.A.*, 152:391–396, 1953.

HAMPSON, J. G. "Hermaphroditic Genital Appearance, Rearing and Eroticism in Hyperadrenocorticism," *Bull. Johns Hopkins Hosp.*, 96:265–273. 1955.

———, MONEY, J., and HAMPSON, J. L. "Hermaphroditism: Recommendations Concerning Case Management," *J. Clin. Endocr. & Metab.*, 16:547–556, 1956.

HAMPSON, J. L., HAMPSON, J. G., and MONEY, J. "The Syndrome of Gonadal Agenesis (Ovarian Agenesis) and Male Chromosomal Pattern in Girls and Women: Psychologic Studies," *Bull. Johns Hopkins Hosp.*, 97:207–226, 1955.

HARLOW, H., and HARLOW, M. "Learning to Love," *Am. Scientist*, 54: 244–272, 1966.

HARNIK, E. J. "Pleasure in Disguise—the Need for Decoration, and the Sense of Beauty,"*Psychoanal. Quart.*, 1:216–264, 1932.

HEATH, R. G. "Electrical Self-Stimulation of the Brain in Man," *Am. J. Psychiat.*, 120:571–577, 1963.

HOAKEN, P. C. S., CLARKE, M., and BRESLIN, M. "Psychopathology in Klinefelter's Syndrome," *Psychosom. Med.*, 20:207–223, 1964.

HOOKER, E. "What Is a Criterion?" *J. Proj. Tech.*, 23:278–281, 1957.

HORNEY, K. "On the Genesis of the Castration Complex in Women," *Int. J. Psycho-Anal.*, 5:50–65, 1924.

———. "The Flight from Womanhood," *Int. J. Psycho-Anal.*, 7:324–329, 1926.

JONES, E. "The Early Development of Female Sexuality," *Int. J. Psycho-Anal.*, 8:459–472, 1927.

———. "The Phallic Phase," *Int. J. Psycho-Anal.*, 14:1–33, 1933.

JONES, H. W., JR., and SCOTT, W. W. *Hermaphroditism, Genital Anomalies and Related Endocrine Disorders*. Baltimore, Md.: Williams & Wilkins Co., 1958.

JOST, A. "Embryonic Sexual Differentiation," in *Hermaphroditism, Genital Anomalies, and Related Endocrine Disorders*, eds. H. W. Jones, Jr., and W. W. Scott. Baltimore, Md.: Williams & Wilkins Co., 1958.

KALLMAN, F. J. "Genetic Aspects of Sex Determination and Sexual Maturation Potentials in Man," in *Determinants of Human Sexual Behavior*, ed. G. Winokur, pp. 5–18. Springfield, Ill.: Charles C Thomas, 1963.

———. "Twin and Sibship Study of Overt Homosexuality," *Am. J. Human Genet.*, 4:136–146, 1952.

KARL, H. J., and MEYER, J. E. "Sexuality in Klinefelter's Syndrome," *Klin. Wschr.*, 42:1172–1179, 1964.

KHAN, M. M. R. "On Symbiotic Omnipotence." Unpublished manuscript, 1965.

——. "The Concept of Cumulative Trauma," *Psychoanal. Study Child*, 18:286–306, 1936. New York: International Universities Press.

——. "The Role of Infantile Sexuality and Early Object Relations in Female Homosexuality," in *The Pathology and Treatment of Sexual Deviation*, ed. I. Rosen, pp. 221–292. London and New York: Oxford University Press, 1964.

KINSEY, A. C., POMEROY, W. B., MARTIN, C. E., and GEBHARD, P. H. *Sexual Behavior in the Human Female*. Philadelphia: W. B. Saunders Co., 1953.

KLEIN, M. "Notes on Some Schizoid Mechanisms," *Int. J. Psycho-Anal.*, 27:99–110, 1946.

——. *The Psychoanalysis of Children*. London: Hogarth Press, 1932.

KNOL, J., and LOS, P. L. "A Mentally Disturbed Patient with Klinefelter's Syndrome," *Ned. T. Geneesk.*, 110/5:242–246, 1966.

KRAFFT-EBING, R. VON. *Psychopathia Sexualis*, pp. 26–29. Brooklyn, N.Y.: Physicians and Surgeons Book Company, 12th ed. rev., 1932.

KRIS, E. "The Nature of Psychoanalytic Propositions and Their Validation," in *Freedom and Experience*, eds. S. K. Hook and M. R. Konwitz. Ithaca, N.Y.: Cornell University Press, 1947.

——. "The Recoveries of Childhood Memories in Psychoanalysis," *Psychoanal. Study Child*, 11:54–88, 1956. New York: International Universities Press.

KVALE, J. N., and FISHMAN, J. R. "The Psychological Aspects of Klinefelter's Syndrome," *J.A.M.A.*, 193:567–572, 1965.

LAVIN, N. I., THORPE, J. G., BARKER, J. C., BLAKEMORE, C. B., and CONWAY, C. G. Behaviour Therapy in a Case of Transvestism," *J. Nerv. Ment. Dis.*, 133:346–353, 1961.

LEIGH, M. *The Velvet Underground*, pp. 80–83. New York: Macfadden-Bartell Corp., 1963.

LEITES, N. "Talking About Identity," Unpublished manuscript, 1967.

LERNER, A. J. *My Fair Lady*. New York: Coward-McCann, Inc., 1956.

LEWIS, M. D. "A Case of Transvestism with Multiple Body-Phallus Identification," *Int. J. Psycho-Anal.*, 44:345–351, 1963.

LICHTENSTEIN, H. "Identity and Sexuality," *J. Am. Psychoanal. Assoc.*, 9:179–260, 1961.

LIEF, H. I., DINGMAN, J. F., and BISHOP, M. P. "Psychoendocrinologic Studies in a Male with Cyclic Changes in Sexuality," *Psychosom. Med.*, 24:357–368, 1962.

LOEWALD, H. W. "Book Review": *Psychoanalytic Concepts and the Structural Theory*, by J. A. Arlow and C. Brenner, *Psychoanal. Quart.*, 35:430–436, 1966.

LORENZ, K. *King Solomon's Ring*. New York: Thomas Y. Crowell Company, 1952.

LUKIANOWICZ, N. "A Rudimentary Form of Transvestism," *Am. J. Psychother.*, 16:665–675,1962.

——. "Survey of Various Aspects of Transvestism in the Light of Our Present Knowledge," *J. Nerv. Ment. Dis.*, 128:36–64, 1959.

——. "Two Cases of Transvestism," *Psychiat. Quart.*, 34:517–537, 1960.

MACALPINE, I., and HUNTER, R. A. "The Schreber Case," *Psychoanal. Quart.*, 22:328–371, 1953.

MACCLEAN, P. D. "Phylogenesis," in *Expressions of Emotions in Man*, ed. P. H. Knapp. New York: International Universities Press, 1963.

MACDONALD, I. J. "Behaviour Therapy in a Case of Transvestism," *Lancet*, i:889–890, 1961.

MANTHEY, H. G. "Psychological Studies in Cases of Male Gonadal Insufficiency," *Acta Endocr.*, 28:213–217, 1958.

MARMOR, J. *Sexual Inversion*. New York: Basic Books, 1965.

MASTERS, W. H., and JOHNSON, V. E. "The Artificial Vagina: Anatomic, Physiologic, Psychosexual Function," *West. J. Surg., Obst. & Gynec.*, 69:192–212, 1961.

——. *Human Sexual Response*. Boston: Little, Brown and Co., 1966.

MATTHEWS, P. C. "Behaviour Therapy (Correspondence)," *Brit. J. Psychiat.*, 110:108, 1964.

MCGUIRE, R. J., and VALLANCE, M. "Aversion Therapy by Electric Shock: A Simple Technique," *Brit. Med. J.*, i:151–153, 1964.

MCKENZIE, R. E., and SCHULTZ, I. M. "Study of a Transvestite. Evaluation and Treatment," *Am. J. Psychother.*, 15:267–280, 1961.

MICHAEL, R. P. "Biological Factors in the Organization and Expression of Sexual Behavior," in *The Pathology and Treatment of Sexual Deviation*, ed. I. Rosen, pp. 24–54. London and New York: Oxford University Press, 1964.

——, and HERBERT, J. "Menstrual Cycle Influences Grooming Behavior and Sexual Activity in Rhesus Monkey," *Science*, 140:500–501, 1963.

MILLER, A., and CAPLAN, J. "Sex-Role Reversal Following Castration of a Homosexual with Klinefelter's Syndrome. Report of an Unusual Case," *Canad. Psychiat. Assoc. J.*, 10:223–227, 1965.

MONEY, J. "Factors in the Genesis of Homosexuality," in *Determinants of Human Sexual Behavior*, ed. G. Winokur, pp. 19–43. Springfield, Ill.: Charles C Thomas, 1963.

——. "Hermaphroditism: An Inquiry into the Nature of a Human Paradox." Unpublished doctoral dissertation, Harvard University, 1952.

——. "Hermaphroditism, Gender and Precocity in Hyperadrenocorticism: Psychologic Findings," *Bull. Johns Hopkins Hosp.*, 96:253–264, 1955.

——, and POLLIT, E. "Cytogenetic and Psychosexual Ambiguity," *Arch. Gen. Psychiat.*, 11:589–595, 1964.

——, and WANG, C. "Human Figure Drawing. I: Sex of First Choice in Gender-Identity Anomalies, Klinefelter's Syndrome and Precocious Puberty," *J. Nerv. Ment. Dis.*, 143:157–162, 1966.

——, HAMPSON, J. G., and HAMPSON, J. L. "An Examination of Some Basic Sexual Concepts: The Evidence of Human Hermaphroditism," *Bull. Johns Hopkins Hosp.*, 97:301–319, 1955.

——, HAMPSON, J. G., and HAMPSON, J. L. "Hermaphroditism: Recommendations Concerning Assignment of Sex, Change of Sex, and Psychologic Management," *Bull. Johns Hopkins Hosp.*, 97:284–300, 1955.

——, HAMPSON, J. G., and HAMPSON, J. L. "Imprinting and the Establishment of Gender Role," *Arch. Neurol. Psychiat.*, 77:333–336, 1957.

——, HAMPSON, J. G., and HAMPSON, J. L. "Sexual Incongruities and Psychopathology: The Evidence of Human Hermaphroditism," *Bull. Johns Hopkins Hosp.*, 98:43–57, 1956.

MOSIER, H. D., SCOTT, L. W., and DINGMAN, H. F. "Sexually Deviant Behavior in Klinefelter's Syndrome," *J. Pediat.*, 57:479–483, 1960.

MUENSTERBERGER, W. "Psyche and Culture: Observations on Some Interrelationships of Sociocultural Institutions and Psychic Structure." Read before the Los Angeles Psychoanalytic Institute-Society, September, 1967.

NIELSEN, J. "Klinefelter's Syndrome and Behaviour," *Lancet*, ii:587–588, 1964.

NORRIS, A. S., and KEETTEL, W. C. "Change of Sex Role During Adolescence," *Amer. J. Obst. Gynec.*, 84:719–721, 1962.

O'DONNELL, T. J. "Current Medical-Moral Comment," *Linacre Quart.*, Feb., 1966, pp. 72–74.

OLDS, J. "Self-Stimulation Experiments and Differential Reward Systems," in *Reticular Formation of the Brain*, eds. H. M. Jasper, L. D. Proctor, R. S. Knighton, W. C. Noshay, and R. T. Costello. Boston: Little, Brown and Co., 1958.

OSTOW, M. "Transvestism (Correspondence)," *J.A.M.A.*, 152:1553, 1953.

OVERZIER, C. "Transvestitism and Klinefelter's Syndrome," *Arch. Psychiat. Newenk.*, 198:198–209, 1958.

PARKES, A. S., and BRUCE, H. M. "Olfactory Stimuli in Mammalian Reproduction," *Science*, 134:1049–1054, 1961.

PARKIN, A. "On Fetishism," *Int. J. Psycho-Anal.*, 44:352–361, 1963.

PARMELEE, A. H., JR., WENNER, W. H., AKIYAMA, Y., SCHULTZ, M., and STERN, E. "Sleep States in Premature Infants," *Devel. Med. & Child Neurol.*, 9:70–77, 1967.

PASQUALINI, R. Q., VIDAL, G., and BUR, G. E. "Psychopathology of Klinefelter's Syndrome. Review of Thirty-one Cases." *Lancet*, ii:164–167, 1957.

PAULY, I. "Male Psychosexual Inversion: Transsexualism," *Arch. Gen. Psychiat.*, 13:172–181, 1965.

PENNINGTON, V. M. "Phrenotropic Medication in Transvestism," *J. Neuropsychiat.*, 2:35–40, 1960.

——. "Treatment in Transvestism," *Amer. J. Psychiat.*, 117:250–251, 1960.

PHILIPPOPOULOS, G. S. "A Case of Transvestism in a 17-Year-Old Girl," *Acta Psychother.*, 12:29–37, 1964.

PLATO, *Symposium* (Jowett trans.), III, 315. New York: Dial Press.

PODOLSKY, E., and WADE, C. *Sexual Sadism: The Sexual Urge of Love and Pain*, p. 123. New York: Epic, 1961.

RABOCH, J., and NEDOMA, K. "Sex Chromatin and Sexual Behavior," *Psychosom. Med.*, 20:55–59, 1958.

RADO, S. "A Critical Examination of the Concept of Bisexuality," *Psychosom. Med.*, 2:459–467, 1940.

RAYMOND, M. J. "A Case of Fetishism Treated by Aversion Therapy," *Brit. Med. J.*, ii:854–857, 1956.

——. "Behaviour Therapy (Correspondence)," *Brit. J. Psychiat.*, 110:108, 1964.

REDMOUNT, R. S. "A Case of a Female Transvestite with Marital and Criminal Complications," *J. Clin. & Exper. Psychopath.*, 14:95–111, 1953.

ROHDE, R. A. "Chromatin-Positive Klinefelter Syndrome: Clinical and Cytogenetic Studies," *J. Chronic Dis.*, 16:1134–1149, 1963.

ROSENFELD, H. "Remarks on the Relation of Male Homosexuality to Paranoia, Paranoid Anxiety and Narcissism," *Int. J. Psycho-Anal.*, 30:36–47, 1949.

ROSKAMP, H. "A Contribution to the Psychopathology of Klinefelter's Syndrome," *Arch. Psychiat. Nerv.*, 199:330–344, 1959.

RUBINSTEIN, L. H. "The Role of Identifications in Homosexuality and Transvestism in Men and Women," in *The Pathology and Treatment of Sexual Deviation*, ed. I. Rosen, pp. 163–195. London and New York: Oxford University Press, 1964.

SCHAEFFER, E. S., and BAYLEY, N. *Maternal Behavior, Child Behavior, and Their Inter-Correlations from Infancy Through Adolescence.* Monograph of the Society for Research in Child Development, 1963.

SCHNEIDER, S. F., HARRISON, S. I., and SIEGEL, B. L. "Self-Castration by a

Man with Cyclic Changes in Sexuality," *Psychosom. Med.*, 27:53–70, 1965.

SCHWABE, A. D., SOLOMON, D., STOLLER, R. J., and BURNHAM, J. "Pubertal Feminization in a Genetic Male," *J. Clin. Endocr.*, 22:839–845, 1962.

SEGAL, M. M. "Transvestism as an Impulse and as a Defense," *Int. J. Psycho-Anal.*, 46:209–217, 1965.

SHERFEY, M. J. "The Evolution and Nature of Female Sexuality in Relation to Psychoanalytic Theory," *J. Amer. Psychoanal. Assoc.*, 14:28–128, 1966.

SHIELDS, R. H. "The Too-Good Mother," *Int. J. Psycho-Anal.*, 45:85–88, 1964.

SPERLING, M. "A Study of Deviate Sexual Behavior in Children by the Method of Simultaneous Analysis of Mother and Child," in *Dynamic Psychopathology in Childhood*, eds. L. Jessner and E. Pavenstedt, pp. 221–242. New York: Grune & Stratton, 1959.

——. "Fetishism in Children," *Psychoanal. Quart.*, 32:374–392, 1963.

——. "The Analysis of a Boy with Transvestite Tendencies," *Psychoanal. Study Child*, 19:470–493, 1964. New York: International Universities Press.

SPITZ, R. "Autoerotism Re-examined: The Role of Early Sexual Behavior Patterns in Personality Formation," *Psychoanal. Study Child*, 17:283–315, 1962. New York: International Universities Press.

STAFFORD-CLARK, D. "Essentials of the Clinical Approach," in *The Pathology and Treatment of Sexual Deviation*, ed. I. Rosen, pp. 57–86. London and New York: Oxford University Press, 1964.

STEKEL, W. *Sadism and Masochism*, I, 50. New York: Liveright Publishing Corp., 1929.

STOLLER, R. J. "A Contribution to the Study of Gender Identity," *Int. J. Psycho-Anal.*, 45:220–226, 1964.

——. "Gender Role Change in Intersexed Patients," *J.A.M.A.*, 188:684–685, 1964.

——. "The Mother's Contribution to Infantile Transvestic Behavior," *Int. J. Psycho-anal.*, 47:384–395, 1966.

STORR, A. Sexual Deviation, p. 47. Baltimore, Md.: Penguin Books, 1964.

WÅLINDER, J. *Transsexualism: A Study of Forty-three Cases*. Göteborg: Scandinavian University Books, 1967.

WALTER, K., and BRAUTIGAM, W. "Transvestitism in Klinefelter's Syndrome," *Schweiz. Med. Wchnschr.*, 88:357–362, 1958.

WAXENBERG, S. E. "Some Biological Correlates of Sexual Behavior," in *Determinants of Human Sexual Behavior*, ed. G. Winokur, pp. 52–75. Springfield, Ill.: Charles C Thomas, 1963.

WEISSMAN, P. "Structural Considerations in Overt Male Bisexuality," *Int. J. Psycho-Anal.*, 43:159–168, 1962.

WHALEN, R. E., and NADLER, R. D. "Suppression of the Development of

Female Mating Behavior by Estrogen Administered in Infancy," *Science*, 141:273–274, 1963.

WHITLOCK, F. A. "(Correspondence)," *Brit. Med. J.*, i:436, 1964.

WINNICOTT, D. W. (1950). "Aggression in Relation to Emotional Development," in *Collected Papers*, pp. 204–218. London: Tavistock, 1958. (Hereafter noted as *CP*.)

———. (1956). "Primary Maternal Preoccupation," in *CP*, pp. 300–305, 1958.

———. (1953). "Transitional Objects and Transitional Phenomena," in *CP*, pp. 229–242, 1958.

———. "The Theory of the Parent-Infant Relationship," *Int. J. Psycho-Anal.*, 41:585–595, 1960.

WOLFF, P. H. *The Causes, Controls, and Organization of Behavior in the Neonate, Psychol. Issues*, vol. V, no. 1, 1966. New York: International Universities Press.

YOUNG, H. Quoted in H. W. Jones, Jr., and W. W. Scott, *Hermaphroditism, Genital Anomalies* . . . (1958), *q.v.*, p. 55.

YOUNG, W. C., GOY, R. W., and PHOENIX, C. H. "Hormones and Sexual Behavior," *Science*, 143:212–218, 1964.

ZILBOORG, G. "Masculine and Feminine," *Psychiatry*, 7:257–296, 1944.

INDEX

Abraham, Karl, 142
Adrenogenital syndrome, ix-x, 57, 238
Aggression, phase-adequate, 123
Amphibia, 4–5
Anxiety, 129, 232, 244, 253, 290
castration, see Castration anxiety
conscious, 144–46
Artistic ability, 145, 195
of transsexuals, 94, 116–17, 126–30, 338–45
Aversion therapy, 243–44, 245–46

Bak, R. C., 119–20, 124
Baker, Dr. Howard J., 75*n*, 79*n*, 80*n*, 81*n*
Bakwin, H., 91
Barr, M. L., 10
Bayley, N., 13–14
Bell, A. I., 48
Bender, L., 91
Benjamin, H., 83, 85, 190*n*, 249–50
Bertram, E. G., 10
Binding perversion, 218–27
dangers of, 221
rarity of, 218
Biological determinism, see Genetics
Birds, imprinting in, 7
Bisexuality, 124
Freudian theory of, 141–42
of mothers, 94–96, 105–6, 112–16, 138–39, 170–75, 298–307, 320
See also Hermaphrodites
Boyhood transsexualism, 89–131, 148, 190, 216–17, 263–64
accident-proneness with, 128
causes adult transsexualism, 133, 136–40
described, 92–94
failure to develop, 170–75
imprinting in, 123
moral position on, 260–61
role of beauty in, 116–18, 137, 296–98
role of skin contact in, 111–12, 124–25, 307–16
taped interviews on, 277–348
therapy for, 251–54
transitional objects in, 124–25, 336–38
transvestism contrasted to, 103–4, 180
Bruce, H. M., 12
Bychowski, G., 142*n*

Call, J., 13, 277
Cappon, D., 232
Castration, 5, 11, 214
of clitoris, 57
of hermaphrodite, 32, 33
of intersexuals, 78, 80
of transsexuals, 104, 187, 192, 286
of transvestites, 188–89, 246, 247
Castration anxiety, xii, 30, 48, 72
loss of identity and, 153
in oedipal phase, 152
of transsexuals, 100–1, 105, 121
of transvestites, 184–85, 215
Castration complex, 53, 58, 60, 63
Freud on, 143
Central nervous system (CNS), 8, 123*n*, 232
effect of hormones on, 5–6
imprinting in, 270
as source of gender identity, 65, 81
Character structure, 37, 105, 142, 162
development of, xiv, 23, 252
feminine, 59, 60
shift in, 161, 242, 253
Charatan, F. B., 92
Childhood (infancy, adolescence), 151, 216–17
of binding pervert, 219–26
biological determinants of sex in, 5, 11, 12–14
of bisexual mothers, 95–96, 112–16, 125, 138–40, 172–73, 175, 298–302, 304–7
conditioning in, 270–71
core identity in, 29–30
of female transvestite, 197–205
of feminine men, 167–69
of hermaphrodites, 257–59
imprinting in, 8, 122–23, 270–71
of male homosexuals, 158–60
of male transvestites, 116, 121, 131, 180–86, 207–12, 242
male vs. female, 263–64, 266–67
of neuter patients, 17–28, 67–81, 83–85, 231–33, 236–40
sense of femaleness in, 50–58, 60–64
sense of maleness in, 39–49
See also Boyhood transsexualism; Oedipal situation; Phallic phase; Symbiosis

377